WHAT YOUR SIXTH GRADER NEEDS TO KNOW

THE
CORE KNOWLEDGE™
SERIES

RESOURCE BOOKS FOR
GRADES ONE THROUGH SIX
BOOK VI

WHAT YOUR SIXTH GRADER NEEDS TO KNOW

FUNDAMENTALS OF A GOOD SIXTH-GRADE EDUCATION

Edited by

E. D. HIRSCH, JR.

Delta
Trade Paperbacks

This book is dedicated in loving acknowledgment to
Polly Hirsch
superb critic and editor, staunch benefactor of the Core Knowledge Foundation,
faithful booster and bucker-up throughout the long labor of all six volumes.

All author's earnings from the sale of this book go to the nonprofit Core Knowledge Foundation, dedicated to the improvement of education for all children. Information about the activities and materials of the foundation are available from the Core Knowledge Foundation, 2012-B Morton Drive, Charlottesville, VA 22901.

A Delta Book
Published by
Dell Publishing
a division of
Bantam Doubleday Dell Publishing Group, Inc.
1540 Broadway
New York, New York 10036

ISBN: 0-385-31467-1

Reprinted by arrangement with Doubleday, a division of Bantam Doubleday Dell Publishing Group, Inc.

Manufactured in the United States of America

Published simultaneously in Canada

August 1995

20 19 18 17 16 15 14 13

RRH

Acknowledgments

This series has depended upon the help, advice, and encouragement of some two thousand people. Some of those singled out here know already the depth of my gratitude; others may be surprised to find themselves thanked publicly for help they gave quietly and freely for the sake of the enterprise alone. To helpers named and unnamed I am deeply grateful.

Project Manager: Tricia Emlet

Editors: Tricia Emlet (Text), Rae Grant (Art), Elaine Moran (Text)

Artists and Writers: Jacques Chazaud (Illustration), Tricia Emlet (Geography, Sayings), Leslie Evans (Illustration), Jonathan Fuqua (Illustration), Julie C. Grant (Illustration), Marie Hawthorne (Science Biographies), E. D. Hirsch, Jr. (Life Science, Physical Science), John Hirsch (Mathematics), John Holdren (About Literature, Stories, Mythology, World Civilization, American Civilization), Jennifer Howard (Speeches, Science Biographies), Blair Logwood Jones (Stories), Phillip Jones (Illustration), Bethanne H. Kelly (Stories), Michael McCurdy (Illustration), Gail McIntosh (Illustration), Elaine Moran (Visual Arts), A. Brooke Russell (Geography, Life Science, Physical Science), Peter Ryan (Music), Lindley Shutz (About Language), Joel Smith (Illustration), Mike Stanford (World Civilization, American Civilization), Alexandra Webber (Illustration), Meg West (Illustration), Perry Whidden (Illustration)

Art and Photo Research: Tricia Emlet, Rae Grant, Elaine Moran, Martha Clay Sullivan

Permissions: Martha Clay Sullivan

Advisers on Multiculturalism: Minerva Allen, Frank de Varona, Mick Fedullo, Dorothy Fields, Elizabeth Fox-Genovese, Marcia Galli, Dan Garner, Henry Louis Gates, Cheryl Kulas, Joseph C. Miller, Gerry Raining Bird, Dorothy Small, Sharon Stewart-Peregoy, Sterling Stuckey, Marlene Walking Bear, Lucille Watahomigie, Ramona Wilson

Advisers on Elementary Education: Joseph Adelson, Isobel Beck, Paul Bell, Carl Bereiter, David Bjorklund, Constance Jones, Elizabeth LaFuze, J. P. Lutz, Jean Osborne, Sandra Scarr, Nancy Stein, Phyllis Wilkin

Advisers on Technical Subject Matters: Richard Anderson, Andrew Gleason, Eric Karell, Joseph Kett, Michael Lynch, Joseph C. Miller, Margaret Redd, Mark Rush, Ralph Smith, Nancy Summers, James Trefil, Nancy Wayne

Conferees, March 1990: Nola Bacci, Joan Baratz-Snowden, Thomasyne Beverley, Thomas Blackton, Angela Burkhalter, Monty Caldwell, Thomas M. Carroll, Laura Chapman, Carol Anne Collins, Lou Corsaro, Henry Cotton, Anne Coughlin, Arletta Dimberg, Debra P. Douglas, Patricia Edwards, Janet Elenbogen, Mick Fedullo, Michele Fomalont, Nancy Gercke, Mamon Gibson, Jean Haines, Barbara Hayes, Stephen Herzog, Helen Kelley, Brenda King, John King, Elizabeth LaFuze, Diana Lam, Nancy Lambert, Doris Langaster,

Richard LaPointe, Lloyd Leverton, Madeleine Long, Allen Luster, Joseph McGeehan, Janet McLin, Gloria McPhee, Marcia Mallard, Judith Matz, William J. Moloney, John Morabito, Robert Morrill, Roberta Morse, Karen Nathan, Dawn Nichols, Valeta Paige, Mary Perrin, Joseph Piazza, Jeanne Price, Marilyn Rauth, Judith Raybern, Mary Reese, Richard Rice, Wallace Saval, John Saxon, Jan Schwab, Ted Sharp, Diana Smith, Richard Smith, Trevanian Smith, Carol Stevens, Nancy Summers, Michael Terry, Robert Todd, Elois Veltman, Sharon Walker, Mary Ann Ward, Penny Williams, Charles Wootten, Clarke Worthington, Jane York

The Three Oaks Elementary School: Constance Jones, Principal; Cecelia Cook, Assistant Principal

Teachers: Joanne Anderson, Linda Anderson, Nancy Annichiarico, Deborah Backes, Katherine Ann Bedingfield, Barbara Bittner, Michael Blue, Coral Boudin, Nancy Bulgerin, Jodene Cebak, Cheryl Chastain, Paula Clark, Betty Cook, Laura DeProfio, Holly DeSantis, Cindy Donmoyer, Lisa Eastridge, Amy Germer, Elizabeth Graves, Jennifer Gunder, Eileen Hafer, Helen Hallman, Donna Hernandez, Kathleen Holzborn, Robert Horner, Jenni Jones, Zoe Ann Klusacek, Annette Lopez, Barbara Lyon, Cindy Miller, Lelar Miller, Laura Morse, Karen Naylor, Joanne O'Neill, Jill Pearson, Linda Peck, Rebecca Poppe, Janet Posch, Judy Quest, Angie Richards, Angie Ryan, April Santarelli, Patricia Scott, Patricia Stapleton, Pamela Stewart, Jeanne Storm, Phillip Storm, Katherine Twomey, Karen Ward

Benefactors: the Dade County School District, the Exxon Education Foundation, the Lee County School District, the National Endowment for the Humanities, the Shutz Foundation

Morale Boosters: Judy Bagley, Polly Hirsch, Robert Payton, Rafe Sagalyn, Nancy Brown Wellin

Our grateful acknowledgment to these persons does not imply that we have taken their (sometimes conflicting) advice in every case, or that each of them endorses all aspects of this project. Responsibility for final decisions must rest with the editor alone. Suggestions for improvements are very welcome, and I wish to thank in advance those who send advice for revising and improving this series.

Contents

I. LANGUAGE ARTS

II. GEOGRAPHY, WORLD CIVILIZATION, AND AMERICAN CIVILIZATION

III. FINE ARTS

IV. MATHEMATICS

V. NATURAL SCIENCES

General Introduction

I. What Is Your Child Learning in School?

I recently received a letter from a parent of identical twins. She wrote to express her dismay that her children, who are in the same grade in the same school, are learning completely different things. How can this be? Because they are in different classrooms; because the teachers in these classrooms have only the vaguest guidelines to follow; in short, because the school, like most in the United States, lacks a definite, specific curriculum.

Many parents would be surprised if they were to examine the curriculum of their child's elementary school. I urge you to ask to see your school's curriculum. Does it say just what specific core of content each child at a particular grade level is expected to learn by the end of the year? Most curricula speak in vague terms of general skills, processes, and attitudes. This vagueness is no virtue. It places unreasonable demands upon teachers and often results in years of schooling marred by repetitions and gaps. Yet another unit on dinosaurs. *Charlotte's Web* for the third time. "You've never heard of the Bill of Rights?" "You've never been taught how to add two fractions with unlike denominators?"

When identical twins in two classrooms of the same school have few academic experiences in common, that is a sign of trouble. When teachers in that school do not know what children in other classrooms are learning on the same grade level, much less in earlier and later grades, they cannot reliably predict that children will come prepared with a shared core of knowledge and skills. The result of this curricular incoherence is that many schools fall far short of developing the full potential of our children.

To address this problem, I started the Core Knowledge Foundation in 1986. This book and its companion volumes in the Core Knowledge Series are designed to give parents, teachers, and through them, children, a carefully sequenced body of knowledge based upon the model curriculum guidelines developed by the Core Knowledge Foundation.

The Core Knowledge curriculum is an attempt to define, in a coherent and sequential way, a body of widely used knowledge taken for granted by competent writers and speakers in the United States. Because this knowledge is taken for granted rather than being explained when it is used, it forms a necessary foundation for the higher-order reading, writing, and thinking skills that children need for academic and vocational success. The universal attainment of such knowledge should be a central aim of curricula in our elementary schools, just as it is currently the aim in all world-class educational systems.

For reasons explained in the next section, making sure that all young children in the United States possess a core of shared knowledge is a necessary step in developing a first-rate educational system.

II. Why Core Knowledge Is Needed

Learning builds on learning: children (and adults) gain new knowledge only by building on what they already know. It is essential to begin building solid foundations of knowledge in the early grades when children are most receptive because research has shown that, for the vast majority of children, academic deficiencies from the first six grades *permanently* impair the success of later learning. Poor performance of American students in middle and high school can be traced directly to shortcomings inherited from elementary schools that have not imparted to children the knowledge they need for further learning.

All of the highest-achieving and most egalitarian elementary school systems in the world (such as those in Sweden, France, and Japan) teach their children a specific core of knowledge in each of the first six grades, thus enabling all children to enter each new grade with a secure foundation for further learning. It is time American schools did so as well, for the following reasons:

(1) Commonly shared knowledge makes schooling more effective. We know that the one-on-one tutorial is the most effective form of schooling, in part because a parent or teacher can provide tailor-made instruction for the individual child. But in a nontutorial situation—in, for example, a typical classroom with twenty-five or more students—the instructor cannot effectively impart new knowledge to all the students unless each one shares the background knowledge that the lesson is being built upon. When all the students in a class *do* share that relevant background knowledge, a classroom can begin to approach the effectiveness of a tutorial. Even when some children in a class don't have elements of the knowledge they were supposed to acquire in previous grades, the existence of a specifically defined core makes it possible for the teacher or parent to identify and fill the gaps, thus giving all students a chance to fulfill their potentials in later grades.

(2) Commonly shared knowledge makes schooling more fair and democratic. When all the children who enter a grade can be assumed to share some of the same building blocks of knowledge, and when the teacher knows exactly what those building blocks are, then all the students are empowered to learn. In our current system, disadvantaged children too often suffer from unmerited low expectations that translate into watered-down curricula. But if we specify the core of knowledge that all children should share, then we can guarantee equal access to that knowledge, and compensate for the academic advantages some students are offered at home. In a Core Knowledge school, disadvantaged children, like *all* children, enjoy the benefits of important, challenging knowledge that will provide the foundation for successful later learning.

(3) Commonly shared knowledge helps create cooperation and solidarity in our schools and nation. Diversity is a hallmark and strength of our nation. American classrooms are usually made up of students from a variety of cultural backgrounds, and those different cultures should be honored and understood by all students. Education should create a *school-based* culture that is common and welcoming to all because it includes knowledge of many cultures, and gives all students, no matter what their background, a common foundation for understanding our cultural diversity.

In the next section I will describe the steps taken by the Core Knowledge Foundation to develop a model of the commonly shared knowledge our children need (which forms the basis for this series of books).

III. The Consensus Behind the Core Knowledge Sequence

The content in this and other volumes in the Core Knowledge Series is based on a document called the *Core Knowledge Sequence*, a grade-by-grade sequence of specific content guidelines in history, geography, mathematics, science, language arts, and the fine arts. The *Sequence* is not meant to outline the whole of the school curriculum; rather, it offers specific guidelines to knowledge that can reasonably be expected to make up about *half* of any school's curriculum, thus leaving ample room for local requirements and emphases. Teaching a common core of knowledge, such as that articulated in the *Core Knowledge Sequence*, is compatible with a variety of instructional methods and additional subject matters.

The *Core Knowledge Sequence* is the result of a long process of research and consensus-building undertaken by the nonprofit Core Knowledge Foundation. Here is how we achieved the consensus behind the *Core Knowledge Sequence*.

First we analyzed the many reports issued by state departments of education and by professional organizations—such as the National Council of Teachers of Mathematics and the American Association for the Advancement of Science—which recommend general outcomes for elementary and secondary education. We also tabulated the knowledge and skills through grade six specified in the successful educational systems of several other countries, including France, Japan, Sweden, and West Germany.

In addition, we formed an advisory board on multiculturalism that proposed specific knowledge of diverse cultural traditions that American children should all share as part of their school-based common culture. We sent the resulting materials to three independent groups of teachers, scholars, and scientists around the country, asking them to create a master list of the knowledge children should have by the end of grade six. About 150 teachers (including college professors, scientists, and administrators) were involved in this initial step.

These items were amalgamated into a master plan, and further groups of teachers and specialists were asked to agree on a grade-by-grade sequence of the items. That sequence was then sent to some one hundred educators and specialists who participated in a national conference that was called to hammer out a working agreement on core knowledge for the first six grades.

This important meeting took place in March 1990. The conferees were elementary school teachers, curriculum specialists, scientists, science writers, officers of national organizations, representatives of ethnic groups, district superintendents, and school principals from across the country. A total of twenty-four working groups decided on revisions in the sequence. The resulting provisional sequence was further fine-tuned during a year of implementation at a pioneering school, Three Oaks Elementary in Lee County, Florida. The result is the *Core Knowledge Sequence* that forms the basis for this series. The *Core Knowledge Sequence* may be ordered from the Core Knowledge Foundation (please see the end of this introduction for the address).

IV. The Nature of This Series

The books in this series are designed to be useful tools for parents and teachers, both at home and in school. They are called "resources" to signal that they do not replace the regular local school curriculum, but rather serve as aids to help children gain some of the important knowledge they will need to make progress in school and be effective in society.

Each book in the Core Knowledge Series presents knowledge upon which later books will build. Our writers have tried their best to make the content interesting, clear, and challenging. We have *not* used discredited grade-level formulas regarding vocabulary and sentence length. Drafts of some materials have been revised on the basis of teachers' experience with children.

Although we have made these books as accessible and useful as we can, parents and teachers should understand that they are not the only means by which the *Core Knowledge Sequence* can be imparted. The books represent a single version of the possibilities inherent in the *Core Knowledge Sequence,* and a first step in the Core Knowledge reform effort. We hope that publishers will be stimulated to offer educational videos, computer software, games, alternative books, and other imaginative vehicles based on the *Core Knowledge Sequence.*

V. What You Can Do to Help Improve American Education

The first step for parents and teachers who are committed to reform is to be skeptical about oversimplified slogans like "critical thinking" and "learning to learn." Such slogans are everywhere, and, unfortunately for our schools, their partial insights have been elevated to the level of universal truths. For example, "What students learn is not important; rather, we must teach students to learn *how* to learn." "The child, not the academic subject, is the true focus of education." "Do not impose knowledge on children before they are developmentally ready to receive it." "Do not bog children down in mere facts, but rather, teach critical-thinking skills."

Who has not heard these sentiments, so admirable and humane, and—up to a point— so true? But these positive sentiments in favor of skills and understanding have been turned into negative sentiments against the teaching of important knowledge. Those who have entered the teaching profession over the past forty years have been taught to scorn important knowledge as "mere facts," and to see the imparting of this knowledge as somehow injurious to children. Thus it has come about that many educators, armed with partially true slogans, have seemingly taken leave of common sense.

Many parents and teachers have come to the conclusion that elementary education must strike a better balance between the development of the whole child and the more limited but fundamental duty of the school to ensure that all children master a core of knowledge essential to their competence as learners in later grades. But these parents and teachers cannot act on their convictions without access to an agreed-upon, concrete sequence of knowledge. Our main motivation in developing the *Core Knowledge Sequence* and this book series has been to give parents and teachers something concrete to work with.

It has been encouraging to see how many teachers, since the first volume in this series was published, have responded to the Core Knowledge reform effort. A small but growing number of schools around the country—over fifty as of this writing, in diverse regions serving diverse populations—are working to integrate the *Core Knowledge Sequence* into their curricula.

Parents and teachers are urged to join in a grass-roots effort to strengthen our elementary schools. The place to start is in your own school and district. Insist that your school clearly state the core of *specific* knowledge that each child in a grade must learn. Whether your school's core corresponds to the Core Knowledge model is less important than the existence of *some* core—which, we hope, will be as solid, coherent, and challenging as the *Core Knowledge Sequence* has proven to be. Inform members of your community about the need for such a specific curriculum, and help make sure that the people who are elected or appointed to your local school board are independent-minded people who will insist that our children have the benefit of a solid, specific, world-class curriculum in each grade.

You are invited to become a member of the Core Knowledge Network by writing the Core Knowledge Foundation, 2012-B Morton Drive, Charlottesville, VA 22901.

Share the knowledge!

E. D. Hirsch, Jr.
Charlottesville, Virginia

How to Use This Book

FOR PARENTS AND TEACHERS

The book you are holding in your hands is an unusual one. It is a collection made for children, but it is not limited to the usual treasury of best-loved stories and poems. In addition to those, it offers engaging accounts of language, literature, history, geography, science, fine arts, and math—the core academic subjects that our children need in the new age of global information. It also contains knowledge that may help them become fulfilled and productive people. Yet it is not a textbook or a workbook filled with exercises. It offers the academic core—the sort of knowledge that the best educational systems are providing children all over the world—written in a lively and effective manner, with tips for making those knowledge domains come alive. But such a book must leave much to you and to the child in the way of additional conversation and practice.

Each book in the *Core Knowledge Series* builds upon knowledge presented in previous books. We know from learning theory that we learn best by building upon what we already know. Hence, this sixth-grade book refers back to previous books. Moreover, the sections of the sixth-grade book also refer you to other sections of the same book. Because subjects and interests cut across disciplines, we encourage you to continue this practice by helping your child see connections between art and math, history and literature, physical sciences and language, just as we have tried to do. And you should also feel free, using the table of contents or the indexes, to make your own connections between the books of the series.

We have tried to make this book attractive and engaging by using an interactive, storybook format. We address the child directly as reader, asking questions and suggesting projects that he or she might do. You can help your child read more actively both by conversing while you are reading and by bringing the subjects up at a later time when connections occur to you. You and your child can read the sections of this book in any order. You do not need to begin at the beginning and work your way through to the end. In fact, we suggest that you skip from section to section, and that you reread as much as the child likes.

To help your child use this book, you might think of it as a guidebook that tries to be as informative and suggestive as possible in a concise format. We encourage you to help your child find ways to open out from this book, exploring further what she or he reads. If possible, take your child to plays, museums, and concerts; help your child find related books (some are suggested here). In short, this guidebook recommends places to visit and describes what is important in those places, but only you and your child can make the actual visit, travel the streets, and climb the steps.

Bon voyage!

I.

LANGUAGE ARTS

Introduction to Stories and Speeches

The selections in this section range from speeches that present the ringing words of admirable real-life heroes to stories that convey the joy and agony of young love. They will appeal to sixth-grade children because the subject matter relates to world events or to the emotions that are beginning to engross young adolescents. While the selections presented here stand on their own, it is likely that children's appreciation of the literature will deepen when they read related sections in this book. For example, Martin Luther King's "I Have a Dream" speech is even more stirring when it is understood in the context of the struggle for civil rights, described in the American Civilization section of this book. And children who appreciate the artistry of *Romeo and Juliet* may enjoy reading about its famous author, William Shakespeare, in the About Language and Literature section of Book Five, or reading our adaptation of Shakespeare's *Julius Caesar*, also in Book Five.

In this book we continue to present excerpted works of great literature, including historically significant speeches. Although it is not within the scope of this series to offer novels in their entirety, we hope that children will be encouraged by the samples they find here to read the full works. Parents and teachers can gauge a child's ability and desire to read complete novels and steer him or her in that direction when the time comes.

Stories and Speeches

Romeo and Juliet

(adapted and retold from the play by William Shakespeare)

Like most of William Shakespeare's plays, Romeo and Juliet *is based on earlier sources, which in this case go back to some stories popular in Italy in the late 1400s. These stories were transformed into a poem in English by a poet named Brooke. Today Brooke's poem has been forgotten, but Shakespeare's play lives on. What makes Shakespeare's play live is its dramatic power and its remarkable language. That language, beautiful as it is, may seem strange to modern readers, especially to young readers encountering the play for the first time. Thus, we have chosen to retell the story here in prose and to weave into it some lines from the original play, with the hope that in time, you will enjoy reading the complete play in Shakespeare's own wonderful words, and perhaps even have the chance to see it acted on stage. You might also enjoy watching the movie of* Romeo and Juliet *directed by Franco Zeffirelli.*

Two households, both alike in dignity,
In fair Verona, where we lay our scene,
From ancient grudge break to new mutiny,
Where civil blood makes civil hands unclean.
From forth the fatal loins of these two foes
A pair of star-crossed lovers take their life;
Whose misadventured piteous overthrows
Doth with their death bury their parents' strife.

Long ago in Italy, in the city of Verona, there dwelled two noble families, the Capulets and the Montagues. For as long as anyone could remember, a feud had raged between these families. They fought with the least provocation: a servant of Capulet would insult a servant of Montague, and this small spark would kindle a blaze of bloodshed and hatred. At last the prince of Verona grew so tired of this feuding that he angrily addressed the heads of the two households. "Old Capulet and Montague," he said, "if ever you disturb our streets again, your lives shall pay the forfeit of the peace."

The two families were then forced to control their mutual hatred. There was no one among them more eager to make peace than Romeo, the son of old Montague, for Romeo was infatuated with a girl named Rosaline, who happened to be Capulet's niece.

One day as Romeo sat pining away with love, he heard that there was to be a feast that night at the house of Capulet. When he learned that Rosaline would be there, Romeo vowed to attend, but in a mask so that no one would recognize him as a Montague. His friends Benvolio and Mercutio agreed to don masks and accompany him.

With their masks in place, they arrived at the Capulets' home just as the dancing began. Romeo looked around the room, hoping to catch sight of Rosaline, but suddenly his eyes fell upon a girl so beautiful that all thoughts of Rosaline flew from his brain forever. "O, she doth teach the torches to burn bright!" he murmured. "Did my heart love till now? Forswear it, sight, for I ne'er saw true beauty till this night."

Capulet's nephew, Tybalt, was standing nearby, and when he heard Romeo's voice, he recognized an enemy behind the mask. Filled with fury, he moved to attack Romeo, but old Capulet restrained him and urged him not to disrupt the feast. Tybalt went away, vowing to take revenge upon Romeo later.

Meanwhile Romeo watched for an opportunity to speak to the unknown girl, and when the next dance had ended, he went forward and took her by the hand. He was so awed by her presence that he felt like a pilgrim, also called a palmer, who had come to pray at a holy shrine. "If I profane with my unworthiest hand this holy shrine," he said, "the gentle fine is this: my lips, two blushing pilgrims, ready stand to smooth that rough touch with a tender kiss."

"Palm to palm is holy palmers' kiss," the girl reminded him.

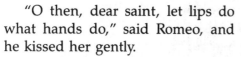

"O then, dear saint, let lips do what hands do," said Romeo, and he kissed her gently.

Just then a woman summoned the girl to speak with her mother. "Who is her mother?" Romeo asked.

"The lady of the house," said the woman. "I nursed her daughter, that you talked withal."

Romeo was stunned. He, a Montague, had fallen hopelessly in love with Juliet, the daughter of old Capulet himself! He left the feast in a state of confusion.

Juliet saw him leaving and sent her nurse to find out his name. When the nurse returned with the news that he was Romeo, the only son of old Montague, Juliet could

hardly believe her misfortune. "My only love sprung from my only hate!" she lamented. "Too early seen unknown, and known too late!"

Romeo kept to himself as he walked home past the Capulets' orchard. Suddenly he stopped. "Can I go forward when my heart is here?" he said. In an instant he had climbed over the orchard wall. He heard his friends Benvolio and Mercutio calling him in the lane, but he did not answer them, and at last they went on. Now Romeo, hidden in the darkness, looked up at the Capulets' house, hoping to glimpse his love. Suddenly he saw her. "What light through yonder window breaks?" he whispered. "It is the east, and Juliet is the sun." He watched as Juliet stood at the balcony, leaning her cheek upon her hand. "O, that I were a glove upon that hand," murmured Romeo, "that I might touch that cheek!"

Juliet sighed longingly. "Romeo, Romeo!" she said aloud, musing to herself. "Wherefore art thou Romeo? Deny thy father, and refuse thy name; or, if thou wilt not, be but sworn my love, and I'll no longer be a Capulet." Romeo listened with happiness as she went on. "'Tis but thy name that is my enemy," she reflected. "O, be some other name! What's in a name? That which we call a rose by any other name would smell as sweet. Romeo, doff thy name, and for thy name which is no part of thee take all myself."

Juliet was startled to hear a man's voice answer from the darkness: "Call me but love, and I'll be new baptized; henceforth I never will be Romeo." Though startled, Juliet was not at all displeased to see Romeo. She asked how he had made his way into the walled garden. "With love's light wings did I o'erperch these walls," he said, "for stony limits cannot hold love out."

The young lovers knew the danger they faced if they were found together, but so strong were their feelings for each other that they talked on and on, confessing their devotion. They vowed to belong to each other forever, and made plans to be married in secret the very next day by Friar Laurence, the priest. Juliet's nurse began calling from within, telling her to come to bed, but the girl could not bear to say goodnight. Again and again she returned to the balcony for one last word. "Parting is such sweet sorrow," she said, "that I shall say goodnight till it be morrow."

The next day, Romeo and Juliet stole to Friar Laurence's rooms. The old friar was surprised at their request. But perhaps, he thought, this bond of love between a Capulet and a Montague would bring an end to the long years of bloody feuding. And so Romeo and Juliet were married in secret.

In the meantime, Juliet's cousin Tybalt, who was still furious with Romeo, had sent him a formal challenge to fight. As Romeo was returning from the secret marriage ceremony, he came upon Tybalt, who had been arguing with Benvolio and Mercutio in the public square.

"Romeo," said Tybalt when he saw him, "thou art a villain."

Romeo had no desire to quarrel with his wife's cousin. "Tybalt, I do protest, I never injured thee," he said, "but love thee better than thou canst devise till thou shalt know the reason of my love."

Mercutio could hardly believe his ears. Could this be his brave friend Romeo, replying so submissively to an insult from a Capulet? Well, he, Mercutio, would respond as the insult deserved. "Tybalt," Mercutio said, "you rat-catcher, will you walk? Good king of cats, I'll have nothing but one of your nine lives."

"I am for you," said Tybalt, drawing his sword.

"Gentle Mercutio, put thy rapier up," pleaded Romeo. But the two hotheads were determined to fight. As they brandished their weapons, Romeo tried to stand between them. Suddenly, with one quick thrust, Tybalt pierced Mercutio's side.

Mercutio sank down, gravely injured. "Why the devil came you between us?" he panted. "I was hurt under your arm."

"I thought all for the best," said Romeo.

Mercutio had grown pale and weak. He was dying. With a last gasp he cried out, "A plague on both your houses!"

When Romeo saw his best friend lying dead, he was filled with rage. "Tybalt," he cried, "Mercutio's soul is but a little way above our heads, staying for thine to keep him company. Either thou, or I, or both, must go with him." He grabbed a sword and plunged at Tybalt. His opponent thrust back. A crowd gathered. The hard clang of sword upon sword split the air. Then Romeo's steel met Tybalt's flesh, and Tybalt fell dead.

At Benvolio's urging, Romeo fled for his life. When the prince of Verona arrived on the scene, Benvolio explained all that had happened. The angry Capulets wanted Romeo put to death, but the prince decreed that since Tybalt shared some guilt in the matter, Romeo would be banished from Verona instead.

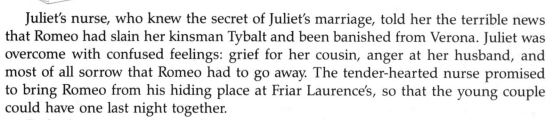

Juliet's nurse, who knew the secret of Juliet's marriage, told her the terrible news that Romeo had slain her kinsman Tybalt and been banished from Verona. Juliet was overcome with confused feelings: grief for her cousin, anger at her husband, and most of all sorrow that Romeo had to go away. The tender-hearted nurse promised to bring Romeo from his hiding place at Friar Laurence's, so that the young couple could have one last night together.

Early the next morning, before the rest of the household was awake, Romeo took sorrowful leave of Juliet, promising that they would someday be reunited. Scarcely had he set off for Mantua when Juliet's parents visited her chamber. They had news that they hoped would cause their daughter to cease mourning for Tybalt. It seemed that Juliet's father had arranged for her to marry the prosperous young Count Paris, who had long adored her. The ceremony was to take place in just a few days.

When Juliet heard this, she felt as if she had been struck. "I will not marry yet," she said firmly. Lady Capulet threw up her hands. The father was furious. And though Juliet begged him on her knees to listen to her, he would not. "Hang thee, young baggage, disobedient wretch!" he shouted. "I tell thee what: get thee to church on Thursday, or never after look me in the face."

Filled with despair, Juliet went to Friar Laurence to seek advice. She told him that she had resolved to kill herself rather than marry Paris. But Friar Laurence, who knew a great deal about the mysterious powers of herbs, proposed another solution. He gave her a vial containing a sleeping potion. Juliet was to drink it before retiring that night. Then she would fall into such a deep sleep, for forty hours, that the next morning she would appear to be dead, and the grieving Capulets would inter her in the family vault. Meanwhile the friar would send for Romeo. When Juliet awakened from her feigned death, Romeo would be there at her side to take her away with him.

The desperate plan filled Juliet with fear, but she agreed. She returned home, pretending that she had done penance for her disobedience, and dutifully agreed to marry Paris. Then she went to bed, drank the vial's contents, and fell into a deathlike sleep.

The next morning Juliet's father was up early to begin the wedding preparations, but his joy soon gave way to horror and grief, for Juliet was found lifeless. Her nurse and her mother were inconsolable, and Count Paris could hardly believe his eyes. All must now prepare not for a wedding, but for a funeral.

When Benvolio heard the sad news of Juliet's "death," he rushed to Mantua to tell Romeo. By an unfortunate accident, the friar's message had never reached Romeo, so he knew nothing about the sleeping potion. When he heard that his beloved Juliet was dead, he cried out, "Is it even so? Then I defy you, stars!" Without Juliet, life seemed empty of meaning; he cared for nothing now, and wanted only to die next to Juliet.

Romeo made his way to an apothecary and purchased a deadly poison. Then he took pen and paper and wrote down all the circumstances of his tragedy, for he wished the truth to be known. Taking these things with him, he rode back to Verona to find the tomb of the Capulets.

Now Romeo entered the dark tomb and looked upon Juliet once more. "O my love, my wife!" he said tenderly. "Death, that hath sucked the honey of thy breath, hath had no power yet upon thy beauty. O, here will I set up my everlasting rest. Eyes, look your last! Arms, take your last embrace! And lips, seal with a righteous kiss a dateless bargain to engrossing death." He raised the cup of poison to his lips, saying, "Here's to my love!" The poison took quick effect. He struggled to place his lips for one last time on Juliet's, and gasped his final words: "Thus with a kiss I die."

When Friar Laurence learned that his letter had never reached Romeo, he hurried to the tomb. What he found there confirmed his worst fears: Romeo was dead, and Juliet was only now beginning to awaken. "A greater power than we hath thwarted our intents," he told her. He heard someone approaching. "Come, come away," he said, fleeing.

But Juliet would not leave. She looked around her and slowly understood what had happened. She took the cup from Romeo's hand. "O churl," she said gently, "drunk all, and left no friendly drop to help me after? I will kiss thy lips; haply some poison yet doth hang on them." She kissed his lips, which were still warm. Suddenly she heard the watchman approaching. "Yea, noise? Then I'll be brief. O happy dagger!" She drew Romeo's dagger from its sheath and stabbed herself to the heart. The watchman entered to find her dead, nestled against Romeo's lifeless body.

When the true story of Romeo and Juliet was made known, their families were stunned and grief-stricken. The prince looked upon the scene of tragedy and said, "Capulet, Montague, see what a scourge is laid upon your hate, that heaven finds means to kill your joys with love. And I for winking at your discords too have lost a brace of kinsmen. All are punished." Then Capulet at last offered Montague his hand, and the two old enemies made a sorrowful pledge of peace. Montague promised to make a gold statue of Juliet, and Capulet promised to place one of Romeo beside it, reminders of the terrible price of their foolish feud.

> Go hence, to have more talk of these sad things;
>   Some shall be pardoned, and some punished;
> For never was a story of more woe
> Than this of Juliet and her Romeo.

Oliver Twist

(retold and excerpted from the novel by Charles Dickens)

In England in the 1830s, the poor and homeless were sent to a dismal place known as the workhouse, where they were made to work slavishly for meager rations and ragged clothes. Oliver Twist *is the story of a sweet-natured orphan who spends his childhood in such a place, after his mother dies giving birth to him there. He and the other orphans are treated cruelly; while their master, Mr. Bumble, lives in comfort, they are practically starved to death. In the scene below, set in the workhouse, when one desperate boy threatens to turn cannibal if he isn't given more porridge, the frightened orphans send Oliver to ask for seconds.*

The room in which the boys were fed was a large stone hall, with a copper at one end, out of which the master ladled the gruel at meal-times. Of this festive composition each boy had one small bowl and no more. The bowls never wanted washing. The boys polished them with their spoons till they shone; and when they had finished this operation (which never took very long, the spoons being nearly as large as the bowls), they would sit staring at the copper with such eager eyes, as if they could have devoured the very bricks of which it was composed.

Boys have generaly excellent appetites. Oliver Twist and his companions suffered the tortures of slow starvation for three months: at last they got so voracious and wild with hunger, that one boy hinted darkly to his companions that unless he had another basin of gruel each day, he was afraid he might some night happen to eat the boy who slept next to him. He had a wild, hungry eye, and they implicitly believed him. A council was held; lots were cast who should walk up to the master after supper that evening, and ask for more; and it fell to Oliver Twist.

The evening arrived; the boys took their places. The master stationed himself at the copper; the gruel was served out. The gruel disappeared. The boys whispered to each other, and winked at Oliver, while his neighbors nudged him. Child though he was, he was desperate with hunger, and reckless with misery. He rose from the table and advanced to the master, basin and spoon in hand. Somewhat alarmed at his own temerity, he said:

"Please, sir, I want some more."

The master, Mr. Bumble, was a fat, healthy man, but he turned very pale. He gazed in stupefied astonishment on the small rebel for some seconds, and then clung for support to the table. The assistants were paralyzed with wonder, the boys with fear.

"What!" said the master at length, in a faint voice.

"Please, sir," replied Oliver, "I want some more."

The master aimed a blow at Oliver's head with the ladle. Then he grabbed Oliver tightly by the arms, and shrieked aloud for his own master, the beadle.

"I beg your pardon, sir! Oliver Twist has asked for more!"

There was a general start. Horror was depicted on every face. An animated discussion took place, and Oliver was ordered into instant confinement. The very next morning a bill was pasted on the outside of the gate, offering a reward to anyone who would take Oliver Twist off the hands of the parish. In other words, five pounds and Oliver Twist were offered to any man or woman who wanted an apprentice to any trade, business, or calling.

Oliver escapes the workhouse only to encounter worse trials. Eventually he is taken in by a band of thieves led by a merry but evil old man named Fagin. Fagin tries to corrupt the unsuspecting Oliver by sending him out for the day with two young pickpockets, Charley Bates and a sly character in a top hat and baggy clothes known as the Artful Dodger. "The Artful" makes off with a gentleman's silk handkerchief, leaving the innocent Oliver to be cornered by an angry crowd and taken before the authorities. But Mr. Brownlow, the victim of the theft, convinces them of Oliver's innocence. He treats the boy kindly and even takes him to his home, where Oliver enjoys the loving attention of the motherly housekeeper, Mrs. Bedwin. His newfound happiness ends abruptly one day when, while delivering some books for Mr. Brownlow, Oliver is recaptured by two of Fagin's gang, the cruel Bill Sikes and his girlfriend, Nancy.

Oliver was walking along thinking how happy and contented he ought to feel, when he was startled by a young woman screaming out very loud, "Oh, my dear brother!" And he was stopped by having a pair of arms thrown tight round his neck.

"Don't," cried Oliver, struggling. "Let go of me. Who is it? What are you stopping me for?"

"Oh my gracious!" said the young woman, "I've found him! Oh! Oliver! Oliver! Oh, you naughty boy, to make me suffer such distress on your account! Come home, dear, come." The young woman burst into another fit of crying.

"What's the matter, ma'am?" inquired a woman standing nearby.

"Oh, ma'am," replied the young woman, "he ran away, near a month ago, from his parents, who are hard-working and respectable people; and went and joined a set of thieves and bad characters; and almost broke his mother's heart."

"Young wretch!" said the woman.

"Go home, you little brute," said another.

"I am not," replied Oliver, greatly alarmed. "I don't know her. I haven't a sister, or father and mother either. I'm an orphan."

"Only hear him, how he braves it out!" cried the young woman.

"Why, it's Nancy!" exclaimed Oliver, who now saw her face for the first time.

"You see, he knows me!" cried Nancy, appealing to the bystanders. "Make him come home, good people, or he'll break my heart!"

"What the devil's this?" said a man, bursting out of a beer-shop. It was Bill Sikes. "Young Oliver! Come home to our poor mother, you young dog!"

"I don't belong to them. I don't know them. Help! help!" cried Oliver, struggling in the man's powerful grasp.

"Help!" repeated the man. "Yes, I'll help out, you young rascal! What books are these? You've been stealing 'em, have you? Give 'em here." With these words, the man tore the volumes from Oliver's grasp and struck him on the head.

Stupefied by the blows and the suddenness of the attack, terrified by the brutality of the man, what could one poor child do? No help was near; resistance was useless. In another moment, Oliver was dragged into a labyrinth of dark streets.

At length the three turned into a filthy narrow street and stopped before the door of a shop that was in a ruinous condition. Bill Sikes seized the boy by the collar, and all three went quickly inside the house.

They waited in a dark passage while the person who had let them in chained and barred the door. It was John Dawkins, otherwise known as the Artful Dodger. Holding a candle before him, he led them down a flight of stairs to a low, earth-smelling room, where they were received with a shout of laughter.

"Oh, my wig!" cried Charley Bates. "Here he is! Oh, Fagin, look at him! Look at his togs! Superfine cloth, and the heavy swell cut! Oh, my eye, what a game! And his books, too! Nothing but a gentleman, Fagin! I can't bear it. Hold me, somebody, while I laugh it out." He laid himself flat on the floor and kicked in an ecstasy of facetious joy. Then, jumping to his feet, he snatched the candle from the Artful Dodger and, advancing to Oliver, viewed him round and round. Meanwhile Fagin, taking off his nightcap, made a great number of low bows to the bewildered boy.

"Delighted to see you looking so well, my dear," said Fagin with mock concern. "The Artful shall give you another suit, my dear, for fear you should spoil that Sunday one."

At that instant the Artful Dodger furthered Fagin's merriment by searching Oliver's pockets and drawing forth a five-pound note. "Hallo, what's that?" inquired Sikes, stepping forward as Fagin seized the note. "That's mine."

"No, no, my dear," said Fagin. "Mine, Bill, mine. You shall have the books."

"Hand over, I tell you!" retorted Sikes. "Give it here, you avaricious old skeleton, give it here!" Sikes plucked the note from between Fagin's finger and thumb and, looking the old man coolly in the face, folded it up small and tied it in his neckerchief. "That's for our share of the trouble," said Sikes, "and not half enough, neither. You may keep the books, if you're fond of reading. If you ain't, sell 'em."

"They belong to the old gentleman," said Oliver, wringing his hands, "to the good, kind, old gentleman who took me into his house. Oh, pray send them back;

send him back the books and money. Keep me here all my life long; but pray, pray send them back. He'll think I stole them; the old lady, all of them who were so kind to me, will think I stole them. Oh, do have mercy upon me, and send them back!" With these words, Oliver fell upon his knees at Fagin's feet and beat his hands together in perfect desperation.

"The boy's right," remarked Fagin, looking covertly around and knitting his shaggy eyebrows into a hard knot. "You're right, Oliver, you're right; they *will* think you have stolen 'em. Ha! ha! It couldn't have happened better, if we had chosen our time!"

Oliver jumped to his feet and tore wildly from the room, uttering shrieks for help. Fagin and his two pupils darted out in pursuit and soon returned, dragging Oliver with them.

"So you wanted to get away, my dear, did you?" said Fagin, taking up a jagged and knotty club which lay in a corner of the fireplace. "Wanted to get assistance, eh? Called for the police, did you? We'll cure you of that, my young master."

He inflicted a smart blow on Oliver's shoulders with the club, and was raising it for a second, when Nancy, rushing forward, wrested it from his hand. She flung the club into the fire, with a force that brought some of the glowing coals whirling out into the room.

"I won't stand by and see it done, Fagin," cried the girl. "You've got the boy. What more would you have? Let him be—let him be—or I shall put that mark on some of you, that will bring me to the gallows before my time."

"You're a nice one," said Sikes, "to take up the humane and gen-teel side! A pretty subject for the child, as you call him, to make a friend of!"

"God almighty help me, I am!" cried the girl passionately, "and I wish I had been struck dead in the street before I had lent a hand in bringing him here."

"Come, come," said Fagin, "we must have civil words."

"Civil words, you villain! Yes, you deserve 'em from me. I thieved for you when I was a child not half as old as this!" she cried, pointing to Oliver. "I have been in the same trade, and in the same service, for twelve years since. It is my living; and the cold, wet, dirty streets are my home; and you're the wretch that drove me to them long ago, and that'll keep me there, day and night, day and night, till I die!"

"I shall do you a mischief worse than that, if you say much more!" Fagin snarled.

The girl made such a rush at Fagin as would probably have left marks of her revenge upon him, had not her wrists been seized roughly by Sikes. She made a few ineffectual struggles, and fainted.

Fagin smiled, relieved to have the disturbance over. Then, retrieving his club from the fire, he said, "Charley, show Oliver to bed."

"I suppose he'd better not wear his best clothes tomorrow, Fagin, had he?" inquired Charley Bates.

"Certainly not," replied Fagin, reciprocating the grin with which Charley put the question.

Charley took the candle and led Oliver into an adjacent kitchen, where there were two or three rough beds. Here, with many uncontrollable bursts of laughter, Charley produced the identical old suit of clothes which Oliver had so much congratulated himself upon leaving behind. "Pull off the smart ones," said Charley, "and I'll give 'em to Fagin to take care of."

Poor Oliver unwillingly complied. Rolling up the new clothes under his arm, Charley departed from the room, leaving Oliver in the dark and locking the door behind him. Oliver was sick and weary, and he soon fell sound asleep.

Oliver endures even worse trials to come, but in the end all works out well, as you can find out by reading Oliver Twist.

The Secret Garden
(retold with excerpts from the novel by Frances Hodgson Burnett)

The Secret Garden, *which tells the story of a young girl named Mary Lennox, describes a kind of place that all of us would like to be able to escape to once in a while.*

When the novel begins, Mary is living in India with her parents. A plague of cholera leaves her an orphan. She goes to live with a minister and his family, but the children in this family call her "Mistress Mary Quite Contrary" because she is so stubborn and haughty. Soon she is sent to England to live at Misselthwaite Manor with her eccentric uncle, Mr. Archibald Craven.

The episodes that follow introduce Mary and her early life at Misselthwaite Manor, where her uncle leaves her on her own. At first, Martha, the housemaid, and Ben Weatherstaff, the gardener, are her only acquaintances in the large, quiet house. Arriving as she does in the chill of winter, Mary finds the house and grounds dreary, and does not even want to go outside. But things change when one day she hears of a mysterious garden different from all the rest.

(In the selection below, "Ayah" means nursemaid in India, and "Mem Sahib" is what a servant would call the lady of the house. A "moor" is a kind of English prairie—open, rolling land covered with shrubs and grasses.)

When Mary Lennox was sent to Misselthwaite Manor to live with her uncle, everybody said she was the most disagreeable-looking child ever seen. It was true, too. She had a little thin face and a little thin body, thin light hair and a sour expression. Her hair was yellow, and her face was yellow because she had been born in India and had always been ill in one way or another. Her father had held a position under the English Government and had always been busy and ill himself, and her mother had been a great beauty who cared only to go to parties and amuse herself. She had not wanted a little girl at all, and when Mary was born she handed her over to the care of an Ayah, who was made to understand that if she wanted to please the Mem Sahib she must keep the child out of sight as much as possible. But when the cholera broke out in its most fatal form and people were dying like flies, Mary woke one morning to find that she had neither father nor mother left.

And so, when Mistress Mary arrived at Misselthwaite Manor, she had perhaps never felt quite so contrary in all her life. From the window of her room in the manor, she could see a great climbing stretch of land which seemed to have no trees on it, and to look rather like an endless, dull, purplish sea.

"What is that?" she said to the housemaid, who had come into her room to light the fire.

"That's th' moor," said Martha, in her Yorkshire way of speaking. "Does tha' like it?" she asked with a good-natured grin.

"No," answered Mary. "I hate it."

"That's because th'art not used to it," Martha said, "But tha' will like it."

"Who is going to dress me?" demanded Mary.

Martha stared. "Can't you put on your own clothes?"

"No," answered Mary, quite indignantly. "I never did in my life. My Ayah dressed me, of course."

"Well," said Martha, "it's time tha' should learn. It'll do thee good to wait on thyself a bit."

"It is different in India," said Mistress Mary disdainfully.

At first each day that passed for Mary was exactly like the others. She pushed away her breakfast and then gazed out of the window across to the huge moor which seemed to spread out and climb up to the sky.

One day Martha said to Mary, "You wrap up warm an' run out an' play you. It'll do you good."

"Out? Why should I go out on a day like this?" Mary replied in her contrary fashion.

"Well, if tha' doesn't go out th'lt have to stay in, an' what has tha' got to do?"

Mary glanced about her. Perhaps it would be better to go and see what the gardens were like.

"Who will go with me?" she inquired.

"You'll go by yourself," Martha answered. "My brother Dickon goes off on th' moor by himself an' plays for hours. That's how he made friends with th' pony. He found it on th' moor with its mother when it was a little one an' he began to make friends with it an' give it bits o' bread an' pluck young grass for it. And it got to like him so it follows him about an' it lets him get on its back. Dickon's a kind lad an' animals likes him."

It was really this mention of Dickon which made Mary decide to go out, though she was not aware of it. She began to feel a slight interest in Dickon, and as she had never before been interested in any one but herself, it was the dawning of a healthy sentiment.

"If tha' goes round that way tha'll come to th' gardens," Martha said, pointing to a gate in a wall of shrubbery. She seemed to hesitate a second before she added, "One of th' gardens is locked up. No one has been in it for ten years."

"Why?" asked Mary in spite of herself.

"Mr. Craven had it shut when his wife died so sudden. He won't let no one go inside. It was her garden. He locked th' door an' dug a hole an' buried th' key."

Martha found Mary's coat and hat for her and showed her the way downstairs. Mary turned down the walk which led to the door in the shrubbery. She could not help thinking about the garden which no one had been into for ten years. She wondered what it would look like and whether there were any flowers still alive in it.

At the end of the path she was following, she saw a long wall with ivy growing over it. She went toward the wall and found that there was a green door in the ivy, and that it stood open. This was not the closed garden, evidently. Mary went down the path and found herself in an orchard. There were walls all round it also and trees trained against them, and there were bare fruit trees growing in the winter-browned grass. She noticed that the wall did not seem to end with the orchard but to extend beyond it as if it enclosed a place at the other side. She could see the tops of trees above the wall, and when she stood still she saw a bird with a bright red breast sitting on the topmost branch of one of them, and suddenly he burst into his winter song—almost as if he had caught sight of her and was calling to her.

She stopped and listened to him and somehow his cheerful, friendly little whistle gave her a pleased feeling—even a disagreeable little girl may be lonely, and the big bare moor and big bare gardens had made this one feel as if there was no one left in the world but herself. The bright-breasted little bird brought a look into Mary's sour little face which was almost a smile. Perhaps he lived in the mysterious garden and knew all about it.

She thought of the robin and of the way he seemed to sing his song at her, and as she remembered the treetop he perched on she stopped rather suddenly on the path.

"I believe that tree was in the secret garden—I feel sure it was," she said. "There was a wall round the place and there was no door."

She walked back to the first garden she had entered and there she found the old gardener, Ben Weatherstaff, digging. He turned about and began to whistle—a low soft whistle. Almost the next moment, she heard a soft little rushing flight through the air—and it was the bird with the red breast flying to them, and he actually alighted on the big clod of earth quite near the gardener's foot.

"Where has tha' been, tha' cheeky little beggar?" chuckled the old man to the bird.

"Will he always come when you call him?" Mary asked almost in a whisper.

"Aye, that he will. I've knowed him ever since he was a fledgling."

The robin hopped about busily pecking the soil. Mary thought his black dewdrop eyes gazed at her with great curiosity. It really seemed as if he were finding out all about her. She went a step nearer to the robin and looked at him very hard.

"I'm lonely," she said.

She had not known before that this was one of the things which made her feel sour and cross. She seemed to find it out when the robin looked at her and she looked at the robin.

Just that moment the robin gave a little shake of his wings and flew away.

"He has flown over the wall!" Mary cried out, watching him. "He has flown into the orchard—he has flown across the other wall—into the garden where there is no door!"

"He lives there," said old Ben, "among th' old rose-trees there."

"I should like to see them," said Mary. "There must be a door somewhere."

Ben drove his spade deep and said, "There was ten year' ago, but there isn't now. None as any one can find, an' none as is any one's business. Don't you be a meddlesome wench an' poke your nose where it's no cause to go."

The robin sang loudly. "It's in the garden no one can go into," Mary said to herself. "It's in the garden without a door. He lives in there. How I wish I could see what it is like!"

Mary continued to go out, exploring the grounds of Misselthwaite Manor. The big breaths of rough fresh air blown over the heather filled her lungs with something which was good for her whole thin body and whipped some red color into her cheeks and brightened her dull eyes. After a few days spent almost entirely out of doors, Mary wakened one morning knowing for the first time what it was to be hungry. When she sat down to her breakfast she did not glance disdainfully at her porridge and push it away, but took up her spoon and began to eat it and went on eating it until her bowl was empty.

One day the rain poured down in torrents, and when Mary looked out of her window the moor was almost hidden by gray mist and clouds. There could be no going out today. But Martha told her that her younger brother, Dickon, did not mind the wet. "He goes just th' same as if th' sun was shinin'. He once found a little fox cub half drowned in its hole and he brought it home in th' bosom of his shirt to keep it warm. He's got it at home now."

Mary begged Martha to tell her more about Dickon and his animals. "I like Dickon," said Mary, "even though I've never seen him."

"Well," said Martha stoutly. "I've told thee that th' very birds likes him an' th' rabbits an' wild sheep an' ponies, an' th' foxes themselves. I wonder," Martha said, staring at Mary reflectively, "what Dickon would think of thee?"

"He wouldn't like me," said Mistress Mary in her stiff, cold little way. "No one does."

"How does tha' like thyself?" inquired Martha.

Mary hesitated, and answered, "Not at all, really."

One day Mary went out into the gardens and there found old Ben Weatherstaff. "Springtime's comin'," the gardener said. "Cannot tha' smell it?"

Mary sniffed the air and said, "I smell something nice and fresh and damp."

"That's th' good rich earth," he answered. "It's in a good humor makin' ready to grow things. In th' flower gardens out there things will be stirrin' down below in th' dark. Th' sun's warmin' 'em. You'll see bits o' green spikes stickin' out o' th' black earth after a bit."

As they talked the robin flew to them. "Are things stirring down below in the dark in that garden where the robin lives?" Mary asked.

"Ask him," said Ben Weatherstaff. "He's the only one as knows. No one else has been inside it for ten years."

Ten years was a long time, Mary thought. She had been born ten years ago.

The robin let her come very close as he scratched for worms, and she began to think of all the things she now liked—the bird, Martha, the stories about Dickon, and playing out-of-doors. Just then, she saw that the robin was scratching in a hole, and that in the newly turned soil lay something like a ring of rusty iron or brass. She knelt to pick it up, and found herself looking at an old key which looked as if it had been buried a long time.

"Perhaps it has been buried for ten years," she said in a whisper. "Perhaps it is the key to the garden!"

After she had looked at the key quite a long time, she walked to the wall and looked at the ivy growing on it. She could not see a door beneath the dark green leaves, but she put the key in her pocket and made up her mind to keep it with her always, so that if she ever found the door she would be ready.

That night, Mary offered to go one day and tell Martha's many brothers and sisters stories about India. "It is quite different from Yorkshire," said Mary. "I never thought of that before." She was thinking of so many new things!

Martha gave Mary a skipping rope with striped red and blue handles, and taught the little girl to skip. In the morning, as she counted and skipped all around the garden, the robin appeared and she followed him down the walk with little skips.

"You showed me where the key was yesterday," she said. "You ought to show me the door today; but I don't believe you know!"

Mary Lennox had heard a great deal about magic in her Ayah's stories, and she always said that what happened almost at that moment was magic.

A gust of wind swept down the walk and swung aside some loose ivy. Mary jumped forward and caught it, because underneath she saw the round knob of a door. Her heart began to thump and her hands to shake a little in excitement. The robin sang and twittered as if he, too, were excited. It was the lock of the door which had been closed ten years. Mary put her hand in her pocket, drew out the key, put it in the lock, and turned it. She took a deep breath and looked to see if anyone was coming. No one was, so she pushed back the door, which opened slowly—slowly.

Then she slipped through it, and shut it behind her, and stood with her back against it, looking about her and breathing quite fast with excitement, and wonder, and delight.

She was standing *inside* the secret garden.

It was the sweetest, most mysterious-looking place any one could imagine. The high walls which shut it in were covered with the leafless stems of climbing roses. All the ground was covered with grass of a wintry brown and out of it grew clumps of bushes which were surely rose-bushes if they were alive. There were other trees in the garden, and climbing roses had run all over them and swung down long tendrils which made light swaying curtains. Mary did not know whether they were dead or alive, but their thin gray branches looked like a sort of hazy mantle spreading over everything. This hazy tangle from tree to tree made it all look so mysterious. It was different from any other place Mary had ever seen in her life.

"How still it is!" she whispered. "I am the first person who has spoken in here for ten years." Even though it was all quite strange and silent, she did not feel lonely at all.

"It isn't a quite dead garden," she cried out softly to herself. "Some of these roses may be alive. Oh! I can't tell; but so many other things are alive."

She did not know anything about gardening, but it looked to her as if the small green plants she saw poking through the dirt needed to breathe. She searched about until she found a rather sharp piece of wood and knelt down and dug and weeded until she had made nice little clear places around all the plants. She went from place to place, digging and weeding, until it was past the time for midday dinner. She had been actually happy the whole time.

"Martha," she said when she returned, red-cheeked and bright-eyed, "I wish I had a little spade." She knew she must be careful of the secret kingdom she had found, so that Mr. Craven would not get a new key and lock it up forever. She really could not bear that. She said, "If I had a little spade I could dig somewhere and perhaps make a little garden."

Martha stopped to think. "The shop at Thwaite sells packages o' flower seeds, an' little garden sets with a spade an' a rake an' a fork, all tied together. We could ask Dickon, who oft walks over to town, to buy the tools an' the seeds."

"If I have a spade," Mary thought, "I can make the earth nice and soft and dig up weeds. If I have seeds and can make flowers grow the garden won't be dead at all—it will come alive."

Martha said Dickon would bring the things to the manor when he had bought them. "Oh!" exclaimed Mary. "Then I shall see him! I never saw a boy that foxes and crows love. I want to see him very much."

For the next week the sun shone on what Mary now called The Secret Garden. It seemed like a fairy place, different from the rest of Mary's world. Mary was a determined little person, and now that she had something interesting to be determined about, she was very much absorbed. She worked and dug and pulled up weeds; it seemed to her a fascinating sort of play. Sometimes she stopped digging to look at the garden and tried to imagine what it would be like when it was covered with thousands of lovely things in bloom.

One day, as Mary skipped round the laurel-hedged walk which curved round the secret garden, she heard a low, whistling sound and wanted to find out what it was. It was a very strange thing indeed. A funny-looking boy of about twelve was sitting under a tree, playing a wooden pipe. His cheeks were as red as poppies, and never had Mistress Mary seen such round and such blue eyes in any boy's face. A brown squirrel was watching him from the tree trunk, a pheasant peeked out from a nearby bush, and quite near the boy two rabbits were sitting up, as if they and the other animals were drawing near to watch and listen to him. He got up slowly, so as not to frighten the animals, and said, "I'm Dickon. I know tha'rt Miss Mary."

He spoke to her as if he knew her quite well, but she felt a little shy. As he explained the seeds and the garden tools to her, she wished she could talk as easily and nicely as he did. He showed her mignonette seeds, and poppy seeds, and seeds for all kinds of lovely flowers.

"See here," said Dickon. "I'll plant them for thee myself. Where is tha' garden?"

Mary had never thought of anyone asking her about this. "I don't know anything about boys," she said slowly. "Could you keep a secret, if I told you one? If anyone should find out, I believe I should die!" She said the last sentence quite fiercely.

Dickon looked puzzled, but answered good-humoredly, "I'm keepin' secrets all th' time. If I couldn't keep secrets from th' other lads, about birds' nests an' wild things' holes, there'd be naught safe on th' moor. Aye, I can keep secrets."

"I've stolen a garden," said Mary, very fast. "It isn't mine. It isn't anybody's. Nobody wants it, nobody cares for it, nobody ever goes into it. Perhaps everything in it is dead already; I don't know." She began to feel as contrary as she had ever felt in her life. "Nobody has any right to take it from me when I care about it and they don't." She burst out crying.

"Where is it?" asked Dickon softly.

Mistress Mary felt quite contrary still, but she said, "Come with me and I'll show you."

She led him round the laurel path and to the walk where the ivy grew so thickly. Dickon felt as if he were being led to look at some strange bird's nest and must move softly. When she stepped to the wall and lifted the hanging ivy he started. There was a door and Mary pushed it slowly open and they passed in together, and then Mary stood and waved her hand round defiantly.

"It's this," she said. "It's a secret garden, and I'm the only one in the world who wants it to be alive."

While Mary watched him, Dickon looked and took in all the gray trees with their gray creepers, the tangle on the walls, and the stone seats in the garden. "I never thought I'd see this place," he said in a whisper. "Martha told me about it once. There'll be nests here come springtime. It'd be th' safest nestin' place in England."

Mary put her hand on his arm without knowing it. "These rosebushes—are they alive? Is that one quite alive—quite?"

Dickon smiled. "It's as wick as you or me," he said, and Mary remembered that Martha had said "wick" meant "alive." They ran eagerly from bush to bush, and then Dickon noticed the clearings around the young plants and asked Mary if she had done that work.

"Yes," she said. "But I don't know anything about gardening."

"Tha' did right," said Dickon. "A gardener couldn't have told thee better. Now they'll come up like Jack's beanstalk. There's a lot of work to do here!"

Mary thought that she had never seen such a funny boy, or such a nice one. "Will you come and help? Oh, do come, Dickon!"

"I'll come every day if tha' wants me, rain or shine," he answered. "But I don't want to make it look all clipped. It's nicer like this, all runnin' wild."

"Don't let us make it tidy," said Mary. "It wouldn't seem like a secret garden if it was tidy." Then Mary did a strange thing. She leaned forward and asked him a question she had never dreamed of asking any one before. And she tried to ask it in Yorkshire because that was his language, and in India a person was always pleased if you knew his dialect.

"Does tha' like me?" she said.

"That I does. I likes thee wonderful!"

Then they worked harder than ever, and when it was time for Mary to go, she went slowly to the wall. Then she stopped and went back.

"Whatever happens, you—you never would tell?" she said.

He smiled encouragingly. "If tha' was a missel thrush an' showed me where thy nest was, does tha' think I'd tell anyone? Not me," he said. "Tha'art as safe as a missel thrush."

And she was quite sure she was.

Animal Farm

(Chapter One from the novel *Animal Farm* by George Orwell)

When George Orwell, a modern writer, wrote Animal Farm, *he was doing what many storytellers had done for centuries before him. Many storytellers from many different times and places have told tales with animals as the main characters.*

Do you remember Aesop's fables from ancient Greece, like "The Fox and the Grapes" or "The Hare and the Tortoise"? Have you read stories of Anansi the Spider, from the African and African-American traditions? How about tales of Coyote, who turns up in many tales told by Native Americans in the Northwest and Southwest?

Why have so many storytellers told tales about animals? Well, one reason is that they're really telling us about people. In an animal story, the storyteller is saying, "Take note: this story isn't just about animals. It's also about people, maybe even you!"

In George Orwell's Animal Farm, *the animals talk and act in ways that reveal a lot about people, especially how people behave when they gain power over other people.*

George Orwell was an English writer, born in 1903. Orwell was a participant in, or a witness to, many of the disturbing events in the twentieth century. He saw firsthand how Britain could oppress the people in its colonies. He fought (and was wounded) in the Spanish Civil War. He saw Hitler's rise to power.

Orwell's experiences led him to become a political writer. He had, as he described it, a "desire to push the world in a certain direction, to alter other people's idea of the kind of society that they should strive after." Most of all, Orwell wanted to push people to strive against totalitarianism—against the belief that people should be totally ruled by an all-powerful government, sometimes under the control of a power-hungry leader like Hitler in Germany or Stalin in what was the Soviet Union.

Animal Farm *is a book written in defiance of totalitarianism. Here we reprint just the first chapter, in which a boar named Old Major urges the animals to rise up against the humans.*

Mr. Jones, of the Manor Farm, had locked the henhouses for the night, but was too drunk to remember to shut the popholes. With the ring of light from his lantern dancing from side to side, he lurched across the yard, kicked off his boots at the back door, drew himself a last glass of beer from the barrel in the scullery, and made his way up to bed, where Mrs. Jones was already snoring.

As soon as the light in the bedroom went out there was a stirring and a fluttering all through the farm buildings. Word had gone round during the day that old Major, the prize Middle White boar, had had a strange dream on the previous night and wanted to communicate it to the other animals. It had been agreed that they should all meet in the big barn as soon as Mr. Jones was safely out of the way. Old Major was so highly regarded on the farm that everyone was quite ready to lose an hour's sleep in order to hear what he had to say.

At one end of the barn, on a sort of a raised platform, Major was already ensconced on his bed of straw, under a lantern which hung from a beam. He was twelve years old and had lately grown rather stout, but he was still a majestic-looking pig, with a wise and benevolent appearance in spite of the fact that his tushes had never been cut. Before long the other animals began to arrive and make themselves comfortable after their different fashions. First came the three dogs, Bluebell, Jessie, and Pincher, and then the pigs, who settled down in the straw immediately in front of the platform. The hens perched themselves on the windowsills, the pigeons fluttered up to the rafters, the sheep and cows lay down behind the pigs and began to chew the cud. The two cart horses, Boxer and Clover, came in together, walking very slowly and setting down their vast hairy hoofs with great care lest there should be some small animal concealed in the straw. Clover was a stout motherly mare approaching middle life, who had never quite got her figure back after her fourth foal. Boxer was an enormous beast, nearly fourteen hands high, and as strong as any two ordinary horses put together. A white stripe down his nose gave him a somewhat stupid appearance, and in fact, he was not of first-rate intelligence, but he was universally respected for his steadiness of character and tremendous powers of work. After the horses came Muriel, the white goat, and Benjamin, the donkey. Benjamin was the oldest animal on the farm, and the worst-tempered. He seldom talked, and when he did, it was usually to make some cynical remark—for instance, he would say that God had given him a tail to keep the flies off, but that he would sooner have had no tail and no flies. Alone among the animals on the farm he never laughed. If asked why, he would say that he had nothing to laugh at. Nevertheless, without openly admitting it, he was devoted to Boxer; the two of them usually spent their Sundays together in the small paddock beyond the orchard, grazing side by side and never speaking.

The two horses had just lain down when a brood of ducklings, which had lost their mother, filed into the barn, cheeping feebly and wandering from side to side to find some place where they would not be trodden on. Clover made a sort of wall around them with her great foreleg, and the ducklings nestled down inside it and promptly fell asleep. At the last moment Mollie, the foolish, pretty white mare who drew Mr. Jones's trap, came mincing daintily in, chewing at a lump of sugar. She took a place near the front and began flirting her white mane, hoping to draw attention to the red ribbons it was plaited with. Last of all came the cat, who looked round as usual for the warmest place, and finally squeezed herself in between Boxer and Clover; there she purred contentedly throughout the Major's speech without listening to a word of what he was saying.

All the animals were now present except Moses, the tame raven, who slept on a perch behind the back door. When the Major saw that they had all made themselves comfortable and were waiting attentively, he cleared his throat and began:

"Comrades, you have heard already about the strange dream that I had last night.

But I will come to the dream later. I have something else to say first. I do not think, comrades, that I shall be with you for many months longer, and before I die, I feel it my duty to pass on to you such wisdom as I have acquired. I have had a long life, I have had much time for thought as I lay alone in my stall, and I think that I may say that I understand the nature of life on this earth as well as any animal now living. It is about this that I wish to speak with you.

"Now, comrades, what is the nature of this life of ours? Let us face it: our lives are miserable, laborious and short. We are born, we are given just so much food as will keep the breath in our bodies, and those of us who are capable of it are forced to work to the last atom of our strength; and the very instant that our usefulness has come to an end we are slaughtered with hideous cruelty. No animal in England knows the meaning of happiness or leisure after he is a year old. No animal in England is free. The life of an animal is misery and slavery: that is the plain truth.

"But is this simply part of the order of nature? Is it because this land of ours is so poor that it cannot afford a decent life to those who dwell upon it? No, comrades, a thousand times no! The soil of England is fertile, its climate is good, it is capable of affording food in abundance to an enormously greater number of animals than now inhabit it. This single farm of ours would support a dozen horses, twenty cows, hundreds of sheep—and all of them living in a comfort and a dignity that are now almost beyond our imagining. Why then do we continue in this miserable condition? Because nearly the whole of the produce of our labor is stolen from us by human beings. There, comrades, is the answer to all our problems. It is summed up in a single word—Man. Man is the only real enemy we have. Remove Man from the scene, and the root cause of hunger and overwork is abolished forever.

"Man is the only creature that consumes without producing. He does not give milk, he does not lay eggs, he is too weak to pull the plow, he cannot run fast enough to catch rabbits. Yet he is lord of all the animals. He sets them to work, he gives back to them the bare minimum that will prevent them from starving, and the rest he keeps for himself. Our labor tills the soil, our dung fertilizes it, and yet there is not one of us that owns more than his bare skin. You cows that I see before me, how many thousands of gallons of milk have you given during the last year? And what has happened to that milk which should have been breeding up sturdy calves? Every drop of it has gone down the throats of our enemies. And you hens, how many of those eggs ever hatched into chickens? The rest have all gone to market to bring in money for Jones and his men. And you, Clover, where are those four foals that you bore, who should have been the support and pleasure of your old age? Each was sold at a year old—you will never see one of them again. In return for your four confinements and all your work in the fields, what have you ever had except your bare rations and a stall?

"And even the miserable lives we lead are not allowed to reach their natural span. For myself I do not grumble, for I am one of the lucky ones. I am twelve years old and have had over four hundred children. Such is the natural life of a pig. But no animal escapes the cruel knife in the end. You young porkers who are still sitting in front of me, every one of you will scream your lives out at the block within a year. To that horror we all must come—cows, pigs, hens, sheep, everyone. Even the horses and the dogs have no better fate. You, Boxer, the very day that those great muscles of yours lose their power, Jones will sell you to the knacker, who will cut your throat and boil you down for the foxhounds. As for the dogs, when they grow old and toothless, Jones ties a brick round their necks and drowns them in the nearest pond.

"Is it not crystal clear, then, comrades, that all the evils of this life of ours spring from the tyranny of human beings? Only get rid of Man, and the produce of our labor would be our own. Almost overnight we would become rich and free. What then must we do? Why, work day and night, body and soul, for the overthrow of the human race! This is my message to you, comrades: Rebellion! I do not know when the Rebellion will come, it might be in a week or in a hundred years, but I know, as surely as I see this straw beneath my feet, that sooner or later justice will be done. Fix your eyes on that, comrades, throughout the short remainder of your lives! And above all, pass on this message of mine to those who come after you, so that future generations shall carry on the struggle until it is victorious.

"And remember, comrades, your resolution must never fail. No argument must lead you astray. Never listen when they tell you that Man and the animals have a common interest, that the prosperity of the one is the prosperity of the others. It is all lies. Man serves the interests of no creature except himself. And among us animals let there be perfect unity, perfect comradeship in the struggle. All men are enemies. All animals are comrades."

At this moment there was a tremendous uproar. While Major was speaking four large rats had crept out of their holes and were sitting on their hindquarters listening to him. The dogs had suddenly caught sight of them, and it was only by a swift dash for their holes that the rats saved their lives. Major raised his trotter for silence.

"Comrades, here is a point that must be settled. The wild creatures, such as rats and rabbits—are they our friends or our enemies? Let us put it to the vote. I propose this question to the meeting: Are rats comrades?"

The vote was taken at once, and it was agreed by an overwhelming majority that rats were comrades. There were only four dissentients, the three dogs and the cat, who was afterwards discovered to have voted on both sides. Major continued.

"I have little more to say. I merely repeat, remember always your duty of enmity towards Man and all his ways. Whatever goes upon two legs is an enemy. Whatever goes upon four legs, or has wings, is a friend. And remember also that in fighting against Man, you must not come to resemble him. Even when you have conquered him, do not adopt his vices. No animal must ever live in a house, or sleep in a bed, or wear clothes, or drink alcohol, or smoke tobacco, or touch money, or engage in trade. All the habits of Man are evil. And above all, no animal must ever tyrannize over his own kind. Weak or strong, clever or simple, we are all brothers. No animal must ever kill any other animal. All animals are equal.

"And now, comrades, I will tell you about my dream of last night. I cannot describe that dream to you. It was a dream of the earth as it will be when Man has vanished. But it reminded me of something I had long forgotten. Many years ago, when I was a small pig, my mother and the other sows used to sing an old song of which they knew only the tune and the first three words. I had known that tune in infancy, but it had long since passed out of my mind. Last night, however, it came back to me in a dream. And what is more, the words of the song also came back— words, I am certain, which were sung by the animals of long ago and have been lost to memory for generations. I will sing you that song now, comrades. It is called 'Beasts of England.'"

Old Major cleared his throat and began to sing. His voice was hoarse, but he sang well enough, and it was a stirring tune, something between "Clementine" and "La Cucaracha." The words ran:

> Beasts of England, beasts of Ireland,
> Beasts of every land and clime,
> Hearken to my joyful tidings
> Of the golden future time.
>
> Soon or late the day is coming,
> Tyrant Man shall be o'erthrown,
> And the fruitful fields of England
> Shall be trod by beasts alone.
>
> Rings shall vanish from our noses,
> And the harness from our back,
> Bit and spur shall rust forever,
> Cruel whips no more shall crack.
>
> For that day we all must labor,
> Though we die before it break;
> Cows and horses, geese and turkeys,
> All must toil for freedom's sake.
>
> Beasts of England, beasts of Ireland,
> Beasts of every land and clime,
> Hearken well and spread my tidings
> Of the golden future time.

The singing of this song threw the animals into the wildest excitement. Almost before Major had reached the end, they had begun singing it for themselves. Even the stupidest of them had already picked up the tune and a few words, and as for the clever ones, such as the pigs and dogs, they had the entire song by heart within a few minutes. And then, after a few preliminary tries, the whole farm burst out into "Beasts of England" in tremendous unison. The cows lowed it, the dogs whined it, the sheep bleated it, the horses whinnied it, the ducks quacked it. They were so delighted with the song that they sang it right through five times in succession, and might have continued singing it all night if it had not been interrupted.

Unfortunately the uproar awoke Mr. Jones, who sprang out of bed, making sure that there was a fox in the yard. He seized the gun which always stood in the corner of his bedroom, and let fly a charge of number 6 shot into the darkness. The pellets buried themselves into the wall of the barn and the meeting broke up hurriedly. Everyone fled to his own sleeping place. The birds jumped onto their perches, the animals settled down into the straw, and the whole farm was asleep in a moment.

In later chapters, the animals do rebel and take over the farm. But then two pigs, named Napoleon and Snowball, begin to struggle for leadership. Although the animals began by declaring that "all animals are equal," their ideals are betrayed when Napoleon takes charge and declares, "Some animals are more equal than others." You can read about all this in Animal Farm.

Anne Frank: The Diary of a Young Girl
(retold with excerpts from the B. M. Mooyart–Doubleday translation)

In the American Civilization section of this book, you can read about World War II and one of the most appalling crimes committed in this century: the Holocaust. The Holocaust is what we call the Nazi attempt to exterminate all Jewish people and others who were considered "inferior" by their leader, Adolf Hitler.

Anne Frank, a German Jewish girl, was a victim of the Holocaust; she died in a concentration camp when she was sixteen. Before being captured in 1944, she and her family spent two years in Amsterdam hiding from the Nazis. They lived with several friends, cramped together in a secret apartment in a warehouse. During this difficult time, Anne kept a diary, which she addressed as "Dear Kitty." Her diary was found and published after the war as The Diary of a Young Girl.

Dear Kitty,
It has been nearly two years since the Nazis summoned my sister Margot for deportation and Daddy led us to the "secret annex," a hiding place he had set up in the attic of his company's warehouse. I wasn't surprised that Pim (Daddy) had provided for our safety, but none of us guessed that we would still be here now. It's not so bad really. There are three rooms for the eight of us—Mother, Daddy, Margot, and me, Mr. and Mrs. Van Daan and their son, Peter, and Mr. Dussel the dentist, who Daddy kindly decided to take in. I share my room with Mr. Dussel (who makes

Anne Frank wrote on her own photograph: This is a photo as I would wish myself to look all the time. Then I would maybe have a chance to come to Hollywood.
  Anne Frank,
  10 Oct. 1942

the most awful fuss over everything!), but at night, when the English planes drop their bombs and the guns fire and the walls shudder, I dart into Daddy's bed until the bombardment ends.

During the day, we can't make any noise for fear that one of the warehouse workers will hear us and turn us in—no footsteps, no conversation, no water, not even a visit to the lavatory. So I try to keep busy. Margot and I study so that we won't be behind when the war is over. Plus, I have heaps of hobbies: writing, which hardly counts as a hobby, and diagramming the family trees of the royal families from information I find in the newspapers. I copy down their biographies. Also, history and mythology. And then I'm mad on film stars, books, and reading (they smuggled in Spenser's *Art History* for my fifteenth birthday!). I also help Mrs. Van Daan come up with new ways to prepare the potatoes (they have grown the most elaborate fungus!) and ways to stifle the stench of the kale.

We get some news of the outside from the radio and the kind Mr. Kraler, Mr. Koophuis, Meip, and Ellie, who bring us food supplies and newspapers. The situation has only grown worse. The Nazis wait to raid a house until they know they'll catch the greatest number of Jews at home. I can't listen for long. It makes me too sad. I am afraid. I dream about my dear friend Lies, knowing that my fate would have been hers had we not gone into hiding, and I feel guilty, and I weep that I can't do anything.

It's a wonder that I haven't lost my ideals, because they seem impossible to carry out. Yet I keep them, because I think that, in spite of everything, people really are good at heart. I simply can't build up my hopes on a foundation consisting of confusion, misery, and death. I see the world gradually changing, I hear the ever-approaching thunder, which will destroy us too, I can feel the sufferings of millions, and yet, if I look up into the heavens, I think that it will all come right, that this cruelty too will end, and that peace and tranquillity will return again.

I Know Why the Caged Bird Sings
(excerpted from the autobiography by Maya Angelou)

Maya Angelou, who was born in 1928, writes in the prologue to her first autobiographical book, I Know Why the Caged Bird Sings, *"Growing up is painful for the Southern Black girl." She goes on to describe the difficulties she faced, some of which were social—the result of a society still permeated by racism and prejudice—and some of which were personal, such as having to deal with an abusive stepfather. Here we present a selection from the book's opening chapters. In loving detail Maya Angelou describes life at her grandmother's store in Arkansas during the Depression, and she also offers a glimpse into the early reading of the child who would grow up to become a celebrated American writer. (Note: For the meaning of the title* I Know Why the Caged Bird Sings, *see Paul Laurence Dunbar's poem "Sympathy," which you can read in this book. For the source of the line from Shakespeare quoted at the end of this selection, see Shakespeare's "Sonnet Number 29.")*

When I was three and Bailey four, we had arrived in the musty little town, wearing tags on our wrists which instructed—"To Whom It May Concern"— that we were Marguerite and Bailey Johnson Jr., from Long Beach, California, en route to Stamps, Arkansas, c/o Mrs. Annie Henderson.

Our parents had decided to put an end to their calamitous marriage, and Father shipped us home to his mother. A porter had been charged with our welfare—he got off the train the next day in Arizona—and our tickets were pinned to my brother's inside coat pocket.

I don't remember much of the trip, but after we reached the segregated southern part of the journey, things must have looked up. Negro passengers, who always traveled with loaded lunch boxes, felt sorry for "the poor little motherless darlings" and plied us with cold fried chicken and potato salad.

Years later I discovered that the United States had been crossed thousands of times by frightened Black children traveling alone to their newly affluent parents in northern cities, or back to grandmothers in southern towns when the urban North reneged on its economic promises.

The town reacted to us as its inhabitants had reacted to all things new before our coming. It regarded us a while without curiosity but with caution, and after we were seen to be harmless (and children) it closed in around us, as a real mother embraces a stranger's child. Warmly, but not too familiarly.

We lived with our grandmother and uncle in the rear of the Store (it was always spoken of with a capital s), which she had owned some twenty-five years.

Early in the century, Momma (we soon stopped calling her Grandmother) sold lunches to the sawmen in the lumberyard (east Stamps) and the seedmen at the cotton gin (west Stamps). Her crisp meat pies and cool lemonade, when joined to her miraculous ability to be in two places at the same time, assured her business success. From being a mobile lunch counter, she set up a stand between the two points of fiscal interest and supplied the workers' needs for a few years. Then she had the Store built in the heart of the Negro area. Over the years it became the lay center of activities in town. On Saturdays, barbers sat their customers in the shade on the porch of the Store, and troubadours on their ceaseless crawlings through the South leaned across its benches and sang their sad songs of the Brazos while they played juice harps and cigar-box guitars.

The formal name of the Store was the Wm. Johnson General Merchandise Store. Customers could find food staples, a good variety of colored thread, mash for hogs, corn for chickens, coal oil for lamps, light bulbs for the wealthy, shoestrings, hair dressing, balloons, and flower seeds. Anything not visible had only to be ordered.

Until we became familiar enough to belong to the Store and it to us, we were locked up in a Fun House of Things where the attendant had gone home for life.

Each year I watched the field across from the Store turn caterpillar green, then gradually frosty white. I knew exactly how long it would be before the big wagons would pull into the front yard and load on the cotton pickers at daybreak to carry them to the remains of slavery's plantations.

During the picking season my grandmother would get out of bed at four o'clock (she never used an alarm clock) and creak down to her knees and chant in a sleep-filled voice, "Our Father, thank you for letting me see this New Day. Thank you that you didn't allow the bed I lay on last night to be my cooling board, nor my blanket my winding sheet. Guide my feet this day along the straight and narrow, and help me to put a bridle on my tongue. Bless this house, and everybody in it. Thank you, in the name of your Son, Jesus Christ, Amen."

Before she had quite arisen, she called our names and issued orders, and pushed her large feet into homemade slippers and across the bare lye-washed wooden floor to light the coal-oil lamp.

The lamplight in the Store gave a soft make-believe feeling to our world which made me want to whisper and walk about on tiptoe. The odors of onions and oranges and kerosene had been mixing all night and wouldn't be disturbed until the wooden slat was removed from the door and the early morning air forced its way in with the bodies of people who had walked miles to reach the pickup place.

"Sister, I'll have two cans of sardines."

"I'm gonna work so fast today I'm gonna make you look like you standing still."

"Lemme have a hunk uh cheese and some sody crackers."

"Just gimme a coupla them fat peanut paddies." That would be from a picker who was taking his lunch. The greasy brown paper sack was stuck behind the bib of his overalls. He'd use the candy as a snack before the noon sun called the workers to rest.

In those tender mornings the Store was full of laughing, joking, boasting, and bragging. One man was going to pick two hundred pounds of cotton, and another three hundred. Even the children were promising to bring home fo' bits and six bits.

The champion picker of the day before was the hero of the dawn. If he prophesied that the cotton in today's field was going to be sparse and stick to the bolls like glue, every listener would grunt a hearty agreement.

The sound of the empty cotton sacks dragging over the floor and the murmurs of waking people were sliced by the cash register as we rang up the five-cent sales.

If the morning sounds and smells were touched with the supernatural, the late afternoon had all the features of the normal Arkansas life. In the dying sunlight the people dragged, rather than their empty cotton sacks.

Brought back to the Store, the pickers would step out of the backs of trucks and fold down, dirt-disappointed, to the ground. No matter how much they had picked, it wasn't enough. Their wages wouldn't even get them out of debt to my grandmother, not to mention the staggering bill that waited on them at the white commissary downtown.

The sounds of the new morning had been replaced with grumbles about cheating houses, weighted scales, snakes, skimpy cotton, and dusty rows. In later years I was to confront the stereotyped picture of gay song-singing cotton pickers with such inordinate rage that I was told even by my fellow Blacks that my paranoia was embarrassing. But I had seen the fingers cut by the mean little cotton bolls, and I had witnessed the backs and shoulders and arms and legs resisting any further demands.

Some of the workers would leave their sacks at the Store to be picked up the following morning, but a few had to take them home for repairs. I winced to picture them sewing the coarse material under a coal-oil lamp with fingers stiffening from the day's work. In too few hours they would have to walk back to Sister Henderson's store, get vittles and load, again, onto the trucks. Then they would face another day of trying to earn enough for the whole year with the heavy knowledge that they were going to end the season as they started it: without the money or credit necessary to sustain a family for three months. In cotton-picking time the late afternoons revealed the harshness of Black southern life, which in the early morning had been softened by nature's blessing of grogginess, forgetfulness, and the soft lamplight.

During these years in Stamps, I met and fell in love with William Shakespeare. He was my first white love. Although I enjoyed and respected Kipling, Poe, Butler,

Thackeray, and Henley, I saved my young and loyal passion for Paul Laurence Dunbar, Langston Hughes, James Weldon Johnson, and W. E. B. Du Bois' "Litany at Atlanta." But it was Shakespeare who said, "When in disgrace with fortune and men's eyes." It was a state with which I felt myself most familiar. I pacified myself about his whiteness by saying that after all he had been dead so long it couldn't matter to anyone anymore.

Bailey and I decided to memorize a scene from *The Merchant of Venice*, but we realized that Momma would question us about the author and that we'd have to tell her that Shakespeare was white, and it wouldn't matter to her whether he was dead or not. So we chose "The Creation" by James Weldon Johnson instead.

John F. Kennedy: Inaugural Address

John F. Kennedy was only forty-two when he was inaugurated as president of the United States on January 20, 1961—the youngest person ever elected to the presidency. In his Inaugural Address (excerpted below), Kennedy spoke of "a new generation of Americans," younger people like himself who had inherited the leadership of the country. As he spoke, Kennedy described the vision that he hoped would guide that new generation through the darkness of the Cold War and into a new day of worldwide freedom, democracy, and cooperation.

We observe today not a victory of party but a celebration of freedom—symbolizing an end as well as a beginning—signifying renewal as well as change. For I have sworn before you and Almighty God the same solemn oath our forebears prescribed nearly a century and three quarters ago.

The world is very different now, for man holds in his mortal hands the power to abolish all forms of human poverty and all forms of human life. And yet the same revolutionary beliefs for which our forebears fought are still at issue around the globe. . . .

We dare not forget today that we are the heirs of that first revolution. Let the word go forth from this time and place, to friend and foe alike, that the torch has been passed to a new generation of Americans—born in this century, tempered by war, disciplined by a hard and bitter peace, proud of our ancient heritage, and unwilling to witness or permit the slow undoing

John Fitzgerald Kennedy.

of those human rights to which the nation has always been committed, and to which we are committed today, at home and around the world.

Let every nation know, whether it wishes us well or ill, that we shall pay any price, bear any burden, meet any hardship, support any friend, or oppose any foe to assure the survival and the success of liberty.

This much we pledge—and more.

To those old allies whose cultural and spiritual origins we share, we pledge the loyalty of faithful friends. . . .

To those people in the huts and villages of half the globe struggling to break the bonds of mass misery, we pledge our best efforts to help them help themselves . . . because it is right. If a free society cannot help the many who are poor, it cannot save the few who are rich. . . .

Finally, to those nations who would make themselves our adversary, we offer not a pledge but a request: that both sides begin anew the quest for peace, before the dark powers of destruction unleashed by science engulf all humanity in planned or accidental self-destruction.

We dare not tempt them with weakness. . . . But neither can two great and powerful groups of nations take comfort from our present course—both sides overburdened by the cost of modern weapons, both rightly alarmed by the steady spread of the deadly atom, yet both racing to alter that uncertain balance of terror that stays the hand of mankind's final war.

So let us begin anew—remembering on both sides that civility is not a sign of weakness, and sincerity is always subject to proof. Let us never negotiate out of fear. But let us never fear to negotiate.

Let both sides explore what problems unite us instead of belaboring those problems which divide us. . . .

All this will not be finished in the first one hundred days. Nor will it be finished in the first one thousand days, nor in the life of this administration, nor even perhaps in our lifetime on this planet. . . .

Now the trumpet summons us again . . . as a call to bear the burden of a long twilight struggle, year in and year out . . . a struggle against the common enemies of man: tyranny, poverty, disease, and war itself.

Can we forge against these enemies a grand and global alliance, North and South, East and West, that can assure a more fruitful life for all mankind? Will you join in that historic effort? . . .

The energy, the faith, the devotion which we bring to this endeavor will light our country and all who serve it—and the glow from that fire can truly light the world.

And so, my fellow Americans, ask not what your country can do for you; ask what you can do for your country.

My fellow citizens of the world: ask not what America will do for you, but what together we can do for the freedom of man.

Finally, whether you are citizens of America or citizens of the world, ask of us here the same high standards of strength and sacrifice which we ask of you.

Martin Luther King, Jr.: "I Have a Dream"

Here is a selection from the great speech that the Reverend Martin Luther King, Jr., delivered to an audience of over 200,000 people who, on August 28, 1963, had gathered at the Lincoln Memorial in Washington, D.C. (You can read more about Dr. King and the civil rights movement in the American Civilization section of this book.) Dr. King's emotional speech invokes the spirit of the Declaration of Independence and of Lincoln's Gettysburg address. It weaves in the poetry and powerful rhythms of the King James Bible (Dr. King was a Southern Baptist minister). The words that Dr. King repeated—"I have a dream"—continue to inspire Americans to keep alive King's dream of a country that overcomes its divisions and learns to live together in love and harmony.

Five score years ago, a great American, in whose symbolic shadow we stand, signed the Emancipation Proclamation. This momentous decree came as a great beacon of light of hope to millions of Negro slaves who had been seared in the flames of withering injustice. It came as a joyous daybreak to end the long night of captivity.

But one hundred years later, the Negro still is not free. One hundred years later, the life of the Negro is still sadly crippled by the manacles of segregation and the chains of discrimination. One hundred years later, the Negro lives on a lonely island of poverty in the midst of a vast ocean of material prosperity. One hundred years later, the Negro is still languished in the corners of American society and finds himself in exile in his own land.

So we've come here today to dramatize a shameful condition. In a sense we have come to our nation's capital to cash a check. When the architects of our republic wrote the magnificent words of the Constitution and the Declaration of Independence, they were signing a promissory note to which every American was to fall heir. This note was a promise that all men, yes, black men as well as white men, would be guaranteed the unalienable rights of life, liberty, and the pursuit of happiness. . . . Instead of honoring this sacred obligation, America has given the Negro people a bad check, which has come back marked "insufficient funds." We refuse to believe that there are insufficient funds in the great vaults of opportunity of this nation. And so we've come to cash this check—a check that will give us upon demand the riches of freedom and the security of justice.

We have also come to this hallowed spot to remind America of the fierce urgency of now. . . . Now is the time to make real the promises of democracy; now is the time to rise from the dark and desolate valley of segregation to the sunlit path of racial justice; now is the time to lift our nation from the quicksands of racial injustice to the solid rock of brotherhood; now is the time to make justice a reality for all God's children. It would be fatal for the nation to overlook the urgency of the moment. This

Martin Luther King, Jr., speaking at the March on Washington.

sweltering summer of the Negro's legitimate discontent will not pass until there is an invigorating autumn of freedom and equality.

Nineteen sixty-three is not an end but a beginning. And those who hope that the Negro needed to blow off steam and will now be content, will have a rude awakening if the nation returns to business as usual.

But there is something I must say to my people, who stand on the warm threshold which leads into the palace of justice. In the process of gaining our rightful place we must not be guilty of wrongful deeds. . . .

Let us not seek to satisfy our thirst for freedom by drinking from the cup of bitterness and hatred. We must forever conduct our struggle on the high plain of dignity and discipline. We must not allow our creative protest to degenerate into physical violence. Again and again we must rise to the majestic heights of meeting physical force with soul force.

The marvelous new militancy which has engulfed the Negro community must not lead us to a distrust of all white people, for many of our white brothers, as evidenced by their presence here today, have come to realize that their destiny is tied up with our destiny, and they have come to realize that their freedom is inextricably bound to our freedom. . . . We cannot walk alone.

And as we walk, we must make the pledge that we shall always march ahead. We cannot turn back. . . . No, we are not satisfied, and we will not be satisfied until justice rolls down like waters and righteousness like a mighty stream. . . .

So I say to you, my friends, that even though we must face the difficulties of today and tomorrow, I still have a dream. It is a dream deeply rooted in the American dream that one day this nation will rise up and live out the true meaning of its creed—we hold these truths to be self-evident, that all men are created equal.

I have a dream that one day on the red hills of Georgia, sons of former slaves and sons of former slave owners will be able to sit down together at the table of brotherhood. . . .

I have a dream that my four little children will one day live in a nation where they will not be judged by the color of their skin but by the content of their character. I have a dream today!

I have a dream that one day, down in Alabama . . . little black boys and black girls will be able to join hands with little white boys and white girls as sisters and brothers. I have a dream today! . . .

I have a dream that one day every valley shall be exalted, every hill and mountain shall be made low, the rough places shall be made plain, and the crooked places shall be made straight, and the glory of the Lord will be revealed and all flesh shall see it together.

With this faith we will be able to work together, to pray together, to struggle together, to go to jail together, to stand up for freedom together, knowing that we will be free one day. This will be the day when all of God's children will be able to sing with new meaning—"My country 'tis of thee; sweet land of liberty; of thee I sing; land where my fathers died, land of the pilgrim's pride; from every mountain side, let freedom ring." . . .

So let freedom ring from the prodigious hilltops of New Hampshire.

Let freedom ring from the mighty mountains of New York.

Let freedom ring from the heightening Alleghenies of Pennsylvania.

Let freedom ring from the snowcapped Rockies of Colorado.

Let freedom ring from the curvaceous slopes of California.

But not only that.

Let freedom ring from Stone Mountain of Georgia.

Let freedom ring from Lookout Mountain of Tennessee.

Let freedom ring from every hill and molehill of Mississippi, from every mountainside, let freedom ring.

And when we allow freedom to ring, when we let it ring from every village and hamlet, from every state and city, we will be able to speed up that day when all of God's children—black men and white men, Jews and Gentiles, Catholics and Protestants—will be able to join hands and to sing in the words of the old Negro spiritual, "Free at last, free at last; thank God Almighty, we are free at last."

Introduction to Poetry
FOR PARENTS AND TEACHERS

In sixth grade we continue to offer a selection of poems that use strong rhythm and rhyme as well as engaging narratives, on the premise that children delight in the music and fun of spoken language. One way to bring children into the spirit of poetry is to read it aloud to them; another is to encourage them to speak it aloud so they can directly experience the sounds of language.

Poetry is also a way for children to understand the power of language to create vivid word pictures. We have included several selections that are notable for their powerful imagery. With these poems, children can begin to enjoy the play between literal and figurative language.

A child's knowledge of poetry should come first from pleasure and only later from analysis. But certain basic concepts, like meter and rhyme schemes, can help parents and children, or students and teachers, talk about particular effects that enliven the poems they like best. In conjunction with the poetry in this section, adults and children may want to read the About Literature section in this book, which discusses poetic structure, rhyme scheme, and meter. In addition, adults and children may wish to refer to the American Civilization section to learn about the Harlem Renaissance as they read the poetry of one of its leading figures, Langston Hughes. Or they may wish to talk about how Maya Angelou's poem "Caged Bird" relates to her novel *I Know Why the Caged Bird Sings*, excerpted in our Stories and Speeches section.

A Few Poems for Sixth Grade

Poems of Inspiration and Reflection

Life Is Fine
by Langston Hughes

I went down to the river,
I set down on the bank.
I tried to think but couldn't,
So I jumped in and sank.

I came up once and hollered!
I came up twice and cried!
If that water hadn't a-been so cold
I might've sunk and died.

But it was
Cold in that water!
It was cold!

I took the elevator
Sixteen floors above the ground.
I thought about my baby
And thought I would jump down.

I stood there and I hollered!
I stood there and I cried!
If it hadn't a-been so high
I might've jumped and died.

But it was
High up there!
It was high!

So since I'm still here livin',
I guess I will live on.
I could've died for love—
But for livin' I was born.

Though you may hear me holler,
And you may see me cry—
I'll be dogged, sweet baby,
If you gonna see me die.

Life is fine!
Fine as wine!
Life is fine!

A Psalm of Life

by Henry Wadsworth Longfellow

Tell me not, in mournful numbers,
Life is but an empty dream!—
For the soul is dead that slumbers,
And things are not what they seem.

Life is real! Life is earnest!
   And the grave is not its goal;
Dust thou art, to dust returnest,
   Was not spoken of the soul.

Not enjoyment, and not sorrow,
   Is our destined end or way;
But to act, that each to-morrow
   Find us farther than to-day.

Art is long, and Time is fleeting,
   And our hearts, though stout and brave,
Still, like muffled drums, are beating
   Funeral marches to the grave.

In the world's broad field of battle,
   In the bivouac of Life,
Be not like dumb, driven cattle!
   Be a hero in the strife!

Trust no Future, how'er pleasant!
   Let the dead Past bury its dead!
Act,—act in the living Present!
   Heart within, and God o'erhead!

Lives of great men all remind us
   We can make our lives sublime,
And, departing, leave behind us
   Footprints on the sands of time;

Footprints, that perhaps another,
   Sailing o'er life's solemn main,
A forlorn and shipwrecked brother,
   Seeing, shall take heart again.

Let us, then, be up and doing.
   With a heart for any fate;
Still achieving, still pursuing,
   Learn to labor and to wait.

A Song of Greatness

(A Chippewa song, translated by Mary Austin)

When I hear the old men
Telling of heroes,
Telling of great deeds
Of ancient days,
When I hear them telling,
Then I think within me
I too am one of these.

When I hear the people
Praising great ones,
Then I know that I too
Shall be esteemed,
I too when my time comes
Shall do mightily.

Lift Ev'ry Voice and Sing

by James Weldon Johnson

This poem was written in 1900 for a celebration of the birthday of Abraham Lincoln. Johnson's brother, J. Rosamond Johnson, set the words to music, and the result became known as the national anthem of African-Americans.

Lift ev'ry voice and sing,
Till earth and heaven ring,
Ring with the harmonies of Liberty,
Let our rejoicing rise
High as the list'ning skies,
Let it resound loud as the rolling sea.
Sing a song full of the faith that the dark past has taught us
Sing a song full of the hope that the present has brought us
Facing the rising sun of our new day begun,
Let us march on till victory is won.

Stony the road we trod
Bitter the chast'ning rod,
Felt in the days when hope unborn had died;

Yet with a steady beat
Have not our weary feet
Come to the place for which our fathers sighed?
We have come over a way that with tears has been watered
We have come, treading our path thro' the blood of the slaughtered,
Out from the gloomy past, till now we stand at last
Where the white gleam of our bright star is cast.

God of our weary years,
God of our silent tears,
Thou who hast brought us thus far on the way;
Thou who hast by Thy might,
Led us into the light,
Keep us forever in the path, we pray.

Lest our feet stray from the places, our God, where we meet Thee,
Let our hearts, drunk with the wine of the world, we forget Thee;
Shadowed beneath Thy hand, may we forever stand,
True to our God, true to our native land.

The Road Not Taken
by Robert Frost

Two roads diverged in a yellow wood,
And sorry I could not travel both
And be one traveller, long I stood
And looked down one as far as I could
To where it bent in the undergrowth;

Then took the other, just as fair,
And having perhaps the better claim,
Because it was grassy and wanted wear;
Though as for that the passing there
Had worn them really about the same,

And both that morning equally lay
In leaves no step had trodden black.
Oh, I kept the first for another day!
Yet knowing how way leads on to way,
I doubted if I should ever come back.

I shall be telling this with a sigh
Somewhere ages and ages hence:
Two roads diverged in a wood, and I—
I took the one less travelled by,
And that has made all the difference.

Poems Old and New

All the World's a Stage

These lines, from William Shakespeare's play As You Like It, *are spoken by a grumpy, cynical character by the name of Jacques. Here are the meanings of some words and phrases that may be unfamiliar to you:* pard *(leopard);* jealous in honor *(eager to pursue fame, sensitive about one's reputation);* capon *(a kind of chicken);* wise saws *(wise sayings);* pantaloon *(a familiar and ridiculous character in Italian comedies, usually portrayed as a skinny, silly, ill-dressed old man);* sans *(without).*

All the world's a stage
And all the men and women merely players:
They have their exits and their entrances;
And one man in his time plays many parts,
His acts being seven ages. At first the infant,
Mewling and puking in the nurse's arms.
Then the whining school-boy, with his satchel
And shining morning face, creeping like snail
Unwillingly to school. And then the lover,
Sighing like furnace, with a woeful ballad
Made to his mistress' eyebrow. Then a soldier,
Full of strange oaths, and bearded like the pard,
Jealous in honor, sudden and quick in quarrel,
Seeking the bubble reputation
Even in the cannon's mouth. And then the justice,
In fair round belly with good capon lined,
With eyes severe and beard of formal cut,
Full of wise saws and modern instances;
And so he plays his part. The sixth age shifts
Into the lean and slippered pantaloon,
With spectacles on nose and pouch on side,
His youthful hose, well saved, a world too wide
For his shrunk shank; and his big manly voice,
Turning again toward childish treble, pipes

And whistles in his sound. Last scene of all,
That ends this strange eventful history,
Is second childishness and mere oblivion,
Sans teeth, sans eyes, sans taste, sans everything.

I Like to See It Lap the Miles
by Emily Dickinson

I like to see it lap the miles,
And lick the valleys up,
And stop to feed itself at tanks;
And then, prodigious, step

Around a pile of mountains,
And, supercilious, peer
In shanties by the sides of roads;
And then a quarry pare

To fit its sides, and crawl between,
Complaining all the while
In horrid, hooting stanza;
Then chase itself down hill

And neigh like Boanerges;
Then, punctual as a star,
Stop—docile and omnipotent—
At its own stable door.

Father William
by Lewis Carroll

"You are old, Father William," the young man said,
   "And your hair has become very white;
And yet you incessantly stand on your head—
   Do you think, at your age, it is right?"

"In my youth," Father William replied to his son,
   "I feared it might injure the brain;
But now that I'm perfectly sure I have none,
   Why, I do it again and again."

"You are old," said the youth, "as I mentioned before,
 And have grown most uncommonly fat;
Yet you turned a back somersault in at the door—
 Pray, what is the reason of that?"

"In my youth," said the sage, as he shook his gray locks,
 "I kept all my limbs very supple
By the use of this ointment—one shilling the box—
 Allow me to sell you a couple."

"You are old," said the youth, "and your jaws are too weak
 For anything tougher than suet;
Yet you finished the goose, with the bones and the beak—
 Pray, how did you manage to do it?"

"In my youth," said his father, "I took to the law,
 And argued each case with my wife;
And the muscular strength which it gave to my jaw
 Has lasted the rest of my life."

"You are old," said the youth, "one would hardly suppose
 That your eye was as steady as ever;
Yet you balanced an eel on the end of your nose—
 What made you so awfully clever?"

"I have answered three questions, and that is enough,"
 Said his father, "don't give yourself airs!
Do you think I can listen all day to such stuff?
 Be off, or I'll kick you down stairs!"

This Is Just to Say
by William Carlos Williams

I have eaten
the plums
that were in
the icebox

and which
you were probably
saving
for breakfast

Forgive me
they were delicious
so sweet
and so cold

The Raven

by Edgar Allan Poe

Once upon a midnight dreary, while I pondered, weak and weary,
Over many a quaint and curious volume of forgotten lore,
　While I nodded, nearly napping, suddenly there came a tapping,
　As of some one gently rapping, rapping at my chamber door.
"'Tis some visitor," I muttered, "tapping at my chamber door—
　　　Only this, and nothing more."

Ah, distinctly I remember it was in the bleak December,
And each separate dying ember wrought its ghost upon the floor.
　Eagerly I wished the morrow;—vainly I had sought to borrow
　From my books surcease of sorrow—sorrow for the lost Lenore—
For the rare and radiant maiden whom the angels name Lenore—
　　　Nameless here for evermore.

And the silken sad uncertain rustling of each purple curtain
Thrilled me—filled me with fantastic terrors never felt before;
　So that now, to still the beating of my heart, I stood repeating,
　"'Tis some visitor entreating entrance at my chamber door—
Some late visitor entreating entrance at my chamber door;—
　　　This it is, and nothing more."

Presently my soul grew stronger; hesitating then no longer,
"Sir," said I, "or Madam, truly your forgiveness I implore;
    But the fact is I was napping, and so gently you came rapping,
    And so faintly you came tapping, tapping at my chamber door,
That I scarce was sure I heard you"—here I opened wide the door—
                    Darkness there, and nothing more.

Deep into that darkness peering, long I stood there wondering, fearing,
Doubting, dreaming dreams no mortal ever dared to dream before;
    But the silence was unbroken, and the stillness gave no token
    And the only word there spoken was the whispered word, "Lenore!"
This I whispered, and an echo murmured back the word, "Lenore!"—
                    Merely this, and nothing more.

Back into the chamber turning, all my soul within me burning,
Soon again I heard a tapping somewhat louder than before.
    "Surely," said I, "surely that is something at my window lattice:
    Let me see, then what thereat is, and this mystery explore—
Let my heart be still a moment and this mystery explore;—
                    'Tis the wind and nothing more."

Open here I flung the shutter, when, with many a flirt and flutter,
In there stepped a stately raven of the saintly days of yore;
    Not the least obeisance made he; not a minute stopped or stayed he;
    But, with mien of lord or lady, perched above my chamber door—
Perched upon a bust of Pallas just above my chamber door—
                    Perched, and sat, and nothing more.

Then this ebony bird beguiling my sad fancy into smiling,
By the grave and stern decorum of the countenance it wore,
    "Though thy crest be shorn and shaven, thou," I said, "art sure no craven,
    Ghastly grim and ancient raven wandering from the Nightly shore—
Tell me what thy lordly name is on the Night's Plutonian shore!"
                    Quoth the Raven, "Nevermore."

Much I marvelled this ungainly fowl to hear discourse so plainly,
Though its answer little meaning—little relevancy bore;
    For we cannot help agreeing that no living human being
    Ever yet was blest with seeing bird above his chamber door—
Bird or beast upon the sculptured bust above his chamber door,
                    With such name as "Nevermore."

But the raven, sitting lonely on the placid bust, spoke only
That one word, as if his soul in that one word he did outpour.
    Nothing further then he uttered—not a feather then he fluttered—
    Till I scarcely more than muttered, "Other friends have flown before—
On the morrow *he* will leave me, as my Hopes have flown before."
             Then the bird said, "Nevermore."

Startled at the stillness broken by reply so aptly spoken,
"Doubtless," said I, "what it utters is its only stock and store,
    Caught from some unhappy master whom unmerciful Disaster
    Followed fast and followed faster till his songs one burden bore—
Till the dirges of his Hope that melancholy burden bore
             Of 'Never—nevermore.'"

But the Raven still beguiling all my fancy into smiling,
Straight I wheeled a cushioned seat in front of bird, and bust and door;
    Then upon the velvet sinking, I betook myself to linking
    Fancy unto fancy, thinking what this ominous bird of yore—
What this grim, ungainly, ghastly, gaunt and ominous bird of yore
             Meant in croaking "Nevermore."

This I sat engaged in guessing, but no syllable expressing
To the fowl whose fiery eyes now burned into my bosom's core;
    This and more I sat divining, with my head at ease reclining
    On the cushion's velvet lining that the lamplight gloated o'er,
But whose velvet violet lining with the lamplight gloating o'er,
            She shall press, ah, nevermore!

Then methought the air grew denser, perfumed from an unseen censer
Swung by Seraphim whose footfalls tinkled on the tufted floor.
   "Wretch," I cried, "thy God hath lent thee—by these angels he hath sent thee
   Respite—respite and nepenthe, from thy memories of Lenore!
Quaff, oh quaff this kind nepenthe and forget this lost Lenore!"
                Quoth the Raven, "Nevermore."

"Prophet!" said I, "thing of evil!—prophet still, if bird or devil!—
Whether Tempter sent, or whether tempest tossed thee here ashore,
   Desolate yet all undaunted, on this desert land enchanted—
   On this home by Horror haunted—tell me truly, I implore—
Is there—*is* there balm in Gilead?—tell me—tell me, I implore!"
                Quoth the Raven, "Nevermore."

"Prophet!" said I, "thing of evil—prophet still, if bird or devil!
By that Heaven that bends above us—by that God we both adore—
   Tell this soul with sorrow laden if, within the distant Aidenn,
   It shall clasp a sainted maiden whom the angels name Lenore—
Clasp a rare and radiant maiden whom the angels name Lenore."
                Quoth the Raven, "Nevermore."

"Be that word our sign in parting, bird or fiend," I shrieked, upstarting—
"Get thee back into the tempest and the Night's Plutonian shore!
   Leave no black plume as a token of that lie thy soul hath spoken!
   Leave my loneliness unbroken!—quit the bust above my door!
Take thy beak from out my heart, and take thy form from off my door!"
                Quoth the Raven, "Nevermore."

And the Raven, never flitting, still is sitting, *still* is sitting
On the pallid bust of Pallas just above my chamber door;
   And his eyes have all the seeming of a demon's that is dreaming,
   And the lamplight o'er him streaming throws his shadow on the floor;
And my soul from out that shadow that lies floating on the floor
                Shall be lifted—nevermore!

Sympathy

by Paul Laurence Dunbar

I know what the caged bird feels, alas!
   When the sun is bright on the upland slopes;
When the wind stirs soft through the springing grass,
And the river flows like a stream of glass;
   When the first bird sings and the first bud opes,
And the faint perfume from its chalice steals—
I know what the caged bird feels!

I know why the caged bird beats his wing
   Till its blood is red on the cruel bars;
For he must fly back to his perch and cling
When he fain would be on the bough a-swing;
   And a pain still throbs in the old, old scars
And they pulse again with a keener sting—
I know why he beats his wing!

I know why the caged bird sings, ah me,
   When his wing is bruised and his bosom sore,—
When he beats his bars and he would be free;
It is not a carol of joy or glee,
   But a prayer that he sends from his heart's deep core,
But a plea, that upward to Heaven he flings—
I know why the caged bird sings!

Caged Bird

by Maya Angelou

A free bird leaps
on the back of the wind
and floats downstream
till the current ends
and dips his wing
in the orange sun rays
and dares to claim the sky.

But a bird that stalks
down his narrow cage
can seldom see through
his bars of rage
his wings are clipped and
his feet are tied
so he opens his throat to sing.

The caged bird sings
with a fearful trill
of things unknown
but longed for still
and his tune is heard
on the distant hill
for the caged bird
sings of freedom.

The free bird thinks of another breeze
and the trade winds soft through the sighing trees
and the fat worms waiting on a dawn-bright lawn
and he names the sky his own.

But a caged bird stands on the grave of dreams
his shadow shouts on a nightmare scream
his wings are clipped and his feet are tied
so he opens his throat to sing.

The caged bird sings
with a fearful trill
of things unknown
but longed for still
and his tune is heard
on the distant hill
for the caged bird
sings for freedom.

·Woman Work

by Maya Angelou

I've got the children to tend
The clothes to mend
The floor to mop
The food to shop
Then the chicken to fry
The baby to dry
I got company to feed
The garden to weed
I've got the shirts to press
The tots to dress
The cane to cut
I gotta clean up this hut
Then see about the sick
The cotton to pick

Shine on me, sunshine
Rain on me, rain
Fall softly, dew drops
And cool my brow again.

Storm, blow me from here
With your fiercest wind
Let me float across the sky
'Til I can rest again.

Fall gently, snowflakes
Cover me with white
Cold icy kisses and
Let me rest tonight.

Sun, rain, curving sky
Mountain, oceans, leaf and stone
Star shine, moon glow
You're all that I can call my own

Stopping by Woods on a Snowy Evening
by Robert Frost

Whose woods these are I think I know.
His house is in the village though;
He will not see me stopping here
To watch his woods fill up with snow.

My little horse must think it queer
To stop without a farmhouse near
Between the woods and frozen lake
The darkest evening of the year.

He gives his harness bells a shake
To ask if there is some mistake.
The only other sound's the sweep
Of easy wind and downy flake.

The woods are lovely, dark and deep,
But I have promises to keep,
And miles to go before I sleep,
And miles to go before I sleep.

Harlem
by Langston Hughes

What happens to a dream deferred?

Does it dry up
like a raisin in the sun?
Or fester like a sore—
And then run?
Does it stink like rotten meat?
Or crust and sugar over—
Like a syrupy sweet?

Maybe it just sags
like a heavy load.

Or does it explode?

The Negro Speaks of Rivers
by Langston Hughes

I've known rivers:
I've known rivers ancient as the world and older than the
   flow of human blood in human veins.

My soul has grown deep like the rivers.

I bathed in the Euphrates when dawns were young.
I built my hut near the Congo and it lulled me to sleep.
I looked upon the Nile and raised the pyramids above it.
I heard the singing of the Mississippi when Abe Lincoln
   went down to New Orleans, and I've seen its muddy
   bosom turn all golden in the sunset.

I've known rivers:
Ancient, dusky rivers.

My soul has grown deep like the rivers.

Introduction to Mythology

FOR PARENTS AND TEACHERS

The first four myths here come to us from ancient Greece by way of Rome, in particular the Latin poet Ovid. Ovid, who lived during the time of Augustus, collected a great many myths and wrote them in books. The book by Ovid upon which our retellings are based is called *Metamorphoses*, a title that suggests that many of the characters in these myths undergo dramatic changes. (You're probably familiar with one natural metamorphosis, in which a caterpillar becomes a butterfly.)

The fifth myth in this section, *Cupid and Psyche*, comes to us by way of the Latin writer Apuleius, who lived in the second century A.D.

Because our retellings here are derived from Latin sources, we use the names given to the gods by the Romans—for example, Jupiter instead of the Greek name Zeus, and Pluto instead of Hades.

Classical Myths About Love

Apollo and Daphne

Daphne (DAF-nee), daughter of the river god, was beautiful, strong, and agile. Like the goddess Diana, she loved to hunt. With her hair streaming wildly behind her, Daphne would run like the wind through the forest in swift pursuit of an unlucky stag, who was sure to fall when pierced by an arrow from her bow.

Daphne loved her freedom. Her father would often say, "My beautiful daughter, it is time for you to take a husband and bear me a grandson." But Daphne would laugh and reply, "I have no need of husband or marriage!"

One day while Daphne was hunting, Apollo, the sun god, caught sight of her. He admired her strength and speed. Then suddenly he felt a sharp piercing sensation, and what had been warm admiration burst into the searing flame of love.

Apollo, you see, had been struck by an arrow shot by the god of love, Cupid, whom even the gods cannot resist.

Cupid had decided to make Apollo his target, because Apollo had made the mistake of laughing at Cupid. Apollo, himself a great archer whose arrows had brought death to a giant serpent called Python, had come upon Cupid with his bow and arrows and laughed aloud, saying, "Be careful that you don't hurt yourself, boy!" Cupid gave an angry flutter of his wings and muttered, "You'll soon see that my arrows are stronger than yours!"

And so it was that when Apollo caught sight of Daphne, Cupid made good on his threat. He struck Apollo with a golden-tipped arrow, which causes deep and burning love. At the same time, he struck Daphne with a lead-tipped arrow, which hardens the resolve to resist all love.

"Stop!" Apollo cried out to Daphne and began to run after her. But when Daphne realized she was being chased, she ran even faster. "Wait!" cried Apollo. "Do you know who you're running from? I am no servant or shepherd; I am a son of Jupiter."

Hearing this, Daphne knew she could not escape. But she had lived free all her life, and would not give up her freedom now. So she ran faster still. Even the swiftest mortal, however, cannot outrun a god, and soon Daphne felt her legs weakening and her breath growing short. Just when she could run no farther, she reached the banks of the river that ran through her father's forest. "Father, oh, Father, help me!" she cried.

The words had hardly left her lips when she felt her once swift feet root themselves to the ground and her arms begin to stiffen. Then her skin turned to bark and her hair to leaves. And where once had run a beautiful, graceful girl, there now stood a beautiful, graceful tree, a laurel.

Apollo wrapped his arms around the trunk and felt a still beating heart inside. Then he cried out, "From this day forth, the laurel shall be my tree. Look for its shining green leaves on my lyre and quiver. Weave it into wreathes to crown the brows of heroes and poets." And Apollo himself wore on his head a wreath made of the laurel's evergreen leaves, a sign of his love for Daphne.

Orpheus and Eurydice

Orpheus (OR-fee-us) was a son of the Muses, the goddesses who sang so sweetly that their very name has given us the word "music." The music of Orpheus could soothe a savage beast. When he touched the strings of his lyre, the fiercest lion would cease his roar, the animals of the forest would gather to listen, the trees would bend their branches near, and even the rivers would turn from their beds to catch a strain of the sweet song.

People everywhere were charmed by the music of Orpheus. So when Orpheus fell in love with a maiden named Eurydice (yoo-RID-ih-see), he had only to play his lyre to win her heart. Yet even his sweetest song could not undo the terrible calamity that struck during their wedding ceremony: as Orpheus's bride walked across the grass, a snake pierced her foot with its venomous bite. Orpheus swept Eurydice into his arms and cried aloud, but in vain. The spirit of Eurydice had already fled to the underworld, the cold realm of the dead.

Stricken with grief, Orpheus wandered the forests playing songs so sad that all who heard him wept. One day, as Orpheus played his doleful music, he thought, "If I can charm the souls of the living, then perhaps I can also charm the souls of the dead. I will go to the underworld and try with my music to persuade Pluto, king of that dark realm, to give Eurydice back to me."

And so Orpheus was ferried across the black waters of the River Styx, which separates the world of the living from the world of the dead. As he descended on the dark and misty path to the underworld, he played such sad music that even the phantoms were moved to tears, and Cerberus, the vicious three-headed watchdog of the underworld, quietly let him pass.

Then he came to the throne of the dread king, Pluto. He touched the strings of his lyre and told of his loss of Eurydice. He sang of his lasting love, of his deep grief. "I beg you," he said, "if in this dark and confused realm you know anything of love, let my Eurydice return to life." Pluto, usually merciless, was moved and granted Orpheus's request, but with one condition. "On your journey back," Pluto commanded, "you must not look back, not even once, or she will vanish from your side forever."

Eurydice was brought forth, and she and Orpheus began to climb the steep path, always looking forward. The way was hard, and Orpheus's heart was torn by the sounds of the faltering steps behind him. If only he could turn and extend a loving hand! They struggled on and were nearing the light when, perhaps on some impulse of love, perhaps out of fear that he had already lost her, Orpheus looked back—only to see, just as Pluto had warned, Eurydice fade like a wisp of smoke carried away on the wind. Helpless, she was pulled back to the realm of the dead.

As his beloved's cry of farewell rang in Orpheus's ears, he crumpled over his lyre and wept. For a second time he had lost Eurydice—for a second time, and forever.

Echo and Narcissus

When Narcissus was born, all who saw him marveled at his beauty. When he grew to be a youth, all who saw him fell in love with him. But Narcissus, vain and conceited, showed love for no one. He would not give even a glance to many a heart-broken maiden.

One day his beauty melted the heart of a lovely nymph named Echo. Once she saw Narcissus, she followed him everywhere. But she could not tell him of her love, for though she longed to speak, she could only repeat the last words of what was said to her.

How had this come to pass? It was because of Juno, queen of the gods. Juno often left Olympus, the home of the gods, to wander the hillsides in search of her husband, Jupiter, who had a fondness for the nymphs who dwelt in the woods. Just when Juno was about to find her husband, Echo would appear and take her aside to distract her with a stream of lively and amusing chatter until the nymphs and Jupiter had gotten away. When Juno discovered what was going on, she punished Echo. "You have spoken too many words," said Juno, "and now you shall speak only the last words you hear."

And so poor Echo could follow Narcissus, but she could say nothing to him.

One day Narcissus got lost in the forest and cried out, "Hello, is there anyone here?"

"Here, here," Echo replied, hidden behind some trees.

"Ho, there! Where are you?" Narcissus called.

"Where are you?" answered Echo.

Narcissus could see no one, so he called out again, "Are you close at hand?"

"Close at hand," came the reply.

Narcissus went toward the voice. "Are you the one who calls me?" he asked.

"Who calls me," Echo answered.

"I am Narcissus," the youth replied.

"Narcissus," said Echo, and, unable to restrain herself, she rushed toward him with open arms.

Narcissus leaped back. "Get away!" he cried. "Not one step closer. I shall go my own way, and I forbid you to stay with me!"

"Stay with me!" said Echo. Her heart broke as she watched Narcissus turn and walk away. In grief and pain, she wandered through the forest alone.

Narcissus continued to spurn all those who offered him their love. Then one day while he was hunting, he stopped to take a drink from a clear still pool. As he bent his head toward the silvery water, he saw a beautiful face looking back at him, and he fell in love—with his own reflection! Now Narcissus knew the desire and longing he caused in others. He stared at the beautiful image in the water and even tried to kiss it, but the touch of his lips disturbed the surface, and the beautiful image vanished in a blur of ripples.

When the water stilled and the reflection returned, Narcissus could not tear himself away. He longed for that which he could never possess. For many days he pined away, and grew weak and thin. Echo came near him, but she could not help him: she could not speak, and his gaze remained fixed on his own image. Finally, with his dying breath he gasped, "My love, my love." Echo could only reply, "My love."

Grief-stricken, poor Echo wasted away until nothing was left of her but her voice, which still haunts dark caves and lonely hillsides.

By the side of the pool where Narcissus died there grew a lovely flower, with a yellow center ringed by delicate white petals— it was a Narcissus, still known to this day by the name of the beautiful but vain youth who died for love of his own reflection.

Pygmalion

Once there lived a sculptor by the name of Pygmalion (Pig-MALE-ee-un) who made statues of surpassing beauty. Pygmalion had no wife; he was perfectly happy to live alone, working all day at his art and dreaming each night of the still fairer forms he would someday carve out of stone.

"You must be lonely," his friends would say. "Why don't you get married and raise a family?"

Pygmalion would always reply, "My art is wife and child to me."

Pygmalion set to work on a statue made out of the finest marble. As he chipped away at the stone, his mind began to be filled with a vision of a maiden more beautiful than any living woman. He worked on and on, never pausing for food or rest, until finally there stood before him, in smooth hard marble, the embodiment of his vision.

Pygmalion loved this statue as other men love a woman of flesh and blood. She seemed so real to him. He even spoke to her, but of course she gave no answer. He reached out to touch her, half expecting her to return the gesture, but he felt only cold, hard stone. He told her how lovely she looked and brought her presents. He draped a beautiful necklace over her, and half expected, half hoped to hear her thank him. But she remained silent and still.

His friends noticed that a change had come over the sculptor. "Tell us about your new statues," they said. But Pygmalion, driven to distraction by his own creation, only replied, "Never again shall I fashion marble into shapes of beauty."

One night, exhausted by hopeless longing, Pygmalion fell asleep at the feet of the statue. From above, Venus, the goddess of love and beauty, looked down and took pity. "Let love kindle life," she said. "Live, Galatea [Gal-uh-TAY-uh], and bring joy to the heart of Pygmalion."

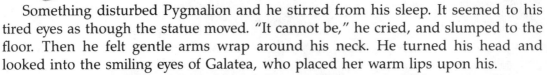

Something disturbed Pygmalion and he stirred from his sleep. It seemed to his tired eyes as though the statue moved. "It cannot be," he cried, and slumped to the floor. Then he felt gentle arms wrap around his neck. He turned his head and looked into the smiling eyes of Galatea, who placed her warm lips upon his.

Venus blessed the marriage of Pygmalion and Galatea. A child was soon born to them, and they lived happily for many years. Some say that when Pygmalion died and his spirit left this world, Galatea's spirit accompanied his while her body returned to the form her husband had shaped—a statue of smooth marble, placed above the sculptor's resting place in a quiet garden.

Cupid and Psyche

Once there was a king who had three daughters. The youngest, named Psyche (SY-kee), was the most beautiful of all—so beautiful, in fact, that people began to say that she was even more beautiful than Venus, the goddess of beauty and love.

When Venus heard these claims, she was filled with jealousy. In a rage she went to her son, Cupid, and said, "Shoot the girl with one of your arrows and make her fall in love with the most wretched and hideous man on earth."

Obediently, Cupid took his bow and arrows and flew down to earth. Just as he was taking aim to shoot Psyche, his finger slipped and he pricked himself with the tip of his own arrow—and so he himself fell deeply in love with Psyche!

Cupid then had a message sent to Psyche's family, informing them that it was the will of the gods that Psyche would marry no mortal; instead, she must go to the mountaintop and meet the husband destined for her—a terrible monster.

Although her parents and friends wept, Psyche went bravely to meet her fate. When she reached the mountaintop it was dark. She felt a warm wind surround her and suddenly found herself in a magnificent palace. Although she saw no one, she heard friendly voices speak: "Whatever you desire, you have but to ask, and we will provide." After a warm bath and a delicious meal, accompanied by sweet music that seemed to surround her but come from nowhere, Psyche fell asleep. That night, and for many nights afterward, she was visited in the darkness by Cupid, who always left before the morning light.

Psyche loved her unseen husband well, and for a time she did not press him to show his face or tell his name. "Why should you wish to see me?" her husband asked. "You know that I love you, and all I ask is that you love me." For a while this arrangement satisfied Psyche, but as time passed she became more curious, and even fearful. What if her husband were in fact a hideous monster?

One night Psyche waited until her husband was asleep. Then she lit a lamp and brought it close to his face. When she saw not a hideous monster but the sweet, fair face of the god of love himself, her hand trembled with delight—and a drop of hot oil fell from the lamp onto Cupid's shoulder. Cupid awoke with a start. Seeing what Psyche had done, he said, "I loved you and asked only for your trust; but when trust is gone, so love must depart." And away he flew, back to his mother, Venus. The jealous goddess greeted her son with a burst of rage for deceiving her, then locked him in her palace.

As soon as Cupid left Psyche, the magnificent palace vanished, leaving the poor girl alone on the cold mountaintop. Night and day, without rest, Psyche wandered in search of her lost love. At last, in desperation, she went to the temple of Venus. The goddess did not greet her kindly. "You dare to come seeking a husband, you plain and haggard wretch?" Venus sputtered. "Come, I will make you at least worthy of being a servant, by teaching you hard work and diligence." And so Venus gave Psyche an impossible task: the goddess set before the poor woman a huge pile of the seeds of various grains—wheat, millet, barley, and more. "Put each of these grains into a separate pile of its own kind by morning," Venus said, laughing, then disappeared.

Psyche hung her head; she knew the task was hopeless. But as a tear dropped from her eye, she noticed a seed moving, then many more, in various directions. An army of ants, thousands and thousands of them, had come to her aid, each carrying a seed to the proper pile. Within hours, the work was done.

When Venus returned, she was furious. "Very well, someone has helped you," she said. "But your next task will not be so easy. Take this box and go to the underworld, and ask the queen of that realm, Proserpina [pro-SUR-pea-nah], to put in the box a little of her beauty for you to bring back to me."

Psyche set off, full of fear, for how often was it that a mortal returned from a descent to the underworld? How would she get there, and what terrors would she encounter along the way? Suddenly she heard a voice speaking to her. It told her to take a coin to give to Charon, the ferryman, who would carry her across the River Styx, and to take a cake to calm Cerberus, the three-headed watchdog of the underworld. "And this above all," said the voice, "once Proserpina has placed some of her beauty in the box, do not open it."

Psyche agreed, and her journey to the underworld went safely as foretold, with Proserpina willingly agreeing to give some of her beauty to Venus. But as Psyche rushed to return the box to Venus, she could not help wondering about what was inside. Surely it would do no harm for her to avail herself of the slightest touch of divine beauty, and perhaps it would even help restore her charms and so win back Cupid. She lifted the lid—and out wafted a deep and heavy sleep. Psyche fell senseless to the ground.

Meanwhile, Cupid's wound had healed, and his love for Psyche had returned, stronger than ever. He longed to see her, and he managed to escape the palace of Venus through a window. No sooner had he flown out than he saw Psyche lying motionless. Alighting beside her, he embraced her. He took the heavy sleep from her body and put it back into the box. "See what your curiosity brings you," he said, smiling. "Now take this box to my mother as you promised. I will return shortly, and all will be well."

Overjoyed, Psyche hurried to fulfill her task. Cupid flew to Jupiter and begged the king of the gods to bless his marriage with Psyche. Jupiter agreed, and even went further: he brought Psyche to Olympus and had her drink some of the ambrosia of the gods, which made her, like her husband, an immortal. Even Venus could not object to her son marrying a goddess. And so, in the marriage of Cupid and Psyche, Love and the Soul (which is what "Psyche" means) were happily united at last.

Introduction to Language and Literature

FOR PARENTS AND TEACHERS

In the sixth grade, besides examining a couple of important punctuation marks (the colon and semicolon), students begin to look at grammar as it relates to style. In particular, by learning about different kinds of sentences, children can become more aware of how they construct their own sentences, and of the pleasure that comes from reading skillfully varied sentences in a good piece of writing.

In the classroom, grammar instruction is an essential part—but only a part—of an effective language arts program. In sixth grade children should continue reading and writing often and in a variety of genres. They should be regularly involved in the writing process: inventing topics, discovering ideas in early drafts, doing research when necessary, revising toward a polished final draft, all with encouragement and guidance along the way.

In this section we also introduce students to some terms that will help them analyze poetry and appreciate the careful craft that goes into the writing of many poems.

Learning About Language

Is It a Sentence? Dependent and Independent Clauses

Did you ever read one of those beginner's books full of short, choppy sentences like these?

See the dog. The dog barks. The dog barks at the cat. The cat runs. Run, cat, run!

It's a good thing all books aren't written like that! Short, simple sentences have their place: they can be informative and effective. But good writers use a variety of sentence structures, mixing short and long, simple and complex.

We're going to take a look at four basic kinds of sentences, but before we can do that, we need to understand what a clause is. A clause is a group of words with a subject and a predicate. Here's a clause:

while Felicia waited for the bus

What's the subject of that clause? It's "Felicia." The predicate is "waited." Here are some more clauses. Can you find the subject and predicate in each?

> unless it rains today
> although his zipper broke
> when the teacher fainted

If someone came into the room and announced, "Unless it rains today," how would you respond? Perhaps something like this: "Yes, go on. Unless it rains today *what?*" Try reading each of the above clauses aloud. Do you notice how each leaves you hanging, wanting to know more? That's because none of those clauses expresses a complete thought. A clause that expresses an incomplete or partial thought is called a dependent clause.

A dependent clause is not a complete sentence; it can't stand on its own. A dependent clause depends on another group of words to express a complete thought, and thus to make a complete sentence.

Let's complete the dependent clauses above. For example:

While Felicia waited for the bus, she dug in her purse to find another quarter.
We're going to have a picnic *unless it rains today.*

You try completing the others.

Now look at the words we've used to complete the dependent clauses:

She dug in her purse to find another quarter.
We're going to have a picnic.

Those clauses *can* stand on their own. Each one forms a sentence that expresses a complete thought. A clause that can stand on its own and that expresses a complete thought is called an independent clause. In the following sentence, the independent clause is italicized:

The Trojans were winning the war until Achilles returned to battle.

Try identifying the dependent and independent clauses in the following sentence:

When Sojourner Truth spoke, her powerful words moved everyone in the audience.

Four Kinds of Sentences

By mixing dependent and independent clauses, you can make different kinds of sentences. A sentence with one independent clause is called a simple sentence. For example:

She jumped.

A simple sentence doesn't have to be so short. For example, here's another simple sentence:

She jumped over the high bar with the grace and strength of a powerful deer.

Sometimes you can't get everything you need to say into a simple sentence. Then you might use a compound sentence, which has two or more independent clauses. For example:

She jumped over the high bar with the grace and strength of a deer, but her teammate slipped and fell to her knees.

Jesse decided to leave the party early, and I decided to follow soon after.

I could tell Mandy to meet us at the museum, or we could all get together later at the restaurant.

Notice that in the compound sentences above, the independent clauses are held together by a comma working with a conjunction:

You can use a comma and a conjunction to join the independent clauses in a compound sentence, or you can use the punctuation mark called a semicolon, which looks like a comma with a period on top of it:

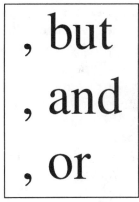

For example:

Jesse decided to leave the party early; I decided to follow soon after.

She jumped over the high bar with the grace and strength of a deer; her teammate slipped and fell to her knees.

A comma alone is *not* enough to join two independent clauses. In the examples above, if you used a comma instead of a semicolon, you'd be making a mistake known as a comma-splice:

Comma-splice

Jesse decided to leave the party early, I decided to follow soon after.

You can correct a comma-splice by adding a conjunction or by using a semicolon.

Comma splice: It was a long time until lunch, I was hungry.
Correct: It was a long time until lunch, *but* I was hungry.
Correct: It was a long time until lunch; I was hungry.

You could also create a different kind of sentence, one that mixes a dependent clause with an independent clause, like this:

Although it was a long time until lunch, I was hungry.

A sentence with an independent clause and at least one dependent clause is called a complex sentence. In this case, "complex" doesn't necessarily mean "difficult." In fact, a complex sentence might be easier to understand than two simple sentences, because a complex sentence can clarify the relation between separate thoughts. For example:

[two simple sentences] The coach decided to pull the star player out of the game. We won by ten points.
[one complex sentence] Although the coach decided to pull the star player out of the game, we won by ten points.

You can also make what is called a compound-complex sentence by joining two or more independent clauses with one or more dependent clauses, like this:

Although the coach decided to pull the star player out of the game, we won by ten points, and we remained the district champions for the third year in a row.

You've learned about four different kinds of sentences: simple, compound, complex, and compound-complex. Now, the important thing is not to go around labeling the different sentences that you read, but to use different kinds of sentences when you write. Good writers use a variety of sentence structures. Let's look at how a great writer, Mark Twain, varies his sentences in this paragraph from *The Adventures of Tom Sawyer*. It describes how Tom feels on a Monday morning when he doesn't want to go to school. Read it aloud to get a better sense of the varied length and rhythm of the sentences.

Tom lay thinking. Presently it occurred to him that he wished he was sick; then he could stay home from school. Here was a vague possibility. He canvassed his system. No ailment was found, and he investigated again. This time he thought he could detect colicky symptoms, and he began to encourage them with considerable hope. But they soon grew feeble, and presently died wholly away. He reflected further. Suddenly he discovered something. One of his upper front teeth was loose. This was lucky; he was about to begin to groan, as a "starter," as he called it, when it occurred to him that if he came into court with that argument, his aunt would pull it out, and that would hurt. So he thought he would hold the tooth in reserve for the present, and seek further.

Like Mark Twain, you can use a variety of sentences when you write, and so give your sentences an effective rhythm and pace—almost like a good song.

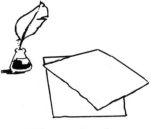

The Colon

A short while ago you read about the semicolon, a punctuation mark you can use to join two independent clauses. Now let's find out about the punctuation mark called the colon. Here's how we show a colon:

A colon is sometimes used between two independent clauses, when the second independent clause explains or closely develops the first. For example:

 The invention of the automobile changed the way people think about distance: whereas once people wouldn't hesitate to walk a mile, now they can't imagine going that far any way but on wheels.

Another common use for the colon is to introduce something that follows, especially a list or a series of items. A colon says, "Pause for a second; something is about to follow."

Ms. Diaz suggested three topics for our reports: cloning, Pavlovian conditioning, and natural selection.

For the field trip, please bring the following: a lunch, a notebook, and your best behavior.

Learning About Literature

Can You Analyze a Poem and Enjoy It Too?

About two hundred years ago, an English poet by the name of William Words-worth wrote that "we murder to dissect." He meant that in order to study and analyze a living thing, first we have to kill it.

Some people feel that what Wordsworth said applies to more than what goes on in a laboratory. They think that Wordsworth, as a poet, saw a poem as a living thing. And they worry that to analyze a poem—to study it in detail, to look closely at specific lines and words—is to dissect the poem, which would mean, unfortunately, to take all the life out of it. These people feel that poetry is something you should read (and write) not with your mind but with your heart. Poetry, they say, is more a matter of emotions than of thinking.

In some ways, that's true. When you first read a poem, you probably read it for enjoyment. When you first start to talk about it, probably the questions that come to mind are "Do I like this poem? How does it make me feel?"

But then another question often occurs, a question that moves you from feeling into thinking: "What does the poem mean?" As soon as you start thinking about that question, you have to go back to the poem itself. You have to linger over certain lines and words. You begin to wonder why the poet used those particular words, in that particular order. For example, you might wonder why Robert Frost repeated the same line at the end of "Stopping by Woods on a Snowy Evening." Here are the last four lines of that poem:

> The woods are lovely, dark, and deep,
> But I have promises to keep,
> And miles to go before I sleep,
> And miles to go before I sleep.

There are good reasons that Frost repeats a line. And the place to look for those reasons is in the poem, in specific words and lines.

But wait a minute—now you're analyzing the poem. Does that mean you've mur-dered it to dissect it? No, not if you don't go over-board. Instead, it means that you are being respectful to the poet. You are acknowledging that he didn't just slap any old words down on a page but carefully chose and arranged certain words, just as a painter would carefully choose certain paints or a furniture maker would carefully choose the right pieces of wood—or just as you would carefully choose exactly the words you want in writing a poem of your own.

You'll find that you can enjoy many poems even more if you look at the craft that went into making them. You might even find that this kind of study, far from killing a poem, breathes life into it, because it brings you closer to the poet who shaped its words.

In looking at the craft of making a poem, you will find it helpful to know a few terms that describe some of the specific ways in which poets structure their words.

Structure in Poetry

Stanza

When you hear a song on the radio, you might notice that often the vocalist sings a group of related lines, then pauses for some instrumental music, then sings another group of lines, often in the same form as the first group.

Similarly, in poetry, related lines are grouped together in stanzas. Usually one stanza is separated from another by a space on the page. Like most poets of the past, some modern-day poets write poems in which each stanza is of equal length, which gives the poem a definite shape and rhythm. For example, if you look at Robert Frost's "Stopping by Woods on a Snowy Evening" (page 50), you'll notice it has four stanzas. If you're discussing this poem, you can help others understand your way of reading it by saying something like "I think the first stanza starts out bright and cheery, but by the last stanza the mood has changed."

There's a special kind of stanza that is generally not separated from the others. This kind of stanza is called a couplet, and consists of only two lines that rhyme with each other. Maya Angelou's "Woman Work" begins with a series of couplets:

I've got the children to tend
The clothes to mend
The floor to mop
The food to shop
Then the chicken to fry
The baby to dry . . .

Many poems written in England during the seventeenth and eighteenth centuries consisted almost entirely of couplets. The rhyming lines in a couplet often tend to tie together a thought in a nice neat package. Many couplets are still remembered and quoted today, such as this one by the English poet Alexander Pope:

Hope springs eternal in the human breast:
Man never is, but always to be blest.

Rhyme Scheme

Not all poems rhyme, but those that do will often repeat rhymes in a regular pattern within each stanza. This pattern of rhyming words makes up a poem's rhyme scheme. In some poems, the rhyme scheme is very regular and predictable. For example, look at the first two stanzas of "Father William," by Lewis Carroll:

"You are old, Father William," the young man said,
  "And your hair has become very white;
And yet you incessantly stand on your head—
  Do you think, at your age, it is right?"

"In my youth," Father William replied to his son,
  "I feared it might injure the brain;
But now that I'm perfectly sure I have none,
  Why, I do it again and again."

To describe the pattern in a rhyme scheme, we use the letters of the alphabet, and assign a new letter to each rhyme within a stanza. Let's assign a letter to the rhyming words in the first stanza of "Father William":

A   said
B   white
A   head
B   right

Now, if you look at the rhyming words in the second stanza, you'll see that the same pattern is repeated.

A   son
B   brain
A   none
B   again

So we say that the rhyme scheme of "Father William" is A-B-A-B.

Now let's look at a poem by Robert Frost, "Stopping by Woods on a Snowy Evening," in which the rhyme scheme varies from stanza to stanza. Notice how the last word in the third line of one stanza sets up the rhyme in the following stanza.

Whose woods these are I think I know	A
His house is in the village, though;	A
He will not see me stopping here	B
To watch his woods fill up with snow.	A
My little horse must think it queer	B
To stop without a farmhouse near	B
Between the woods and frozen lake	C
The darkest evening of the year.	B
He gives his harness bells a shake	C
To ask if there is some mistake.	C
The only other sound's the sweep	D
Of easy wind and downy flake.	C
The woods are lovely, dark, and deep,	D
But I have promises to keep,	D
And miles to go before I sleep,	D
And miles to go before I sleep.	D

If you read Frost's poem aloud, it might sound almost like casually spoken words. But by noticing the rhyme scheme, you can see that Frost was not writing casually at all: he carefully chose and arranged every word. You can enjoy just reading Frost's poem aloud and hearing the simple words and pleasing rhymes. And you can enjoy

thinking and talking with others about questions like why Frost chose to end the poem with four repeated rhymes.

Meter

Think of what happens when you listen to music. You might find yourself tapping your feet or drumming your fingers in time to the beat. You do that because you can feel the rhythm, the regular beat in the music.

Something similar happens in a lot of poetry, in which the regular beat is called the meter. In a way, meter is a measure of how your voice rises and falls when you read a poem. As you read, your voice rises on what are called the stressed syllables, and it falls on what are called the unstressed syllables. This may be hard to hear at first. One way to tune your ear to the rise and fall of your voice is to practice by exaggerating when you read aloud some lines of poetry. For example, here are the first two lines of a poem by Emily Dickinson. They are marked to signal what to do with your voice. Let your voice rise on the stressed syllable, marked "—," and let your voice fall on unstressed syllables, marked " ⌣ ." Make it obvious; ham it up.

⌣ — ⌣ — ⌣ — ⌣ —
I like to see it lap the miles,

⌣ — ⌣ — ⌣ —
And lick the valleys up . . .

Of course, you don't always want to exaggerate the meter when you read aloud, because you'll end up sounding "singsongy." But by noticing the meter, you can see again how a poet carefully chooses words to give a poem a certain sound and rhythm.

Just as music can be played in many rhythms, so poetry can be written in many different meters. The most common meter in poetry written in English is called iambic (eye-AM-bic), and consists of one unstressed syllable followed by one stressed syllable. Much of Shakespeare's verse is iambic. The lines by Emily Dickinson quoted above are iambic, as is this line by Robert Frost:

Whose woods these are I think I know

Although poets who write in English often use the iambic meter, they also use many others. You can hear how a meter different from iambic sounds by reading aloud this familiar line:

'Twas the night before Christmas, and all through the house

Can you mark the stressed and unstressed syllables in this line from Edgar Allan Poe's "The Raven"?

Once upon a midnight dreary, while I pondered, weak and weary . . .

Free Verse

Many modern poems, including perhaps some of your favorites, do not have a regular meter or rhyme scheme. These poems are written in what is called free verse. Most poets who write in free verse choose their words as carefully as those who write in regular meter and rhyme. In this book, you can read an amusing short poem in free verse by William Carlos Williams, as well as a great poem by Langston Hughes called "The Negro Speaks of Rivers." In the opening lines of Hughes's free verse poem, you can see and hear how the length and rhythm of the lines vary.

I've known rivers:
I've known rivers ancient as the world and older than the
    flow of human blood in human veins.

My soul has grown deep like the rivers.

Introduction to Sayings

FOR PARENTS AND TEACHERS

Every culture has phrases and proverbs that make no sense when carried over literally into another culture. Many children may not need this section; they will have picked up these sayings by hearing them at home and among their friends. But the category of sayings in the *Core Knowledge Sequence* has been the one most appreciated by teachers who work with children from home cultures that differ from the standard culture of literate American English.

Sayings and Phrases

All for one and one for all

This saying means that all the members of a group must work for the good of each individual member, and each individual must work for the good of the group as a whole.

As the Red Dragons headed onto the field, the soccer coach reminded them, "All for one and one for all!"

All's well that ends well

This saying from Shakespeare means that if something finally succeeds, then the difficulties or mistakes along the way can be forgotten.

At the school dance, Jake managed to step on Alice's toes, spill punch on her dress, and tear his pants. But when the evening ended and Alice said, "I hope you'll ask me out again," Jake sighed to himself, "All's well that ends well."

The best-laid plans of mice and men go oft awry

A poet named Robert Burns wrote this line in a poem titled "To a Mouse." "Awry" means turned or twisted to one side. The speaker in the poem ruins the mouse's nest while plowing a field. He explains to the creature that even when you put a great deal of careful planning and effort into something (like building a nest), you may not end up with the result you want.

Hundreds of men planned and built the Tower of Pisa, but it ended up leaning anyway. The best-laid plans of mice and men go oft awry.

A bird in the hand is worth two in the bush

When people say this, they mean that it is much better to be content with what you have than to go chasing after something that may be out of reach: you might end up with nothing.

The excited contestant on the game show had just won a car.

"And now," said the host, "you can keep the car, or you can give it back and spin the wheel again to try for an even bigger prize!"

"Thanks," replied the contestant, "I'll keep the car. A bird in the hand is worth two in the bush."

Don't cut off your nose to spite your face

Sometimes out of anger or for revenge we do things that actually end up hurting us rather than making us feel better. We use this expression to warn against such behavior.

Sam was angry. "I studied really hard for that math test and my grade was terrible. So you know what I'm going to do for the next test? I'm not going to study at all."

"Oh, come on, Sam," said Dana. "Don't cut off your nose to spite your face."

Don't look a gift horse in the mouth

This saying means that you shouldn't fault something that is given to you, or criticize the giver. It comes from the practice of checking a horse's teeth and gums before buying it to see how healthy it is.

"Alec, I can't believe you're giving me your old bike! Thanks!" Stacie said as she jumped on and began to play with the gears. "Say, do all the gears work?"

"Don't you know better than to look a gift horse in the mouth, Stacie?" said Alec, disappointed. "The bike may be old, but it'll get you where you want to go."

A fool and his money are soon parted

This saying means that a person who is foolish with his money won't hold on to it for very long. People usually say it as a warning.

The first time Noah got paid for mowing a neighbor's yard, he wanted to rush out and buy something—anything! But he remembered his big brother saying that a fool and his money are soon parted, and he decided to save his money for something worthwhile.

A friend in need is a friend indeed

Some people are your friends when you are happy but avoid you when you are having trouble. This proverb explains that a true friend is the one who sticks around when you are in need of help, comfort, or anything else.

Every day while Mr. Gainey was sick, his neighbor Charles went to his house to cook for him and read to him. Charles really proved that a friend in need is a friend indeed.

Good fences make good neighbors

This saying suggests that by clearly marking the boundaries between yourself and other people, you can stay on better terms with them. It comes from a poem by Robert Frost.

"Marcus borrows so many books from me that I can't find my own books when I need them," moaned Phillip.

"You know," said his father, "good fences make good neighbors. Why don't you tell Marcus he can only borrow one book at a time? Then you'll know what he has, and you won't feel so angry with him."

He who hesitates is lost

If you wait before you do something, it may be too late. People use this saying to urge someone into action or to comment on a lost opportunity.

Erika looked sadly out the window at the falling snow and then said, "Grandma is right—she who hesitates is lost. I kept meaning to plant daffodil bulbs under my window, but now the ground will be frozen all winter."

He who laughs last laughs best / To have the last laugh

People often ridicule new projects or ideas. But in the end, when something works, the person who took it seriously gets the best laugh of all—one that proves him right.

"My neighbors think I'm silly for practicing my climbing on the garden wall," Kyle said. "But the day I reach the summit of Mount Everest, I'll have the last laugh."

Hitch your wagon to a star

This saying means that you should aim as high as you can.

Robert practiced his jump shots and free throws every day. "Someday," he said to his father, "I'm going to make the high school team."

"Why stop there?" said his father with a laugh. "Hitch your wagon to a star: shoot for the NBA!"

If wishes were horses, beggars would ride

This proverb comes from past times, when horses were a primary means of transportation and many people were too poor to own them. It means that if wishes were easy to achieve, then everyone would have everything they want.

"I wish I had a million dollars," said Cal.

"Sure," said Alicia, "and if wishes were horses, beggars would ride."

The leopard can't change its spots

When people say this, they mean that it's impossible to change or hide a particular trait, because that trait is part of what makes that someone or something what it is.

"I wish Marcia would be on time for once," said Kelly. "A leopard can't change its spots," commented Jonathan. "I say next time we tell her the meeting starts half an hour earlier than it does."

Little strokes fell great oaks

A task may seem overwhelming, but if you break it into manageable smaller tasks and persevere, you can complete it.

When the students volunteered for the housing program, they couldn't imagine what their hammering, sawing, and plastering would do. But little strokes fell great oaks, and in the spring five new houses were ready for families to occupy.

Money is the root of all evil

This proverb means that greed for money can sometimes motivate people to do things that they wouldn't otherwise do.

"Mrs. Alvarado, it says here that some factories dump poisonous waste into rivers. Don't they care about the wildlife and the people who use the water?"

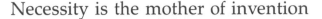

Bill's teacher explained, "It's cheaper to dump the waste than to dispose of it safely. Some factories care more about their profits than they do about rivers."

"No wonder people say money is the root of all evil," Bill mused.

Necessity is the mother of invention

People often come up with new ideas, new ways of doing things, or new things because they need to solve a problem.

"Rosie, you should see Ted's new bed. It's up on a platform," said Raymond. "And he even built a desk and book shelves underneath!"

"What a good idea," replied Rosie. "The last time I saw Ted he was complaining about how small his room is. I guess necessity really is the mother of invention."

It's not over till it's over

This saying means that you can never be sure what the outcome of something (a football game, a book, or even life) will be until the very end.

"I can't take this movie," Chase whispered to Juan. "The forces of evil are going to win. There's no way the hero can survive in a cave full of poisonous gases."

"Wait and see. I bet he finds a way out," said Juan. "It's not over till it's over."

Nothing will come of nothing / Nothing comes of nothing

This saying tells us that without effort, you can't accomplish anything.

"The band needs a new saxophone player, but I'll never be chosen," said Lauren.

"I think you should try," Midori replied. "Nothing comes of nothing. But if you audition, you might get in."

Once bitten, twice shy

If a dog bites you, you will probably be very careful to stay clear of dogs after that. This saying means that people tend to protect themselves from being hurt, especially if they've been hurt before.

"Why didn't Lee enter the science fair?" asked Jim. "The volcano she made last year was great."
"Once bitten, twice shy," said Jenna. "She heard some kids making fun of her entry last year, so she wouldn't enter this year."

Procrastination is the thief of time

Procrastination means putting things off. If you put off doing something, then you may not have enough time left to do it once you finally get started. Thus, procrastination "steals" your time.

"I thought you came up here to study for your spelling test," said Maria's brother, "and here you are cleaning your room."
"I can't study in a messy room," Maria protested.
"If you keep cleaning you won't have any time left to study: procrastination is the thief of time, you know."

The proof of the pudding is in the eating

This saying means that you can't judge something until you try it.

"Zach told me the new space adventure movie is great," said Lydia.
"Well, I usually don't like the same movies he does," Seth answered. "But the proof of the pudding is in the eating. Let's go see it tonight."

Rome wasn't built in a day

Do you remember the story of ancient Rome? It took many people many decades to build that imperial city. People use this expression to mean that it takes a long time to achieve great things. They often use it to counsel patience.

Anna looked up from the rows of seeds she was planting. "Oh, the garden will never be finished!"
"Cheer up," her uncle said. "After all, Rome wasn't built in a day. By August you'll have the best beans, tomatoes, and squash you've ever tasted!"

A stitch in time saves nine

By taking a little care early, you may save yourself a lot of trouble later. This saying is similar to "An ounce of prevention is worth a pound of cure." Can you see how the proverb is based on the activity of sewing?

Marie's father was reading the yellow pages. "What are you looking for, Dad?" she asked.

"I'm looking for a chimney sweep. We need to get the chimney cleaned before too much soot builds up inside. A chimney fire can ruin a chimney or worse. A stitch in time saves nine, I always say."

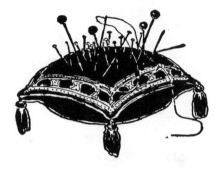

Strike while the iron is hot

To work on metal, a blacksmith heats the metal and then strikes it with a huge mallet. Cold metal isn't easily shaped. So people use this saying to mean that you should do something while circumstances are in your favor.

"Maggie sure is in a good mood today," thought Luke. "I think I'll strike while the iron is hot and ask her if I can borrow her chess set."

There's more than one way to skin a cat

There are many ways to accomplish something or take care of a difficult situation. If one way doesn't work, you can always try another.

"What am I going to do?" said Kristen with a sigh. "I need to learn these verbs for the Spanish test tomorrow, but I've been reading the list over and over and I still can't remember them."

"There's more than one way to skin a cat," replied her sister. "Let's make up sentences for each verb. Maybe that will help."

Truth is stranger than fiction

Things that happen in real life can be more unusual or surprising than things that people make up in stories.

When I read that the same couple had been married three times, once in an airplane, once in a hot-air balloon, and once in an elevator, I decided that truth really is stranger than fiction!

To have a bee in your bonnet

If a bee flew into your hat, wouldn't you be intent on getting it out? People say that someone has a bee in her bonnet if she is annoyed by or obsessed with something.

"The school nurse really has a bee in his bonnet about healthy food. But I'll be glad if he gets the cafeteria to offer a salad bar at last."

To bite the dust

When someone is defeated, we sometimes use this saying. It orginated from physical combat, when people fell facedown in the dust.

"Despite a valiant effort, the Blue Demons bite the dust, and our own Bobcats have won again!" cheered the announcer.

Catch as catch can

This phrase describes a situation in which someone must make do with whatever is available at the moment.

"We don't have as many instruments as we do students," said the music teacher, "so bring in your kazoos, your harmonicas, even empty coffee cans. It's pretty much catch as catch can, but we'll still sound great."

Eat humble pie

"Humble" means "modest." Humble pie, which originally had no relation to being humble, was a meat pie made of animal intestines. The expression "eat humble pie" came to stand for the unpleasant situation in which you are forced to admit your mistakes or weaknesses.

Carlos bragged that he was the fastest runner in the school, but he had to eat humble pie when he came in last at the time trials.

Give the devil his due

This proverb means that even if you don't like someone, you can still give that person credit for his or her good points.

Everyone agrees that the new math teacher assigns a lot of homework. But you have to give the devil his due—all of us have learned a lot of math!

Nose out of joint

Someone's nose is out of joint (that is, not in its normal position) if he or she is annoyed.

>   Ian and Chung Ho were playing backgammon. "Hold on, you can't take all of those pieces," said Chung Ho irritably.
>   "Don't get your nose out of joint," Ian said. "I'm just separating the red pieces from the black pieces."

On tenterhooks

People use this idiom to mean "nervously waiting for something to happen."

Elizabeth waited for the cast list to be posted. As the minutes passed, she grew more and more anxious. At last Mrs. Marks came out of the office and taped it to the door.
"Thank goodness, I got a part!" cried Elizabeth. "I was on tenterhooks all morning."

Pot calling the kettle black

Since most pots and kettles were once made of the same black metal, this phrase is used when you criticize someone for having a fault that you yourself possess.

Matt and Gino were eating potato salad at a family picnic.
"You're really wolfing it down!" said Matt.
"Listen to the pot calling the kettle black!" said Gino. "You've eaten twice as much as I have."

R.I.P.

This abbreviation for "Rest in Peace" is commonly used on gravestones.

As she walked through the colonial cemetery, Nora saw many stones ornately carved with the letters *R.I.P.*

Rule of thumb

In contrast to an official rule or an exact measurement, a rule of thumb is a general principle or a rough estimate that has been shown by experience to work.

"I'm going to get some potato chips. Want some?" Dorothy asked her brother.
"Nope, my rule of thumb while I'm training for the race is 'Don't eat anything you enjoy too much,'" said Andrew.

Tempest in a teapot

A tempest is a very large storm, and a teapot is quite small. We use this expression when a large commotion is made over something pretty little.

"Being Rapunzel for Halloween was my idea. Mandy stole my idea, and I'm never going to speak to her again," Janice shouted.
"Don't make a tempest in a teapot," said Janice's sister. "A costume isn't worth losing your best friend over."

Tenderfoot

A tenderfoot is a person who doesn't have very much experience at something.

After Pete and Joe had pitched their tent, Pete began to hoist the food bag into a tree.
"What are you doing that for?" asked Joe.
"So the raccoons and bears don't get your breakfast, tenderfoot," replied Pete, laughing.

Wolf in sheep's clothing

This phrase describes someone who appears to be harmless or friendly but who is really dangerous or untrustworthy. It comes from a fable by Aesop.

"I can't believe Ron took my idea for his history report. He said he was just interested in hearing about what I was working on. What a wolf in sheep's clothing!"

Foreign Words and Phrases

Gracias

This word means "thank you" in Spanish.

"Gracias," Jane started her letter to her pen pal in Peru. "I loved your description of Machu Picchu. One day I hope you can take me there and show me around as well in person as you did in your letter."

Mademoiselle, Madame, Monsieur

These are French words for Miss, Mrs., and Mr.

Merci

This word means "thank you" in French.

Señorita, Señora, Señor

These are Spanish words for Miss, Mrs., and Mr.

Touché

Fencers use this word from the French language when they hit their opponents, so we say *touché*, when we accomplish something difficult or make a clever counter-response in an argument.

II.

GEOGRAPHY, WORLD CIVILIZATION, AND AMERICAN CIVILIZATION

Introduction to Geography

FOR PARENTS AND TEACHERS

This section on geography introduces children to the complex processes involved in the making of maps. It explains the need for flat maps of our round planet and the distortions that occur in various map projections. From the diagrams children will see that to make maps cartographers rely on geometry as well as accurate measurements. The section also discusses different types of deserts, surveys the deserts of the world, and explains the weather patterns and human actions behind both the formation and the spread of deserts.

It would be helpful to your child to have a globe and a large world map available while reading this section. In addition to the books in this series, a helpful resource is *World Newsmap of the Week/Headline Focus*, a weekly newsmagazine for elementary school students and teachers (Weekly Reader Corporation, 4343 Equity Drive, P.O. Box 16600, Columbus, OH 43216. Subscription cost for 1992–93 school year was $69.95.).

For those with IBM or IBM-compatible personal computers, P.C. Globe, Inc., of Tempe, Arizona, offers GeoJigsaw, an on-screen puzzle with twelve different themes ($39.95 suggested retail price). Many children also enjoy the various Carmen Sandiego games produced by Broderbund Software, which are widely available.

Geography

ROUND EARTH, FLAT MAP

Have you ever compared a globe and a flat map, noting the differences in size of the world's largest land masses? Look, for example, at how much larger Greenland appears on a flat map than on a globe. On some maps it is larger than South America!

These differences in size result from distortions that occur when mapmakers represent our round earth on a flat piece of paper. If you could remove the entire peel from an orange in one piece, what would happen if you tried to flatten it? It would crack and split, wouldn't it? The peel could flatten without cracking only if the areas at the orange's "poles" could stretch. Let's think about this another way. Take a large sheet of paper and wrap it around the globe, touching the globe at all points along the equator. Right away you can tell two things: that the paper forms a tube or cylinder, and that the tube does not touch the globe at all at the poles. Now, pretend your globe is hollow and made of clear plastic. On the plastic are opaque

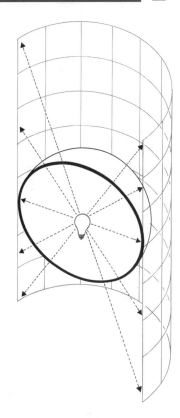

outlines of the world's land masses. If you put an electric light in the middle of this hollow, clear globe, the light would cast the shadows of the globe's features onto the paper tube. Only where the paper fits fairly closely would both the sizes and the shapes of the shadows be accurate.

Now think about how areas near the poles are represented on the globe and the tube. Whereas on the globe all the lines of longitude meet in a single point at the pole, on the paper tube the lines of longitude would stretch apart to look vertical and parallel. That's why Greenland and Alaska look so big on many flat maps.

On what part of the cylinder will the shadows cast by the light bulb most accurately represent the globe's features? Most distort the globe's features?

Cartographers and Projections

Mapmakers are known as cartographers. If you break that word in two it becomes "carto" and "grapher," or, "one who graphs, or draws, charts." Cartographers don't draw their charts or maps using a hollow globe with a light inside. Instead they use the rules of mathematics that go along with simple geometric shapes—such as the sphere, cylinder, cone, or plane—to draw maps on flat pieces of paper.

Different kinds of maps are called "projections." If you have ever watched a filmstrip or slides at school, you may already know the meaning of that word. A film or slide projection is the image, enlarged and sent out by a machine called a projector, that you see displayed on a screen. A map projection is an image of the earth's round surface displayed on a flat piece of paper.

The Mercator Projection

The Flemish cartographer Gerardus Mercator was the first to project the earth's surface onto a flat map. Made in the 1500s, his is still the best-known map projection of the world, although much detail has been added as more information from explorers, sailors, surveyors, and others was gathered.

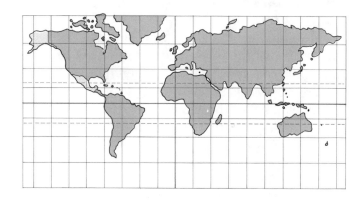

On the left you see how Gerardus Mercator projected the globe's features onto a cylinder. On the right, a finished Mercator projection map laid out flat.

Mercator's projection was made onto a cylinder like the one in the exercise above. This kept shapes accurate, but gradually stretched lines of latitude and longitude until size was tremendously enlarged at the Poles. So, for example, Alaska looks much larger than Mexico on the Mercator projection even though Mexico really has more square miles of land. Generally speaking, you can trust the Mercator projection between the Tropics of Cancer and Capricorn. Note that this is the same area where your paper fit most closely to the globe.

In addition to shape, direction on Mercator's map is also accurate, so the map is helpful in ship navigation.

Conic and Plane Projections

If you twisted a piece of paper into the shape of a cone and put it over a part of the globe, you would end up with a conic projection. In this projection, the map is most accurate where the cone touches the sides of the globe, usually in the middle latitudes (which would be near the Tropic of Cancer, if the cone is placed on top of the globe like a hat, or the Tropic of Capricorn, if the globe is placed on top of the cone like a scoop of ice cream). As you move away from the area where the cone touches the paper, however, distortion increases, so conic projections are rarely used for world maps. Instead, they focus on small parts of the globe, such as the United States.

If you put a flat piece of paper against the globe, it would touch the globe at one point only, like the polar projection of the North Pole in the diagram here. These

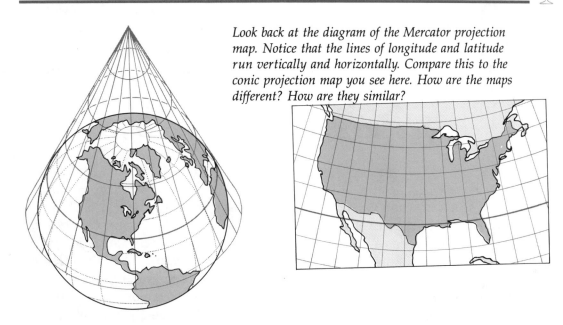

Look back at the diagram of the Mercator projection map. Notice that the lines of longitude and latitude run vertically and horizontally. Compare this to the conic projection map you see here. How are the maps different? How are they similar?

maps are accurate only in the center, near where the plane of the paper touches the globe. They are therefore useful for mapping particular points such as the poles. They show accurate distances and shapes at the point, but elsewhere both shape and distance are distorted.

There are many other types of map projections, each one distorting some portion

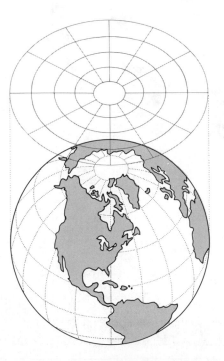

Would this polar projection map be your first choice if you wanted to learn about the geography of Mexico? Why?

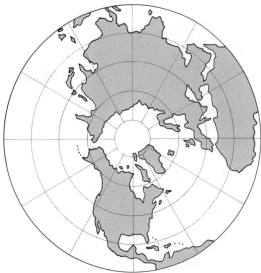

of the globe. With all their distortion, you might wonder, "Why bother with maps at all?" But the distortions we've been explaining here do not affect most everyday uses of maps. If you're hiking on forest trails or looking for a museum in an unfamiliar city, maps still come in handy.

DESERTS OF THE WORLD

What Is a Desert?

What do you think of when you hear the word "desert"? We usually think of deserts as hot, dry places, but notice that the map above shows both hot and cold deserts. Scientists define deserts as areas of land where less than ten inches of rain falls per year and few plants can grow. In arctic and antarctic regions, there is very little rain. Precipitation is almost always frozen in the form of ice or snow, and because it stays frozen on the ground, plants cannot use it to grow. So these regions are considered deserts and given the special label "cold desert" to describe their temperatures, which can range from 10 to 50° F. in summer and from −50 to 10° F. in winter.

Hot deserts, on the other hand, have high temperatures—usually over 75° F. in the shade every day—although they may be cold at night or in the winter. As with

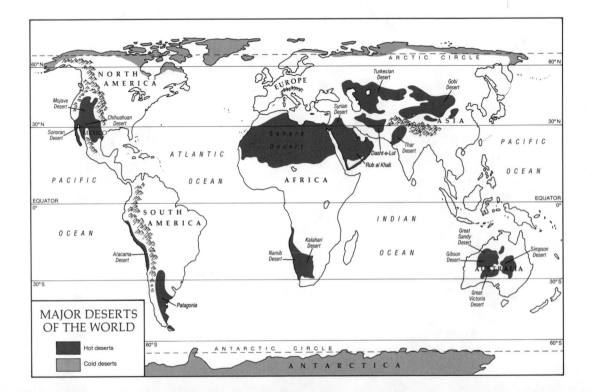

MAJOR DESERTS
OF THE WORLD

Hot deserts

Cold deserts

Who Lives in the Desert?

Desert plants and animals adapt to the heat and lack of rain in their environment in fascinating ways. For example, the acacia tree sends its roots down over one hundred feet to reach groundwater, and cactus leaves are reduced to thin spines to cut down on water loss. (These sharp spines also protect the cactus from thirsty or hungry desert animals.) Many desert animals do not drink water at all. Instead they get all their water from the foods they eat. Others can go without food and water for many days. The Arabian camel, for example, can go without water for over two weeks, and when it must go without food, it relies on the fat stored in its hump.

Choose one of the hot deserts labeled on the map above, and find out more about its environment and the kinds of plants and animals that live there. You can find this information in a book about deserts, or in an encyclopedia under the name of the desert you choose, or under the entry "Deserts." Write a short report on the living creature you find most interesting, and, if you like, present it to your class or to your friends and family.

This jackrabbit has developed a special way to keep cool in the hot deserts of the American Southwest. His ears, tall and thin, provide a large surface area for releasing heat.

The Joshua tree is a familiar sight in hot desert landscapes from southwestern Utah to the Mojave Desert. What do you notice about its "leaves" and bark?

cold deserts, there is usually little water available for plant growth. But contrary to what many people think, hot deserts are not lifeless wastelands. They are home to a fascinating variety of plants and animals that have learned to adapt to the lack of water and harsh temperatures. Also, they are not necessarily made up of endless, shifting sand dunes. In many hot deserts, wind has blown the sand away, leaving bare rock, boulders, and gravel. Some deserts have steep, rocky mountains, while others are flat.

A cold desert on Coulman Island, off the coast of Antarctica.

Sand dunes in the hot desert of Death Valley, on the California-Nevada border.

In the following sections, we will concentrate on hot deserts, learning where the largest ones are located, and why and how they were formed.

Where Are the Deserts?

When you look at the map of the world's deserts, you may notice that all the hot deserts are found about the same distance north or south of the equator. Find the Sonoran and Chihuahuan deserts of North America. They both lie about 30° north of the equator. Now look at the Atacama Desert of South America. It is found near the thirtieth parallel

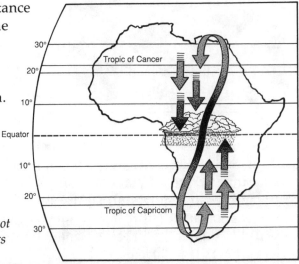

Two reasons deserts form: little rainfall and removal of moisture. Incoming air loses its moisture as precipitation before it reaches the desert regions, so little rain falls there. And hot dry air, moving back toward the equator, sucks moisture out of the desert landscape.

south of the equator. Similarly, the Sahara and the Rub' al-Khali deserts of northern Africa and nearby Saudi Arabia are 30° north of the equator, while the Kalahari Desert of southern Africa is about 30° south of it. The Gobi Desert of central Asia lies a little farther than 30° north, at about 45°, while the Great Sandy and Gibson deserts of Australia fall back into the pattern, lying 30° south of the equator. This pattern is no coincidence. Look at the diagram on the previous page to see why.

Weather Patterns and the Formation of Deserts

A weather pattern created by the moist air and the hot temperatures at the equator contributes to the creation of the hot deserts that ring our planet. Remember learning about air masses, air movement, and fronts in Book Four of this series? You read that hot air holds more moisture than cold air and that hot air can be pushed upward by cooler, heavier air underneath it. (It might be helpful to review the sections in Book Four about air movement to aid your understanding of the following material.)

As you know, the air masses at the equator are hot. They contain a lot of moisture from the many lakes, rivers, and oceans nearby. Because these moist air masses are warmed rapidly at the equator, they begin to rise. As this hot moist air rises it cools and begins to spread north and south. The moisture in the air collects into huge clouds. When these clouds become so heavy that they can't hold any more water, they drop it in the form of rain. Generally, this rain occurs in a broad band between the Tropic of Cancer and the Tropic of Capricorn.

By the time the cool air masses reach 30° latitude (both north and south), where most of the world's hot deserts are, they have lost all their moisture, and no rain falls. The dense, high pressure air masses sink toward the earth, where they are heated again. As they are heated, they become low pressure systems and flow back toward the equator, pushed along by the cooler, high pressure systems that are sinking behind them. Along the way to the equator, the warm, dry, low pressure systems suck up any moisture in desert areas like a sponge. (Remember, hot air can hold a lot of moisture.) This moisture is not deposited until the warm air again begins to rise at the equator, and the cycle starts over. Can you see how over years and years this weather pattern could make a desert?

There's an interesting way in which the same weather pattern maintains these deserts. Have you ever been to a desert? Did you see any clouds hanging overhead? Or can you find any pictures of deserts that have clouds in them? By the time air masses reach the desert, they have lost their moisture. So there are rarely clouds over deserts to block the sun. The sun beats down relentlessly on the already dry earth, evaporating any moisture and keeping it a desert. The lack of clouds over deserts also explains why some are so cold at night. In other places, clouds help trap the hot air that rises from the earth's surface as it cools at night. But in the desert, without a blanket of clouds hot air escapes very quickly into the atmosphere, and the desert cools rapidly.

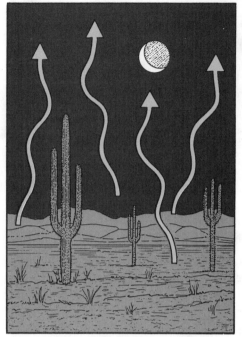

Without cloud cover at night, deserts lose hot air and cool rapidly.

Cloud cover traps hot air and directs it back toward the earth.

More Reasons Deserts Are So Dry

As we just read, the earth's general weather patterns are responsible for the formation of the world's hot deserts, but in addition, there are other things that keep moist air from reaching the areas that have become deserts. Sometimes, for example, these areas are far from large bodies of water such as seas. As warm, moist air over the sea makes its way onto land, it is cooled. It loses its moisture in the form of rain before it reaches places that are far inland. Look again at the map of the world's deserts. Notice how far inland the Gobi Desert is. The air that reaches the Gobi Desert has lost all of its moisture by the time it gets there.

But you'll notice on the map that some deserts, such as the Atacama in South America, are near the sea. Here the prevailing winds blow in the opposite direction, from land to sea, and there is a mountain range blocking their path. In the case of the Atacama desert, any moisture the air has picked up over the land is lost on the east side of the Andes Mountains. As the warm air meets the mountain slope, it rises and cools, dropping all its moisture as rain or snow on the side facing the wind. By the time it reaches the Atacama, the air is dry. In some parts of this desert, until 1974 rain had not been reported for over four hundred years!

Even in areas where winds blow from the sea onto land, deserts can form if there is a mountain range between these lands and the sea. Winds coming from the sea and carrying moisture lose that moisture as rain on the side of the mountain that

Deserts in a rain shadow. Rain falls on the mountainsides that face a water source, rather than on the sheltered side of the mountains.

faces the winds. By the time the winds reach the sheltered side of the mountains, they are dry. Deserts formed for this reason are said to be in a rain shadow. The Sonoran Desert, which extends from northwestern Mexico into the southwestern United States, lies in a rain shadow.

People Can Make Deserts

People have caused several deserts to form or expand. The Thar desert in western India was created by people where no desert existed before. Two thousand years ago it was a forest. And the Sahara in Africa has been greatly expanded by poor farming practices. During the time of the Roman Empire, the northern Sahara was a temper-ate area good for farming. The Romans cut hillside forests for firewood and to make fields. They also plowed the land too much, so that there was nothing to hold the soil in place and prevent it from being carried away by wind and rain. Domesticated animals overgrazed grassy areas, which also exposed the topsoil to wind and rain. Soon there was no topsoil left, and most plants couldn't grow. Because there were few plants to hold moisture, water

White Sands National Monument, part of the Sonoran Desert, is in a rain shadow. In the background you can see clouds forming over the mountains. But where will the rain from these clouds fall?

evaporated quickly. Over thousands of years—a relatively short time in the earth's history—the climate changed from moist and temperate to hot and dry. The damaged land quickly turned to desert.

Spreading Deserts

L*ike the Thar and the Sahara, other deserts throughout the world continue to spread because of human activities. The spread of deserts, known as desertification, is a global problem that affects two thirds of the world's nations.*

Go to the library and do some research to find out why desertification is a problem and what is being done about it. Most books on deserts include at least one chapter about desertification. You might try The Spread of Deserts *by Ewan McLeish (Wayland Publishers Ltd., "Conserving Our World" series) and* Expanding Deserts *by Paula Hogan (Gareth Stevens Children's Books, "Environmental Alert!" series). In addition, you can write to organizations such as Children of the Green Earth (P.O. Box 95219, Seattle, WA 98145), Oxfam America (115 Broadway, Boston, MA 02116), or CARE (660 First Avenue, New York, NY 10016) for further information about desertification.*

Make a map of the world's deserts. (You can copy the map in this section.) Then mark the areas threatened by desertification. How much land is threatened? In how many countries? Is there a threat of desertification in our country?

Introduction to World Civilization

FOR PARENTS AND TEACHERS

If you have a world map or globe that's even a few years old, then parts of it, as you may know, are already out of date. There is no more "Soviet Union," or a single country called Yugoslavia. The dramatic historical changes of our time—what schools sometimes call "current events"—are more than a matter of shifting names and boundaries. Newspapers, magazines, and television bring us painful stories and pictures of the people whose lives are affected—sometimes lost—in these struggles and changes.

It is worth keeping in mind the lives and difficulties of these people as we look back on the story of the recent past covered in the following section. The story introduces political, military, and economic struggles that, with only slight adaptations, could be illustrated by many of the images we see on television news shows today. The often fierce struggle for power and resources, and the unleashing of new powers in the Industrial Revolution, have had consequences that we can see all around us. Parents and teachers are encouraged to talk with children about what these struggles and changes meant for the people who experienced them, and what they mean for us today. In these discussions, one can be guided by the wisdom expressed in these words of Maya Angelou, spoken in the poem she delivered at the inauguration of President Bill Clinton:

> History, despite its wrenching pain,
> Cannot be unlived, but if faced
> With courage, need not be lived again.

World Civilization

THE STRUGGLE FOR INDEPENDENCE IN THE AMERICAS

Every July 4, Americans celebrate Independence Day. In the middle of all the fireworks and songs, we remember that once this nation was not a nation at all but, like many other lands in North and South America, a colony under the control of a faraway government.

In the late 1700s, many people living in the Americas began to rebel against their European rulers. The colonists in North America were the first to defeat their European (specifically, English) rulers and gain independence. Within fifty years,

This map shows you the countries of Latin America and the dates they became independent of European rule.

many people in the vast region made up of Mexico, Central America, and South America would gain independence from the European powers of Spain and Portugal.

After the United States, the next colony to win its independence was Haiti. Haiti is a country on the large island of Hispaniola in the Caribbean. In the 1600s it had been settled by the French, who brought slaves from Africa to work on sugar plantations. They brought so many slaves that the Africans outnumbered the French by ten to one.

In 1791, just fifteen years after the North American colonists rebelled against England, the slaves of Haiti rose up against their masters. Their leader, a former slave named Toussaint L'Ouverture (too-SAHN LOO-vair-tyur), was the son of an African king and a brilliant military leader. He abolished slavery and declared himself governor of Haiti. Later, when a French army invaded Haiti in 1801, Toussaint was captured and sent to France, where he died in prison. But his memory lived on. His followers defeated the French army the next year, and in 1804 the rebels declared the independence of Haiti.

Toussaint L'Ouverture is remembered as the liberator of Haiti.

Colonial Mexico

From the 1500s to the 1800s, the land we know as Mexico was a Spanish colony called "New Spain." (You may recall reading in Book Five of this series how the Spanish explorer Cortés conquered the country by overthrowing the great empire of the native Aztecs.) New Spain was the largest and most important of all Spanish colonies. It was a huge land that included not only present-day Mexico but also the areas that became the states of California, Nevada, Arizona, Utah, New Mexico, Texas, and part of Colorado.

The population of New Spain was clearly divided into four groups. The group a person belonged to was determined by two things: the person's racial background and place of birth. The most powerful group was the Spaniards, people born in Spain and sent to rule the colony. Only Spaniards could hold high-level jobs in the colonial government. Members of the second most powerful group, called creoles, were people of Spanish background who had been born in Mexico rather than in

Spain. Many creoles were prosperous landowners and merchants. But even the most wealthy creoles had very little say in the government, which was controlled by the Spaniards.

The third group, the mestizos, had a much lower position in colonial society. The word *mestizo* means "mixed," and a person was a mestizo if some of his or her ancestors were Spanish and some were Indians. The mestizos were looked down upon by both the Spaniards and Creoles, who held the racist belief that people of "pure" European background were superior to everyone else.

The poorest, most oppressed group in New Spain was the Indians, the original people of the land. The other groups constantly mistreated and took advantage of them. Indians were forced to work as laborers on the ranches and farms (called "haciendas") of the Spaniards and creoles.

The "lower" groups—creoles, mestizos, and Indians—often disagreed among themselves. But all three resented the small minority of Spaniards who had all the political power. By the early 1800s, many native-born Mexicans were beginning to think that Mexico should become independent of Spain, as the United States had recently become independent of England. The man who finally touched off the revolt against Spain was a Catholic priest, Father Miguel Hidalgo y Costilla (he-DAL-go ee coss-TEE-ya). Hidalgo is remembered today as the "Father of Mexican Independence."

Miguel Hidalgo

Hidalgo was a dedicated scholar who had studied the writings of Thomas Jefferson and Tom Paine, and of the leaders of the French Revolution. These revolutionary writings helped convince him that Mexico should be free. Hidalgo also had great sympathy for the poorest, most downtrodden Mexicans. Although he himself was a creole, he lived and worked among the Indians and earned their respect and loyalty.

On September 16, 1810, Hidalgo gathered a group of his followers, most of them poor Indians. He spoke of the injustice and oppression that Spain had brought to Mexico. Then he cried, "Will you free yourselves? Will you recover the lands stolen three hundred years ago from your forefathers by the hated Spaniards? We must act at once!" (Today Hidalgo's speech is known to every student in Mexico, and September 16 is celebrated as Mexico's Independence Day.)

Within months Hidalgo gathered tens of thousands of Indians into his rebel army. At first the rebels surged across the countryside, capturing every town in their path. Several times they defeated small forces of Spaniards. But their success did not last long. The rebel forces were untrained and poorly armed, whereas the Spaniards were well equipped and well trained. The rifles, clubs, and

Miguel Hidalgo.

knives of the Indians were no match for the Spanish artillery. In a great battle, Hidalgo's army was beaten and scattered in January, 1811.

Hidalgo and the other leaders of the rebellion tried to escape to the United States, where they hoped to win American aid for their cause. But they were ambushed and captured on the way. Hidalgo was tried for treason, found guilty, and sentenced to die by firing squad. He faced death bravely, placing his hand over his heart so that the firing squad could take better aim.

Mexico Achieves Independence

Although Hidalgo was dead, the rebellion lived on. One of Hidalgo's followers, Father José María Morelos, was determined to keep fighting. Like Hidalgo, Morelos was a Catholic priest sympathetic to the plight of the Indians. He turned a part of Hidalgo's defeated army into a tough, disciplined band of guerrillas. (Guerrillas are fighters who are not part of a regular, formal army.) This group fought on against the Spaniards for another four years.

José María Morelos.

The rebellion was not popular with all Mexicans. Many people were shocked by the violence and disorder it brought to the country. The creoles in particular were suspicious of Morelos and his followers. Most of the rebels were Indians, a group the creoles considered "inferior." Also, there was a great deal of tension between the creoles, who were middle-class or wealthy, and the rebels, who were poor and resentful of the creoles' wealth. The creoles worried that if the rebellion were successful, their property might be taken from them and divided among the rebels.

The rebellion was further weakened when the rebel leaders began quarreling among themselves. Then, in 1815, Morelos was captured by the Spaniards; like Hidalgo, he was executed by a firing squad.

It seemed as though the rebellion was doomed to fail. But the people's desire for freedom did not fade. In 1820 the independence movement got an unexpected new leader: Colonel Agustín de Iturbide (ee-tour-BEE-thuh), an officer in the Spanish army who had helped defeat the first Indian rebels. Suddenly he turned against the Spanish government and declared that Mexico ought to be free. Unlike Hidalgo and Morelos, he appealed to both the upper classes and the poor. And he had the power of the army behind him. In 1821, Iturbide marched into the capital, Mexico City, and took control of the government from the Spanish authorities. Mexico was finally independent of Spain.

Mexico now had its own government, but at first it was not a good one. Iturbide quickly became a dictator. He had himself proclaimed "emperor" of Mexico, copying the ceremony used by Napoleon when he had had himself proclaimed emperor of France. No one was allowed to speak out against Iturbide. He filled his government with corrupt officials, who became rich by taking bribes and making dishonest business deals.

By 1823, Mexicans of all classes were fed up with Iturbide's corrupt and oppressive rule. They overthrew the emperor and sent him into exile. In 1824, Mexico was proclaimed a republic. The new government adopted a constitution partly modeled on the Constitution of the United States, which guaranteed basic human rights and divided the responsibilities of government between a central authority and a number of smaller units known as states.

Santa Anna

Despite its newly won independence, Mexico remained a deeply divided nation. The Spaniards, creoles, mestizos, and Indians continued to quarrel with each other. And the new constitution led to arguments between those who wanted more power for the state governments and those who wanted more power for the central government.

All this quarreling made Mexico's government extremely unstable, and revolutions broke out frequently. One group of revolutionaries would overthrow the government and rule for a few months or years, then they would be overthrown in another revolution. The Mexican army, however, remained consistently powerful. This put the country at the mercy of the *caudillos* (cow-THEEL-yos), power-hungry military leaders like Iturbide.

One important caudillo was a general named Santa Anna. From the 1830s to the 1850s, Santa Anna was the most powerful man in the country. But he was a terrible leader. He was dishonest and used his office to make himself rich. He was also incredibly vain, erecting statues of himself all over Mexico and forcing people to address him as "Your Most Serene Highness." Santa Anna had no real beliefs or principles; all he cared about was keeping himself in power. His leadership was a great disaster for Mexico. In fact, it was partly because of his bad leadership that Mexico lost *half* of its total territory to the United States.

War with the United States

In the 1820s, U.S. settlers began moving into the Mexican territory of Texas. At first the settlers were content to live under the new Mexican republic. But when Santa Anna came to power, he laid down oppressive new laws, making the settlers so resentful of his government that finally, in 1836, they declared Texas to be independent of Mexico.

Santa Anna led an army into Texas to punish the rebels. At a fortress called the

After his defeat, Santa Anna (center in white pants) surrenders to the wounded Sam Houston, leader of the American forces. The man at the right with his hand to his ear is "Deaf" Smith, a famous scout who served with Houston.

Alamo, his troops defeated a vastly outnumbered force of Texans. All of the Texas rebels were killed, but their courage in the face of great odds inspired a rebel battle cry: "Remember the Alamo!" A few months later, the Texans got their revenge. One day, when Santa Anna's troops were resting in their camp, the Texans launched a surprise attack and defeated the Mexicans.

After this defeat, Santa Anna agreed to grant Texas its independence. Meanwhile, more and more Americans were moving westward: do you recall reading about "manifest destiny" in Book Four of this series? Americans were settling in Mexican territory, not just in Texas but also in California and the area that would become the states of Arizona, Nevada, and New Mexico. Many Americans began to think that this vast region should belong to the United States rather than to Mexico. The Mexicans, of course, disagreed. The two nations grew hostile toward each other, and when the United States admitted Texas into the Union in 1845, Mexico was deeply angered. The following year, war broke out between the two countries.

American armies attacked Mexico by land and sea. The Mexicans fought bravely, but their leader, Santa Anna, made foolish military mistakes and quarreled with other Mexican leaders. Finally, in September 1847, the Americans captured Mexico City and the war came to an end. Mexico was forced to give up all the land north of the Rio Grande river—about half its total territory.

For many generations, Mexicans felt bitter and angry about this war. They were angry at Santa Anna for his incompetent leadership, but even angrier at the United States. In the United States, the war of 1846–1848 is called the Mexican-American War; but in Mexico, it is called the American Invasion.

Benito Juárez

When Santa Anna was in power, many Mexicans opposed him, including a young lawyer named Benito Juárez (WAH-rez). In 1853, Juárez was thrown in jail for speak-

Benito Juárez.

ing out against Santa Anna. But he escaped from prison and made his way to New Orleans, where he supported himself by working in a cigar factory.

Shortly after Juárez returned to Mexico in 1855, Santa Anna fell from power and a democratic government was organized. Juárez joined the government, and in 1858 he became president of Mexico.

Juárez was not at all like Santa Anna. Whereas Santa Anna was crooked, Juárez was famous for his sincerity and honesty. The vain Santa Anna had dressed in gaudy uniforms; Juárez dressed in plain black clothes. Santa Anna had ruled as a dictator, but Juárez governed Mexico democratically. Under Juárez, Mexicans enjoyed freedom of speech and could criticize the government without fear of harm. Juárez also showed great concern for the plight of Mexico's poor. Juárez came from a poor Indian family, and he never forgot his background. He set out to correct one of the worst injustices in Mexico at the time: most of the land was owned by a few wealthy people, while most of the workers were poor farmers who owned no land and were treated like slaves. The wealthy owners of the gigantic haciendas wouldn't allow the workers to leave and seek work elsewhere. While the landowners lived in luxury, the workers lived in shacks without floors or windows. Juárez fought for new laws that would force the landowners to sell their lands, thus giving the farmers a chance to own a little land of their own and work their way out of poverty.

Not everyone supported Juárez's ideas for social reform. In fact, for three years he fought a civil war against his opponents in the government. But after Juárez won the civil war, he realized that Mexico's problems—especially poverty—were too large to be solved quickly. After Juárez died in 1872, his ideals continued to inspire later generations, and today Juárez is the most honored of all of Mexico's past leaders.

Dictatorship and Revolution

After Juárez's death, his democratic government was replaced by a new dictator, a general named Porfirio Díaz who ruled Mexico for more than thirty years. Díaz tried to make Mexico a modern, prosperous nation. He built railroads and developed natural resources such as mines and oil fields. He invited Europeans and Americans to buy land and set up businesses in Mexico. As a result, the nation as a whole became more prosperous.

But many Mexicans, especially in the countryside, were still terribly poor. Unlike Juárez, Díaz showed no concern for the landless farm workers. Instead, he allowed wealthy landowners to buy even more land, and the farm workers became poorer

Not everyone benefited equally from Mexico's increased prosperity. These Yaqui Indians, shown in a temporary camp, lost not only their lands but also their freedom.

and more desperate. Indians, too, suffered more oppression under Díaz. Indian lands were stolen and given to friends of the dictator. One group of Indians, the Yaquis, refused to give up their lands. To punish them, Díaz had thousands of Yaquis forced into slavery in a region far from their home.

Díaz ruled Mexico until the year 1910, when a great revolution broke out against his dictatorship. The revolution had different leaders in different parts of Mexico. Two of the most famous leaders were Pancho Villa and Emiliano Zapata. As a young man, Villa had been a bandit, supporting himself by robbing trains and banks. During the revolution, he proved himself a skillful guerrilla leader. He was cruel and ruthless but also very brave, and his followers loved him. Zapata was a more idealistic leader than Villa. Like Juárez, he came from a poor family of Indian descent, and he cared for the landless poor: his battle cry was "Land and liberty!"

By 1911, Díaz's dictatorship was overthrown, but the fighting went on. The revolution became a civil war between different groups of revolutionaries. This conflict lasted for ten years and cost almost a million lives. But it ended with the establish-ment of a new form of government in Mexico. The revolutionaries drew up a new constitution, one that guaranteed democracy and promised a better life for the country's poor. This constitution forms the basis of Mexico's present-day government.

The Zapatistas, followers of Zapata, were peasants who fought in the Mexican Revolution.

The Revolutions in South and Central America

As we have seen, Mexico's war for independence from Spain began in the year 1810. At almost the same time, the Spanish colonies in South America began their own struggles for independence.

In the northern part of South America, the revolution against Spain was led by Simon Bolívar. Bolívar, who came from a wealthy Venezuelan family, was a brilliant general and an inspiring leader. At one time in the middle of the war, as Bolívar was eating dinner with some of his followers, he suddenly leaped up on the table and began stalking back and forth. He cried, "As I cross this table from one end to the other, I shall march from the Atlantic to the Pacific, from Panama to Cape Horn, until the last Spaniard is expelled!"

Again and again Bolívar's troops won victories over the larger, better-armed forces of Spain. Thanks to his leadership, a vast region in northern South America won its independence. Today this region includes the countries of Venezuela, Colombia, Ecuador, and Peru, as well as the country named for Bolivar, Bolivia. Throughout South America, Bolivar is still referred to as "the Liberator."

In the southern part of the continent, the revolution was led by another great leader, José de San Martín, whose forces liberated the countries of Argentina and Chile. Though he was the son of a Spanish official, San Martín yearned to see his homeland free of Spanish rule. Like Bolívar, San Martín was an awe-inspiring general. At one point, in order to attack the Spanish forces in Chile, he had to lead his army on a great journey over the towering Andes mountains, a feat comparable to the famous crossing of the Alps by Hannibal (which you read about in Book Three).

Simon Bolívar.

Thanks to Bolívar and San Martín, all of the Spanish colonies in South America became independent nations. But independence did not bring democracy. Throughout the 1800s, most South American countries were ruled by a series of caudillos, or military dictators. Often one caudillo would rule for only a short time before being overthrown by another, even more ruthless, leader. Simon Bolívar and José de San Martín had dreamed of a free, peaceful, prosperous South America. But the leaders who came after them betrayed that dream.

A Prince Brings Independence to Brazil

One important South American nation had never been colonized by Spain. This was the vast country of Brazil, which had been claimed by Portugal. When Brazilians watched other South Americans struggling for freedom, they were inspired to fight for their own independence. Oddly enough, it was a Portuguese prince who helped them achieve it.

Prince Pedro, the son of the Portuguese king, lived in Brazil, which he ruled in the name of his father. Pedro loved Brazil and was well liked by its people. As time went by, he began to sympathize more and more with the Brazilians who wanted to be independent.

In 1822 the Portuguese government ordered Prince Pedro to return to Portugal. But Pedro refused the order, crying, "I remain!" (Today in Brazil, Pedro's response is celebrated on "I Remain Day.") A few months later, Pedro declared the independence of Brazil. He was crowned emperor of the new country, and promised to rule as a constitutional monarch—a ruler whose powers are limited by a constitution. Thanks to Prince Pedro, Brazil achieved independence without having to suffer years of bloody warfare, as did the other South American nations. As an independent nation, Brazil would face many challenges in the years ahead, especially with regard to its long practice of importing slaves into the country.

Prince Pedro.

At about the same time that South Americans were fighting for freedom, the peoples of Central America (the region of North America between Mexico and South America) also declared their independence from Spain. At first Central America was a single country, but it later broke into five separate nations: Costa Rica, El Salvador, Guatemala, Honduras, and Nicaragua. By 1825, Spain had been driven from both American continents.

Latin America and the United States

In the United States, most people sympathized with the revolutionaries in Latin America. In 1823 the American president James Monroe made a famous declaration to Congress, in which he warned Europe to keep its hands off North and South America. "The American continents," Monroe declared, ". . . are henceforth not to be considered as subjects for future colonization by any European powers." This warning (as you might recall from Book Four) became known as the Monroe Doctrine.

At first most Latin Americans welcomed the Monroe Doctrine. They were glad that the United States was offering to help defend them against European aggression. But as time went on, Latin Americans began to take a less positive view of the United

States. In the late 1800s, American businessmen started making heavy investments in Latin America. Some Latin Americans thought these businessmen were trying to buy control of their countries. Then (as you may recall from Book Five of this series), starting with the Spanish-American War of 1898, the United States began to get heavily involved in Latin American political affairs. The United States took Cuba and Puerto Rico away from Spain, and encouraged Panama to break away from Colombia. Later, U.S. Marines were sent to occupy Nicaragua and the Dominican Republic.

Sometimes the United States got involved in these countries to protect American businesses; at other times it got involved in the name of human rights. Either way, many Latin Americans resented U.S. interference in their affairs. Perhaps, they thought, America had only warned Europe to keep its hands off Latin America so that the United States could get its own hands on it. Many Latin Americans worried that the United States was becoming as aggressive an empire-builder as the European countries had been in years past.

BACK IN EUROPE

Europe After Napoleon

Let's think back: the American Revolution began in 1776. Fifteen years later, the Haitians began their fight for freedom, the first in a series of Latin American struggles for independence.

Across the Atlantic, the French Revolution, which began in 1789, led to the Napoleonic Wars, which continued until 1815. (You read about the events of these years in Book Five of this series.) From 1789 to 1815, Europe was in turmoil. In many countries people rebelled against the established governments. Great armies clashed all over the continent. Not until 1815—when an alliance of powers (England, Austria, Prussia, and Russia) defeated the forces of the French leader, Napoleon, at the famous battle of Waterloo—was Europe again at peace.

The years following 1815 were in many ways a time of looking backward. The rulers of the countries that defeated Napoleon wanted to turn back the clock to a time before the French Revolution. They wanted Europe to be ruled by kings and emperors rather than by representatives of the people. They were afraid of the democratic ideas that had been unleashed by the American and French Revolutions, and they wanted to prevent the majority of people from having a say in how they were ruled.

In France, a new monarchy replaced the one that had been overthrown in 1789. But the desire for democracy remained strong, so strong that in 1848 a new revolution broke out in France, and once again the king was overthrown. Inspired by events in France, people in other European countries rose up against their rulers. Revolutions broke out in Italy, Germany, and the Austrian Empire (which later became the nations of Austria, Hungary, and Czechoslovakia).

In country after country, however, the armies of the kings put down the revolutionaries. It would be a long time before democracy would come to some European countries, and it would come through slow changes and reforms, not all at once in a revolution. In the meantime, however, another kind of revolution was taking place, one that would permanently change the lives of Europeans, and have far-reaching effects around the world.

The Industrial Revolution

If a European person from the Middle Ages were somehow magically transported to the early 1700s, she would see people living and working in familiar ways. Before 1750, most Europeans still lived in the countryside and worked on the land. They made the goods they needed, such as clothes and furniture, by hand or with small, simple machines. They didn't travel much, and when they did, the going was slow, on foot or on horseback.

But, if our time-traveler from the Middle Ages were to land around 1800, she would find herself in a strange and surprising world. She would see new machines that could do the work of hundreds, even thousands, of people. She would see people leaving the countryside and traveling on fast, noisy, smoke-belching machines that would probably frighten her, but which you'd recognize as railroad trains. These trains carried many people to the rapidly growing cities, where the workers tended the new machines in large buildings called factories.

Before the Industrial Revolution most Europeans lived in the countryside and worked on the land.

The Industrial Revolution changed where and how people lived: many moved into the cities and worked in factories.

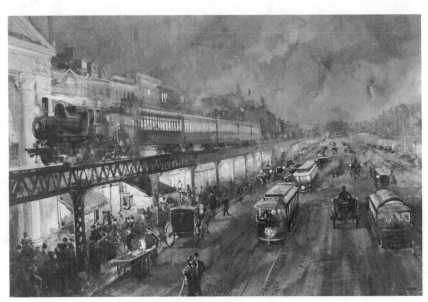

All of these changes make up what we call the Industrial Revolution. The Industrial Revolution began in England around 1750, and then spread gradually to other European countries. Partly because of its head start in the Industrial Revolution, England became an especially powerful country in the 1800s.

The Industrial Revolution was, as we will see, a revolution with both good and bad effects. Let's look at the industry that first adopted the new and faster ways of making things: the textile industry in England.

The English Textile Industry

Today, if you need a new shirt, you probably go to a store with a clothing section. On shelves or racks you can see dozens of piles of shirts in many different sizes and colors. But who made those shirts?—not to mention the pants, dresses, socks, and hundreds of other articles of clothing in the store? Most likely not the people in the store. The shirt you buy is the end-product of manufacturing processes that were developed for the first time back in England during the Industrial Revolution.

In the mid-eighteenth century, one of the main products produced by English workers was cloth, especially cotton cloth. Have you ever seen raw cotton? It doesn't look much like cloth. It looks like a puffy web of thin, fuzzy strands. To make cloth, you must first spin these fuzzy strands into yarn. Then you can weave this yarn into cloth. In the 1760s, English inventors developed new machines that made it possible to spin the cotton much faster than ever before. For a while, these new machines made it possible for workers to spin cotton into yarn much faster than the weavers could turn the yarn into cloth. Then, in the 1780s, another English inventor came

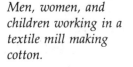

Men, women, and children working in a textile mill making cotton.

up with a new, more powerful loom (weaving machine) that made weaving just as fast as spinning.

But now, the spinners and weavers couldn't get enough cotton fiber to feed their speedy new machines. The cotton fiber, as you may know, grows on a plant: when you pick the fiber, you also get a lot of seeds along with it. Before the fiber can be used, it must be separated from the seeds. In the 1790s, an American, Eli Whitney, invented a machine called a cotton gin, which quickly separated the cotton fiber from the seeds. Now the whole process of making cotton was rapid and efficient.

What happened first in the textile industry happened over and over in other industries during the Industrial Revolution: one invention led to another, and another, and another.

The Steam Engine

Factory owners now had big, powerful new machines that could do the work of many people. But it took a great deal of energy to run the machines. The first factories were run by water power. Workers built a large wheel alongside a river or stream: the flowing water would turn the wheel, creating energy to drive the machines. But to take advantage of water power, you had to build a factory next to a river or stream, which limited where you could build a factory and how many you could build.

All this changed, however, in the late 1700s, when a man named James Watt invented a new kind of engine run by steam. Because steam can be made anywhere by boiling water, steam-powered factories could be built anywhere. By 1800 there were over one thousand steam engines in England, and factories were spreading all over the country. Steam remained the most important source of energy until the 1900s, when electrical energy came into widespread use.

The Railroad

The steam engine also made possible a dramatic new form of transportation: the railroad. Even before 1800, England had railways, but these were just lines of iron track along which carts could be pulled by horses. Then, in the early 1800s, English engineers invented the locomotive, a steam engine on wheels that could pull much heavier loads than any horse, and pull them more swiftly. Early locomotives traveled between 20 and 40 miles an hour—not as fast as a car travels on a modern highway, but much faster than a horse.

Soon trains were being used to carry passengers as well as goods. By 1850, Britain had more than 6,000 miles of railroad track. The railway system made English industry more successful by making it faster and cheaper to transport goods. It connected remote, distant parts of the country with the great cities. Because railway travel was cheap, it allowed even poor people to travel and experience new things.

Most people were delighted by this new form of transportation. One Englishman remembered how he would visit the countryside just to catch a glimpse of passing trains:

> I went into the country for a week . . . and saw the white steam shooting throughout the landscape of trees, meadows and villages, and the long train, loaded with merchandise, men and women and human enterprise, rolling along under the steam. I had seen no sight like that; I have seen nothing to excel it since. In beauty and grandeur, the world has nothing beyond it.

But not everyone welcomed the railroad. Some people insisted that trains were too noisy, too dirty, and too dangerous. They worried that a rock on the tracks might cause a train wreck, that a spark from an engine might cause a forest fire, or even that cows in the fields might be driven crazy by the noise of passing trains! But

Try to imagine what a change the invention of the steam-powered locomotive brought about: both people and goods could travel farther, faster, and more cheaply than before.

such fears did not stop the railroad. Soon it was England's most important form of transportation.

The Plight of the Factory Workers

Gradually, the Industrial Revolution spread, and most of the world's nations began to change to the new ways of manufacturing and transportation. The Industrial Revolution came to different countries at different times, and took different forms. By the middle of the 1800s, Western Europe and the northeastern United States were becoming industrialized. Southern and Eastern Europe followed decades later. It was not until the 1900s that most Asian and African nations began to industrialize.

As the Industrial Revolution spread, it brought great benefits, but it also brought great hardships to many people. While the Industrial Revolution created new jobs, especially jobs tending the new machines, it also did away with old jobs. For example, making furniture once required skilled craftsmen who worked carefully and slowly by hand; the new machines, however, put these skilled craftsmen out of work. In the early 1800s, some of the unemployed workers turned to violence. Some, called "Luddites" (after an English worker named Ned Ludd), showed their anger by smashing machines and burning factories. Those Luddites who were caught by the authorities were severely punished; some were even hanged.

Many people, hoping to find high-paying jobs and a better life, moved from the country to the towns and cities where factories were springing up. These factory towns, as they were sometimes called, were not ready for so many people at once: from about 1800 to 1850, in one English city, Birmingham, the population grew from 73,000 to 250,000! There were not enough jobs or housing for all these people. Whole families crowded into a single room, while others were left homeless, wandering the bleak, polluted streets of towns like this one described by the English writer Charles Dickens in his novel called *Hard Times* (1854):

It was a town of red brick, or of brick that would have been red if the smoke and ashes had allowed it. . . . It was a town of machinery and tall chimneys, out of which interminable serpents of smoke trailed themselves for ever and ever, and never got uncoiled. It had a black canal in it, and a river that ran purple with ill-smelling dye, and vast piles of buildings full of windows where there was a rattling and trembling all day long, and where the piston of the steam engine worked monotonously up and down like the head of an elephant in a state of melancholy madness. It contained several large streets all very like one another, and many small streets still more like one another, inhabited by people equally like one another, who all went in and out at the same hours, with the same sound upon the same pavements, to do the same work, and to whom every day was the same as yesterday and tomorrow, and every year the counterpart of the last and the next.

Every day and every year the same: life for the factory workers was an exhausting routine. What are you doing at five o'clock in the morning? If you were a factory laborer in the early 1800s, you would be on your way to work, trudging through dark, dirty streets. Once in the factory, you would stand in one place all day, running a machine. You would work for very low pay from fourteen to sixteen hours a day, six days a week (more than twice as long as the average American works today). Your ears would hurt from the constant noise, your lungs would grow weak from the stale air, and your spirit would sink from the same dreary routine, day after day.

But you wouldn't dare miss a day or show up late for work. If you did, you might have to pay a fine. For showing up only twenty minutes late, you could lose a quarter of a day's pay. You could also be fined if you were caught talking to another worker or sitting down on the job. And if you complained or talked back to your boss, you would be fired on the spot.

Your work, besides being dreary and low-paying, might also be dangerous. Standing on your feet sixteen hours each day, year after year, could lead to crippled legs or a deformed spine. If you let your mind wander for just a moment, part of your body might get caught in the machine, and, like thousands of workers each year, you could lose a finger, hand, or arm. If you were injured or crippled in an accident at work, then you were out of a job, with no way to make a living. (In America today, a disabled worker can receive a payment from the government.)

You might think that, if you had lived in the early 1800s, all this wouldn't apply to you, since you're probably not much more than twelve years old, with a lot of school left before you hold a full-

Factory workers labored long hours in noisy, dirty, often dangerous conditions for low wages.

time job. But one of the worst aspects of the early factories—and what led many people to call for changes and reforms—was the shocking mistreatment of the many laborers who were your age and younger.

Child Labor

Because factory workers earned such low wages, they often had to put their children to work in order to make ends meet. Even before the Industrial Revolution some children had helped support the family, but they usually did so by helping on the farm, in the home, or in the shop. Now children—some as young as five years old—were sent off to work in the factories. There they would work the same long hours as adults, be exposed to the same dangers and diseases, and of course receive no education.

Some factories were kind to their child workers. But others treated them very harshly. One Englishman, who had worked in a factory when he was seven years old, recalled that his hours were from five in the morning to eight at night, with one solitary break of thirty minutes at noon. He had to eat any other meals in snatches, without interrupting his work. He remembered that, starting at about three in the afternoon, he would get very tired, and could hardly keep his eyes open by six or seven in the evening. But if he started to doze off, he would be painfully awakened by an "overlooker" whose job it was to "strap" the children—to beat them in order to keep them alert.

When stories like this became widely known, people were outraged. In the 1830s the English government began making laws to protect child workers. One law said that no one under the age of nine could work in the factories. Another law, passed in the 1840s, said that children under thirteen could work no more than thirty-six hours a week. Things gradually became better for children who worked until, in the 1900s, England and other countries passed laws doing away completely with most child labor.

In addition to working in factories, children like these boys worked long hours in mines.

(Today in Europe and the United States, children are not allowed to work in most jobs. Some are permitted to work, usually by helping on the family farm, but only if they also go to school.)

The Idea of Laissez-Faire

At about the same time that society was changing because of the Industrial Revolution, many people's ideas were changing because of a popular new economic idea called laissez-faire (LESS-ay FAIR). Laissez-faire—which is French for "to let alone"—is the idea that government should not make rules or laws to affect the economy, but instead should just leave it alone.

Until the late 1700s, the economy of England was tightly controlled by the government, which limited the amount of interest that banks could charge, laid down rules about the way employers should treat their workers, and set strict standards for how some products should be made. The government set up trade monopolies, giving certain companies the sole right to trade with certain parts of the world. (Do you remember the English East India Company?) To protect English manufacturers, the government set high tariffs, or taxes, on goods imported from foreign countries.

Then in the late 1700s, an English writer named Adam Smith published a book called *The Wealth of Nations,* in which he argued that government controls were hurting the economy. Smith said that individuals should be let alone to make their own economic decisions—to decide what products to make, how to make them, and what to charge for them. Smith believed this economic freedom would make people more creative and hard-working, because they would be motivated by the opportunity to try new ideas and make more money. If the government would leave people alone to pursue their own economic goals, said Smith, then more people would get involved in inventing, manufacturing, and trading products, and as a result, society as a whole would become wealthier.

In the years after Smith's book was published, the idea of laissez-faire became more and more popular. Many of the old laws controlling the economy were abolished. The new freedom to invent and invest helped spur the Industrial Revolution, creating, as Adam Smith had predicted, vast new wealth.

But it also created the harsh conditions some employers maintained in the factories. These employers were believers in laissez-faire. They fought against laws that would make things better for factory workers, saying that it was none of the government's business how much their workers were paid or how many hours a day they worked. For obvious reasons, the idea of laissez-faire was more popular among employers than their workers.

Capitalism and Socialism

As the Industrial Revolution spread and laissez-faire economic ideas grew more popular, England and other nations grew wealthier. But that wealth was not equally shared. An English politician and novelist named Benjamin Disraeli (diz-RAE-lee) wrote that England was becoming "two nations, between whom there is . . . no sympathy"; these two nations, said Disraeli, were *"the rich and the poor."*

Many people began to argue about what kind of economic system would be best for the industrialized nations with their growing wealth and inequality. Most people argued for one of two economic systems: either the existing system, called "capitalism," or a very different system, called "socialism."

What is the "capital" in capitalism? Capital is wealth, either in the form of money or what money can buy: land, ships, factories, works of art, etc. A capitalist economic system is built upon the idea of "private property," meaning that individuals or groups of individuals can own capital, and can decide how they want to use their wealth. Those who believe in laissez-faire capitalism say that people should be free to do whatever they want with their wealth, without any government control. In a capitalist system, people often use their wealth to try to make more wealth: they are driven by what is called the "profit motive," a desire to acquire more wealth.

In a capitalist economy, people are free to buy and sell just about anything. What will people buy and sell? How much will a buyer pay? How much profit can a seller make? These and other questions depend upon what is called "the law of supply and demand." Imagine, for example, that you were one of the first manufacturers to supply new machines to spin cotton. Many people were demanding to buy such machines, so you could charge a high price and make a big profit. But as more people bought the machines, the demand for them would go down; as other manufacturers offered similar machines for sale, the supply would go up—and soon, you would be making smaller profits, and probably looking for another way to gain wealth.

In a capitalist economy, people sell more than machines and products: they also sell their labor. They offer their skills and time in exchange for pay. How much pay? That depends on supply and demand. How did the law of supply and demand affect the thousands of laborers who flooded English cities like Birmingham in the 1800s? (How does it affect many teenagers today who are out of school during the summer and looking for summer jobs?)

You can trace the beginnings of capitalism back to the towns that developed in the Middle Ages, and to the growth of trade in countries like Italy during the Renaissance (see books Four and Five of this series). The United States today is a capitalist country, though our capitalist system is not completely laissez-faire: some laws, for example, control the ways people can use their money, or the minimum wage that employers can pay, or the precautions manufacturers must take to ensure workers' safety or to decrease pollution from factories.

Compared to our current capitalist economy, the capitalist system in England during the 1800s was more laissez-faire. The system was attacked by many people. Critics of capitalism argued that as long as economic decisions were left to individuals rather than the government, then the rich would get richer and the poor would get poorer. To stop this growing inequality, some people offered an alternative to capitalism, called "socialism."

Socialists believed that the government should take over the economy and run it for the benefit of all people. Socialists said the workers or the government should own the factories and fairly distribute the factories' products, and that the country's wealth should be more fairly divided among all its citizens.

One of the most important socialist thinkers was a German writer named Karl Marx. He believed that society was divided into two main classes—the *bourgeoisie* (BOOR-shwa-ZEE) and the proletariat. The bourgeoisie was made up of the middle and upper classes; the proletariat was made up of the lower classes, or workers.

Karl Marx.

According to Marx, members of the bourgeoisie had all the property and all the power. They oppressed and exploited the proletariat. For example, factory owners took advantage of their workers by paying them much less than their labor was worth.

Marx believed that the proletarian class was constantly struggling to win its rights from the bourgeoisie. Marx referred to this conflict as the "class struggle." He predicted that the class struggle would end in a great revolution, in which the proletariat would overthrow the bourgeoisie and take over the government. The new proletarian government would establish a society completely based on socialism. Private property would be abolished, and society's wealth would be equally distributed.

Marx's version of socialism was called "communism." In 1848 he published a book called *The Communist Manifesto* (a "manifesto" is a statement of beliefs or principles). Marx called for workers all over Europe to rise up and overthrow the bourgeoisie. He ended his call to arms with these famous words: "Workers of the world, unite! You have nothing to lose but your chains, and a world to win."

The Communist revolution did not occur as Marx had hoped. As the late 1800s wore on, European workers did begin to win more rights, not through violent revolutions but by joining labor unions or electing leaders who supported their cause. It was not until the 1900s, long after Marx's death, that Communists forcefully seized power in certain countries. And the major Communist revolutions did not occur in industrialized Europe, as Marx had predicted, but in underdeveloped Russia and China.

THE BRITISH EMPIRE

As you've read, the Industrial Revolution first got underway in England. This head start gave an advantage to England and its neighboring countries, Scotland and Wales, which had joined with England by 1707 to form Great Britain (you may also hear these countries referred to as the United Kingdom, which includes Northern Ireland). Great Britain—or Britain, for short—became the most prosperous and powerful country in Europe. The British used their power to take over many faraway lands as colonies.

In the 1800s and early 1900s, Britain ruled an empire that included countries on

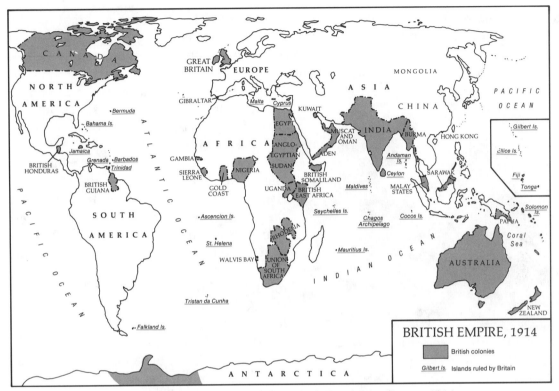

This map shows the reach of the British Empire in the year 1914.

every continent. In North America, the British ruled Canada. In South America, they ruled British Guiana, the Honduras in the West Indies, and several islands including Jamaica. In Africa, they ruled Egypt as well as the countries that are now called Sudan, Uganda, Kenya, Nigeria, Gambia, Sierra Leone, Gold Coast, and South Africa. In Asia, they ruled India, Burma, and the Malayan peninsula. In the South Pacific, they ruled Australia and New Zealand. At the end of the 1800s, almost *one quarter* of the human race lived under the British flag. It was said that "the sun never set on the British empire." In other words, because Britain ruled lands all around the globe, the sun was always shining somewhere on British territory.

Queen Victoria

The greatest years of the British empire were those when a remarkable woman sat on the English throne. Queen Victoria was monarch of Great Britain from 1837 until her death in 1901—a reign of sixty-four years. This period is often called the Victorian Age.

For many centuries England had been ruled by kings and queens. But in the 1800s it was becoming a more democratic nation, and Queen Victoria had much less political power than the monarchs who came before her. In her time, most of the power was in the hands of the Parliament, a body of elected representatives similar to the U.S. Congress. Yet the monarch was still the symbol of the nation, and Queen Victoria had great influence over her people.

Queen Victoria in her customary black clothes of mourning.

The queen was a stern and serious woman. One reason she was so serious was that she had suffered a great loss. When she was twenty years old, she married a German prince named Albert. Victoria and Albert were deeply in love, and their marriage was extremely happy. In 1861, after they had been married for twenty-one years, Albert died, leaving Queen Victoria heartbroken. For the rest of her life, the lonely Victoria mourned his loss. It was customary in those days for a widow to dress in black for a short time after the death of her husband. But Queen Victoria dressed in black for *forty years*. And for forty years, as another sign of her grief, she wrote her letters on white paper edged in black.

Even before Prince Albert died, Queen Victoria was known as a very serious woman. She had a strong sense of duty and worked very hard at all her tasks. In her diary she wrote, "I *love* to be employed; I *hate* to be idle." She never forgot that she was Britain's queen and always acted with great dignity. Victoria had high ideals and moral standards that sometimes made her seem stuffy. She was also very sure of herself. She always thought that she was right, and she expected everyone to agree with her.

The people who built the British empire had many of the same qualities as Queen Victoria. They were serious, determined, and hardworking. Many of them had high ideals, and they too were very sure of themselves. They thought that, as Englishmen, they knew better than anyone else how things should be done. They thought that they could run countries all over the world better than the people who already lived in those countries.

British Imperialism

When a nation builds an empire by conquering and ruling other countries, it is practicing imperialism. Today almost no one is in favor of imperialism, but in the 1800s, in Europe and especially in Great Britain, the idea of improving people by ruling over them was extremely popular.

Many English people felt that it was Britain's destiny to rule over much of the world, and that Britain had the right to rule because of its superior culture. People who felt this way usually had the racist idea that Africans and Asians were "inferior" to Europeans. Because the Industrial Revolution had not yet reached Africa and Asia, they did not have factories, steam engines, or railroads. Imperialists used this as evidence that Asians and Africans were "backward" or "primitive." They thought it was the duty of Europeans, like the British, to bring their "superior" way of life to non-European peoples.

The British writer Rudyard Kipling wrote a famous poem, "The White Man's Burden," to express this idea. (By "burden," Kipling meant a heavy responsibility.) In part, the poem reads:

> Take up the White Man's burden,
> Send forth the best ye breed,
> Go, bind your sons to exile
> To serve your captives' need.

In the countries they ruled, the British built ports and roads as well as factories, schools, and churches. But the British did not provide these benefits for free. They forced the native peoples to pay taxes to support British rule. At the same time, they used the colonies to increase the wealth of England. The native peoples were forced to work to produce raw materials that the British would then take to their factories in England. Then the British would turn around and bring their manufactured goods back to the colonies, where they would charge the native peoples high prices to buy them.

Imperialism had long-lasting effects in the African and Asian colonies, even after the colonies gained their independence from Britain. Since the wealth went to the British rulers and a few native people who collaborated with them, the majority of people in these colonies were reduced to living in poverty. In some cases, the imperialists caused huge ecological damage, leaving the landscape scarred and barren. Imperialism denied the right of every country to govern itself: in the African and Asian colonies, native people, no matter how talented, were rarely allowed to serve in the colonial government. Finally, by sending out the degrading message that people of darker complexions were "inferior" to their lighter-skinned rulers, imperialists caused deep anger and resentment that persist to this day.

British Rule in India

England's largest and most important colony was India, which an English writer would later call "the jewel in the crown" of the British empire. This vast country is bigger than the whole continent of Europe. It is the home of an ancient, deeply religious civilization with many magnificent temples and great works of religious art. (Perhaps you remember reading about India in Book Two of this series, which introduced you to the caste system, the Hindu religion, and King Asoka.)

A view of Madras, India in the early 1800s.

At first, the English had ruled India through a private company called the East India Company. In the 1600s this company established large-scale trade with India. Over the next century the company's trading posts turned into settlements, which grew larger and larger. Then the company formed its own army, and gradually gained more and more Indian territory, both through treaty and through conquest.

By the late 1700s the East India Company was coming under criticism. Word got back to England that many of the company's officials were greedy, dishonest, and cruel to their Indian subjects. The British government put controls on the activities of the company. Now the government became involved in running the territories along with the company. Meanwhile those territories kept expanding. By the middle of the 1800s the British controlled all of India.

Many Indians naturally resented British rule. The British put many Indians out of work: peasant families who had long made their living by selling cloth they spun by hand found themselves out of business when the British brought in cheaper cloth manufactured by machines. The British refused to allow Indians to hold any high government posts. They looked down on the religious practices and customs of the Indians.

The Indians' religious beliefs provided the spark that in 1857 ignited a great uprising against the British called the "Sepoy Rebellion." Most Indians were—and still are—either Hindus or Muslims. There is a long and continuing history of conflict between Indian Hindus and Muslims, though one similarity in their religions brought a group of them together against the British. Hindus are forbidden to eat the meat of cows, and Muslims are forbidden to eat the meat of pigs. Keep this in mind as we look at how the Sepoy Rebellion started.

The rebellion involved Indian soldiers, called "sepoys," who served in the British Army. The British issued the sepoys a new kind of rifle: to load this rifle, a soldier first had to bite off the tip of a greased bullet. The sepoys heard a rumor that the bullets had been greased with the fat of pigs and cows. This shocked and angered them: they thought that the British were deliberately forcing them to violate their religious beliefs.

The men in one sepoy unit refused to use the new bullet, so the British had the

Fighting during the Sepoy Rebellion was fierce.

sepoys' leaders arrested. Then the sepoys killed their British officers, and the rebellion began. It quickly spread to different parts of India. The conflict raged for eighteen months, with both the British and the Indian rebels committing terrible brutalities. The British were especially angered when one group of sepoys massacred hundreds of English captives, including many

Gandhi: Nationalism and Independence

In the late 1800s, many Indians began to feel strong feelings of nationalism—pride in, and devotion to, their country. They wanted India to become an independent, self-governing nation, free of British domination. In 1885 Indian nationalist leaders formed the Indian National Congress (later called the Congress Party). Many of these leaders had been educated in Britain, and at first they limited their cause to asking that Indians be given better positions in the colonial government. But in the early 1900s, the Congress Party began calling for complete independence from Britain.

From the 1920s on, a deeply religious man named Mohandas Gandhi emerged as the leader of the Congress Party and the strongest voice for Indian independence. Gandhi did not call for an armed revolution against the British; on the contrary, he urged Indians to overcome British rule by using "civil disobedience"—nonviolent protests and peaceful resistance to unjust laws and oppressive actions. (Gandhi's tactics of civil disobedience later inspired the great American civil rights leader, Martin Luther King, Jr.)

Mohandas Gandhi urged Indians to live simply and to overcome British rule through nonviolent protest. He always wore the traditional Indian garb you see here, called a dhoti.

Since the British relied upon Indians to do most of the work, Gandhi called on the Indians to refuse to work and instead devote themselves to prayer and fasting (not eating) for a day. He urged Indians to boycott (refuse to use or buy) British cloth, and instead to weave their own cloth by hand at home. He would sometimes endanger his own life by fasting for five or six days at a time to protest against British injustice.

Thanks largely to Gandhi's heroic efforts, India finally won its freedom in 1947.

women and children. For their part, the British often executed their sepoy captives by tying them to the mouths of cannons and then blowing them to pieces.

By the end of 1858 the Sepoy Rebellion had been defeated. Many people in England blamed the conflict on the oppressive policies of the East India Company. So the British government declared that from then on it would govern India directly. Queen Victoria was named Empress of India, a title she was very proud of. She declared that Indians would enjoy complete freedom of worship, as well as equality under the law. Although the English honored their promise not to interfere with Indian religious practices, they never treated Indians as their equals.

The British in Australia

Australia was another vast country under British rule. But it was a very different kind of colony from India. Whereas India was one of the most crowded places on earth, Australia was one of the most sparsely populated. In the 1800s, India had a population of about 300 million people. But when the British began settling Australia in the late 1700s, there were only a few hundred thousand native Australians. These native peoples, or "aborigines," lived in small, scattered settlements.

The British government was first interested in Australia because it was so vast and empty. It seemed like a perfect place to establish a penal colony (a faraway place where criminals could be removed from society). People convicted of crimes in England were sent to Australia, where they were put to work in labor camps. Once they served out their sentences, few convicts could afford the long, expensive voyage home. So they settled down to live and work in Australia.

Most of Australia's early settlers were convicts. But in the 1800s, ordinary Englishmen began to immigrate there. This trickle of settlers became a flood in the 1850s when gold was discovered, only two years after the famous California gold rush of 1849. Soon tens of thousands of Englishmen set out for Australia, hoping to make their fortune in the gold fields.

As the English population grew, the white settlers came into increasing contact with the aborigines, which proved to be a great misfortune for those peoples. Most whites felt a sense of superiority to the dark-skinned natives. If settlers wanted aborigine land, they simply took it and

The original Australians, called aborigines, were forced into the dry harsh interior of the continent when British settlers took over coastal areas.

Gold miners in Australia. After gold was discovered, immigrants from Britain poured into Australia to make their fortunes. Many of these people became settlers because they did not find enough gold to pay their return fare home.

often murdered the aborigines who refused to leave their land. Other native people died of diseases such as smallpox, which the settlers had brought from Europe. By the late 1800s, the population of Australia was almost entirely of English descent.

The British government did not openly approve of the exploitation of the aborigines. But it clearly reflected the racist views of the period by allowing Australia, unlike India, a large degree of self-government. The British thought that because most Australians were white, they could be trusted to govern themselves, whereas the nonwhite Indians could not.

Britain and China: The Opium Wars

In the 1800s more people lived in China than in any other country in the world. China was the home of one of the world's oldest and most glorious civilizations. In earlier books in this series, you read about the construction of the amazing Great Wall of China during the Han dynasty. You read about the T'ang and Sung dynasties, and how the Chinese invented or improved upon the inventions of many things we take for granted, including the printing press, the magnetic compass, and gunpowder. For more than two thousand years, the Chinese had created wonderful poetry, pottery, and paintings. The brilliant achievements of Chinese culture influenced all the countries of eastern Asia.

The Chinese were extremely proud of their achievements. They considered their culture the greatest in the world. They called their country "The Middle Kingdom," and saw themselves as being at the center of all things. They tended to look down on foreign customs and ideas, and referred to all non-Chinese people as "barbarians."

Before the 1800s the Chinese had only limited contact with Europeans. European merchants wanted to trade with China, but the Chinese government wanted to keep out foreign goods and ideas, so it put strict limits on trade with Europe. In the late 1700s, the British tried to convince the Chinese to trade more heavily with them. The Chinese emperor refused the British request. He proudly declared, "We possess all things and have no need for your country's manufactures."

There was one thing in particular that the Chinese leaders wanted to keep out of their country: a drug called opium, made from a certain kind of poppy flower. People used opium to make them feel good, but the drug is highly addictive: people who use it begin to crave it all the time, and soon they become addicts—they feel they can't live unless they have more and more of the drug. European merchants—mostly British—had discovered that they could make huge profits by selling opium in China. The Chinese government was worried that so many Chinese were becoming addicted to the drug. "Opium," one official declared, "poisons the empire." The Chinese government banned the importation of opium, though European merchants continued to smuggle it into the country.

In 1839 the Chinese government tried to crack down on the opium trade. Large shipments were seized from British merchants and destroyed. This led to conflict with the British government, which took the side of its merchants. Opium was sold legally in Great Britain, and the English saw no reason that it shouldn't be sold in China as well. For three years the British and the Chinese fought an on-again, off-again battle. This "Opium War" ended in 1842 with a victory for the British, who then forced the Chinese to open a number of ports to trade with the West. But the Chinese would never forget the Opium War. They would remember with anger that Europeans had won the right to "poison" the Chinese people with drugs.

A British gunboat fires on Chinese junks during the Opium War. Though the two sides fought on and off for several years, most of the battles were one-sided. The British had iron-covered steam-powered boats and modern artillery; the Chinese had wooden boats of ancient design.

The Boxer Rebellion

Now that Great Britain had opened China to trade, merchants from other countries arrived. More and more Chinese cities were declared "treaty ports," cities where foreigners were allowed to live by the terms of a treaty between the Chinese emperor and foreign governments. Often a treaty port had large groups of English, French,

Russians, Italians, Germans, and others all living in separate sections of the city. Each of these sections was run by the foreigners themselves rather than by the Chinese authorities. It was as if a number of different countries were setting up small colonies inside China's cities.

Many Chinese resented this. They also resented the growing influence of Western ideas and religious beliefs. Along with European merchants had come Christian missionaries, who tried to get the Chinese to give up their traditional religions and become Christians. Some Chinese did convert to Christianity, but they were often looked on as traitors who had turned against their country and its ways.

At the end of the 1800s a radical religious group tried to drive Christians and foreigners from China. This group called itself the Fists of Righteous Harmony, because its members were skilled in a traditional kind of hand-to-hand fighting. They became known more simply as the Boxers. The Boxers practiced secret rituals that only members were permitted to see, including one ritual that was supposed to make their bodies invulnerable to bullets. Their beliefs made them brave and reckless fighters.

In the late 1890s, there were terrible droughts and famines in Northern China: the Boxers blamed these on the presence of the foreigners

Members of the Fists of Righteous Harmony, or Boxers, believed the ancient Chinese arts of self-defense would protect them from guns.

and their strange religion. Boxer leaders declared: "The Catholic and Protestant religions being insolent to the gods, and extinguishing sanctity, rendering no obedience to Buddha, and enraging Heaven and Earth, the rain clouds no longer visit us; but eight million Spirit Soldiers will descend from Heaven and sweep the Empire clean of all foreigners. Then will the gentle showers once more water our lands."

In 1899 the Boxers began their campaign to "sweep the empire clean." They started by murdering missionaries and Chinese Christians. Thousands of people were killed. They also attacked European merchants and their families. Those who escaped fled to Peking, the Chinese capital, where they took shelter in the European legations. (Legations are places where diplomats—representatives of foreign countries—live and work.) For two months, foreigners and Christians were trapped inside the legations by the Boxers. Finally they were rescued by an army made up of troops from many nations, including England, France, Germany, Japan, Russia, and the United States. The foreign troops crushed the Boxer uprising.

To punish the Chinese for the rebellion, the Western powers forced them to sign a harsh agreement. According to this agreement, China had to apologize to the Europeans and pay huge fines to them. It also had to allow European troops to be stationed in Peking and other important cities. The Chinese were humiliated by this agreement, which forced them to bow to the "barbarians." Many Chinese people blamed their government for being too weak to stand up to the foreigners. They argued that China should replace its ancient monarchy with a more modern and effective form of government.

In 1911 a great revolution broke out, and the following year the revolutionaries forced the last emperor from his throne. They declared that China was now a republic. Tragically, however, China never got the better government its people hoped for. Instead, the country suffered through four decades of civil war. In 1949 a group of Chinese Communists took power and put an end to all the fighting. But after coming to power, the Communists slaughtered millions of their countrymen and set up an absolute dictatorship. Although the Communists brought peace to China, they also brought tyranny. (You can read more about Chinese Communism on page 194 of this book.)

AFRICA

The Slave Trade Ends but Europeans Remain

In Book Five of this series, you read about the beginnings of the slave trade. You might remember the Portuguese sugar plantations on the island of São Tomé, and how these set a precedent for plantations in South America and the Caribbean islands. You might recall the development of a "triangular trade," in which European traders took slaves from Africa, sold them in the New World, then took goods that were the products of slave labor—sugar, tobacco, cotton—and sold them in Europe. You read about the horrors of the Middle Passage, when slaves were crammed into ships to cross the Atlantic, and many died along the way.

For a long time, from antiquity to the eighteenth century, many people in many countries accepted slavery as just another economic arrangement. But in the eighteenth and nineteenth centuries, some people in Europe and America attacked the immorality and injustice of slavery. In the 1800s they finally began to convince their countrymen that slavery was wrong. Slowly, one by one, countries like Great Britain, France, and the United States stopped importing slaves, which led to the quick decline of the Atlantic slave trade. This was followed later by the abolition of slavery itself. By the mid-1800s most of the Spanish-speaking countries in Latin America had abolished slavery. After our long and bloody Civil War, the United States abolished slavery in 1866 (do you remember the Thirteenth Amendment to the Constitution?). Cuba and Brazil finally abolished slavery in the 1880s.

But even as the Europeans lost interest in Africa as a source of slaves, they were getting more involved in Africa than ever before, for a variety of reasons. Some wanted to become wealthy by trading with the Africans. Some wanted to convert the Africans to Christianity. Others wanted to acquire scientific knowledge. Still others were simply looking for adventure.

At first the Europeans were content to explore and trade. Then they started to "claim" parts of Africa for their own nations. Soon a number of European nations—England, France, Germany, Belgium, and Portugal—were competing to see who could claim the most African land. In the 1880s and 1890s these nations signed a number of treaties with each other. In these treaties, they agreed to divide among themselves almost the entire continent of Africa. No one asked the Africans what *they* wanted, and when the Europeans came to take possession of "their" territories, they frequently found the Africans ready to fight back fiercely.

Missionaries and Explorers

Beginning in the early 1800s, many Christian missionaries went to Africa to convert the people to Christianity. The missionaries were often brave and dedicated people. But they often looked down on the Africans' own religions, which they did not understand. One African told of his boyhood memory of a missionary who came to his village:

> The missionary spoke to us through his interpreter. He denounced our old ceremonious life, the rituals, especially sacrifice. He said that we worshipped wood and stone and graven images. This was not accurate but no one was impolite enough to contradict him. Anyway, it would have been too difficult to make a stranger understand.

Although most Africans preferred to keep their own religions, they often welcomed the missionaries because they were eager to learn more about European ways and European technology.

In addition to the missionaries came explorers, driven by a sense of adventure and curiosity, and hoping to open trade routes into the center of Africa. The interior of Africa was almost completely cut off from the outside world. Very few Europeans had ever seen it, and no one, European or African, had ever made a map of it. On maps of the world, the central part of Africa was simply left blank. Adventurous Europeans wanted to fill in that blank. They wanted to see firsthand the wonders of Africa and describe them to the world.

There was one thing the explorers especially wanted to find—the source, or starting point, of the Nile River. The Nile is the longest river in the world. The first great civilization—that of Egypt—arose along its banks. But neither the Egyptians nor any Europeans had ever followed the river to its source, thousands of miles south in central Africa. In the 1800s many Europeans searched for the source of the Nile. One of them was a Scotsman named David Livingstone, who was unusual in that he was both a great explorer and a great missionary.

"Dr. Livingstone, I Presume?"

From the 1840s to the 1870s, Livingstone explored vast areas of southern, central, and eastern Africa. (Today these areas are the nations of Botswana, Zimbabwe, Mozambique, Zambia, Tanzania, and Zaire.) He carefully mapped the countryside and described the native plants and animals, many of which no white man had ever seen. Once, traveling down the Zambezi River, he was amazed to see what looked like huge columns of smoke rising hundreds of feet into the air. He discovered that what he saw was, instead, the mist from a gigantic waterfall. This great waterfall was more than a mile wide. The local people called it Mosioatunya ("The Smoke That Thunders"). Livingstone gave it an English name, in honor of his queen—Victoria Falls. Today people come to Zambia and Zimbabwe from all over the world to see this natural wonder.

Victoria Falls.

Livingstone was driven by more than curiosity. He was a Christian minister, and he hoped that by "opening up" the heart of Africa, he could encourage more missionaries to come and convert more Africans. He also hoped to attract more European merchants. A healthy trade in goods, he thought, would put an end to the trade in enslaved human beings once and for all. Livingstone hated slavery with all his heart.

Like so many Europeans, Livingstone believed that Africans were less "advanced" than Europeans. Yet he was sincere in his love for Africa and the people he encountered. He learned African languages and accepted African ways of life. As a result, many Africans respected him. Livingstone was even more admired in Great Britain. People looked up to him because he was not only brave but also modest and sincere. He had no desire for wealth or fame, but truly wanted to benefit both Africa and England.

In 1865 he set off on his last great African journey, to find the source of the Nile. For several years he disappeared into the unknown interior to explore the rivers and lakes of eastern Africa. But as months and then years passed with no word from Livingstone, people in the outside world began to worry. Where was the great explorer? Was he alive?

At that time, a young American journalist, Henry M. Stanley, was working for a New York newspaper. Stanley was known as a bold and adventurous reporter. One day his boss met with him and gave him a simple order: "Find Livingstone." So Stanley traveled to Africa and set off on the search. After traveling for many months,

The famous meeting of Stanley (left of center) and Livingstone (right of center).

he found Livingstone in a small village on the shore of Lake Tanganyika. The great explorer was still alive, although he had run out of supplies and was seriously ill with fever. Stanley's description of the meeting later became famous:

I . . . walked deliberately to him, took off my hat, and said:
"Dr. Livingstone, I presume?"
"Yes," said he, with a kind smile, lifting his cap slightly.
. . . I then said aloud: "I thank God, Doctor, I have been permitted to see you."
He answered, "I feel thankful that I am here to welcome you."

Stanley stayed with Livingstone for a few months and then returned home. Livingstone went on with his search for the source of the Nile, which he would never find. (In fact, although Livingstone did not realize it, the source had already been found by another English explorer, John Speke. Speke had discovered a great lake at the head of the Nile, which he named Lake Victoria.) In 1873, worn out by travel and disease, Livingstone died. His African friends sent his body back to England. But first they removed his heart, placed it in a tin box, and buried it in the soil of the Africa he loved.

Europeans in North Africa

While Livingstone and others were exploring central Africa, Britain and France were starting to take over the northern part of the continent that lay on the Mediterranean Sea. In 1830 France invaded Algeria, seizing the city of Algiers. Over the next four decades the French gradually conquered all of Algeria. Then, in the 1880s, they took over the neighboring country of Tunisia.

At about the same time, the English invaded the ancient nation of Egypt. Their main purpose was to protect the Suez Canal, a waterway built in the 1860s that was of vast importance to world trade. By connecting the Mediterranean Sea with the Red Sea, the Suez Canal connected Europe with Asia. Before it was built, ships sailing from Europe to Asia had to sail all the way around Africa. The Suez Canal had become a vital link between England and its most important colony, India.

In 1882 a new ruler came to power in Egypt, one who disliked Europeans. The British feared that he might close the Suez Canal to European shipping, so they sent in troops, who occupied the capital city of Cairo. Although the British never claimed Egypt as a colony, they continued to occupy it for more than half a century.

Industrialism and Nationalism

You've seen how England was able to build up a great empire thanks to its head start in the Industrial Revolution. It wasn't long, however, before other nations in Western Europe caught up. By the 1870s, there were many factories in Western Europe, all with a huge appetite for raw materials such as rubber and palm oil that could be found in the great forests of central Africa. Rubber was used to make many products: shoes, hoses, raincoats, machine belts, and later, tires. Palm oil was turned into grease to make machines run more smoothly.

As the European nations became industrialized, they also became more prosperous. The people in each nation began to feel a strong sense of power and pride in their nation—something like you might feel if you had a favorite team that was winning every game. These strong feelings of nationalism drove many European nations to try to outdo each other in building an empire as great or greater than Britain's. The European nations especially competed with each other for the control of Africa. This race of the European powers in the 1880s and 1890s to take over the continent became known as the "scramble for Africa."

Rubber harvesting in the Congo. These men are thumping rubber plants to remove a milky liquid called latex from the plants. Once separated, the raw latex was formed into hardened balls that were usually carried overland by a caravan of porters. The latex was then shipped to rubber factories that used it for a growing number of products, from waterproofed fabric to shoes.

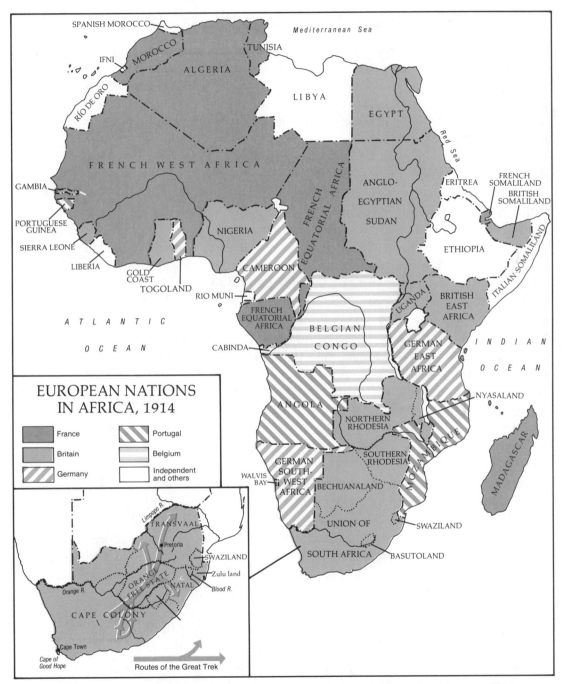

EUROPEAN NATIONS IN AFRICA, 1914

Legend:
- France
- Britain
- Germany
- Portugal
- Belgium
- Independent and others

Routes of the Great Trek

This map shows you how much of Africa was under European control in the year 1914.

The Scramble for Africa

Imagine one day that three strangers—let's call them Boss One, Boss Two, and Boss Three—arrive in your town or city. They proceed to divide your town among them; your street ends up under the control of Boss One, while Boss Two takes over the part of town where your school is located, and Boss Three takes the rest. The Bosses never ask you or anyone else what you think or whether you want to be taken over: they just do it.

Impossible? Well, consider what the European nations did when they gathered at a conference in Berlin beginning in 1884. They met to draw up rules for colonizing Africa. No Africans were invited to the Berlin Conference; no one was concerned with what they thought. In the years following this conference, the Europeans signed a number of treaties in which they awarded each other pieces of Africa. By the beginning of the 1900s, nearly the entire continent was claimed by European nations.

The European countries that gained the most in the scramble for Africa were Britain, France, Germany, and Portugal. Britain claimed among others the areas that are now the nations of Ghana, Nigeria, Kenya, and part of South Africa. Germany claimed what became Togo, Cameroon, Namibia, and Tanzania. France ruled a huge region called French West Africa, including today's Senegal, Mauritania, Mali, Niger, Chad, Ivory Coast, and Guinea. King Leopold II of Belgium claimed for himself a large area around the Zaire (formerly called the Congo) River. Portugal kept control over what are now Angola, Guinea-Bissau, and Mozambique.

Most of Africa would remain under European rule until the 1950s or 1960s.

The Belgians in the Congo

Europeans in Africa were sometimes savage rulers, nowhere more so than in the area called the Congo (today called Zaire). At the Berlin Conference, this huge area was granted to King Leopold II of Belgium as his own private colony. The forests of the Congo were full of a kind of vine from which rubber could be gathered. Leopold let large international companies send troops to the Congo, where they forced the native people to collect the rubber. The soldiers would invade a village and send everyone there into the forest to gather rubber. Anyone who resisted was tortured or killed by the soldiers.

In 1895 an American missionary described the terrible things he had seen in the Congo:

> The soldiers drive the people into the bush. If they will not go they are shot down, and their left hands cut off and taken as trophies to the commissaire [Belgian official]. The soldiers do not care who they shoot down, and they more often shoot poor helpless women and harmless children. These hands,

the hands of men, women and children, are placed in rows before the commissaire, who counts them to see that the soldiers have not wasted the cartridges [bullets].

When news of such cruelty became known, people all over the world were shocked. Even people in the other colonizing nations condemned the actions of King Leopold and his officials. Leopold was forced to turn over control of the colony to the Belgian government in 1908.

African Resistance to European Rule

Again and again, Africans fought against the European invasion of their homelands, but their resistance was rarely effective for long. Most African peoples lived in states much smaller than the nations of Europe. While they could organize armies larger than those the Europeans sent to Africa, they could not defend themselves against the much more modern and powerful weapons of the Europeans. The Africans had spears and, sometimes, rifles; the Europeans had cannons and machine guns. Nevertheless, some African groups fought long and hard against the colonial armies.

In French West Africa, the Mande people had a leader named Samori Touré. For almost ten years, Samori held off the French forces. He led a well-armed force of 30,000 men. But Samori's forces were gradually worn down by the power of the French. By 1898 all that was left of their army was a few scattered bands. In that year the French captured Samori and sent him into exile.

Meanwhile, the British were establishing their rule in the Gold Coast (today's Ghana). A number of African rulers and merchants there had grown wealthy by selling gold, rubber, and palm oil to the Europeans. Some of them made treaties with the British and accepted British "protection"—which in fact meant British rule. But the rulers of the largest state in the region, the Ashanti, refused to sign such a treaty. The Ashanti were sophisticated rulers and traders with a powerful army. When the Ashanti king was offered British "protection," he delivered this dignified and forceful reply:

An Ashanti chief surrounded by family and advisors. This picture was probably taken about 1910, several years after the Ashantis' defeat by the British.

The suggestion that Ashanti in its present state should come and enjoy the protection of Her Majesty the Queen and Empress of India, I may say this is a matter of serious consideration, [but] I am happy to say we have arrived at this conclusion, that my kingdom of Ashanti will never commit itself to any such policy; Ashanti must remain independent as of old, at the same time to remain friendly with all white men. I do not write this with a boastful spirit, but in the clear sense of its meaning. Ashanti is an independent kingdom.

The British did not accept the independence of the Ashanti. In the 1890s, they fought a series of wars against them. Like the Mande, the Ashanti were eventually defeated by the greater strength of the European armies. They held out until 1901, when they were finally forced to surrender to the British.

Europeans in South Africa

South Africa today is a large, wealthy nation at the southern end of the African continent. The majority of its people are black, like most Africans. Unlike most African countries, however, South Africa also has a large white population, descended mostly from English and Dutch colonists. The history of this nation is complicated and tragic. In South Africa, European rule began earlier and lasted longer than anywhere else in Africa. And it led to many bloody conflicts, in which white colonists fought each other as well as blacks.

Before the building of the Suez Canal, ships from Europe had to make a long voyage around Africa to reach Asia. In Book Five, you read about the Portuguese sailors who explored the African coast, and about how Vasco da Gama rounded the southern tip of Africa. This area, called the Cape of Good Hope, became an important place for European ships to stop and take on fresh supplies.

You also read in Book Five about how one group of Europeans, the Dutch—from the seafaring nation of the Netherlands (also called Holland)—came to dominate the trade routes to Asia in the 1600s. In the mid-1600s, the trading company called the Dutch East India Company started a settlement at the Cape of Good Hope. They built a fort and brought many people from Holland to farm the surrounding land. What the farmers grew was partly used to supply the ships that stopped at Cape Town.

The Dutch East India Company brought in more settlers to farm the land. But the land around Cape Town was already being used by the local people, the Khoisan, for cattle grazing. When the Dutch moved onto Khoisan land, the Khoisan fought back, but they were defeated by the Dutch, who had more powerful weapons. Some of the Khoisan moved northward, away from the Dutch colony, while others stayed in the Cape area, where they were forced to become servants or slaves to the Europeans.

In the 1700s the settlers from Holland were joined by others from France and Germany. Gradually the descendants of these Dutch, French, and German settlers began to think of themselves as permanent residents of the Cape, as though they were natives of the land. After 1815 the lives of new settlers were affected by events in Europe. You might remember that, during the time of Napoleon, France and England had fought a long series of wars until the French were finally defeated in 1815. In these wars, Holland had taken the side of France. In order to punish the Dutch, the victorious British seized control of the Dutch colony in southern Africa.

The Dutch resented the English takeover. The Dutch had their own laws, customs, and language: they didn't want to speak English or obey English laws. The Dutch were further angered when, in 1833, Great Britain abolished slavery throughout its empire. The Dutch did not want to give up their African slaves. Many Dutch decided it was time to break away from English rule.

The Boers and the Zulu

In the late 1830s, thousands of Dutch left the Cape Colony and journeyed hundreds of miles north in search of new lands to settle. They traveled in groups of covered wagons, much like those used by settlers in the American West. The journey north was long and hard. It became known as the Great Trek. Trek is a Dutch word meaning "to travel." These settlers became known as *Boers* (BO-ers), the Dutch word for "farmers."

The Boers made the Great Trek to look for new lands to settle.

Zulu warriors.

On their journey the Boers often fought against the Africans whose lands they crossed. They met the strongest resistance when they crossed the lands of the Zulu. The Zulu, who had grown powerful in the early 1800s under a strong leader named Shaka, had a proud tradition as warriors. They were widely feared for the way they handled their *assegais,* short spears used for stabbing. Again and again the Zulu attacked the Boers, killing many of them and making off with their oxen and other animals.

Finally one Boer leader gathered a force of five hundred men and set out to defeat the Zulu. He brought along cannons as well as smaller guns. On the banks of a river, the Boers set up a strongly protected camp. They were soon surrounded by Zulu. Wave after wave of Zulu warriors attacked, only to be cut down by the cannons and muskets of the Boers. Three thousand Zulu were slaughtered. Later, the river where the battle was fought was given a new name: Blood River.

After the battle of Blood River, the Boers and the Zulus made a peace treaty that enabled the Boers to settle in an area where they would be free of British rule. To the north of British territory they set up two new colonies, the South African Republic (later called the Transvaal) and the Orange Free State. The British had meanwhile set up a new colony, Natal, to the east of the Cape Colony. Now the southern end of Africa was divided into four colonies, two British and two Boer. At first these colonies lived in peace, but, as you will soon see, this peace would not last.

Cecil Rhodes

Today South Africa is the world's largest producer of diamonds. It was in the late 1860s that the country's rich diamond fields were first discovered. A little boy, the son of a Boer farmer, found a shiny stone lying on a riverbank. He and his brothers played jacks with it for a while. Then they took it to their mother. She showed it to a friend, who recognized it as a diamond. Soon several more stones were found, and a "diamond rush" was on. Thousands of prospectors flocked to the diamond fields hoping to become rich. One of these was a young Englishman named Cecil Rhodes.

Rhodes made his fortune in the diamond fields, and eventually became owner of the world's largest diamond company. Then in the 1880s came the discovery that the South African land was also rich in gold. Rhodes got involved in gold mining, too, and further increased his wealth.

Meanwhile Rhodes went into politics. His greatest ambition was not to make money but to increase the size and power of the British empire. He was a fanatical imperialist who strongly believed in England's destiny to rule "less civilized" countries. He once wrote, "I contend that we [the English] are the first race in the world, and the more of the world we inhabit, the better it is for the human race." Rhodes dreamed that England would eventually colonize China, Japan, and South America. He even dreamed that the United States would be brought back into the British empire!

Cecil Rhodes (seated left) wanted to expand British control over all of Africa.

But first, Rhodes thought, the British should conquer Africa. They ruled Egypt in the north and the Cape Colony in the south; now they should conquer the lands in between. To advance this plan, Rhodes formed a group called the British South Africa Company to build a railroad from the Cape of Good Hope all the way north to Cairo. This group sent British settlers into the lands north of the Boer states. There they bullied or tricked the rulers of the African states into giving up much of their land. The new settlements became the colonies of Northern and Southern Rhodesia, named in Rhodes's honor. Today these are the nations of Zambia and Zimbabwe.

In 1890, Rhodes became prime minister of the Cape Colony. He decided that it was time Britain added the Boer colonies to its empire. He especially wanted to take over the Transvaal, where most of the gold mines were located. Some of his followers launched a raid on the Transvaal but they were easily defeated by the Boers. Rhodes was heavily criticized for giving his followers the idea to attack the Transvaal. He was forced to give up the office of prime minister. Just a few years later, however, the British government sent its armies to carry out Rhodes's plan.

The Boer War

After the raid on the Transvaal, the Boers expected another attack by the British. For greater strength, the Boers in the Transvaal and the Orange Free State joined together against the British. In October 1899 when the English stationed their troops on the border of the Transvaal, the Boers, convinced that the English were about to invade, declared war.

The British called this war the Boer War, while the Boers considered it a "war for freedom." Most people in Europe and the United States sympathized with the Boers: they were the "underdogs," a small group fighting against a huge empire. But black

South Africans did not agree. They took no part in this fight between two groups of white men. If they did favor one side or another, they chose the British, for the Boers were infamous for their cruelty to blacks.

Because the Boers knew the countryside better, they won the first battles. But the British kept sending more troops and weapons to South Africa, and gradually wore down the Boers. The Boers broke into small bands of guerrilla fighters who ambushed British soldiers, attacked British outposts, blew up bridges, and tore up railroad tracks. The British knew the guerrillas were getting shelter and supplies from Boers living on the farms in the region. So the British burned the farms of the Boers, leaving thousands of families without homes.

The British took the homeless women and children to crowded, dirty camps. Soon disease broke out in these camps, and thousands of Boers—mostly children—died of typhoid, scarlet fever, or malaria. In South Africa today, descendants of the Boers still remember these camps with bitterness and anger.

A scene from the Battle of Mujaba Hill, an early battle in the war between the Boers and the British.

In 1902 the Boers and the British finally signed a peace treaty. The experience of the war left the Boers with a feeling of great loyalty to each other: they thought of themselves not as Dutch but as "Afrikaners," as natives of the land they had lost to the British.

In 1910, the British combined the British and Afrikaner colonies into the Union of South Africa. The British promised to respect the Afrikaners' customs and their Dutch-based language, called Afrikaans. And the British allowed the Afrikaners, who now held many important government posts, to continue their practice of keeping the government in the hands of the white population. Though the majority of the country was black, they were given no say in the government of the Union of South Africa. In fact, the white South African government passed a number of laws designed to keep control over the blacks.

In the gold and diamond industries, blacks were allowed to take only the dirtiest, lowest-paying jobs. Black workers were not allowed to form unions. Many were forced to live on "reserves" which, like American Indian reservations, were in poor, remote areas.

Apartheid in South Africa

In the decades after 1910, the South African government instituted even more oppressive measures against the majority black population. In the 1940s the government introduced apartheid (*uh-PART-hite*), which means "apartness" in Dutch. Apartheid was a rigid system of racial segregation designed to help white Afrikaners recover from their defeat by the British, but at the expense of the blacks. Under apartheid, blacks and whites were to stay completely separate. They could not ride on the same buses, live in the same neighborhoods, or swim on the same beaches. They could not eat in the same restaurants or go to the same schools. People of different races were not allowed to marry each other. And blacks could not vote or hold good, well-paying jobs.

In the 1950s and 1960s most African countries became independent of European rule. But in South Africa, three to four million whites found their comfortable lives depending on continued rule over fifteen to twenty million impoverished blacks. People all over the world condemned the racism of apartheid and white-controlled government. It was not until the late 1980s, however, that the system began to change. Many apartheid laws were abolished. Blacks were given more rights and were promised a voice in the government. Yet some whites remained strongly opposed to these changes. The struggle for racial equality and democracy continues in South Africa today.

JAPAN

The Opening of Japan

In the 1800s most Asian nations were victims of European imperialism. They were either colonized, like India and Africa, or bullied and humbled, like China. One of the few exceptions was Japan. The Japanese beat the Europeans at their own game: like the European countries, Japan became a modern, industrialized nation, and then an imperialist power.

But the Japanese had to scramble to catch up with the Europeans. In the mid-1800s, Japanese society was pretty much as it had been in feudal times (which you read about in Book Five of this series). The Japanese had been sealed off from contact with the outside world for almost two centuries. Japanese rulers in the early 1600s had banned all foreigners from Japan because they saw foreign ideas, including the Christian religion, as a threat to their culture. These leaders had said, in no uncertain terms, "So long as the sun warms the earth, any Christian bold enough to come to Japan . . . even if he be the god of the Christians, shall pay for it with his head."

At the same time, the leaders forbid the Japanese people to travel outside Japan, or even to build a ship big enough to sail to another country! Almost all trade with the outside world ground to a halt. You've read before about how countries develop when they exchange goods and ideas, but no new goods or ideas could get into

Commodore Perry arrives in Japan.

Japan at this time. While Europe proceeded into the Industrial Revolution, Japan still lived with the technology of the Middle Ages.

Then one day in 1853, a strange sight confronted the people in the Japanese capital city. There in the bay floated four large ships: two had sails, but the other two moved without sails. These ships had chimneys that poured out clouds of smoke. They were strange and frightening to the Japanese, who had never heard of ships powered by steam. They called them "the black ships of evil appearance."

They turned out to be United States warships. The United States had sent a naval officer, Commodore Matthew Perry, to meet with Japanese leaders. He was carrying a letter from the American president, which asked that the Japanese open trade with the United States. Perry delivered the letter, then sailed away, saying that he would return in a year for the Japanese response.

The Japanese leaders did not want to open Japan to the outside world. But they had heard of the European conquests elsewhere in Asia. They had seen Perry's steamships. They knew that the Europeans and Americans had the military strength to conquer Japan. So to keep from being colonized, the Japanese gave in. When Perry returned, they agreed to start trading with the United States.

To celebrate the agreement, the Japanese and Americans gave each other gifts. The Japanese gave the Americans beautiful handmade objects—swords, fans, silk robes, porcelain cups. The Americans gave the Japanese guns, a telescope, a clock, and a telegraph. They also gave them seventy feet of railway track and a miniature (one-quarter-size) locomotive. The Japanese studied these gifts carefully.

The Meiji Restoration and the Modernizing of Japan

Within a few years the Japanese had reopened trade with a number of countries. Foreigners were allowed to live in Japan, and even the Christian missionaries returned. These changes opened Japan to the world but also led to the overthrow of the Japanese government.

Japan has always been a monarchy, headed by an emperor or empress who, according to the Japanese religion, is a divine, godlike being, descended from the Goddess of the Sun. At the time that Perry reached Japan, however, the emperor had no real power. For several hundred years, the most powerful man in Japan had been the shogun, or military dictator. But this changed after the opening of Japan. The shogun then in power was a weak leader who had already lost the respect of many of his warriors. After the country was opened, many people called him a coward for giving in to the foreigners, and his power was undercut even more. In 1868 the shogun was overthrown by warriors who rallied around the emperor.

The emperor was a fifteen-year-old boy who had come to the throne in the preceding year. He was known as the Emperor Meiji. (Meiji was not his name, but a title meaning "Enlightened Rule.") The year 1868 is remembered as the year of the Meiji Restoration because the emperor had been "restored," or brought back, to a position of real power as Japan's ruler. Meiji ruled Japan for the next forty-five years with intelligence and great dignity. The Japanese came to admire their Emperor Meiji as much as the English admired their Queen Victoria.

Meiji's first task was to unify the country under his rule. In the 1860s much of Japan was still run by feudal lords, who were like the noblemen of the Middle Ages in Europe. Each lord ruled his own estate, or fief, and had his own private army. Meiji made the lords give up their fiefs and broke up the private armies so that a new, national army could be formed. Now the emperor and his advisers had power over the whole country.

The Emperor Meiji was determined to shape Japan into a modern, industrialized nation. He was convinced that this was the only way Japan could avoid being colonized. When the emperor came to power, he took an oath which declared, "The bad customs of past ages shall be abolished, and our government shall tread in the paths of civilization and enlightenment." The oath continued, "We shall endeavour to raise the prestige and honor of our country by seeking knowledge throughout the world."

Japan's Emperor Meiji.

So Japanese leaders were sent to Europe and America to learn about Western ideas and Western technology. Meanwhile, Europeans and Americans were brought to Japan to train Japanese engineers and manufacturers. They also trained Japanese soldiers and sailors in the most modern ways of fighting wars.

Japan Becomes a World Power

During the 1870s and 1880s, Japan steadily became an industrialized nation. By 1890 the country had more than two hundred steam-powered factories. It also had railways, steamships, and telegraph lines and was building a powerful army and navy. Japan was catching up to Europe. Now, like the European nations, it wanted new sources of raw materials and new markets for its goods. It wanted to expand overseas.

The first place into which Japan expanded was Korea, a nation located on a peninsula between China and Japan. For a long time Korea had been partly independent and partly controlled by China. The Japanese decided to drive the Chinese out, so in 1894 they went to war with China. With their more modern army, the

Japanese easily defeated their larger neighbor. The peace treaty that was signed between China and Japan recognized the independence of Korea. As time went on, however, Japan took increasing control of Korea.

Ten years later, in 1904, Japan again fought a war over Korea, this time against Russia. The Russian empire was expanding in Asia, and it seemed about to spread into Korea. To prevent this, the Japanese declared war. They knew this would be a tougher fight than their war with the Chinese. Russia was a huge and powerful Western nation with a modern army and navy. Japan appeared to be the underdog. People in England

TERRITORIES CONTROLLED
BY JAPAN (1905)

▨ Extent of Japanese Empire by 1905

This map shows you the lands under Japanese control by the end of 1905.

and the United States admired "gallant little Japan." But the Russians looked down on the Japanese. Russian soldiers sang a song that said, "A Japanese is nothing but a mosquito"—just waiting to be squashed.

It is true that the Japanese had a smaller army and navy than the Russians. But they also had determined, well-trained soldiers, led by a group of brilliant generals and admirals. One of these leaders was Admiral Heihachiro Togo. Admiral Togo was skilled in the latest ways of naval warfare. For seven years he had studied under the British, who had the world's most powerful navy. Now he sailed out to meet the Russians, who had sent their European fleet halfway around the world to attack the Japanese.

Before the battle, Togo sent a message to his sailors: "The country's fate depends upon this battle. Let every man do his duty with all his might." The great Battle of the Sea of Japan began in the morning and raged until sunset. By the time it was over, the Russians had lost nearly all of their ships and almost five thousand men, whereas only one hundred and sixteen Japanese had been killed. The Russian navy was crippled. The Japanese had won one of the greatest sea battles in history.

The Japanese had meanwhile won several tough victories on land against the Russians. By late 1905 the war was over. Russia and Japan signed a peace treaty, which gave the Japanese control over Korea. Even more important, it gave the Japanese a tremendous sense of pride. In only fifty years, a "backward" Asian nation had risen to beat one of the major powers of Europe. From then on, Japan would be respected as a world power.

With their new sense of pride, Japanese leaders set out to build their own empire. Eventually that empire included much of eastern Asia and the South Pacific. It continued to expand until the Japanese were defeated in a war with the United States. (For more on the Japanese empire and World War II, see the American Civilization section of this book.)

EUROPE, NATIONHOOD, AND WAR

Nationalism and the Unification of Italy

One of the major forces in European life in the 1800s was nationalism. As you've read, nationalism means a strong sense of pride in one's country. But nationalism also refers to the political idea that each separate people who are bound by a shared language and traditions should have its own separate nation.

In the 1800s some of the peoples of Europe—such as the French and the English—had their own nations. But others did not. For example, much of central Europe was ruled by the Austrian empire. This huge state included many different peoples—Germans, Italians, Hungarians, Poles, Czechs, Serbs, and others—each with its own language and traditions. In the 1800s many of these peoples developed nationalistic ideals and began the struggle to become independent nations.

One successful struggle was waged in Italy. The Italians were a people with their own distinct language and culture, but they had never had a unified, independent nation. In the early 1800s, Italy was made up of a number of different states. Furthermore, large parts of the country were controlled by foreigners. Southern Italy was ruled by a line of Spanish kings known as the Bourbons; much of northern Italy was run by the Austrians.

The 1850s, however, saw the rise of two nationalist leaders, Giuseppe Garibaldi and Count Camillo di Cavour. Cavour and Garibaldi were very different men: Cavour was a sly, cautious diplomat, and Garibaldi was a bold adventurer who had been a pirate as a young man, raiding ships off the coast of South America. The Italian people were eager to fight for what Garibaldi called "the sacred cause of nationality." While Cavour conducted negotiations to unify northern Italy, in the south thousands of Italian patriots, called Red Shirts, rallied to the battle cry of Garibaldi, who said, "Let him who loves his country in his heart, and not with his lips only, follow me." By 1861, the Italian people were united as a nation at last.

Giuseppe Garibaldi, the Italian nationalist leader.

Bismarck and the Unification of Germany

To the north of Italy lived another people who had never been united as a nation. These were the Germans. The country of the Germans was not ruled by foreigners, as was Italy. But it was even more divided than Italy. In the early 1800s this country was divided into *thirty-nine* separate states. The largest and most powerful of these was Prussia. In the 1860s, the king of Prussia appointed a new prime minister, a nationalist named Otto von Bismarck who was determined to create a unified Germany.

Prussia was a partially democratic country, with an elected parliament, but Bismarck was a ruthless leader who distrusted democracy and disliked politicians. According to Bismarck, all politicians did was argue and bicker; they never got things done. Bismarck thought that the best way to get things done was to use force. In a famous speech he declared, "The great questions of the time are not decided by speeches and majority decisions . . . but by iron and blood."

It was through the "iron and blood" of war that Bismarck brought about the

Otto von Bismarck (seated left) created a united German empire.

unification of Germany. He had convinced the separate states that they were surrounded by hostile countries, and talked them into forming an alliance for their own protection. In 1870, he persuaded the allied states to invade France. Within a few months the Germans had crushed the French army and captured the French ruler. Then they surrounded Paris, the capital of France, and refused to let food supplies into the city. The people of Paris were starved into submission. The Germans forced the French to sign a humiliating peace treaty and to pay large fines. The treaty also forced the French to give up a large piece of territory, Alsace-Lorraine, on the border between France and Germany.

By defeating France, Bismarck had shown the separate German states what they could accomplish when they united. In 1871 the states agreed to become parts of a unified Germany. The Prussian king, Wilhelm I, was declared *kaiser* (emperor) of the German *reich* (empire). ("Kaiser" is the German form of "caesar," the title by which the ancient Roman emperors had been known.) Bismarck still held most of the real power. Under his leadership, Germany grew more and more prosperous. The Industrial Revolution had come to Germany late, but once the nation was unified, the pace of industrialization speeded up. By the early 1900s, Germany was the greatest industrial power in Europe.

In 1890 Kaiser Wilhelm I died, and a new kaiser, Wilhelm II, came to the throne. Bismarck was forced from office because he and the new kaiser disagreed about many things, especially about whether Germany should expand overseas. Bismarck thought that Germany had no need of colonies. But Wilhelm II dreamed of a great German empire that would rival the British empire. Wilhelm's imperialist ambitions eventually helped bring on a worldwide war.

Europe Moves Toward War

Kaiser Wilhelm II knew that if Germany was to become, like Britain, a ruler of vast territories in Africa and Asia, Germany would have to build up its navy first. He realized that it was the mighty navy of the British that allowed them to control the oceans and maintain a grip on their faraway colonies. So Wilhelm set out to challenge Britain's control of the seas, declaring, "The trident must pass into our hands!" (Do you recall, from Book Two in this series or other readings, the sea god of the ancient Greeks, Poseidon—called Neptune by the Romans—and what he held as a symbol of his power over the seas?)

The Germans began a huge program of shipbuilding. After only a few years, Germany had the largest navy in the world next to Britain's. Soon Germany and Britain were locked in a "naval race" to see which nation could build more warships.

As they competed, the Germans and the English came to dislike and distrust each other more and more. Besides the English, other Europeans were also hostile to the Germans. The French bitterly remembered the invasion of 1870, and how the Germans had starved the people of Paris and taken the French lands of Alsace-Lorraine. The French were hungry for revenge.

To make matters worse, the European nations began to take sides with each other, forming dangerous alliances—dangerous because if one nation went to war, then its allies would be drawn in as well. On one side stood the alliance of Britain, France, and Russia. Against them stood Germany and its powerful ally, Austria-Hungary.

Austria-Hungary and Russia began to quarrel. The quarrel arose over what were called the Balkan states in southern Europe. These countries—including Bosnia, Herzegovina, Serbia, Bulgaria, and Rumania—had been part of the Ottoman Empire. In Book Four of this series, you read about how the Islamic Turkish people called Ottomans conquered Constantinople and changed its name to Istanbul, then went on to establish a vast empire around the Mediterranean Sea. By the nineteenth century, the Ottomans were losing control of their empire, which people began to call "the sick man of Europe." In the late 1800s the Balkan countries won their independence from the Ottoman Turks. Both Russia and Austria-Hungary wanted these Balkan countries (which would give them access to the Mediterranean Sea), and both thought they had the right to control them. Russia became especially angry when, in 1908, Austria-Hungary took over Bosnia and Herzegovina.

On one side, then, stood Germany and Austria-Hungary. On the other side stood France, Britain, and Russia. All of these nations were proud, powerful, and heavily armed. All felt bitterness and anger against their opponents. All watched each other suspiciously. Back in 1879, Bismarck had written words that still applied to the tense situation in Europe in the early 1900s: "The great powers of our time are like travelers, unknown to one another, whom chance has brought together in a carriage. They watch each other, and when one of them puts his hand into his pocket, his neighbor gets ready his own revolver in order to be able to fire the first shot."

The first shot was fired, in a way nobody expected, in June of 1914, in the little country of Bosnia.

World War I Begins

In the Bosnian city of Sarajevo, in June of 1914, seven young men spread out along a route in the city that would be traveled by the heir to the throne of Austria-Hungary, the Archduke Francis Ferdinand, who was visiting Bosnia with his wife that day.

These seven young men were assassins, some with bombs, some with pistols. They belonged to a group of revolutionaries who were part of a strong nationalist movement based in Bosnia's neighboring country, Serbia. The goal of this movement was to unite the Slavic people of southern Europe. Slavs are the varied descendants of a people who lived in central Europe in ancient times then migrated to different regions, where they developed distinct cultures and traditions. Besides the Slavs in southern Europe, there are a great many people of Slavic descent in Poland, Russia, Ukraine, the former Czechoslovakia and other countries.

The Slavs in Serbia wanted to unite with other southern Slavic states—including Bosnia and Herzegovina, which, in 1914, were under the rule of Austria-Hungary. The leaders of Austria-Hungary saw the Serbian nationalists as a threat, and were eager to find an opportunity to take over Serbia, just as they had taken over Bosnia and Herzegovina. That opportunity was provided by the young conspirators who, on June 28, 1914, lay in wait for Archduke Ferdinand.

The archduke and his wife, Sophie, were in the second of four cars traveling through the unguarded streets of Sarajevo. They passed the first conspirator, who, for some reason, did nothing. But the second conspirator was ready to act: as the archduke's car approached, he took aim and heaved his bomb. The bomb bounced off the archduke's raised arm and exploded in the street, injuring some bystanders. The archduke was unhurt; his wife was grazed on the face by a splinter. The man who threw the bomb was arrested by the police.

The archduke's car sped past three other assassins on the way to city hall. The archduke was upset but went ahead with his planned meeting with the city's leaders. After the meeting, he expressed fear of another attack: he was assured that he was safe, since the police had arrested the would-be assassin, and surely any accomplices had run away by now. The archduke asked to be taken to the hospital to check on the condition of the bystanders injured by the bomb. He told his wife to remain behind, but she insisted on going with him.

The car passed the sixth conspirator, who did nothing. Then the driver, realizing he had made a wrong turn, stopped the car—just a few feet from the seventh assassin, a nineteen-year-old man named Gavrilo Princip. Princip fired two shots: one struck the archduke, one struck his wife. Both shots were deadly.

The New York Times *reports the assassination of Archduke Ferdinand and his wife, Sophie.*

Princip is not to blame for "starting" the war that would soon come: the causes, as you've seen, are much more complex than that. Though people were shocked by the assassination, no one thought it would have almost global consequences. In fact, when the emperor of Austria-Hungary heard the news that the heir to his throne had been murdered, he wasn't even very upset. The assassination provided Austria-Hungary the opportunity it was looking for to take over Serbia. Because Princip and his fellow conspirators had been trained and armed by revolutionaries in Serbia, Austria-Hungary blamed Serbia for the archduke's murder. One month after the killing, the Austrians declared war on the Serbs. Now Russia stepped in. The Russians knew that Austria could easily conquer Serbia, and they refused to allow Austria to swallow up another piece of the Balkans. As the Russians prepared for battle, both Germany and Austria-Hungary declared war on Russia. Then Russia's allies, Britain and France, declared war on Germany and Austria.

The great war between the European powers had finally come. Many people welcomed it. All over Europe young men rushed to join the army, full of patriotic pride. One French soldier described marching off to battle:

Our hearts beat with enthusiasm. . . . My muscles and arteries tingle with happy strength. The spirit is contagious. . . . We are carried away by . . . the mystery that the future holds, the thought of glorious adventure, and the pride of being chosen to share it.

But others realized that the war would not be a "glorious adventure." Sir Edward Grey, the British foreign minister, had worked hard to prevent the outbreak of war. When Britain declared war on Germany, Grey said, "The lamps are going out all over Europe; we shall not see them lit again in our lifetime."

The war lasted four years. As it went on, it drew in more and more nations. The Allied Powers (Britain, France, and Russia) were joined by Italy, Japan, and the United States. The Central Powers (Germany and Austria-Hungary) were joined by Turkey and Bulgaria. The war affected so many people that it came to be known as the Great War, and later as the First World War. It ended in 1918 with the defeat of Germany and its allies, but not before ten million lives were lost. Edward Grey was right: Europe had been plunged into darkness.

The American Civilization section of this book begins with the story of how the United States was drawn into World War I.

Introduction to American Civilization

FOR PARENTS AND TEACHERS

The story of American Civilization in the twentieth century is a story with a global context. Early in the century, our country entered a great war that forever changed our place in the world. No longer able or willing to remain an isolated power, the United States became a central player on the world stage. American politics, industry, and social developments affected not just our own citizens, but peoples around the world. Just as importantly, events in other countries—from the Russian Revolution to the rise of Hitler—affected the lives and history of Americans.

The story of our nation in the twentieth century includes not just two world wars but also the Korean War, the Vietnam War, and a war without shooting, the Cold War. On the home front, our story includes the Great Depression, the New Deal, the struggle for civil rights, the women's movement, and important technological developments—some which made our lives easier, and one—the atom bomb—which threatened life itself.

The story we tell here culminates with the celebration in 1976 of our bicentennial. But American history doesn't end there: it continues to be written, and we read it daily in newspapers and magazines, and hear it on the evening news. It is our hope that children who have read this book and earlier volumes in this series will have a sense of the past that affords them a strong foundation for understanding our history as it unfolds in the present global context.

In this book, we have made a choice to introduce certain events—such as World War I, the Russian Revolution, and World War II—within the context of the story of American Civilization in the twentieth century. We do this because to tell the story of America's increasingly complicated relations with the rest of the world, it is necessary to know something about important events in other lands. Our intention here is simply to introduce these events. In later grades, it will be important for students to examine the history of other peoples and nations in greater depth and from a variety of perspectives. Our hope is that the foundations of knowledge provided here will make students both more interested and capable as they build their knowledge in later years.

American Civilization

WORLD WAR I

The Deadliest War Ever

In 1914 a great war broke out in Europe. (If you haven't already read the World Civilization section of this book, which explains the causes of this war, you should do so before going on here.) It involved so many nations of the world that it was called the Great War, or the World War. Later, after a second such war, it came to be called the First World War or World War I.

European nations began the conflict. On one side were the Allies, led by France and Britain; on the other were the Central Powers, led by Germany. Then, in 1917, after three years of fighting in Europe, the United States entered the war on the side of the Allies, an event that would turn out to be one of the most important in our history. From that time on the United States would be more deeply involved in the affairs of foreign countries than ever before. After World War I, America would be a power on the world stage: its actions would affect people all over the globe, and its responsibilities would weigh heavily on many people's lives at home.

World War I gun crew in a war-torn landscape.

More soldiers died in World War I than in any other war in history. This war was so bloody and destructive because soldiers used many new weapons that were products of the industrial era. Tanks and airplanes were used for the first time in battle (though they didn't greatly affect the outcome of the war, because the first tanks and airplanes were rather simple, ineffective machines). Submarines proved a deadly new weapon at sea. Huge cannons hurled explosive shells farther than was ever possible before. In some battles thousands of soldiers were blinded, wounded, or killed by a terrible new weapon, poison gas.

The greatest loss of life, however, was caused by one weapon: the machine gun. In earlier wars—even in our Civil War, the bloodiest war in history before World War I—a soldier's rifle could fire only one shot at a time. But in World War I a machine gun could fire more than four hundred bullets a minute. A single machine gunner could shoot down dozens, or even hundreds, of charging soldiers.

Because both the Allies and the Central Powers were well equipped with machine guns, both armies found it almost impossible to move forward. The war soon bogged down into a draw, with soldiers on each side stuck in protective ditches called "trenches." These trenches were separated from each other by a stretch of ground called No Man's Land. Life in the trenches was grim, dirty, and boring. Fleas and lice bit the soldiers; rats stole their food. When it rained the trenches filled with water and mud. From time to time one side or the other would launch a great assault on the enemy's trenches. These attacks usually ended in the slaughter of thousands of the attackers, who were mowed down by enemy machine guns as they charged

From this picture of Allied soldiers, you can see what close quarters the trenches were.

across No Man's Land. Once, when the British tried to storm the German line, twenty thousand English soldiers were killed in a single day.

American Neutrality

Americans were horrified by the brutality of the conflict. Most Americans were thankful to be living in a peaceful country, a whole ocean away from the fighting. Most Americans agreed with the decision of the United States government to remain neutral, which means not to take a side in a fight. But as time went on, more people became sympathetic to the Allied cause. Americans felt tied to England because Englishmen and Americans spoke the same language, and because a number of basic American ideas and institutions had their roots in England. Also, many Americans sympathized with France, where the battles were being fought, because they admired French culture and remembered how the French had helped them win the Revolutionary War. Then, too, France and England had forms of government that were more democratic than the imperial government of Germany, and Americans thought that democracy was the best form of government.

But in the end it was two things the Germans did that made Americans angry enough to go to war against Germany. The first was to sink a ship. The second was to send a telegram.

The Sinking of the *Lusitania*

In 1914 when the war began, the British had the most powerful Navy on earth. They stationed ships off the German coast, setting up a naval blockade to prevent vessels from carrying goods into Germany. The Germans, with their much smaller Navy, had no way of defeating the mighty British warships and breaking the blockade. So, in order to strike back, they decided to set up their own blockade around England—an *underwater* blockade.

The Germans had far fewer surface ships than the British, but they had plenty of submarines, or as the English called them, "U-boats" (from a German word meaning "undersea boat"). The German Navy declared that it would use its U-boats to sink ships trying to carry goods into England, and warned that anyone traveling on an English supply ship was risking his life.

One day in May 1915, the British passenger ship *Lusitania* was steaming across the Atlantic on its way from New York City to England. Suddenly the captain heard one of his officers cry, "Torpedo coming!" Before the captain had time to react, the torpedo, fired by a German U-boat, smashed into the center of the ship and exploded. The

A German U-boat surfaces in rough waters.

Lusitania immediately started to go down. It sank in less than twenty minutes—so quickly that many of the passengers were unable to get into the ship's lifeboats.

Over a thousand passengers were killed, most of them ordinary men, women, and children who were not involved in the war. One hundred and twenty-eight of the dead were Americans. When people back in the United States learned of this disaster, they reacted with outrage. American newspapers called the German sailors "pirates" and "murderers." The American government complained to the German government, but the Germans pointed out that the people on the *Lusitania* had been warned, and furthermore, that the ship had been carrying arms for the Allies. Hoping to avoid killing civilians in the future, the Germans gave new, stricter orders to their U-boat captains. But Americans would not soon forget the *Lusitania*.

America Enters the War

For over a year American anger at Germany went on simmering; then, in early 1917, German actions brought it to a boil. First the German government announced that it would once again instruct U-boat captains to sink any ship sailing toward England. Second, the Germans sent a telegram to a German diplomat in Mexico. This telegram offered a secret deal to the Mexican government. If Mexico would join the war on the side of the Central Powers, then Germany would help the Mexicans get back the territories they had lost to the United States in the Mexican-American War—territories that had become the states of Arizona, New Mexico, and Texas.

Some British spies found out about this telegram and informed the U.S. government. Now most Americans were furious with Germany, including the American president, Woodrow Wilson. Until now, Wilson had argued that the United States should stay out of the conflict in Europe. Even after the sinking of the *Lusitania*, he said, "There is such a thing as a man being too proud to fight. There is such a thing as a nation being so right that it does not need to convince others by force." But now the president changed his mind. In April 1917, he asked Congress to declare war on Germany. In his speech before Congress, Wilson proclaimed, "The world must be made safe for democracy"—in other words, Germany, which was trying to conquer democratic nations like England and France, must be defeated. Most members of Congress agreed with Wilson, and a few days after the president's speech America was officially at war. About two million men joined the military as volunteers; almost three million more were eventually drafted. But it would be many months before American soldiers were trained and would actually take part in the fighting. In the meantime, something happened in Russia that was bad news for the Allies and good news for the Germans.

Revolution Comes to Russia

Russia, which was fighting on the side of the Allies, was a huge and powerful country. But in many ways it was also a backward country. Most people were poor and uneducated. They were ruled by a czar and an undemocratic government that denied its people many basic human rights. The war against the Germans made the poor people of Russia even poorer; many came close to starving. Finally, in 1917, the people rose up and overthrew the czar. This came to be known as the Russian Revolution.

At first it seemed as if Russia might become a democracy, but after eight months a group called the Bolsheviks came to power. They would prove to be even more undemocratic and tyrannical than the old rulers of Russia.

The Bolsheviks adopted their ideas from Karl Marx (whom you read about in the World Civilization section of this book). Marx's ideas gave rise to the movement known as communism. Marx thought it was wrong that some people were poor while others were rich, and that the rich had power over the poor. He believed that the workers of the world would someday unite to overthrow the rich ruling class, and that finally, after many struggles and conflicts, a classless society would emerge.

Spurred on by Marx's ideas, the Bolsheviks called on the working class to rise up against the ruling class. In October of 1917, the Bolsheviks took over Russia. They were led by a fiery revolutionary named Lenin. In the years ahead, under Lenin's rule, the Bolshevik Party emerged victorious in a bloody civil war in which millions of Russians died. The Bolsheviks changed their name to the Communist Party and

Lenin, his worker's hat in hand, addresses a crowd of rebellious workers.

renamed the Russian Empire the Soviet Union. A "soviet" was a council of workers, and the Communists favored these councils as a means for the people to participate in government. But while the Communists claimed to rule in the name of the majority of Russians, who were workers and peasants, they were in fact a small minority who kept power for themselves.

When Lenin first took control in 1917, the hungry and war-weary Russian people were attracted by his promise of "Peace, Land, and Bread." Lenin's government signed a peace treaty with Germany, which meant that Russians were no longer fighting on the side of the Allies. This allowed millions of German troops to leave eastern Europe, where they had been fighting the Russians, and join the fight against the British and French. For a time it looked as if Germany might win the war; German troops pushed deep into France, coming within fifty miles of Paris, the French capital.

The End of the War

When the first American troops arrived in France in 1917, an American officer declared, "Lafayette, we are here." He was referring (as you might remember from Book Four in this series) to the Marquis de Lafayette, a French nobleman who had fought on the American side during the Revolutionary War. By coming to the aid of France, the officer suggested, America was returning a great favor.

The arrival of American troops helped turn the tide of the war. The Americans, who were fresh and full of energy, fought fiercely against their German enemies, who were worn out by almost four years of combat. The presence of the Americans also raised the spirits of the French and British troops, and they began to fight more effectively. Together, the British, French, and Americans stopped the German advance and then drove the German army back toward the French border. After this defeat Germany realized that it was never going to win the war, and it offered to make peace with the Allies. In November 1918 the shooting stopped.

Representatives from twenty-seven countries met near Paris at the enormous palace called Versailles (which you might remember reading about in Book Five of this series). Here—on June 28, 1919, the fifth anniversary of the assassination of Francis Ferdinand at Sarajevo—they signed a treaty called the Treaty of Versailles. This treaty dealt harshly with Germany; it forced the Germans to say that they alone were guilty of starting the war, and it forced them to agree to pay billions of dollars in fines to the Allies. Many Germans were angered by the treaty, because they didn't think they were the only ones to blame for the war.

There was also a more positive side to the agreement made at Versailles. It set up an organization called the League of Nations. This was to be a great assembly in which all nations could get together to settle their conflicts peacefully. Those who favored the League of Nations hoped that it would mean the end of war, or at least the kind of terrible war that Europe had just suffered.

It was the American president, Woodrow Wilson, who had come up with the

In the famous Hall of Mirrors at Versailles, world leaders came together to sign the treaty ending World War I. Woodrow Wilson is seated, fifth from the left.

idea of the League of Nations. But he was unable to convince his own countrymen that they should join the League. Many Americans felt that the United States should always be able to do what it wished without asking permission of other nations, so the Senate refused to approve the Treaty of Versailles. Americans also felt that the United States had already gotten too deeply involved in the affairs of far-off countries. President Wilson, a man of high ideals who had hoped that World War I would be "the war to end war," was heartbroken at the failure of the United States to join the League.

AMERICA AFTER WORLD WAR I

America Turns Inward

The rejection of the League of Nations was only one sign of increasing "isolationism" in America. Isolationists wanted the United States to be isolated, or separated, from the problems and conflicts of the rest of the world.

One way the government tried to isolate the United States was to limit the number of immigrants who could enter the country. Before World War I, many thousands of people, perhaps some of your ancestors, had come to America seeking freedom and opportunity. A sharp increase in immigration in the late nineteenth century led some groups to urge the government to restrict immigration.

It might seem strange that in our nation, with a population consisting largely of recent immigrants and the descendants of past immigrants, people would feel so suspicious of "foreigners." Nevertheless, after World War I, when many Americans feared a flood of immigrants from the war-torn countries of Europe, Congress passed laws saying that only a small number of people would be allowed to immigrate into the United States each year.

The new laws were especially designed to keep out those whose religious and political ideas might differ from those of most Americans. Many prejudiced people believed that only Protestants of Northern European descent were "true" or "pure" Americans. They were especially suspicious of immigrants from Southern and Eastern Europe, who were often Catholic or Jewish. You may recall reading in Book Five of this series about the Ku Klux Klan, a group that had been founded after the Civil War to terrorize Southern blacks. In the 1920s the Klan was reborn, but now it attacked Catholics and Jews as well as black people.

Do you remember these words inscribed on the Statue of Liberty: "I lift my lamp beside the golden door"? After World War I, the "golden door" was partially closed, keeping out many, while others got in only to find a cold and hostile welcome.

Prosperity and Progress

Though the 1920s was a difficult decade for many minorities, it was a time of widespread prosperity and technological progress. Most Americans had more money to spend, and manufacturers produced more new things for them to buy.

By the 1920s most American homes had electricity. Americans could now enjoy a number of things that made life more comfortable—not just electric light and heat but also new machines like the vacuum cleaner, the washing machine, and the refrigerator. (Before refrigerators, people kept food cool in ice boxes that had to be regularly filled with big blocks of ice.)

But the machine that really changed American life in this time was the automobile. Gasoline-powered automobiles were first sold in the 1890s, although they were so expensive that only the wealthy could afford them. Then in 1908 an American busi-

nessman named Henry Ford began to manufacture a car called the Model T. The Model T wasn't very pretty, and it only came in one color, black. But it was well built and cheap enough for the average person to afford. It soon became the most popular automobile in America.

A few years later Ford figured out a new way to manufacture cars by using an assembly line. Instead of having an individual worker put together a whole product, in the assembly line system many workers assemble a product one piece at a

Workers on an assembly line efficiently put together a Model A Ford.

time as it proceeds along a moving line. At different stations along the line, each worker adds another piece to the product. After Henry Ford figured out this efficient system, he was able to produce cars quickly and sell them cheaply.

Heroes of the Air

Have you ever flown in a modern passenger jet, the kind that holds hundreds of people? Maybe you've even been on a flight where you could sit back and watch a movie, and enjoy the meal brought to you by a friendly flight attendant.

Air travel has come a long way since Wilbur and Orville Wright made their pioneering flights in the early 1900s. (You can read more about the Wright Brothers in the Stories About Scientists at the end of this book.)

In the 1920s airplanes were still small and fragile, and it took courage to fly them, especially over long distances. In the year 1927, a young American named Charles Lindbergh astonished the world by flying all by himself from New York City to Paris, France. To make the journey Lindbergh had to fly for thousands of miles over the stormy North Atlantic ocean. He had to stay awake and alert for thirty-three hours straight. Toward the end of the flight he was so sleepy that he had to pull his eyelids open with his fingers. With his little plane shaking in the wind, he flew around icebergs and through rain clouds. For part of the way he had to fly through a thick fog that kept him from seeing where he was going; several times he nearly crashed into the ocean. You can see why after he landed safely in France, Lindbergh was given the nickname "Lucky Lindy"! After his return to the United States, Lindbergh was cheered as a national hero, and his plane—the Spirit of St. Louis—became the most famous aircraft in the world.

In the decade after Lindbergh's feat, a woman pilot named Amelia Earhart became as famous as Lindbergh. In 1932 she accomplished her own solo flight across the Atlantic, flying from Canada to Ireland. Later she became the first person to fly solo from California to Hawaii. Finally, in 1937, Earhart attempted her greatest feat—to fly all the way around the world.

With a co-pilot she set off from California, flying east. She flew to Florida, then down to South America and across the Atlantic to Africa. From there, her route took her across the Middle East, and then on to India, Southeast Asia, and Australia. Everywhere she went she was greeted by people who admired her and were keeping track of her great adventure. But in July 1937, six weeks after Earhart set out, people around the world were saddened to learn that her plane had disappeared somewhere in the South Pacific. Her last radio message said that she was lost and running out of fuel. Earhart and her co-pilot had made it more than three quarters of the way around the world before they disappeared. To this day no one knows exactly what happened to them.

Charles Lindbergh and his plane, Spirit of St. Louis.

The automobile changed the lives of Americans forever. Americans liked the speed and convenience of auto travel, the freedom of being able to go anywhere on their own at any time. They liked being able to live in the countryside and drive to the city to work. This new way of getting around was so popular that by the end of the 1920s the auto industry employed more workers than any other industry in the United States.

New Forms of Entertainment

Many new inventions gave Americans new ways to spend their leisure time. In the 1920s families would gather nightly around their radios—just as families today gather around the TV set—to hear broadcasts of news and music, as well as comedy shows,

 religious shows, and programs for children. In this period, too, many people first started going to the movies. But the movies in the 1920s were very different from the movies of today. For one thing, they were filmed in black and white. Before 1927 all movies were silent—they had no sound-tracks, which meant that you could see what was going on but not hear it. When an actor spoke, words would appear on the screen so that you could see what he had said. Often a musician would play a piano or organ in the theater to provide music to go along with the picture.

The movies of the 1920s included Westerns, love stories, adventures set in exotic lands, and stories based on tales from the Bible. But perhaps the best-loved movies were the comedies. For a while these comedies offered only slapstick humor, in which peo-ple would get into crazy car chases or hit each other in the face with pies. But then came a series of great comedies starring an actor named Charlie Chaplin. Chaplin played a character who came to be called the "Little Tramp"—a poor, shy, unlucky little man who would get into lots of trouble and then get out of it by the end of the movie. In the twenties, people all over the world became familiar with the Little Tramp. They recognized him by his square moustache, his round-topped bowler hat, his baggy pants, and the cane he swung as he walked along. Moviegoers would laugh at his antics but root for him at the same time, because he would always bounce back from di-saster and because he never lost his dignity or his sense of hope.

Charlie Chaplin as the Little Tramp in the movie City Lights.

While Chaplin made people laugh, many of his

comedies also made them think. For example, in one movie called *Modern Times* (now available on videotape), Chaplin took a humorous look at the modern assembly line. Sure, the assembly line made it possible to produce goods quickly and cheaply, but what did it mean for workers? When you see the Little Tramp develop a variety of bizarre nervous twitches, you have to laugh, but you also get a sense of what it means to perform the same tedious task over and over, day after day.

The Roaring Twenties

The 1920s are sometimes called the "Roaring Twenties," because for many people, especially young people, they were such exciting, fast-paced times. In this period young Americans started to rebel against some of the strict rules of behavior that older Americans had lived by. Many of them decided that it was more important to enjoy life than to work hard. For many young Americans of the middle and upper classes, the decade of the twenties was like one long party.

It was a party where people drank lots of alcohol, even though it was now against the law to do so. For many years advocates of the "temperance" movement had attacked the use of alcohol. They pointed out that drinking alcohol was unhealthy, and that people often committed violent crimes when they drank too much. In 1919 Congress passed the Eighteenth Amendment to the U.S. Constitution: this amendment prohibited (banned) the making and selling of beer, wine, and alcohol everywhere in the United States. The years during which this ban was in effect are known as the period of Prohibition. Prohibition lasted from 1920 to 1933, when Americans voted to ratify the Twenty-first Amendment to the Constitution, which repealed the Eighteenth Amendment (to repeal a law is to declare it no longer in effect).

Although Prohibition cut down on the number of Americans who drank alcohol, many went on drinking in secret. Often when something is forbidden it becomes more attractive; and now people, especially young people, began to think of drinking as something daring and exciting to do. They started going to illegal drinking places called "speakeasies." Alcohol was supplied to the speakeasies by men known as "bootleggers," who either made their own illegal liquor or smuggled it in from foreign countries. (The term "bootlegger" comes from the old smuggler's trick of hiding a bottle inside the leg of a boot.)

Speakeasies were usually noisy and crowded. Customers listened to loud music, and drank and danced for hours on end. Many of the customers were young women, and this was something new. Before World War I, women were not supposed to drink in public, and most bars would let in only men. But now women were becoming more independent in lots of ways. (You may recall reading in Book Five of this series about how American women won the right to vote in 1920.)

The fun-loving, carefree young women who frequented speakeasies were often called "flappers." Flappers not only drank but also smoked cigarettes and wore

heavy makeup—two more things that were thought to be very daring for women to do. Flappers also wore their clothes in a carefree way. Before World War I, women had usually worn dresses that completely covered their legs, but now the flappers began wearing dresses that only came down to their knees. Older people were shocked by these short new dresses. In fact, flappers and their male friends did many things just because they wanted to shock their elders: that was part of the spirit of the Roaring Twenties.

This cover of Life *magazine from 1928 shows a flapper and her partner dancing the night away.*

African-Americans Move North

As you've seen, the years after World War I were years of great prosperity for many Americans. New industries were thriving, especially in the North. These industries needed workers, but, with the new restrictions on immigration, there were fewer people coming from Europe to work in American factories. The prospect of jobs and a better way of life attracted many African-Americans to leave their homes in the rural South and move to the great cities of the North. They came North looking not only for good jobs, but also because they believed they would encounter less racial prejudice in the North.

Many African-Americans headed for Chicago and New York City—so many that during the 1920s the black population of New York grew by six times (from about fifty thousand to over three hundred thousand). Most of these newcomers made

Marcus Garvey

In the early 1920s many African-Americans were influenced by the ideas of a man named Marcus Garvey. Garvey urged African-Americans to be proud of their blackness and of their African roots. He also argued that American blacks should help establish a free black nation in Africa. At this time much of Africa was ruled by European colonizers. But Garvey declared, "We are going to Africa to tell England, France, and Belgium to get out of there." Garvey had his own fleet of steamships, with which he planned to take a large group of African-Americans "home" to Africa. But this plan never worked. Although many black Americans admired African culture, most felt that their real home was in the United States and they were determined to gain their rights and make their contributions as Americans.

their homes in a New York City neighborhood called Harlem. Harlem would in time become a great center of African-American culture. In Harlem African-Americans found a new sense of independence and of pride in their traditions.

The Harlem Renaissance

Although Garvey's "back–to–Africa" movement did not achieve its political goals, the powerful idea of black pride would influence a bold new generation of African-American artists and help to bring about what is sometimes called the "Harlem Renaissance." (A "renaissance" is a period during which artists, writers, and scholars are especially brilliant and creative. You may recall reading in Book Five of this series about the Renaissance in Europe several centuries earlier.) The Harlem Renaissance celebrated the emergence of "the New Negro"—of the African-American who was, in the words of one historian, "black and proud, politically assertive and economically independent, creative and disciplined." (The term "Negro" was commonly used to refer to African-Americans at the time, though it is no longer generally accepted today.)

One of the leading figures of the Harlem Renaissance was the poet Langston Hughes. (You can read some of his poems in Books Five and Six of this series.) Hughes declared that black artists and writers should work to please themselves, not to please white people:

> We young Negro artists who create now intend to express our individual dark-skinned selves without fear or shame. If white people are pleased we are glad. If they are not, it doesn't matter. . . . We build our temples for tomorrow, strong as we know how, and we stand on top of the mountain, free within ourselves.

African-American artist Archibald Motley evoked the feeling of Harlem street life in the 1920s in this painting.

Some of Hughes's poems protest against inequality in America; others celebrate the vitality of life in black communities like Harlem; others express ideas and feelings that apply to all people regardless of race. Many of his poems reflect black culture by their form as well as by their subject matter; for instance, some of his poems imitate the rhythm of popular African-American forms of music, especially jazz and the blues.

Another important poet of the Harlem Renaissance was Hughes's friend, Countee Cullen. As a college student at New York University, Cullen won prizes for his poetry. After receiving a graduate degree from Harvard University, he went on to teach in the New York City public schools and continued to write poetry. Compared to the poems of Langston Hughes, Cullen's poems are in a more traditional style. In a poem called "Heritage," he thought about what Africa might mean to a modern black American:

> One three centuries removed
> From the scenes his father loved,
> Spicy grove, cinnamon tree,
> What is Africa to me?

(You might remember reading another poem by Cullen in Book Five of this series.)

While Hughes and Cullen were writing their poems in Harlem, a young woman named Zora Neale Hurston was one of the few African-Americans studying at nearby Barnard College. She had come north from Eatonville, a small, all-black town in Florida. At Barnard she studied the science of anthropology, which deals with the customs and traditions of people. She decided to use her skills as an anthropologist to explore the culture of her own hometown in Florida. So she returned to Eatonville to collect the traditional folktales of her people. She listened to people telling wonderful stories like "How the Woodpecker Nearly Drowned the Whole World" and "Why the Porpoise Has His Tail on Crossways." She recorded these stories in a book called *Mules and Men*, which helped people understand and appreciate the traditional black culture of the South. A few years later she wrote her most famous book, *Their Eyes Were Watching God*, about the struggles and triumphs of a young black woman living in Florida.

The Great Depression

In the 1920s, most Americans lived better than ever before. But the decade of the 1930s was just the opposite—a time of great economic hardship and widespread poverty. During the 1930s millions of Americans lost their jobs and their homes, and had to struggle to feed themselves and their families. This period of hardship and poverty became known as the "Great Depression."

Historians still argue over what caused the Great Depression, but most agree that in the twenties, American industry grew too rapidly. As more and more people bought new products like cars and refrigerators, more and more factories were built to make these products. But at a certain point there were more products than people could buy. Sooner or later the factories would have to stop producing at such high levels, and the people who worked in them would lose their jobs.

Another problem was that people got into the habit of spending more money than they had. Because people thought that times would continue to get better and better, they thought that they would always have more money than they had before. So if they saw something they wanted to buy, they borrowed money to pay for it, or paid for it "on installment" (a little bit at a time). In doing this, many people went further and further into debt, which was dangerous because if people's incomes went down instead of up, they would be stuck with debts they were unable to pay. With companies producing more goods than people could buy, and people spending more money than they really had, the stage was set for economic disaster.

Many people also became reckless with their money in another way. They began to invest heavily in the stock market. When you buy a bit of stock—called a "share"—in a company, it's as if you own a little piece of the company. By buying stock in a company, you invest money that helps the company grow, and when the company makes a profit, you, as a stockholder, are entitled to a share of the profit. The price of a share of stock goes up and down depending upon how well the company is doing: if the company is growing and making big profits, then the price of its stock will go up. If you buy stock in a company when it is still small and not very well known, you might pay a low price for the stock, let's say, for example, five dollars per share. If the company then goes on to become very successful, the price of the stock will go up, and one way you can make money is to sell your shares of stock at the new high price of, say, twenty-five dollars per share. For every share you sell, you make a profit of twenty dollars.

Normally you buy stock in a company because you think it makes a good product that people want to buy, and you want to share in the profits that result from the sale of that product. But in the 1920s, when American companies were making high profits and the price of stocks was going up and up, people began to gamble on the price of stocks. Instead of investing in a company so that they could share in its profits, people began to buy stocks just so they could sell them later when their price had gone up. More and more people began "playing" the stock market this way—not just wealthy people but millions of ordinary working men and women, who invested their life savings in stocks.

The problem was, as more and more people played the stock market, they were willing to pay much more for stocks than they were really worth. They kept gambling that stock prices would go even higher. But by the end of the twenties stocks were dangerously overvalued, or inflated. The whole stock market was like a big balloon getting ready to burst. It finally burst in October 1929, when the price of stocks started to fall rapidly. For example, a share in U.S. Steel (an excellent company) cost $262 in 1929; by 1932 it was worth only $22.

People who had invested in the stock market panicked; they tried to sell their stocks before the prices went down further. But with everyone trying to sell, almost no one wanted to buy.

The "crash" of the stock market—which came to be called "the Crash of '29"—helped bring on the Great Depression. In the 1930s, many people went broke. They lost the houses and cars they could no longer afford to make payments on. Even people who were not impoverished were afraid to buy new things. Factory warehouses were already too full of unsold goods. Hardly anybody was buying, and factories started to lay off workers. Then the laid-off workers could not afford to buy things made by other workers, and more and more factories shut down. By the end of 1932 about one in four American workers had lost his job. Suddenly millions of Americans had no way to pay for even the basic necessities of life.

If you walked through a large American city in the early thirties, you would see the frightening results of the Depression. You would see people standing patiently in lines that stretched for blocks, waiting to be served a bowl of soup. Beggars would come up to you, asking, "Brother, can you spare a dime?"—a line heard so often in the thirties that it became the title of a popular song. On certain sidewalks you would see men standing behind crates full of apples, trying to earn a few cents by selling fruit. The man who sold you an apple today might have been a factory worker or a teacher or a banker just a few months before.

If you walked to the outskirts of the city, you would see dozens or hundreds of homeless people camped in shacks made out of scraps of wood and metal. And if you passed the city dump, you would see the hungriest, most desperate people picking through the garbage for something to eat.

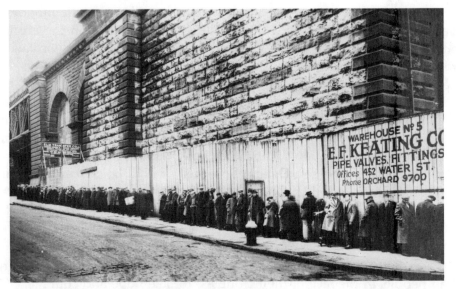

Hungry people wait in a breadline in New York.

President Hoover, third from left, meets with business leaders appointed to help ease unemployment during the Depression.

Herbert Hoover

The Great Depression was a terrible thing, and when terrible things happen to people they look around for someone to blame. Many Americans blamed the Republican president, Herbert Hoover, who had been elected in 1928. After all, they thought, the president was the leader of the country, so he must have led it in the wrong direction. People bitterly referred to the homeless camps as "Hoovervilles." An empty pocket turned inside-out was a "Hoover flag." The newspapers that homeless people slept under were "Hoover blankets."

This was not really fair. President Hoover was a kind man who cared deeply about human suffering. In fact, he had become famous for leading the effort to send food to hungry Europeans during World War I. But like most Republicans of his time, he believed that government should not get too involved in the economy. He believed in America's traditional free enterprise system, in which individual businessmen, rather than the government, should make most economic decisions. So when the Depression came he helped business owners get loans, and he urged them not to lay off workers. But he rejected the idea that government should aid the unemployed directly by giving them money or making jobs for them. Most Americans thought that Hoover was not doing enough to help the victims of the Depression, and in the presidential election of 1932 they voted him out of office. The new president was a Democrat, Franklin Delano Roosevelt, with a bold plan for coping with the Depression. He called his plan the "New Deal."

The New Deal

When Roosevelt was sworn in as president, he gave a stirring speech. He urged the American people, in the face of their troubles, to take hope and courage. "The only thing we have to fear," he declared, "is fear itself." He promised to "wage war" against the Depression, to treat it as if it were a foreign enemy that had invaded the land. And he noted, "Our greatest primary task is to put people to work."

True to his word, Roosevelt saw to it that the government immediately began putting people to work. One of the first programs set up by the New Deal was the Civilian Conservation Corps (known as the CCC). This program employed young men between the ages of eighteen and twenty-five to work on projects to improve and protect the environment. CCC workers lived in camps on public lands, especially in the national parks. They built trails and bridges, stopped soil erosion, fought forest fires, and planted millions of acres of trees. It was hard but useful and healthy work. The CCC gave millions of frustrated, jobless young men a new sense of pride and satisfaction.

Beginning in 1935, an even bigger jobs program, the Works Progress Administration (WPA), employed construction workers and engineers on new building projects all over the country. Roads, bridges, power plants, school buildings, hospitals, and airports were built or improved with government money. The WPA also gave jobs to artists. Musicians and actors went out to perform in large and small communities, some of which had never before seen a professional performance. Writers put together a series of guidebooks about different parts of the country. Painters splashed brilliant, colorful murals on the walls of public buildings. (Some of these can still be seen in post offices and other buildings around the country.) Never before had the American government done so much to help the arts.

But Roosevelt's New Deal programs went beyond the creation of jobs. One bold program, the Tennessee Valley Authority (TVA), was set up to improve the lives of millions of people in the poverty-stricken Tennessee Valley (an area that includes parts of seven Southern states). The TVA taught farmers in the region better ways to grow their crops. It constructed great dams along the local rivers to protect against the flooding that destroyed the farmers' crops. And it built electric power plants, harnessing the power of the rivers to bring electricity to the homes in the area. (Before the TVA was set up, only two of every hundred local homes had electric power.) The TVA gave new life to the whole region.

One of the most remarkable engineering achievements of the twentieth century, the Golden Gate Bridge, was completed during the Depression without any money from New Deal programs. Built from 1933 to 1937, this suspension bridge stretches 4,200 feet across the entrance to the San Francisco Bay, where the bay meets the Pacific Ocean. Like the Statue of Liberty, the Golden Gate Bridge has become a symbol of American possibility: it is, said the chief engineer of the bridge, "like a mighty door, swinging wide into a world of wonders."

Some people thought that under Roosevelt the federal government was growing too big and too powerful. They mocked all the new agencies—known by their initials, CCC, WPA, TVA and many more—joking that Roosevelt had cooked up a big pot of "alphabet soup." But for other people, especially poor people, the New Deal showed that America could be a caring country.

Social Security

Perhaps the most important of the New Deal programs was Social Security. Before Social Security existed, Americans worried that they would not be able to support themselves if they lost their jobs or if they were unable to work due to age or illness. A worker who lost his job could turn to local groups that provided charity or "relief," but many Americans were ashamed to ask for help because they had been brought up to believe that people should take care of themselves.

Then in 1935 Congress passed the Social Security Act. This law said that most workers had to pay a small part of their income into a special government fund. Then if the worker lost his job, the government would pay him money out of the fund. This way he could support himself while he looked for another job. If the worker became ill or he reached the age of retirement, the government would use the fund to send him regular payments for the rest of his life. Now Americans knew that if they lost their jobs or grew too old to work, they would still be able to survive. And they were not ashamed to take Social Security because they knew that they had worked to earn it.

The "Indian New Deal"

During the New Deal years, the federal government passed the Indian Reorganization Act, also known as the "Indian New Deal." This act was the result of the tireless efforts of a man named John Collier, whom President Roosevelt had appointed in 1933 as Commissioner of Indian Affairs.

Collier's Indian Reorganization Act put an end to the Dawes Act of 1887, also called the General Allotment Act (which you read about in Book Five of this series). The Dawes Act ordered that the lands owned in common by all members of a tribe be broken into 160-acre pieces to be allotted to individual Indians, on the theory that making Indians into private landowners would bring them into the mainstream of American society. But the real effect of the Dawes Act was to take land from the Indians, in part because after each Indian had received a 160-acre allotment, the remaining tribal land was sold to whites; and in part because some Indians so desperately needed money that they sold their allotments to whites.

In 1934, the Indian Reorganization Act stopped the allotment of Indian land, and it set aside a fund of money to help buy land for Indian tribes and individuals. John Collier's plan also gave tribes some power to govern themselves in accord with their specific tribal rules and customs. And the plan stated that qualified Native Americans would be picked first to fill jobs in the Bureau of Indian Affairs. To Collier's disappointment, however, Congress refused to approve any programs to help preserve the distinct customs and traditions of different Native American peoples.

The Dust Bowl and the "Okies"

The New Deal was a bold plan that gave hope and confidence to most Americans. But it did not immediately end the Depression, and hard times continued through the 1930s. For some people things got even worse as the decade went on.

In 1934 and 1935 a terrible drought struck the farms of the Great Plains, a huge grassland region covering parts of Texas, Oklahoma, Kansas, Nebraska, Colorado, and the Dakotas. Month after month went by without rain. Crops dried up and died in the fields. Then the soil itself got so dry that it blew away on the wind, sometimes sweeping gigantic clouds of dirt across the land, turning the sky dark as night in the middle of the day. People had to wear handkerchiefs over their mouths to keep

Franklin and Eleanor Roosevelt

Franklin Delano Roosevelt, who led America through the Depression years, was the only man to be elected president four times—in 1932, 1936, 1940, and 1944. (When Roosevelt was sworn in for his third term, Chief Justice Hughes joked, "Mr. President, this is getting to be a habit.") FDR, as he was known to almost everyone, had great energy and imagination. He also had an unusual ability to communicate effectively with the American people. Once a week he gave a talk on the radio. Speaking in a friendly, informal way, he told the American people about his most recent ideas and plans. These radio talks were known as "fireside chats" because they made people feel as if they were sitting at home with the president, chatting by the fireplace.

FDR was popular with most Americans, but not with all. Some felt that, with all his new programs, he was taking on too much power. They accused him of wanting to be a dictator. Also, many wealthy people detested Roosevelt. They thought that his economic ideas were destroying the free enterprise system that gave people the opportunity to become rich. FDR himself came from an extremely wealthy family that had already produced one president, FDR's distant cousin, Theodore Roosevelt. Though FDR never suffered from poverty, he was well acquainted with personal

Franklin Roosevelt liked to get out among the people. The sight of the president seated in an open car and surrounded by friendly crowds became very familiar during this popular president's years in office.

hardship. At the age of thirty-nine he was stricken with polio, a terrible disease that partly paralyzed his arms and legs. Doctors thought that he was completely disabled and would have to give up his political career. FDR refused to accept their opinion. As he got better he started exercising his upper body, pushing himself against great pain. Gradually he regained control of his arms, and built them up until they were as strong as a boxer's. His legs did not improve as much. For the rest of his life he could walk and stand only with the help of braces or crutches.

FDR's wife, Eleanor Roosevelt, was one of our most remarkable First Ladies. Even more than FDR himself, Eleanor was concerned about the suffering of the nation's poor. She traveled all over the country to see how the New Deal programs were working. She became the "eyes and ears" for her husband, who could not travel as widely because of his disability.

Eleanor showed a special concern for the problems of women and African-Americans. She helped women get jobs in government, and she spoke to women's groups across the country. She was friends with many well-known women, including Amelia Earhart, who gave her a ride in her plane. *At the same time she often invited African-American leaders to dinner at the White House. These invitations shocked many people, especially in the South, where whites and blacks were still strictly segregated. Eleanor once attended a meeting in Birmingham, Alabama, where the audience was divided into a white section and a black section. Eleanor sat in the black section with a friend, and when some officials asked her to move to the white area, she angrily picked up her chair and set it down in the aisle, right between the two sections.*

First Lady Eleanor Roosevelt greets her friend, Dr. Mary McLeod Bethune, during a visit to a dormitory for African-American women who took part in the war effort.

from choking on all the dirt in the air. Months went by and, as dust storm followed dust storm, people all over the country came to know this unfortunate region as the Dust Bowl. (In Book Four of this series you can read about how farming techniques of the time were in part responsible for the formation of the Dust Bowl.)

Like everyone else, the farmers of the Great Plains had suffered the effects of the Depression. But now they were completely wiped out: their farms were literally blowing away. Thousands of farm families left their homes in the Great Plains and fled westward, hoping to find jobs on the rich farms of California. There they became migrant (traveling) workers, laboring at low-paid, temporary jobs. They might pick fruit at harvest time and then be jobless the rest of the year, living in their cars or in miserable camps by the roadside. Because farm workers were not covered by the new Social Security laws, they got little help from the government. For some people, the "Okies" (so-called because many of them came from Oklahoma) showed how terrible things had become in America: a group of once proud and self-sufficient farmers were now living like serfs in the Middle Ages. The author John Steinbeck wrote one of the most famous American novels, *The Grapes of Wrath,* about the suffering and endurance of the migrant workers.

A migrant family says grace before their meal by the roadside.

THE ROAD TO ANOTHER WAR
Hitler's Rise to Power in Germany

Through most of the 1930s, Americans were too worried about problems at home to pay much attention to the rest of the world. But other countries were also undergoing terrible troubles. When the Great Depression came to the United States in 1929, it quickly spread to the European nations as well. The suffering was especially great in Germany, where more than one third of German workers lost their jobs. Like Americans, Germans wanted a strong leader to lead them out of the Depression. In 1933, the same year that Roosevelt took office in America, a man named Adolf Hitler came to power in Germany. But he was a very different kind of leader from Roosevelt.

Hitler quickly made himself the absolute dictator of Germany. He destroyed all political parties except his own, the National Socialist (or Nazi) Party. Hitler stirred up strong feelings of nationalism in the German people (in the World Civilization section of this book, you saw how nationalism was one cause of World War

Hitler, left, and other Nazi leaders in 1939.

I); most Germans, who felt bitterness at the humiliating terms imposed on them by the Treaty of Versailles at the end of World War I, were ready to respond to Hitler's appeal to their pride. Hitler declared the beginning of a great new era of German history, which he called the Third Reich ("Reich" is German for empire). Hitler believed that under his rule, Germany would become a great empire, surpassing both the earlier Holy Roman Empire and the German empire formed in the nineteenth century under Bismarck.

Under the Third Reich, Hitler promised, Germany would become the most powerful nation in the world. One Nazi slogan went, "Today Germany, tomorrow the world." Like Roosevelt, Hitler put the unemployed to work. But unlike Roosevelt, he put them to work making weapons and vehicles for the military. His goal was to build up the German Army so that it would be strong enough to conquer all of Europe.

Hitler and the Nazis came to power partly by making the Germans feel proud, and partly by stirring up hatred. They encouraged hatred of those nations—Britain, France, and the United States—that had beaten Germany in World War I. But above all Hitler stirred up hate against a group that was a small minority in Germany: the Jews.

Hitler blamed all of Germany's problems on the Jews. The Jews, he said, were not "pure" Germans. "Real" Germans, he claimed, belong to a "master race" called the Aryans. According to Hitler, Jews were an inferior race that was trying to take over Germany. All this was completely false, but many Germans came to believe it. A terrifying period of persecution began: Jews all over Germany were fired from their jobs and beaten in the streets. Then in 1935

To segregate Jews, Germans forced them to wear a yellow star sewn onto their clothes, or sometimes painted yellow crosses on their backs.

the German government passed a set of laws taking away the civil rights of Jews and forbidding Jews to marry non-Jews, so that the so-called Aryan "race" would stay "pure." Later in this section, you will learn how this systematic hatred and persecution of the Jews would lead to one of the most horrendous acts in history.

World War II Begins

In 1938 Hitler began his march to conquer the world. In that year the German Army conquered first Austria and then what until recently was called Czechoslovakia. Germany's old enemies, Britain and France, stood by nervously. They realized that if Germany were allowed to go on invading its neighbors, their own countries would soon lie in the path of conquest. So when the Germans invaded Poland in September 1939, Britain and France declared war on Germany. The Second World War had begun.

At the beginning of the war the Germans seemed unstoppable. Hitler had built up the most powerful army in Europe, and now it swept across the continent with frightening speed. The Germans themselves called their way of fighting *Blitzkrieg*, or "lightning war." In April 1940 the Germans conquered Denmark and Norway. The following month they captured Belgium and Holland, and then invaded France

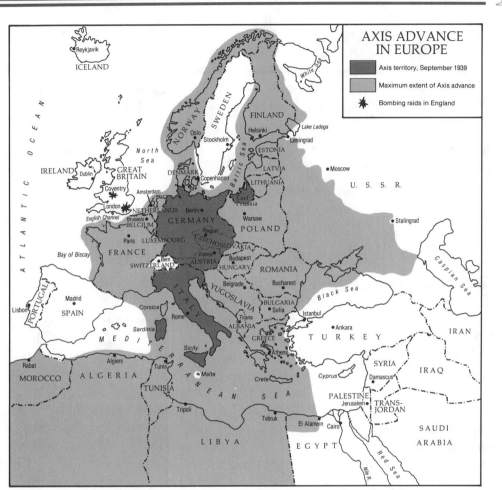

AXIS ADVANCE IN EUROPE

- Axis territory, September 1939
- Maximum extent of Axis advance
- ★ Bombing raids in England

By September of 1939 Hitler and the Nazi Party had conquered much of Europe, as you can see from this map.

itself. Within a few short weeks the German Army succeeded in doing what it had failed to do through all the years of World War I: it conquered France.

Now Hitler dominated almost all of Europe, as he had sworn to do. Britain alone continued to resist him. Because Britain was an island, it was difficult for an army to invade

Fire fighters in London battle a blaze after a bombing raid.

it. But airplanes could cross the English Channel easily. So Hitler directed his air force to bomb the British until they surrendered. For months in what came to be known as the Battle of Britain, the Germans rained bombs on England, killing thousands of men, women, and children. But the British refused to give in. Winston Churchill, the prime minister of England, declared in a famous speech:

> We shall defend our island, whatever the cost may be, we shall fight on the beaches, we shall fight on the landing grounds, we shall fight in the fields and in the streets, we shall fight in the hills; we shall never surrender.

In the same speech, Churchill made a prediction. Sooner or later, he said, as in World War I, America would once again come to the rescue of Europe.

Should America Fight?

In the United States, the majority of the people sympathized with Britain's lonely fight. But not many Americans were eager to go to war again. They remembered the horrors of World War I and many people were still isolationists. They thought that the United States could stay removed from Europe's troubles, safe behind its ocean barrier.

President Roosevelt disagreed. To FDR, Germany's conquests threatened the survival of democracy. He denied the idea that America could remain "a lone island" of peace in a world at war. "The world has grown so small," he said, "and weapons of attack so swift that no nation can be safe." FDR convinced Congress that America should aid Britain by sending weapons and supplies. He said that this was like helping your neighbor when his house catches on fire. You should be glad to lend him your garden hose so that the fire doesn't spread to your own house.

At the same time, FDR argued, America had to build up its own defenses. In the period after World War I the American military had grown small and weak. Now FDR started a great program of rearmament. Almost a million men were drafted into the armed services. America, FDR declared, must become "the arsenal of democracy." (An arsenal is a place where weapons are stored.) Factories all over the country began building ships, planes, and tanks. With all the new work going on, the American economy began to finally recover from the Depression.

For the sake of democracy Americans were willing to make the United States an "arsenal." But they were not yet ready to fight. It took a military attack on American soldiers to convince Americans to enter the war. That attack came not from the Germans but from their Asian allies, the Japanese.

Pearl Harbor Pushes America to War

About the same time that the Nazis took over Germany, a group of military men came to power in Japan. This new military government dreamed of ruling Asia just as the Nazis dreamed of ruling Europe. Like the Germans, the Japanese began by invading their neighbors.

In 1937 the Japanese launched a major invasion of China. The Chinese people, under their leader Chiang Kai-shek (CHANG KIGH-shek), fought back fiercely. But the Japanese Army was powerful and determined. In 1940, after three years of bloody fighting, the Japanese controlled much of eastern China. In the same year, Japan formed a military alliance with Germany.

In the United States, President Roosevelt watched the Japanese advance with great concern. He declared that Japan was an "aggressor nation," as dangerous as Germany. Then, in the summer of 1941, Japan occupied Indochina (the present-day countries of North and South Vietnam, Laos, and Cambodia). Now the Japanese were poised to strike at Malaya, Indonesia, and the Philippines (where the United States had important military bases). Roosevelt responded by forbidding the export of oil, iron, and rubber to Japan. Without these raw materials, the Japanese war machine could not run. FDR warned that trade would not start again until the Japanese withdrew from both China and Indochina.

The Japanese government would not accept American interference in its plan for conquest. It decided to go to war against the United States. And it struck the first, crippling blow in a surprise attack on Pearl Harbor, a U.S. Navy base on the island of Oahu in Hawaii, and headquarters of the Navy's Pacific Ocean fleet.

On Sunday morning, December 7, 1941, the base at Pearl Harbor was calm and peaceful. Few men were on duty; soldiers and sailors were sleeping late or getting ready for church. The admiral who commanded the fleet was dressing for a game of golf.

Suddenly, at five minutes before eight in the morning, planes filled the sky. At first the men on the ground thought that the American air force was practicing, but then some of the planes started to dive toward the earth. They came so close to the ground that the American servicemen could see the symbol painted on each plane: a red circle, standing for the "rising sun" of Japan. An officer sent out the radio message: "AIR RAID, PEARL HARBOR. THIS IS NOT A DRILL." Men rushed

A scene after the Japanese air raid on Pearl Harbor: the small boat is picking up survivors from the burning USS West Virginia.

to their duty stations while the Japanese pilots swooped down at them, machine guns blazing. All over the base exploding bombs ripped the ground. Japanese bombs fell on barracks and houses, killing men in their sleep. They fell on the airfield next to the naval base, destroying dozens of American planes.

For the Japanese pilots, the most important targets were the American warships in the harbor. Bombs and torpedoes rained down on the ships, while the crews scrambled to man their antiaircraft guns. One Japanese pilot scored a direct hit on the battleship *Arizona*. (Battleships were the biggest, most powerful ships in the U.S. Navy.) An American sailor on another ship said, "That big *Arizona* blew up like a million Fourth of Julys." In a single horrifying moment, more than a thousand American sailors were blown to pieces.

The attack went on for two hours. The Americans fought back as best they could. But they had been caught unprepared, and the Japanese had planned well. By the time the Japanese pilots flew away, they had sunk or badly damaged nineteen ships and killed more than two thousand Americans.

The surprise attack on Pearl Harbor shocked and angered the American people. One day after the attack, President Roosevelt spoke to Congress. With anger in his voice, he proclaimed December 7, 1941, as "a date which will live in infamy." Then he asked Congress to declare war on Japan. Congress passed the declaration immediately. Days later, Japan's allies, Germany and Italy, declared war on the United States. America was once again involved in a world war.

After the Japanese attack, the American people united behind their president. Isolationist feeling disappeared almost overnight. Millions of young men flocked to join the military. "Remember Pearl Harbor!" became a rallying cry.

The Axis Versus the Allies

Now that the United States had entered the war, it faced a military alliance of Germany, Japan, and Italy. Italy was ruled by a dictator named Mussolini, known as "Il Duce," meaning "the leader." Mussolini was the head of the Fascist Party, a group that, like the Nazis, stirred up people with feelings of fierce national pride mixed with a hatred of foreigners. Together these countries—Germany, Japan, and Italy— were known as the Axis powers.

Opposing the Axis was an alliance of the United States, Britain, China, and the Soviet Union. Together these countries were known as the Allied powers. The Allies also included a group known as the Free French—Frenchmen who refused to accept German rule in their country. The leader of the Free French was General Charles de Gaulle, a hero of the First World War. When the Germans took over France, De Gaulle escaped to England. From there he organized a fighting force of Frenchmen living overseas. He also directed groups of French civilians, known as the French Resistance, who fought an underground war against the Germans at home.

By fighting against the Axis, Americans believed they were fighting to preserve democracy. But not all of America's allies were democratic countries. In fact, the Soviet Union was ruled by a brutal dictator, Joseph Stalin, who had killed millions of his own countrymen in order to strengthen his power. Why would the Allies be willing to join forces with such a criminal? The answer takes us into the politics of war, which sometimes leads to unnatural alliances and innocent victims.

The Division of Poland

As you've read, in World War II, the countries fighting against the Axis powers were known as the Allies, which included the Soviet Union—but not at first. Early in the war, the Nazi leader, Hitler, made a deal with the Soviet leader, Stalin. In August 1939 they signed the Nazi-Soviet Non-Aggression Pact. This agreement was a matter of political and military convenience: by agreeing not to fight each other, Germany and the Soviet Union could instead concentrate on taking over and dividing a country they both wanted, Poland.

In early September of 1939, Germany invaded Poland from the west. A short while later the Soviet Union invaded Poland from the east. Overwhelmed, Poland quickly surrendered, and the Soviets proceeded to move into neighboring countries in the North—Latvia, Lithuania, and Estonia—that had strategic access to the Baltic Sea.

Hitler and Stalin's deal to divide Poland did not result in a lasting friendship. Hitler hated communism, and he lusted after the resources of the huge Soviet Union. In 1941, Hitler turned against Stalin: German troops invaded the Soviet Union, and this drove the Soviets to take sides with the Allies.

The Allies were willing to welcome Stalin, even though Stalin had once cozied up to Hitler. British and American leaders overlooked the cruelty of the Soviet government under Stalin because they perceived the Axis powers as a more direct threat. But the military need to have the Soviet Union as an ally pushed American and British leaders into morally questionable positions. This was especially true when President Roosevelt and Winston Churchill rose to defend Stalin against charges that he murdered thousands of Poles.

It was, of all people, Hitler who accused Stalin of committing these murders. Hitler's evidence came from what his German troops discovered in 1943 as they pushed across Russia to the city of Katyn: there, a wolf pawing at the ground led to the uncovering of mass graves in which hundreds of bodies of dead Poles had been buried. Hitler—conveniently ignoring his own practice of mass murder—accused Stalin of murdering the Poles. Stalin denied the accusations. FDR dismissed Hitler's charges as "German propaganda," and Churchill noted only that "nothing will bring them [the dead Poles] back."

The grim truth is that Hitler was right. Just before the Soviet invasion of Poland in 1939, Stalin had rounded up thousands of leading Polish citizens and brought them to Russia to be executed. After the Soviets invaded Poland, Stalin's troops took thousands more Polish officers and citizens to Soviet jails, where they were held only briefly before being shot. But Stalin's horrible crime against the Poles was long ignored as the Allies chose to make the political compromises necessary to fight against their common enemy.

The Axis at High Tide

When America entered the war, the Axis powers seemed to be winning. After conquering its neighbors, Germany had invaded the Soviet Union. The German Army had pushed deep into Soviet territory, coming within twenty-five miles of the capital

JAPANESE EXPANSION

Japanese territory in 1941

Japanese occupied territory in 1942

city, Moscow. Meanwhile, in northern Africa, German forces were battling the British for possession of Egypt (then a British colony). It seemed as if Germany was about to take over Egypt, and with it the Suez Canal, which controls the sea trade between Europe and Asia.

On the other side of the world, the Japanese were just as successful. Within a few months of the attack on Pearl Harbor, they took over the rest of Southeast Asia. After pushing down the Malay Peninsula, they conquered the vast territory of the Dutch East Indies (today called Indonesia). To the west they invaded Burma, advancing to the borders of Britain's huge colony of India. To the east they invaded the Philippine Islands, which had been an American colony and still had large numbers of American troops stationed there. (You may recall reading in Book Five of this series how the United States took over the Philippines after the Spanish-American War.) For six months, outnumbered American and Filipino forces heroically resisted the Japanese, but at last were forced to surrender.

In the Philippines American prisoners of war were treated very cruelly by their Japanese captors. By beating, starving, and sometimes killing their prisoners, Japanese soldiers broke the traditional rules of warfare as spelled out in the Geneva Conventions, a set of rules agreed upon by most countries in the late nineteenth century that called for humane treatment of prisoners, the sick, and the wounded. Americans back home were angered to learn that their men had been treated so brutally. But it was not only captured soldiers who suffered from Japanese cruelty. Throughout Japan's new empire, the citizens of conquered countries—men, women, and children—were treated just as badly. Japanese soldiers had been trained to think of non-Japanese peoples as inferior and so not worthy of any respect.

In Europe, German soldiers had been trained to think of non-Germans in exactly the same way. So, like the Japanese, they became especially cruel conquerors. Wherever Germans ruled, the conquered peoples lived in terror. But no group suffered as much from German cruelty as the Jews.

The Holocaust

As we have seen, Adolf Hitler hated the Jewish people. After the war began, Hitler decided to bring about what he called "the final solution to the Jewish question." This "solution" was as simple as it was horrifying: all the Jews of Europe were to be murdered.

In the early 1940s, the Nazis built prison camps and death camps in Germany and Poland. All over Europe Jews (and other people who didn't fit Hitler's "Aryan" model) were rounded up and sent to these camps. The death camps were like factories for killing. Men, women, and children were herded like cattle into large, empty rooms, called gas chambers. Then the doors were shut and poisoned gas was pumped into the rooms, killing all those inside in minutes. The corpses were taken

Hundreds of women and children lived in a single room at the German concentration camp of Belsen. Hard as it may be to believe, many imprisoned Jews faced even worse conditions.

away and burned to make room for new victims. These gas chambers became a symbol of the evil of Nazism.

Today the mass murder of the Jews is known as the Holocaust (a word meaning "total destruction"). The Holocaust was one of the worst crimes in the history of the world. It was a cold, calm, deliberate attempt to commit genocide—the systematic killing of a whole racial or cultural group. The Holocaust claimed the lives of six million Jews—two thirds of the Jewish population of Europe.

During World War II, few Americans knew about the existence of the death camps. But at the end of the war, when American troops entered the camps, even the toughest soldiers were shocked by what they found there. At the camp called Buchenwald, soldiers found something that especially appalled them. It was a bin full of thousands of pairs of tiny shoes, taken from Jewish babies before they were gassed to death.

When the Allies liberated the concentration camps, they found piles of wedding rings like these, as well as shoes, eyeglasses, and even gold fillings, which the Germans had taken from the Jews to use in their war effort.

The War in Europe and Africa

In 1942, the atrocities of the Holocaust were not well known among the Allied Powers. Their thoughts were on military victory. In order to defeat Germany, President Roosevelt and the British leader Winston Churchill agreed to put their armies under the same command. They also agreed on a plan for the war. The ground war would have to wait, because the German ground forces in Western Europe were too strong to be attacked directly by the British and American armies. The Allies would take some time to build up their forces, and in the meantime, they would bomb Germany as Germany had bombed Britain. They hoped to weaken the will of the German people.

The Allied bombing caused a great deal of damage in Germany, and, just as in Britain, many civilians lost their lives. Still the German armies rolled on. In the summer of 1942 they pushed deep into Egypt. At the same time, the Germans launched a mighty assault against Stalingrad (today Volgograd), a large city in the southern Soviet Union. Hitler believed that he could bring down the Soviet Union by gaining control of the great natural resources of southern Russia, including wheat and oil. Stalingrad was the key to this plan. Stalin, the Soviet dictator for whom the city was named, ordered his troops to hold it at all costs. "Not a step backward!" he cried.

Before the German troops assaulted Stalingrad, their planes bombed much of the city to rubble. But the Russian defenders dug in, hiding in cellars, tunnels, and trenches. When the Germans came, the Russians met them with bullets, riflebutts, and bayonets. The Russians made the Germans pay for every inch of ground. One German officer remembered that it took his men two weeks to capture a single house from the determined Russian troops.

Meanwhile Stalin sent reinforcements to the city, commanded by his best generals. The German advance was halted. Two large Russian forces managed to make a circle around the Germans. The Soviets pounded the trapped enemy with artillery. Then winter came—the Russian winter famous for its terrible cold and great snowstorms (which, you may recall, devastated Napoleon and his troops more than a century earlier). Unable to survive the cold, the German forces surrendered in February 1943. Stalingrad was the first great German defeat, and it helped turn the tide of the war.

So did another Allied victory, over a thousand miles from the snows of Stalingrad, in the blazing desert of North Africa. In a great battle at El Alamein, a British army stopped the German drive through Egypt. Now it was clear that the Germans could be beaten.

The War in the Pacific

The world's largest ocean, the Pacific, lies between Japan and the United States. The Pacific is dotted with thousands of small islands, many of which had been occupied by Japan since World War I. By the time America entered World War II, Japan dominated the western half of the ocean.

Then the Japanese tried to move even closer to the United States. They attacked Midway, a group of islands occupied by the United States. In June 1942, the Japanese and American navies clashed off Midway in a new kind of naval battle, one fought by planes rather than ships. Planes took off from the decks of large ships called aircraft carriers, and attacked the enemy's vessels. In this battle the Japanese lost

A tropical climate made island-hopping difficult for U.S. troops on the Pacific front. Here, a Marine Corps unit must camp on very swampy ground in Guadalcanal.

their four best carriers, and were forced to retreat. The Battle of Midway halted the Japanese advance across the Pacific.

Now the Americans went on the offensive. They began the long process of "island hopping," fighting their way from island to island. Navy ships would carry soldiers and marines to an island occupied by the Japanese. The marines would storm ashore and capture the beaches. Then they would battle their way into the jungles where the Japanese troops were hidden.

The fighting on these Pacific Islands was especially brutal. The Japanese were skilled jungle fighters. They were also brave and dedicated. Again and again they fought to the death, refusing to surrender. But over the next three years the Americans captured island after island, painfully inching toward Japan.

The Home Front

Meanwhile, back in the United States, everyone had joined in the effort to win the war. Civilians bought bonds (small investments in the government) to help pay for the war. They cheerfully accepted shortages of things like meat and gasoline, which had to be sent to the soldiers overseas. People worked day and night in factories, turning out vehicles and weapons for the British, Russian, and American armies.

With so many young men away at war, women flocked to the factories to take their places. During the war years,

Women welders at Ingalls Shipbuilding in Pascagoula, Mississippi.

about six million women joined the labor force, many of them working jobs that women had never held before. A symbol of these new working women was an imaginary character named "Rosie the Riveter." (A rivet fastens pieces of metal together.) Pictures of the time depict Rosie smiling with self-confidence and pride, dressed in overalls and carrying tools, with her hair tied up in a scarf. By doing their jobs so well, said Eleanor Roosevelt, women showed that they were "an indispensable part of the life of the country."

Now Americans overwhelmingly supported the war. Newspapers, radio, and movies told them over and over that they were engaged in a noble battle against a cruel and treacherous enemy. All these powerful feelings stirred up by the war led to an unfortunate injustice against one group of people in America.

The Internment of Japanese-Americans

Large numbers of Japanese-Americans lived on America's West Coast. After the attack on Pearl Harbor, Americans were enraged at the Japanese, and many unfairly turned their anger on Japanese-Americans as well. People said that Japanese-Americans could not be trusted, and accused them of being more loyal to Japan than to the United States. Government officials even claimed that Japanese-Americans were spying for Japan.

The "extraordinary order" signed by President Roosevelt did not specifically order the removal of Japanese-Americans, but it did result in their mass internment. The

A little girl waits to be moved to a resettlement camp with her family.

order said that, to protect "against espionage and against sabotage," military commanders could take people considered dangerous and, without any sort of trial, put them in detention (holding) camps. About two thousand Germans and Italians living in America were declared dangerous enough to be interned in these camps. Their families were given the choice to join them if they wished. But Japanese-Americans were given no choice. More than one hundred and ten thousand Japanese-Americans—men, women, and children—were uprooted from their homes on the West Coast.

Not until the end of 1944 did the government take back the order interning Japanese-Americans. Today most Americans realize that this order was a terrible injustice, an injustice bred by racism. German-Americans and Italian-Americans did not suffer the same extreme treatment. Only people of Asian descent, who looked different from the majority of white Americans, were locked away merely on suspicion of disloyalty. While the United States was fighting for human rights abroad, it had taken away the rights of thousands of innocent people at home.

D-Day

As you have seen, in late 1942 the Allies stopped the German advance in Russia and Egypt. A few months later, the Allies started to take Europe back from the Germans.

In the summer of 1943, the British and Americans invaded Germany's ally, Italy. It took the British and Americans a year to fight their way to Rome, the Italian capital. Then, two days after the capture of Rome, a huge Allied force landed in northern France to mount a gigantic assault against German troops in the area called Normandy. The American general Dwight Eisenhower was in charge of the Allied forces.

On June 6, 1944, a day that would be remembered as "D-Day," the Allied armies struck. At dawn, tens of thousands of Allied troops swarmed onto the beaches of Normandy. At some places the Allies quickly overcame the outnumbered Germans. But at a place called Omaha Beach, American troops met with fierce resistance. The beach was covered with mines, barbed wire, and German "pillboxes"—small forts with machine-gunners inside. From cliffs above the beach, German artillery fire rained down on the American landing craft. Many men were blown up in their boats. Others drowned or were shot as they struggled to wade ashore in their heavy combat gear. Still others were cut down as they moved up the beach.

Slowly and painfully the Americans fought their way ashore. A small, daring group of U.S. Rangers decided to capture the artillery on the cliffs. They scaled the cliffs with ropes, dodging German hand grenades as they climbed. Finally they reached the top and destroyed the German guns.

At the end of a long day of fighting, the Allies

American troops wade to shore from their barge on D-Day.

had taken the beaches of Normandy and moved inland about a mile. In the following weeks more and more Allied troops would land—one million in the first month alone. Over the next few months, this mighty wave would hurl the Germans out of France; by October most of the country was liberated. Meanwhile, the Soviets, having driven the Germans out of Russia, were sweeping across Eastern Europe. By the beginning of 1945 all that remained of the Nazi empire was Germany itself.

Meeting at Yalta

In February, 1945, the three main Allied leaders—Churchill, Roosevelt, and Stalin—met at the city of Yalta in the Soviet Union. Now that Germany was almost defeated, they wanted to make plans for the future. It was agreed that Germany would be occupied by troops from all of the Allied nations. It would be divided into four "zones" or parts, each run by one of the four occupiers—Britain, the United States, France, and the Soviet Union.

Churchill and Roosevelt were also concerned about the fate of the Eastern European nations. These countries had been conquered by the Germans and were now occupied by Soviet troops. Churchill in particular worried that the Nazi domination of Eastern Europe would be replaced by Soviet domination. Stalin had already set up a Communist government in Poland. Under pressure from the other Allied leaders at the Yalta meeting, Stalin had agreed to hold free elections in Eastern Europe after the war. But as Churchill feared, Stalin had no intention of keeping this promise.

Churchill, Roosevelt, and Stalin at the Yalta Conference.

FDR Dies; Truman Becomes President

Harry S Truman's well-known sign, "The buck stops here," indicates his willingness to face and make tough decisions in order to lead our country through one of its most trying periods.

At their meeting in Yalta, Churchill noticed that Roosevelt looked frail and sick. Before the war, the president, despite his disability, had been vigorous and energetic. But the tremendous strain of the past four years had worn him down. When he returned to the United States, he gave a speech to Congress. For the first time, instead of struggling to stand up with the help of braces, FDR spoke from his wheelchair.

One day in April 1945, FDR was having his picture painted by an artist. Suddenly he said, "I have a terrific headache," and fell unconscious. A few hours later he was dead. Americans mourned the man who had led them through the long years of Depression and war, only to die with victory in plain sight.

FDR was succeeded by his vice president, Harry S Truman. (The "S" is spelled without a period because, oddly enough, "S" is not an abbreviation but Truman's whole middle name.) On his first day in office, a reporter asked Truman how he felt about becoming president so suddenly. Truman, who had grown up on a farm, replied, "Have you ever had a bull or a load of hay fall on you?" Although the new president felt crushed by the weight of his responsibilities, in the last months of the war, he would prove to be a tough, effective leader.

Victory in Europe

The war in Europe was rapidly drawing to a close. British and American armies invaded Germany from the west; Russian armies invaded it from the east. At the end of April the Anglo-American and Russian forces came together deep inside Germany, and Germany's capital, Berlin, was falling to Russian troops. A few days after the Allied armies linked up, Adolf Hitler was dead. The German dictator who had plunged the world into war shot himself to avoid being captured by his enemies. On May 7, 1945, Germany surrendered.

The soldiers who died at the Battle of Iwo Jima are commemorated by the Iwo Jima Memorial in Arlington, Virginia. The memorial stands across the river from Washington, D.C.

The surrender of Germany left Japan to fight on alone. But by then Japan too was nearly defeated. For almost three years the Americans had battled their way across the Pacific. Island after island—Guadalcanal, Saipan, Iwo Jima—had fallen after furious fighting. Then, in April 1945, the Americans launched an assault on Okinawa, a large, well-fortified island only four hundred miles south of Japan. It took American soldiers and marines almost three months to fight their way from one end of the island to the other.

Shortly after they captured Okinawa, the American troops learned that Germany had surrendered. Now they started preparing for the invasion of Japan itself. But as it turned out, Okinawa was the last battle of the Pacific war. Japan would be defeated not by an invasion but by the use of a terrible new weapon.

The Atomic Bomb

In the 1930s scientists found that by splitting the nucleus of certain heavy atoms, like uranium 235, they could release an unbelievable amount of energy. Scientists began working on a way to use this new form of energy for military purposes. They hoped to create a "superbomb" that would be more powerful than any weapon that had ever existed. As the war went on, the United States government invested more and more money in this attempt. Then, in 1942, it set up the Manhattan Project, which coordinated the efforts of all the individual scientists working on the atomic bomb.

Scientists in America worked hard on the project partly because they feared that Germany might develop the "superbomb" first. But it was not until Germany had already been defeated that an atomic bomb was ready for testing. In July 1945, the first atomic bomb was set off in the New Mexico desert. It exploded with the force of thirteen thousand tons of ordinary explosive. The whole desert flooded suddenly with a light brighter than the sun. The ground rocked as if hit by a powerful earthquake, then a wind as strong as a hurricane swept across the desert. The explosion released huge amounts of deadly radiation. The scientists saw a gigantic cloud rise high into the air, taking the shape of a mushroom. The vast destructive potential of the bomb made one of the scientists remember a line from the Hindu scriptures: "I am become Death, the shatterer of worlds."

Hiroshima, Nagasaki, and the Surrender of Japan

Meanwhile, despite the defeat of Germany, the Japanese refused to surrender. Beaten on all fronts, Japan had retreated from the territories it had conquered in China and Southeast Asia. But it still had two million soldiers inside Japan itself. Japanese civilians, too, were being armed to resist an invasion. President Truman knew that

A scene from Nagasaki one month after the atom bomb was detonated there.

The mushroom cloud from the second atom bomb dropped on Japan, at the industrial city of Nagasaki.

the Japanese were trained to fight to the death. He believed that Japan could be invaded only at a huge cost in American lives. So in order to force the Japanese to surrender, Truman ordered the dropping of two atomic bombs on Japan.

The first bomb was dropped on August 6, 1945, on the city of Hiroshima. In the first flash of the giant fireball, eighty thousand people died in a single moment. Tens of thousands more died later, from burns or from the effects of radiation. Most of the city was burned to the ground.

Even after the bombing of Hiroshima, the Japanese government rejected American demands for surrender. Three days later a second atomic bomb was dropped, this time on the city of Nagasaki. Finally, the Japanese government, fearing the destruction of the whole country, agreed to surrender to the Allies.

World War II was over. In six years of conflict, some forty million people around the world had lost their lives. A terrifying new weapon had ended one of the most terrible wars in the history of the world.

ALLIES BECOME ENEMIES
The "Superpowers" Square Off

At the end of World War II, the most powerful nations in the world were the United States and the Soviet Union. Although these two "superpowers" had managed to overlook their differences and fight together as allies, once the war ended they became enemies.

The two nations had very different political systems. The United States was (and is) a democratic country with a government freely elected by its citizens, whose individual rights were (and are) guaranteed by the Constitution. But the Soviet Union had become an oppressive totalitarian state, in which all aspects of life—economic, political, and social—were controlled by the government. In the name of "the good of the state," Soviet citizens were denied freedom of speech, freedom of the press, and freedom of religion—rights especially cherished by Americans.

The United States and the Soviet Union also differed in their economic systems. America was (and is) a capitalist country, in which individuals and businesses are free to make many economic decisions. The Soviet Union, however, had a Communist system, in which the government controlled all aspects of the economy. The Communist rulers of the Soviet Union believed that capitalism was evil and must be overthrown wherever it existed. (You can read a more detailed account of the differences between capitalism and communism in the World Civilization section of this book.)

The Truman Doctrine and the Marshall Plan

After World War II, the Soviet Union set up Communist governments in the countries of Eastern Europe. In 1946 the British prime minister, Winston Churchill, declared

The United Nations

When World War II ended, people all over the world hoped for a peace that would last. You might remember that after World War I, people also hoped for a lasting peace, and put their hopes in the League of Nations. The League of Nations was a noble but unsuccessful attempt to establish a body that could unite the various governments of the world. Though the League failed, the idea behind it was reborn after World War II in an organization set up by the Allied powers, called the United Nations.

Today almost all countries of the world belong to the United Nations, which has its headquarters in New York City. The UN, as it is called, tries to maintain peace by helping countries resolve their differences without going to war. The UN also organizes cooperative efforts among various nations to bring help where it is needed, such as, for example, by getting food to people in famine-stricken areas.

Despite its best efforts, the UN has not been very successful in keeping peace around the world. During the UN's early years, its effectiveness was limited because two of its most important members, the United States and the Soviet Union, almost always disagreed.

The UN remains active and important today. Take some time to check in newspapers or news magazines to see what activities the UN has been engaged in recently.

that "an iron curtain has descended over Europe." He meant that Europe was now divided in two, with a strong barrier between the two parts. Western Europe was capitalist and democratic, while Eastern Europe was ruled by Communist governments set up by the Soviets. Churchill went on to say that the Soviets were trying to spread their power even farther. He called on the democratic countries to resist the spread of Soviet power and Communist ideas.

America's president, Harry Truman, agreed with Churchill. In 1947 he proclaimed the Truman Doctrine, which said that the United States would come to the aid of any country threatened by communism. The Truman Doctrine got its first test in Greece, where a Communist group was trying to overthrow the government. The United States sent Greece money to buy military equipment and American officers to work with the Greek Army. By late 1949 the Communists were defeated.

Truman realized that many European countries needed economic aid. Because of World War II, many cities were in ruins, and many factories and roads were destroyed. To help rebuild the economy of Western Europe, the United States began a great program in 1948 called the Marshall Plan (after Secretary of State George C. Marshall). Under the Marshall Plan, the United States spent billions of dollars to rebuild Western Europe. By giving so much money to countries like Britain, France, West Germany, and Italy, the United States made many friends, and made sure that these countries would take America's side in case of a war against the Soviet Union.

The Cold War

The United States and the Soviet Union did engage in a kind of war, but this conflict was very different from World War II: it wasn't a "hot" war with bombs and bullets flying. Instead, it was a long, tense period of hostility that often came dangerously close to war. We call this period of hostility, from 1946 to 1991, the Cold War.

Throughout the Cold War, the Soviet Union encouraged Communist movements throughout the world, and helped Communists come to power in China and other nations. Everywhere Communists came to power, they set up harsh totalitarian governments that took away the rights and freedom of the people.

This map shows the division of Europe after World War II into democratic countries, Communist countries, and nonaligned countries.

Meanwhile the United States tried to prevent the spread of communism. It helped countries that were determined to resist the Soviets. Often the countries the United States supported were democratic, but sometimes the United States supported brutal dictators as long as they were anti-Soviet and anti-Communist.

Although most Americans fiercely opposed communism during the Cold War years, just a couple of decades earlier, especially during the 1930s, some Americans, along with some Europeans as well, sympathized with the ideas of communism and looked to the Soviet Union with great hope. The misery suffered by Americans during the Great Depression made some think that communism, with its commitment to economic equality, offered a better way. They thought that the Russian Revolution of 1917 would lead to the creation of a truly classless society, in which there would be even greater equality than people enjoyed in countries like America and England. But they were disappointed and disillusioned by the actions of leaders like Stalin, under whom life for many in the Soviet Union turned into a nightmare.

A British writer by the name of George Orwell saw very clearly what happens when a revolutionary ideal like equality for all is betrayed by corrupt and power-hungry leaders. He dramatized such a betrayal of ideals in his novel called Animal Farm, *in which a group of animals rise up against their oppressive human owners, only to find themselves later under the even more oppressive rule of the pigs. You can read a selection from* Animal Farm *in the Stories and Speeches section of this book.*

The "Military-Industrial Complex" and the Nuclear Arms Race

During the Cold War the United States and the Soviet Union both built up huge military forces. The United States government spent more and more of its budget on defense: producing weapons, training troops, and making other preparations in case the Cold War should turn hot. Most Americans accepted this military buildup as necessary in order to protect the country and its allies from the Soviets.

But some people worried that the military, along with the businesses that provided it with weapons and supplies, were gaining too much influence over the government. One man who felt this way was Dwight Eisenhower, who had led the Allied troops in Europe in World War II. Eisenhower was such a hero to the American people they elected him president in 1952. He served two terms, and when he left office in 1961 he gave a famous speech in which he pointed out the danger of what he called "the military-industrial complex." Eisenhower warned that the combined power of the military and the weapons industry could grow to someday threaten America's democratic system.

The greatest threat of all in the Cold War years, however, was the danger of a nuclear war. The United States, as you know, had developed the first atomic bombs and dropped two on Japan to end World War II. In 1949, Americans were shocked to learn that the Soviets had developed and tested an atomic bomb of their own. American scientists jokingly called the first Soviet bomb "Joe I" (after the first name of the Soviet dictator, Joseph Stalin). But the fact that the Soviets now had atomic weapons was no joke. As long as the United States was the only country with atomic weapons, the Soviets would not risk war with the United States or its allies. But now that the Soviets had atomic bombs as well, Americans feared that the Soviets might try to attack the United States or Western Europe.

President Truman declared that America would build an even more powerful kind of nuclear weapon. This was to be the hydrogen bomb, or "H-bomb." The H-bomb would work by fusion (bringing atoms together) rather than by fission (splitting atoms apart). In the process it would release far more energy than the original atomic bomb. In 1954, an H-bomb was tested on a deserted island in the Pacific. It exploded with a force one thousand times as great as that of the bomb dropped on Hiroshima. This H-bomb released enough radiation into the air to kill every living person in an area the size of New Jersey.

In the meantime, however, the Soviets had also discovered the secret of making the H-bomb. From now on the Americans and the Soviets would try to stay ahead of each other by building more powerful and effective nuclear weapons. This process became known as the nuclear "arms race."

The arms race affected people even in their day-to-day lives. Some families dug deep in the ground to build bomb shelters, in which they hoped to survive a nuclear war. In American schools, just as you probably go through fire drills today, children would go through drills to practice what to do in case of a nuclear attack. Even as everyday life went on, there was always a lingering anxiety that, at any moment, terrible destruction could fall from the sky.

McCarthyism

From the standpoint of the United States, 1949 was one of the worst years of the Cold War. Not only did the Soviets develop an atomic bomb, but a group of Communists took over the government of China, the most populous country in the world. Then early in 1950, a British scientist was arrested for selling America's atomic secrets to the Soviet Union. Many Americans began to grow suspicious: perhaps the Communists were being helped by other spies and traitors within the United States.

America's setbacks created a climate of fear and suspicion. A Republican senator named Joseph McCarthy decided to take advantage of this atmosphere. McCarthy had served one term as a senator and was worried that he might not be reelected. So he set out to make himself famous. He did this by declaring that the government of the United States was full of Communist agents.

In February 1950, McCarthy gave a speech in which he attacked the government for not standing up to communism. Then he waved a piece of paper over his head. He said, "I have here in my hand a list of 205 [people] who were known to the secretary of state as being members of the Communist Party and who, nevertheless, are still working and shaping policy in the State Department."

This was an outright lie. McCarthy had no such list. No one knows what was really on the piece of paper he waved. McCarthy was a dishonest man who only wanted publicity for himself, but to some people, McCarthy's charges seemed to make sense. If America was losing to the Communists abroad, perhaps it was because the State Department—which deals with foreign affairs—was full of Communists.

McCarthy found that his wild accusations made him popular, so he kept making wilder and wilder ones. In 1951 he said that the secretary of defense was at the head of a Communist plot to take over the government. The charge was ridiculous, but the secretary of defense quit his job. McCarthy had gained the power to ruin careers.

McCarthy's way of smearing people as Communists became known as "McCarthyism." He was not the only one to practice it. Even before McCarthy's rise, suspected Communists were kept out of government jobs. Thousands of people were fired or forced to resign from government positions. Often there was little or no evidence that they had Communist ties. Some people compared this hunt for Communists to the witch-hunts of colonial America, in which many innocent women were hanged or jailed for being "witches."

By the mid-1950s, though, America had turned against McCarthyism. In 1954 McCarthy came up with wild new charges against the U.S. Army, which he said was protecting Communists. When the Senate held hearings on these charges, the hearings were shown on television, and most of the people watching were repelled by McCarthy. They realized now that he was a bully and a liar. The Senate passed a resolution condemning McCarthy, and his own Republican Party turned against him. Dwight Eisenhower, the Republican who had been elected president in 1952, declared that "McCarthy*ism*" had become "McCarthy*wasim*."

The Korean War Begins

The "Communists" McCarthy chased were mostly imaginary. But his witch-hunt was so popular partly because, in the early 1950s, the Cold War briefly turned hot when American troops fought against Communist forces in Korea.

Korea is a country that lies on a peninsula between China and Japan. It was one of the many Asian countries conquered by Japan before the Second World War. After the war, the southern part of Korea was occupied by the United States, while the northern part was occupied by the Soviet Union. As they did in Eastern Europe, the Soviets set up a totalitarian government in North Korea.

In June 1950, the North Korean army suddenly invaded South Korea. The North Koreans quickly captured the South Korean capital of Seoul. Within weeks they had taken over all but the southern tip of the peninsula. President Truman declared, "The attack upon the Republic of Korea makes it plain beyond all doubt that the

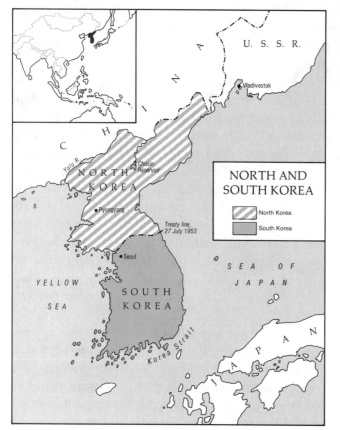

North Korean troops invaded nearly all of South Korea, but were beaten back to the uppermost dotted line. The final truce divided the country in half.

international Communist movement is prepared to use armed invasion to conquer independent nations." With the support of other countries in the United Nations, Truman decided to send American troops to the aid of South Korea.

Three months after the Communist invasion, a large American force landed on the coast of Korea near Seoul. After savage fighting between American and North Korean troops, the city was recaptured by the American forces. As the Americans pushed farther inland, the North Koreans began to retreat. The Americans chased them back into North Korea itself.

Just as quickly as South Korea had fallen to the North Koreans, North Korea fell to the Americans. By the end of October, American troops had driven all the way to North Korea's border with China. It seemed as if the two parts of Korea might now be united under a pro-American government. Then something happened that destroyed this hope—Communist China joined the war.

Korea: Heroism and Frustration

At the end of November 1950, the Chinese struck. Hundreds of thousands of Chinese troops came pouring into North Korea to attack the Americans. Badly outnumbered, the Americans were driven back down the peninsula.

At a place called the Chosin Reservoir, a force of American marines was completely surrounded by Chinese troops. In order to escape, the marines had to fight their way to the sea. For three weeks they trudged across rugged mountains in terrible winter weather. In some places the snow was two or three feet deep. Temperatures fell below zero. Water froze in the men's canteens; their food was too frozen to eat. Many men were crippled by frostbitten feet. All the while the marines were fighting off ferocious Chinese attacks. Despite the valiant efforts of the marines, within a month the Chinese had driven them back into South Korea. Fighting went on in the border area between the two Koreas.

The American commander, General Douglas MacArthur, was angry that the Chinese had driven his troops out of North Korea. He wanted the United States to attack China itself. President Truman refused to do so. He knew that by attacking China, America would risk war with China's ally, the Soviet Union. Such a conflict might become World War III—a world war even more terrible than the first two, since it would be fought with nuclear weapons.

Panmunjom, Korea, site of the armistice ending the Korean War.

By June 1951, the Korean War had become a stalemate. The Chinese could not break through into South Korea; the Americans could not advance into North Korea. Fighting continued off and on until 1953, when a truce was signed. Even today Korea remains divided into two parts. Some Americans were frustrated that the war ended without a clear-cut victory. But others thought that the Korean War had been a success. The United States had stood up to Communist aggression while avoiding war with the Soviet Union.

AMERICAN LIFE IN THE 1950S

A Decade of Prosperity

Despite the battles going on overseas, for most Americans at home the decade of the 1950s was a time of optimism and prosperity. In fact, the United States in this period was by far the most prosperous nation on earth. The Second World War had hurt the economies of Europe and Asia, but it had helped the economy of the United States. It lifted the country out of the Depression, and put almost everybody back to work. Unlike the other nations that fought in the war, the United States was not bombed or invaded and Americans did not have to rebuild their cities, roads, and factories.

During World War II, Americans had little to spend money on. Most of the goods coming out of the factories were sent overseas for the soldiers. So the people at home worked and saved their money. After the war, they had lots of money saved and were ready to start buying things again. In the meantime, millions of fighting men were getting out of the service. After more than three years of war, they were eager to enjoy the things that they had been living without—things like cars, new houses, and electrical appliances. With all this demand for new goods, industry boomed.

The government helped as well. In 1944 Congress passed a law creating a "GI Bill of Rights." (A "GI," for "Government Issue," was slang for an American service-man.) The GI Bill helped veterans finish their educations. When veterans enrolled in colleges or technical schools, the government paid their tuitions, the fees charged by the schools. Millions of veterans took advantage of this program; many went to college who could not otherwise have afforded to do so. The new skills and knowl-edge they gained further strengthened the American economy.

The GI Bill also helped veterans buy their own homes with loans from the govern-ment. By doing so, it fueled the demand for new housing. Soon millions of new homes were being built all over the country. By the end of the 1950s, 60 percent of Americans owned their own homes.

In the Suburbs and on the Road

Most of the new houses built after World War II were built not in large cities but in the surrounding areas, or suburbs. Soon most cities were surrounded by large, middle-class communities. The homes in the suburbs were often in "housing developments" where every house looked like every other house. Still, the suburbs gave more people a chance to own their own homes than ever before.

The growth of the suburbs affected American life in many ways. For one thing, it made the automobile even more important. Americans had always loved their cars, but now they really needed them to get around. Unlike the cities, the new suburbs usually had no mass transportation (buses or trains). By the end of the 1950s, three quarters of American families owned a car.

With so many more people traveling by car, the nation's roads were getting too crowded. In 1956 Congress voted to build a vast system of interstate highways—roads of four lanes or more that would crisscross the country. The interstate highway program would be the largest building program ever undertaken by any government.

Americans drove along their big new roads in big new cars. In the 1950s the automobile became a "status symbol," a way of showing off. People wanted to have larger, more expensive, more luxurious cars than their friends. Cars grew bigger every year, until they were the size of small boats. They came in every color of the rainbow and grew into strange new shapes—some had huge "tail fins" that made them look like giant metal fish. The American automobile had come a long way from Henry Ford's cheap, plain black Model T.

The TV Age Begins

Automobiles were not the only machines Americans spent their money on. In the 1950s American homes were suddenly full of gadgets designed to make life easier—

everything from high-powered washing machines to electric carving knives. Because of all the appliances Americans bought in the 1950s, the use of electricity tripled during the decade. But the gadget that really changed American life was the television set.

Scientists had been experimenting with TV since the 1920s. But it wasn't until the late 1940s that television technology really got off the ground. In the early 1950s, national broadcasting began, and suddenly everyone wanted to own a TV. By the mid-1950s, two thirds of American homes had a set. Now in the evenings families gathered around the television as they used to gather around the radio. Soon Americans were spending almost as much time watching TV every day as they were spending at school or work!

Many people had high hopes for television; it promised to bring the whole world into everyone's home. In the 1940s, one writer predicted that a TV set would be "a combination movie theater, museum, educator, news reporter, playhouse, daily picture magazine, political forum and discussion center, . . . art gallery, . . . opera and ballet theater, plus a few other things rolled into one." But it turned out that most Americans were not very interested in watching things like opera and ballet on TV. The most popular shows were silly comedies, or shows about the adventures of detectives or cowboys. Some people began to refer to TV as the "boob tube."

But not everything on television was junk. Thanks to the news programs on TV, for the first time people could really watch history taking place. Joseph McCarthy suffered his downfall when TV showed him as a liar and a bully. Later, people would begin to support the civil rights movement after TV cameras showed shocking pictures of African-American demonstrators being attacked by police. In 1968 Americans felt proud as they gathered around their TV sets to watch the first American astronauts step onto the moon.

SEGREGATION AND CIVIL RIGHTS

The "Jim Crow" Laws

While the 1950s were good times for most Americans, African-Americans did not enjoy the general prosperity.

From the beginnings of American history, most black people had lived in the Southern states where they had first been brought as slaves to work on plantations. In 1900, about nine tenths of all African-Americans lived in the South. Then, as we have seen, blacks, hoping to find new opportunities, began coming North around the time of World War I. During and after World War II, the stream of northward migration became a great flood. By 1950 almost one third of African-Americans were living outside the South. But many who came North were disappointed to find that they were still not treated as equals. If you had driven through most Northern suburbs in the 1950s, you would not have seen many black faces.

But it was the blacks who stayed behind in the South who were still the most oppressed. In the South, most black people were not allowed a basic right of American citizens: the right to vote. Southern whites used many tricks to keep African-Americans from voting. Sometimes African-Americans were told that they had to pay a "poll tax" in order to vote, a fee that most blacks were too poor to pay. At other times they were forced to take complicated tests that white voters did not have to take. And sometimes African-Americans were simply threatened with violence if they tried to vote.

Furthermore, blacks in the South were held down by a rigid system of segregation (separation) of the races. Blacks were not allowed to mix with whites; they had to live in all-black neighborhoods and go to all-black schools. In fact, the Southern states passed hundreds of laws designed to keep the races separate. Together these were known as "Jim Crow" laws. ("Jim Crow" was an insulting slang term for an African-American.)

Some Jim Crow laws said that whites and blacks had to be kept separate on buses and trains. Others said that hospitals had to have different sections for whites and blacks, or that whites and blacks could not play on the same sports teams. They could not even use the same water fountains or bathrooms. All over the South, public bathrooms were marked with signs saying "Whites Only" or "Colored." Some of the

Jim Crow laws were simply ridiculous—one Alabama law said that no black person was allowed to play checkers with a white person!

But the laws were no laughing matter. They strictly limited the opportunities of African-Americans. Furthermore, they humiliated blacks by telling them they were too "inferior" to mix with white people. They created a system as oppressive and unjust as apartheid in South Africa (see the World Civilization section of this book). In the 1950s, African-Americans' anger at the Jim Crow laws fueled a great movement to end segregation in American life: the civil rights movement.

A man mounts the stairs to the "colored entrance" of a movie theater in Mississippi.

A. Philip Randolph: Pioneer for Civil Rights

It was in the 1950s and 1960s that the civil rights movement would achieve its greatest successes. But the movement had begun long before. Since the time of slavery, African-American leaders like Frederick Douglass and later W. E. B. Du Bois had fought for equal rights for black Americans.

From the 1920s to the 1950s, another leader was especially important in the fight for civil rights. His name was A. Philip Randolph. In the 1920s, Randolph became head of the largest black labor union, the union of railway porters. (Porters are railway workers whose job it is to help passengers.) He would become one of the most powerful figures in the American labor movement. (To review the rise of American labor unions, see the American Civilization section of Book Five in this series.)

During World War II, Randolph was angered by the treatment of black workers in the defense industry. In factories turning out weapons and vehicles for the Allies, African-Americans could get only the worst-paying

Civil rights leader A. Philip Randolph.

jobs, with all of the better jobs going to whites. Randolph met with President Roosevelt and asked him to make this kind of discrimination illegal. The president said he would look into the problem, but he took no action. Randolph declared that he would lead one hundred thousand African-Americans in a great demonstration (mass protest) in Washington, D.C. The president knew that such a demonstration would be highly embarrassing. The United States was fighting against German racism overseas, and now Randolph wanted to call attention to racism at home. So in June 1941 FDR issued an order banning discrimination against workers in government or the defense industry "because of race, creed, color, or national origin."

African-Americans in the Armed Forces

Thanks to Randolph, good jobs in the defense industry were now open to blacks. But African-Americans in the armed forces were still segregated. Throughout World War II, black soldiers served mainly in all-black units. During and after the war, Randolph protested this injustice. In early 1948, he met with President Truman, and asked him to integrate the armed forces. Like President Roosevelt before him, President Truman listened to Randolph's request but put off taking any action. So Randolph traveled around the country, making fiery speeches. He urged young black men to refuse to join the armed forces. Randolph declared:

> We will fill up the jails with young men who refuse to serve. And I am prepared to fight the Jim Crow army even if I am convicted of treason and have to rot in jail. The time has come when we can no longer fight under the flag of segregation.

President Truman gave in. In July 1948 he put out an order ending discrimination in the armed forces. Two years later, when the Korean War broke out, black and white Americans fought side by side.

Jackie Robinson and the Integration of Big League Baseball

Imagine someone telling Michael Jordan, "Sorry, you can't play in the National Basketball Association because you're black." Ridiculous? Yes, though a situation like this existed as recently as the 1940s. At that time, in professional major league baseball, the umpire's cry of "Play ball!" applied only to white players.

African-Americans were not permitted to play in the major leagues, but instead played in a separate league for black players. There was no law against African-Americans playing "big league" baseball; they were kept out by habit and prejudice. Until, that is, the general manager of the Brooklyn Dodgers, Branch Rickey, decided to find a player to break the color barrier in major league baseball.

Rickey found Jack Roosevelt Robinson playing in the "Negro leagues." Jackie Robinson had been a star in baseball, football, basketball, and track at the University of California at Los Angeles: there was no doubt about his athletic ability. But Rickey also wanted something else: a man strong enough not to fight back against the insults and abuse that were sure to come his way as the first African-American in the "big leagues."

At first Robinson was confused: "You don't want a ballplayer who's afraid to fight back, do you?" he asked Rickey. Rickey responded, "I want a ballplayer with enough guts not to fight back." Rickey knew that if Robinson got into fights, then prejudiced whites would take that as proof that black players couldn't get along with white players in the major leagues.

Jackie Robinson accepted the challenge. When he took his place at first base in April of 1947, he was greeted with jeers and insults. But he kept his cool, and gradually, attitudes changed. Already by the end of the 1947 season, four more African-American players joined major league teams. Robinson himself was voted Rookie of the Year. In the 1949 season, he had the highest batting average in the National League, and was voted the league's Most Valuable Player. His determination and ability opened the way for players of all races to succeed in major league professional sports in America.

Brown v. Board of Education

One of the most important civil rights groups today is the National Association for the Advancement of Colored People, or NAACP. You may recall reading in Book Five of this series how the NAACP was founded in 1910 by a group including the great African-American scholar, W. E. B. DuBois. In the early 1950s, the NAACP set out to abolish the system of segregated public education. Many schools in the North, and almost all schools in the South, were segregated. This was especially unfair to black children in the South because the Southern states spent much more money on their all-white schools than they did on their all-black schools.

In order to end the segregation in public schools, the NAACP decided to work through the legal system. In 1954, Thurgood Marshall, a brilliant African-American lawyer, argued a case before the U.S. Supreme Court. The case was *Brown v. Board of Education of Topeka* ("v." stands for "versus," which means "against"). Oliver Brown was an African-American living in Topeka, Kansas; his daughter had been kept out of the local elementary school and forced to attend an all-black school far from her home. Thurgood Marshall argued that this discrimination in schooling went against the U.S. Constitution.

The Supreme Court agreed. It decided that segregated schools violated the rights of African-American students. The people who ran Jim Crow school systems said that they provided "separate but equal" schools for the two races. This was not true, since so much more money was spent on the white schools. But now the Supreme Court said that even if the same amount of money were spent on black and white schools, segregation would still be unfair to black children.

According to the court, segregation gave black children "a feeling of inferiority as to their status in the community that may affect their hearts and minds in a way never to be undone." In other words, the system hurt black children by telling them

they were not good enough to go to school with whites. The justices went on to say, "We conclude that in the field of public education the doctrine of 'separate but equal' has no place. Separate educational facilities are inherently unequal."

After the Supreme Court's decision that American schools must be integrated, when black students tried to enroll in all-white schools, they were sometimes threatened or even attacked. In Mississippi, Tennessee, and Arkansas, police and soldiers had to be called in to protect black students from white mobs.

The decision in *Brown v. Board of Education* marked the beginning of the end of segregated education. It was also a great victory for the NAACP and Thurgood Marshall. Marshall became famous and admired, and in 1967 he would become the first African-American justice of the Supreme Court.

Thurgood Marshall leaving the U.S. Supreme Court after arguing against segregation in Brown v. Board of Education.

Rosa Parks and the Montgomery Bus Boycott

One day in December 1955, an African-American woman named Rosa Parks got on a bus in Montgomery, Alabama. As on all buses in Montgomery, white people were sitting in the front and black people in the back. Parks sat down in a row of seats just behind the "whites only" section. The bus was already crowded.

Two stops later, some more white people got on the bus. One of them couldn't find a seat in the white section. So the bus driver called back to the four people sitting in the first "black" row, ordering them all out of the row so the white man could sit down. Three of the black passengers obeyed him. But the fourth—Rosa Parks—stayed in her seat. She was tired from a long day's work, and she didn't see why she had to stand up just so a white man could sit down. The driver called the police, who arrested Parks because she had broken the Jim Crow law which said that white and black bus passengers had to be separated.

African-Americans all over Montgomery admired Parks's courage and were angered by her arrest. They decided to protest by boycotting the city's bus system. African-Americans refused to ride the buses until black and white passengers were treated equally. Since most bus passengers in the city were black, the boycott would cost the bus company a lot of money.

Still, the bus company refused to do away with its Jim Crow rules. So African-Americans went on with the boycott for more than a year. Instead of taking the bus to work, black people walked or used taxis owned by blacks. The boycott was a hardship, but Montgomery's African-Americans were determined to fight for their rights.

In December 1956, a little over a year after the boycott began, the U.S. Supreme Court made a decision. According to the court, Montgomery's way of segregating buses went against the Constitution. The city's buses had to be integrated; the boycott was over. People all over the country were impressed by the determination of the African-American citizens of Montgomery. They were especially impressed by the young black minister who had led the boycott—Dr. Martin Luther King, Jr.

Rosa Parks is fingerprinted after being arrested for refusing to yield her bus seat to a white person.

Martin Luther King, Jr.

When he led the bus boycott, Martin Luther King, Jr. was only twenty-six years old. King had been born in Atlanta, Georgia, where his father was a minister. King himself became a minister while he was still a student at Morehouse College. Later he went to Boston University, where he received a Ph.D. (A Ph.D. is the highest degree a university can give. King was addressed as "Dr." [Doctor] King because that is the title given to someone who has a Ph.D.)

For several reasons, King would come to be considered the most important of all the civil rights leaders. He was highly educated and a spellbinding speaker. He was courageous, willing to risk jail and even death for the sake of the cause. But perhaps above all, he attracted so many followers because of his high moral ideals. As a Christian, he followed the teachings of Jesus, which say that you should love everyone, even those who persecute you. To his followers in Montgomery he said:

> If we are arrested every day, if we are exploited every day, if we are trampled over every day, don't ever let anyone pull you so low as to hate them. We must use the weapon of love.

The movement King led was strictly nonviolent. King said that African-Americans should not take up weapons, but should fight an unjust system by using the method of "passive resistance." Passive resistance meant quietly but firmly refusing to obey an unjust law. Rosa Parks was practicing passive resistance when she refused to get up from her seat on the bus. If enough people practiced passive resistance, King thought, the unjust laws would have to be changed.

One effective form of passive resistance was the "sit-in." In early 1960, four black college students sat down at a lunch counter in Greensboro, North Carolina. No one

Civil Disobedience: An American Tradition

In encouraging passive resistance, Martin Luther King, Jr., was influenced by the great Indian leader Gandhi (whom you can read about in the World Civilization section of this book). Through Gandhi, King inherited the ideas of a nineteenth-century American writer and philosopher, Henry David Thoreau (1817–62).

For part of his life, Thoreau lived in a small cabin he built by Walden Pond, near Concord, Massachusetts. In 1846, he spent a night in the Concord jail for refusing to pay his taxes. He could not, he said, pay taxes to support a government that allowed slavery and that was engaged in a war to take lands from Mexico (which you read about in Book Four of this series).

To explain his actions, Thoreau wrote a powerful essay called "Civil Disobedience," which influenced Gandhi and others. "Unjust laws exist," said Thoreau; "shall we be content to obey them, . . . or shall we transgress them at once?" If, said Thoreau, a law "requires you to be the agent of injustice to another, then I say, break the law."

The spirit of civil disobedience—of disobeying (by nonviolent means) unjust laws in order to achieve justice—was revived in the American civil rights movement. Those who, with Martin Luther King, Jr., disobeyed Jim Crow laws in the South were putting into practice the principle, as stated by Thoreau, that "it is not desirable to cultivate a respect for the law, so much as for the right."

Demonstrators sit in at a "whites only" waiting area in Birmingham, Alabama.

would wait on them, because only white customers were served there. Though the black students were taunted by white customers, they kept on sitting there until closing time. The next day a larger group of students showed up to "sit in," and the day after that even more students came.

Other people heard of the students' demonstration. All over the South, African-Americans began to "sit in" at restaurants and stores that refused to serve them. By sitting in, the demonstrators were calling attention to the injustice of Jim Crow rules. Martin Luther King, Jr., encouraged this tactic. In October 1960, King himself was arrested for taking part in a sit-in at a department store in Atlanta.

King in Birmingham

In 1963, King led a campaign to end segregation in the large city of Birmingham, Alabama. King called Birmingham the most segregated city in America. The Birmingham police were notorious for their cruel treatment of African-Americans. When King came to Birmingham, he led boycotts, sit-ins, and marches. Once he was arrested and thrown into jail for a week. But nothing would make him or his followers back down.

As the demonstrations went on week after week, the Birmingham police became more and more brutal. They started using fire hoses and police dogs to break up the marches. Snarling police dogs chased black men, women, and children. Fire hoses shot powerful jets of water that knocked the marchers to the ground.

Pictures of segregationist whites cruelly mistreating the black people of Birmingham were printed in newspapers and broadcast on TV screens around the nation. Outraged by what they saw, many Americans condemned the cruelty of the whites and began to sympathize with the African-Americans' demand for equal rights. Within six weeks, the city of Birmingham agreed to end most kinds of segregation:

King and his followers had won. Their victory extended beyond Birmingham: now many Americans, of all races, were convinced that bold new laws should be passed—laws that would end segregation for good.

The March on Washington

In the summer of 1963, Congress was debating whether to pass a sweeping new law called the Civil Rights Act. The labor leader A. Philip Randolph planned a great "March on Washington" in support of the new law.

On August 28, 1963, the march took place in Washington, D.C. It was the largest demonstration ever held in the capital city. More than two hundred thousand people took part; about one quarter of them were white. The marchers carried signs calling for an end to segregation and racism. As they marched, they sang, a spiritual, "We Shall Overcome," the song of the civil rights movement:

> We shall overcome,
> We shall overcome,
> We shall overcome,
> Someday.
> Oh deep in my heart,
> I do believe, that
> We shall overcome
> Someday.

> We'll walk hand in hand,
> We'll walk hand in hand,
> We'll walk hand in hand,
> Someday.
> Oh, deep in my heart,
> I do believe, that
> We shall overcome
> Someday.

At the end of the march, the demonstrators gathered at the Lincoln Memorial. The day was sunny and warm; the mood of the great crowd was hopeful, even joyous. A number of civil rights leaders gave speeches. Then Martin Luther King, Jr., stood up to address the sea of faces. In a deep preacher's voice, echoing Thomas Jefferson, he spoke these passionate words:

Part of the huge crowd at the March on Washington. You can see the Washington Monument rising above the crowd in the distance.

So I say to you, my friends, that even though we must face the difficulties of today and tomorrow, I still have a dream. It is a dream deeply rooted in the American dream that one day this nation will rise up and live out the true meaning of its creed—we hold these truths to be self-evident, that all men are created equal. . . .

I have a dream my four little children will one day live in a nation where they will not be judged by the color of their skin but by the content of their character. I have a dream today!

The people who heard King speak—including millions who watched it on TV—were overwhelmed by the power of his message. Today the words of King's "I have a dream" speech (which you can read in the Language Arts section of this book) are familiar to many Americans.

THE TURBULENT SIXTIES AND AFTER

John F. Kennedy

In the 1960s, the United States had an inspiring young president, John F. Kennedy. Kennedy—who was only forty-three when he was elected in 1960—was our youngest president ever. At his inauguration (the ceremonies that officially marked the beginning of his presidency), he made a speech in which he promised fresh new leadership. "Let the word go forth," he said, ". . . that the torch has been passed to a new generation of Americans." (You can read more of Kennedy's inaugural address in the Language Arts section of this book.)

The youthful president was full of energy. "Vigor" was one of his favorite words. He was always on the move—giving speeches, handing down orders, talking to journalists, meeting with foreign leaders. He never seemed to slow down. At the end of one long day a journalist joked, "[Kennedy] did everything today but shinny up the Washington Monument."

Partly because of his youth, Kennedy was especially popular among young people. They responded to his call to serve the nation when he said, "Ask not what your country can do for you; ask what you can do for your coun-

President John F. Kennedy, right, with his brother Robert Kennedy.

try." Hundreds of idealistic young people joined a new program called the Peace Corps. Peace Corps members went to work in poor countries, especially in Latin America and Africa, where they helped build schools, roads, and hospitals. They helped the people learn new and better ways of farming. They taught subjects like science and English in local schools. Peace Corps volunteers worked very hard for very little money, and they made America many friends overseas.

The Berlin Wall

While Kennedy was president, the Cold War was heating up: relations between the Soviet Union and the United States became especially tense. In fact, it looked for a time as if war might finally break out between the two superpowers.

In 1961 the United States and the Soviet Union quarreled over the German city of Berlin. To understand this quarrel, we have to look back at what happened in Germany after World War II.

After World War II, Germany became a divided country. The western part of Germany became a democratic country, but the eastern part became a Communist state, dominated by the Soviets. Germany's largest city, Berlin, was located deep inside Communist East Germany. But Allied troops—British, French, and American—still occupied part of the city of Berlin. Just as the country of Germany was divided in two, so the city of Berlin was divided. The western part of the city, where the Allied forces remained, became an island of democracy in a Communist country. East Germans who did not want to be ruled by Communists flooded into West Berlin, looking for freedom.

The East German rulers and their Soviet allies were angered by the existence of a free West Berlin. In 1961 the Soviet leader, Nikita Khrushchev, met with President Kennedy and demanded that the United States and its allies pull out of West Berlin. Kennedy refused. It looked as if the argument over Berlin might lead to war. But then the Communists did something dramatic and shocking: they built a wall between the two sections of the city. The wall was topped with barbed wire and guarded by armed soldiers, who were told to shoot any East Germans trying to flee to West Berlin. Over the next three decades almost two hundred people would be killed as they tried to escape over the wall.

The Berlin Wall was a visible reminder to East Europeans of the repressive control exercised by the Soviet Union.

The Berlin Wall was finally torn down in 1989, when the Communist government of East Germany was overthrown. But for nearly thirty years the wall stood as a hated symbol of Communist tyranny.

The Cuban Missile Crisis

Although the Soviets and the Americans did not go to war over Berlin, an even more dangerous conflict arose over Cuba, an island in the Caribbean Sea only a hundred miles from Florida.

For many years Cuba had been ruled by a corrupt and oppressive government. Then in 1959, that government was overthrown by a revolution. The head of the revolutionaries, Fidel Castro, promised to bring democracy to Cuba. Instead he set up a Communist government and allied himself with the Soviet Union. Many Americans were worried that there was now a Communist country in the Western Hemisphere.

In October 1962, the U.S. government learned that the Soviets had set up bases in Cuba, equipped with missiles that could aim nuclear warheads at American cities. President Kennedy refused to tolerate this threat to the United States. He ordered the U.S. Navy to set up a blockade around Cuba, so that Soviet ships could not bring in any more missiles. At the same time he ordered the U.S. armed forces to prepare for a possible invasion of the island.

For a few terrifying days it looked again as if the Soviets and Americans might finally go to war. People all over the world dreaded the coming of a nuclear World War III. A large group of Russian ships was sailing to Cuba and would soon confront the ships of the U.S. blockade. The world held its breath.

Then the Soviet ships suddenly turned around and started home. When he learned of this, this American secretary of state said, "We're eyeball to eyeball and I think the other fellow just blinked." The Soviets were backing down. Khrushchev wrote Kennedy a letter, offering to pull his missiles out of Cuba if Kennedy would end the blockade and agree not to invade the island. Soon the Soviets were packing up the missiles and leaving their bases.

The United States had faced down the Soviet Union, but only after the world had come to the brink of a terrible war. Beginning in 1963, the Americans and the Russians would work out a series of treaties designed to control the use of nuclear weapons. Parly because of these treaties, the United States and the Soviet Union never again came so close to war.

The Space Race Begins

In the 1960s the United States and the Soviet Union were competing in another, less dangerous way—the exploration of outer space. They were engaged in a "space race" and the Soviets had a head start. In 1957, the Soviets had launched the first manmade satellite, known as *Sputnik I*, a little machine about twice the size of a basketball, which they had shot into space on a rocket. *Sputnik* began orbiting the earth like a miniature moon. Over the next few years the Soviets sent up several more satellites.

Many Americans were concerned that the Russians seemed so far ahead of us in exploring space, and became especially worried when, in 1961, the Russians sent a man into space for the first time. President Kennedy immediately dedicated himself to putting America ahead in the space race. He asked Congress to allocate billions of dollars for the National Aeronautics and Space Administration (NASA). And he proposed an ambitious new plan. "I believe," he said, "that this nation should commit itself to achieving the goal, before this decade is out, of landing a man on the moon and returning him safely to earth."

Americans started training a group of military pilots to fly in space. These "astronauts" (a word meaning "star sailors") quickly made themselves heroes to the American people. In May 1961, Alan B. Shepard became the first American in space. "Boy, what a ride!" he said after he came down. An even greater hero was John Glenn, who in February 1962 became the first American to orbit the earth. When he returned to earth, Glenn was given a great parade in New York City. He was also invited to address Congress—an honor usually given only to leaders of foreign countries. Glenn was as famous as Charles Lindbergh after making the first solo flight across the Atlantic. Glenn later became a U.S. senator from his home state of Ohio.

The Assassination of Kennedy

On November 22, 1963, the country was shocked to learn that President Kennedy had been assassinated in Dallas, Texas, where he had gone to give a speech. He was riding in a convertible car with the top down when he was shot in the head. A government commission later concluded that the killer was a man named Lee Harvey Oswald. But, because Oswald himself was shot by an outraged citizen, no one knows for sure why he killed Kennedy.

Back in Washington the president was given a moving funeral. Almost everyone in America gathered around their televisions to watch and mourn. Kennedy's coffin, guarded by soldiers, was drawn slowly through the streets on a caisson (a kind of cart) pulled by a horse. The horse, although it had no rider, wore a saddle. In the stirrups were a pair of empty boots—the ancient symbol of a fallen warrior.

Lyndon Johnson and the Great Society

After the assassination of Kennedy, his vice president, Lyndon Baines Johnson, became president. His background and personality were very different from Kennedy's. Kennedy was from a wealthy Massachusetts family; Johnson's family were middle-class Texans. Kennedy had gone to Harvard, the most famous university in the country; Johnson went to a Texas college that few people had ever heard of. Kennedy enjoyed dressing in a fancy, elegant way; Johnson liked to wear cowboy hats and boots. Many of the people who had admired Kennedy disliked the new president.

Johnson cared deeply about the problems of America's poor. He had first entered politics during the Depression years, during which he saw terrible poverty all around him in Texas and became a strong supporter of Franklin Roosevelt's New Deal. When Johnson became president thirty years later, poverty was not nearly as widespread. But millions of Americans were still poor, and Johnson believed that a country as rich as the United States should make sure that everyone could share in its wealth. Government, he declared, should wage a "war on poverty."

In 1964 Johnson gave a speech to a group of college students. "In your time," he said, "we have the opportunity to move not only toward the rich society and the powerful society, but upward to the Great Society." The Great Society would be the name for Johnson's own plan for change, a kind of new New Deal. When Johnson won the presidential election of 1964, he started to put his plan into effect.

Johnson set up many new antipoverty programs, including a job-training program called the Job Corps, and a program to help people pay for decent housing. An educational program called Head Start was set up to help prepare young children from poor families for school.

Johnson and Civil Rights

When Johnson first became president, some African-Americans were not sure if they should trust him. After all, he was the first Southern president in a century, and African-Americans in the South were still fighting especially hard for their rights. But Johnson, who hated the racism he had seen while growing up in Texas, turned out to be a strong supporter of civil rights.

The two most important laws passed during Johnson's presidency dealt with civil rights. The Civil Rights Act of 1964 made it illegal to discriminate against any person because of race, religion, or the country a person's family came from. After the Civil Rights Act, employers could not discriminate in hiring people. Labor unions could not discriminate in accepting members. Businesses like hotels and restaurants had to serve everyone who could afford to pay.

The country took another step toward equal rights with the passage of the Voting Rights Act of 1965. This law said that all citizens had the right to vote, and put an end to the many tricks that had been used to keep most Southern blacks from voting. If a state refused to let someone register to vote, then the federal government would sign that person up. Now African-Americans all over the country had the power of the ballot. In the next few years more and more African-Americans would be elected to office. In 1965 no American city had a black mayor, but by 1979 African-Americans were mayors in dozens of cities, including such large cities as Atlanta, Detroit, and Los Angeles.

Malcolm X

Though the Civil Rights Act and the Voting Rights Acts were very important laws, they did not end inequality and prejudice against African-Americans. Many African-Americans who had left the South to find a better life in the North instead found racism and inequality there as well. Some African-Americans became impatient with the slow if steady progress of the civil rights movement. They began to feel deep resentment against white people. One group, known as the Nation of Islam, attracted many African-Americans who felt especially bitter about their long history of injustice in the United States.

The Nation of Islam—sometimes also called the Black Muslims—claimed to be followers of the religion of Islam, but in their version of Islam, blacks were superior to whites. In fact, white people were "devils." This went against the real teachings of Islam, which say that men of all races are equal.

Black Muslims rejected integration, which was the goal of civil rights leaders like Martin Luther King. Like Marcus Garvey in the 1920s, Black Muslims thought that blacks should live apart from whites and build up their own communities. In the early 1960s many people joined the Nation of Islam after hearing the speeches of a brilliant young Muslim, Malxolm X.

A leader of the Nation of Islam, Malcolm X, had been born in 1925 as Malcolm Little. He and other members of the Nation of Islam changed their last names to "X" to represent their unknown African ancestors, and to reject what they called the "slave names" imposed upon their ancestors who had been brought to America in chains.

Malcolm's father was a minister who supported the ideas of Marcus Garvey and preached that blacks should be proud of their race. When Malcolm was only six, his father was found dead, his battered body lying across the streetcar tracks. There was little doubt that he had been murdered by whites who didn't like what Reverend Little preached.

When Malcolm entered seventh grade, he was the only African-American in his class. He did very well in school. One day he had a talk with his favorite teacher, who asked Malcolm if he had thought about what kind of career he might enter. Malcolm said that he was thinking of being a lawyer. But his teacher told him that wasn't a "realistic" goal for a black person, and that he should consider something else, like carpentry. Although the teacher encouraged all the white children to pursue their dreams, he advised Malcolm to lower his expectations. From that day on, Malcolm later recalled, "I drew away from white people."

Malcolm later moved to Boston, where he was surprised to find a thriving African-American community in a section of the city called Roxbury. He got a job as a railway porter, and some of his trips took him to New York City, where he discovered the night life of Harlem. He moved to Harlem and unfortunately drifted into the city's underworld: he got into gambling, bootlegging, and selling and using drugs. When he moved back to Boston, he began to commit robberies, in part to buy the drugs he was addicted to. He was caught and sent to prison.

Malcolm X once described his life as "a chronology of . . . *changes.*" One of the most remarkable changes in his life took place in prison. He overcame his drug habit, and then he started to educate himself. Years later, looking back on his life, he said, "My greatest lack has been, I believe, that I don't have the kind of academic education I wish I had been able to get." Understanding the value of a solid academic education, Malcolm X worked hard in prison to pick up where his education had broken off (he had dropped out in the eighth grade). With amazing self-discipline, he copied an entire dictionary, page by page. He read every book he could get his hands on in the prison library.

While in prison, Malcolm X also became a believer in the teachings of the Nation of Islam. When he left prison, he followed the strict code of conduct of the Nation of Islam, and he worked to spread the Black Muslim belief that white people were "devils." He was a powerful speaker, and soon millions of Americans heard his furious words broadcast over radio and television. He was accused of promoting hatred of whites, but he responded, "For the white man to ask the black man if he hates him is just like . . . the wolf asking the sheep, 'Do you hate me?' The white man is in no moral position to accuse anyone else of hate!"

Malcolm X.

In 1964, Malcolm X experienced another one of the dramatic changes in his life, this time as a result of making a pilgrimage to Mecca (in Saudi Arabia), the holy city of Islam. He discovered people of all colors—black, white, brown, red, yellow—united in their faith. When he returned to the United States, he declared that he was now a believer in *nonracial* Islam. He still urged African-Americans to fight for their rights "by any means necessary," but he no longer condemned all white people. "I don't speak against the sincere, well-meaning, good white people," he said. "I have learned that not all white people are racists."

Before Malcolm X could develop his new message, he was shot dead in 1965. He left behind a powerful book about his life, *The Autobiography of Malcolm X.* Near the end of that book, he looked back over his thirty-nine years of life and said, "For the freedom of my 22 million black brothers and sisters here in America, I do believe that I have fought the best that I knew how, and the best that I could, with the shortcomings that I have had."

The Civil Rights Movement Loses a Leader

In the mid-1960s, the civil rights movement was becoming divided. Like Malcolm X, some young blacks in the movement thought that equality was too slow in coming. They began to question Martin Luther King's tactic of passive resistance. Like the Black Muslims, they questioned the goal of integration itself. More and more young blacks began to reject the goal of integration and instead to talk about "black power."

"Black power" meant different things to different people. To some, it meant that blacks should have complete control over their own communities. To others, it meant taking up arms in a violent revolution against whites. Martin Luther King was disturbed by this talk of black power. He urged African-Americans to use peaceful means, and to ally themselves with nonracist whites.

King went on with his work, leading peaceful protests around the country. He knew that he was putting himself at risk. Although he and his followers were nonviolent, they faced violent people who were against the idea of civil rights. Several civil rights workers had been murdered in the early 1960s. For years King had a feeling that he, too, might be murdered. On the day President Kennedy was killed, King said to his wife, "This is what is going to happen to me."

In April 1968, King traveled to Memphis, Tennessee to lead a demonstration for equal pay for black workers. He told an audience that he knew he might not live much longer. And he referred to the Bible story of Moses, the ancient leader of the Jewish people. Moses had led his people on a long journey to the land God had promised to give them. But just before they reached the promised land, Moses died. Before he died, he glimpsed the land from the top of a mountain. In his speech King said:

> Like anybody, I would like to live a long life. . . . But I'm not concerned about that now. I just want to do God's will. And He's allowed me to go up the mountain, and I've looked over, and I've seen the promised land. I may not get there with you. But I want you to know tonight, that we, as a people, will get to the promised land. And so I'm happy tonight. I'm not worried about anything. I'm not fearing any man.

The next day, as King stepped out of his motel room on his way to dinner, he was shot dead by an assassin. Now it was up to other leaders to finish his work—to lead their people into the "promised land" of equality.

Cesar Chavez Organizes Migrant Workers

While the struggle for civil rights had a special urgency for African-Americans, who had behind them the terrible history of slavery, the struggle came to include people of many races: Native Americans, Asian-Americans, Hispanic-Americans, and many more.

One of the fastest-growing groups in America was (and is) the Hispanics, who are people from Spanish-speaking countries, mostly from Mexixo, Cuba, and Puerto Rico, and also from the Caribbean islands, from Central and South America, and from Spain.

In the 1960s, in California and the Southwestern states, the largest minority group was Mexican-American. For over a hundred years, Mexican-Americans had suffered some of the same injustices that Jim Crow laws had inflicted on African-Americans in the South. Often they were forced into segregated schools, or kept out of hotels or restaurants that were reserved for whites.

Because Mexican-Americans did not have the same opportunities as their fellow citizens, they were often forced to take the hard, dirty jobs that others did not want. Many became migrant farm workers who traveled from farm to farm hoping to find work. When they found it, they spent their days bent over in the hot sun, picking fruit and vegetables by hand. It was back-breaking work that paid very little money. Because they could not afford decent housing, the migrants had to live packed together in run-down, overcrowded labor camps.

In the 1960s a Mexican-American named Cesar Chavez led a movement to improve

Beyond the Melting Pot

For many years, people referred to the United States as a "melting pot," a place where people from different countries would all blend together to become Americans. As far back as 1782, a Frenchman who had emigrated to America, Hector St. John de Crèvecoeur, claimed that in America, "Individuals of all nations are melted into a new race of men, whose labors and posterity will one day cause great changes in the world." This idea of the melting pot took for granted that, in coming to America, immigrants and the children of immigrants would abandon the customs and traditions of the countries they had left behind.

But in time, some people began to see the idea of the melting pot as out of date. In 1916, an American writer named Randolph Bourne said that the time had come for Americans "to assert a higher ideal than the 'melting pot.'" In America, said Bourne, the cultures and traditions of immigrants should not be "melted down . . . into a tasteless, colorless fluid." Rather than a melting pot, America should be a colorful tapestry, "a weaving back and forth . . . of many threads of all sizes and colors."

As Bourne saw it, in the tapestry of America, individual threads would remain distinct yet also be woven into a larger whole. This idea of combined separateness and wholeness—of being part of a distinct strand but also part of a larger whole—lies behind the recent practice of different groups within American society referring to themselves as Mexican-American, Korean-American, Cuban-American, Polish-American, and many more. Each group celebrates a distinct heritage, yet all are Americans, part of the colorful and changing tapestry.

Many people still share Bourne's great hope for America as "the first international nation," as a land that can make possible "the peaceful living side by side . . . of the most heterogenous peoples under the sun. . . . It is for the American of the younger generation," said Bourne, to turn this hope into reality.

the lives of migrant workers. Chavez himself came from a family of migrants and knew all about the hardships they faced. As he grew up, Chavez became determined to change things. Once, when he was still a teenager, he was arrested for refusing to leave the "white" section of a movie theater (as Rosa Parks would later be arrested for refusing to leave the "white" section of an Alabama bus).

In the early 1960s, Chavez formed a union of farm workers that eventually became known as the United Farm Workers. The union fought for higher pay and better living conditions for the migrants. Some farmers in California who grew grapes were especially unfair in the way they treated their workers. In 1965, Chavez's union called a strike against the grape-growers. Workers walked off the job and picketed the farms. The strike went on for months and then years. Gradually some of the farmers agreed to raise the pay and living standards of their workers. But other farmers refused to do so.

Cesar Chavez.

Then, in 1967, Chavez called on people everywhere to boycott grapes. No one should buy the fruit, he declared, until all the grape-growers treated their workers fairly. All over the country, people refused to buy grapes and expressed their support for the migrant workers. Finally, in 1970, the growers gave in and signed agreements with the union.

In his actions Chavez had been inspired by the example of the African-American civil rights movement, and by the nonviolent philosophy of Martin Luther King, Jr. Chavez always insisted that his followers avoid violence. He explained, "People associate strikes with violence, and we've removed the violence. Then people begin to understand what we're doing, . . . and after that, they're not afraid." Chavez gained the support of so many Americans because they admired a leader who, like Martin Luther King, was strong but peaceful.

Native Americans: From Termination to Self-Determination

The civil rights movement energized many American Indians to demand more just treatment and policies. In part, American Indians were angry over their long history of exploitation, broken promises, and forced removal at the hands of the United States government. In part they were angry at the policy pursued by the federal government since about 1945, a policy called "termination."

The policy of termination overturned much of John Collier's "Indian New Deal," which had provided special government programs and financial support for Indians. Termination put an end to even the limited tribal self-government allowed under the "Indian New Deal." It subjected tribes and their lands to state laws and taxes. It required that the shared property of the tribe be divided among individual members, thus breaking one of the bonds that held a tribe together. To make matters worse, while the government pursued the policy of termination, it also worked to relocate Indians from reservations to urban areas, thus further breaking the tribal bonds.

The federal government tried to put termination in a positive light by saying that it "freed [Indians] from Federal supervision and control," and that it would fully integrate Indians into American society. In effect, however, termination was a way for the government to save money, while for Indians it was a dangerous threat to their tribal identities and ways of life. Between 1954 and 1966, Congress took action to terminate more than a hundred tribes. The result was increased poverty for many Indians, and a terrible sense of fear and injury at the forced dismantling of a people's way of life.

In the 1960s, Native American civil rights activists began to draw attention to the suffering of many American Indians. Representatives of various tribes worked together to demand that Indians be involved in the design and control of programs that affected them. The U.S. government responded by renewing economic aid and by adopting a new policy, which came to be known as self-determination.

Self-determination, as President Lyndon Johnson explained in 1968, in part meant that Indians would have "an opportunity to remain in their homelands, if they chose, without surrendering their dignity; [and] an opportunity to move to towns and cities of America, if they chose . . ." In 1970, President Richard Nixon affirmed the policy of self-determination, and acknowledged that the earlier policy of termination had been wrong. It was wrong, said the president, to think of government assistance to Native Americans as "an act of generosity," Rather, such support was part of the

Preserving Heritages

In the late 1800s, the U.S. government established boarding schools for young Indians. You read about one, the Carlisle School, in Book Five of this series. At schools like Carlisle, Indian children were not allowed to wear tribal clothes or speak the tribal language. The "education" Indian children received at these schools was designed to wipe out their tribal heritage.

Such practices changed, however, in the mid-1960s, when American Indians began to take part in running their own schools. The first school directed and controlled by Indians was established on the Navajo Reservation in Rough Rock, Arizona. At this school, children learned not only English and math but also Navajo language, history, and customs. Today, many Indian children attend schools that help them preserve a sense of their tribe's people and past, even as they learn some of the same things that children across the nation learn in school.

"solemn obligations" and "specific commitments" of the U.S. government to the Indian peoples.

Self-determination restored federal government support and gave tribes back much control of their local government. Today, American Indians living on reservations have (with some limitations) the right to choose and form their own kinds of government. States cannot regulate how Indians live on reservations or how they use reservation lands. Nor can a state tax Indians living on reservations. Away from a reservation, an American Indian is subject to the same taxes and laws as anyone else. On a reservation, non-Indians must obey a tribe's specific laws and customs.

The War in Vietnam

In the 1960s the United States got involved in a war in Asia that would turn out to be the longest war in the history of our country. The Vietnam War was a bloody and frustrating conflict. And, unlike World War II—which most Americans at home strongly supported—the Vietnam War sharply divided Americans and turned them against each other.

Vietnam is a country in southeastern Asia. Until 1954 it was a colony of France. In that year the French withdrew, leaving Vietnam divided (like Korea) into two countries— a Communist north and a non-Communist south. The North Vietnamese soon began trying to overthrow the government of South Vietnam by arming and training Communist guerrillas to fight the South Vietnamese military. ("Guerrillas" are fighters who are not part of a regular army. They usually fight in small groups and do not wear uniforms. They often pretend to be civilians until they get a chance to strike at their enemy. Many revolutionary groups have waged guerrilla warfare against governments they wanted to overthrow.)

In the early 1960s, President Kennedy sent thousands of American soldiers to South

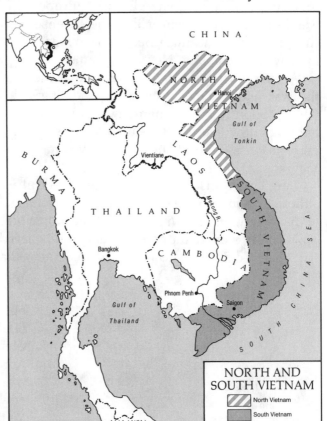

NORTH AND
SOUTH VIETNAM

Vietnam. They were called "advisers," and the American government said their goal was to train and advise South Vietnamese troops. But more than advice would be needed. The Communist guerrillas, known as the Vietcong, were tough and determined. By early 1965 it looked as though they might overthrow the government.

President Johnson was unwilling to let this happen. He believed that if South Vietnam fell to communism, so would other nations in the area, opening the way for Communist China to dominate all of eastern Asia, as

President Johnson greeting troops in Vietnam.

the Soviet Union dominated Eastern Europe. So Johnson decided to throw the whole weight of American power into the defense of South Vietnam. In 1965 he ordered two hundred thousand American troops into the country and sent the American air force to start bombing North Vietnam.

At first most Americans believed that the bombing of North Vietnam would end the war within a few weeks. Instead, it made the Communists fight back more fiercely. Soon North Vietnam's own soldiers, as well as the Vietcong guerrillas, were fighting in the South. The United States stepped up the bombing and sent more and more troops. By 1968 there were over half a million American soldiers in South Vietnam.

The Americans had much more powerful weapons than the Communists, so, although thousands of Americans were being killed, they were killing many more of the enemy. Still the Vietcong and the North Vietnamese showed no sign of backing down. They were dedicated soldiers who believed they were fighting for their country. Their Communist leaders had told them that the Americans, like the French, wanted to rule Vietnam as colonizers.

The American soldiers fought well, but it was a difficult war for them, unlike any war American soldiers had ever fought. In the world wars and in Korea, there was always a "front line," where soldiers clashed with the enemy. But there was no front line in Vietnam, except when Americans

American soldiers in Vietnam.

fought North Vietnamese units head-on. Most of the time the enemy hid in the jungle or disguised himself as a civilian. He seemed to be everywhere and nowhere. Sometimes "he" was even a young woman or an old man. An American officer remembered:

> You never knew who was the enemy and who was the friend. . . . Here's a woman of twenty-two or twenty-three. . . . [S]he watches your men walk down a trail and get killed or wounded by a booby trap. She knows the booby trap is there, but she doesn't warn them. Maybe she planted it herself. . . . The enemy was all around you.

The War at Home: Hawks and Doves

As the years wore on and more Americans died in Vietnam, people at home grew more and more frustrated. A bitter argument arose between two groups of Americans. The "hawks" thought that the United States should keep fighting, and the "doves" thought that we should bring our troops home. (A hawk is a fighting bird, and the dove is an ancient symbol for peace.) The hawks argued that the United States was fighting to save a small, weak country from communism. The most extreme hawks thought that we should invade and conquer North Vietnam. The doves argued that we had gotten involved in a civil war that was none of our business. The most extreme doves thought that the Communist cause was just, and that the Communists should rule all Vietnam.

Antiwar feelings were especially strong on college campuses. Many college students felt that the money spent on the war should be used to fight poverty and racism at home. Also, college students were the right age to be drafted and required to serve in the armed forces. Those who were against the war did not want to be forced to fight in it. Demonstrations against the war broke out at colleges across the country. Sometimes these demonstrations turned violent: students burned buildings and threw rocks at police. The police responded by beating up students.

One student uprising ended in tragedy. In May 1970, there were violent demonstrations at Kent State University in Ohio. The National Guard—a group of citizen-soldiers who serve part time—was called in to protect the campus. A crowd of students started throwing rocks at the guardsmen. Although the soldiers were in no real danger, they had little experience in this kind of confrontation, so they panicked and fired into the crowd. Fifteen students were shot, and four of them died. The deaths at Kent State shocked the country and turned more people against the war.

The Youth Rebellion

In the late 1960s, it was not only college students who were rebelling. All over the country, teenagers and young adults began acting very differently from older people.

A "generation gap" opened up. Young people used special words that parents could not understand. They listened to a new kind of music—rock-and-roll—that parents thought was far too loud and crazy. As you have seen, young Americans also rebelled against their elders during the Roaring Twenties. But the youth rebellion of the 1960s was more extreme. Although many young people were just out to enjoy themselves, others were questioning the basic values of American society.

One group of young people decided that America was a greedy, materialistic, and warlike nation. They declared that they would "drop out" of society and create

The Moon Landing

One of President Kennedy's goals had been to put a man on the moon before 1970. All through the 1960s, American astronauts flew missions from the great space base in Florida, which had been renamed Cape Kennedy in honor of the late president. They flew deeper and deeper into space. Then, just five months before Kennedy's deadline, the goal was reached.

In July 1969, three astronauts—Michael Collins, Buzz Aldrin, and Neil Armstrong—lifted off from Cape Kennedy on a spaceship called the Columbia after Christopher Columbus. The moon is a quarter of a million miles from the earth, but the Columbia covered this vast distance in only four days! On July 20, 1969, the three astronauts were orbiting the moon.

A smaller spacecraft called the Eagle was detached from the Columbia to carry Aldrin and Armstrong down to the surface of the moon. The astronauts aimed the Eagle toward the area called the Sea of Tranquility. At 4:17 P.M., Neil Armstrong broadcast the historic words: "Houston, Tranquility Base here. The Eagle has landed."

Armstrong was the first to leave the Eagle. He carefully climbed down the ladder and, as he took the last step from the ladder to the moon's surface, he said, "That's one small step for a man, one giant leap for mankind." A television camera on the spacecraft allowed hundreds of millions of people all over the world to watch Armstrong as he moved across the gray lunar landscape in his bulky spacesuit.

The astronauts collected samples of moon soil and moon rock for scientists to study. They also raised an American flag (the flag was stiffened by wire so that it would seem to "fly" on the airless moon). But Aldrin and Armstrong were not claiming the moon for the United States. Unlike Columbus and the other explorers of the past, they had not come to take over a territory. Instead they had come to add to man's knowledge of the universe. The moon would remain open to any nation that cared to explore it. Along with the American flag, the astronauts left a small steel sign which read: "Here men from the Planet Earth first set foot on the Moon July 1969. We came in peace for all mankind."

After the Eagle, other manned space flights landed on the moon. Here Astronaut James Irwin salutes the flag during the fourth moon landing, in August 1971.

their own society based on the values of love and peace. These young people left their schools and their jobs and gathered together in cities like San Francisco and New York. There they lived on the streets or in the parks, and had joyful celebrations called "love-ins." These young people became known as "hippies" or "flower children" because of their custom of handing out flowers as a sign of peace and friendship. Many hippies wore beads and headbands; the men often wore long hair and beards. They wanted to look as different as possible from older people and working people.

The high point of the youth movement came in August 1969. Four hundred thousand young people gathered on a farm near Woodstock, New York, to see a rock music festival. For three days they camped out in a huge, muddy field. Hundreds of thousands of strangers came together to listen to rock-and-roll, dance, talk, and enjoy each other's company. The local police were amazed that such a huge crowd could be so peaceful. For three days the people at Woodstock seemed to be living out the hippies' dream: a world of friendship and peace.

But the youth movement had a dark side as well. Many of the teenagers who ran away from home to live the hippy life were too young to take care of themselves. Often they got sick or had to go without food. Sometimes they were the victims of criminals. And often they started using illegal drugs. Some damaged their health or even died from overdoses or from using drugs that had been badly made.

The Vietnam War Ends

In 1968, Richard M. Nixon took office as president of the United States. One of his first actions was to announce that he would "wind down" the war. This meant that he would slowly withdraw American troops. Like President Johnson, he was determined that the Communists not take over South Vietnam. So even as he was bringing soldiers home, he was stepping up the bombing of North Vietnam. He hoped that the bombing would convince the Communists that the costs of the war were too high.

The End of the Cold War

Although American soldiers fought against Communist troops in Vietnam and earlier in Korea, the United States and the Soviet Union never directly engaged each other in battle throughout the long tense years of the Cold War.

You can do some research in the library to learn about how the Cold War came to an end in 1991, when the Soviet Union's Communist government was overthrown by the Soviet people. Today, what was the Soviet Union has broken into a number of independent (and sometimes hostile) nations, including Russia, Ukraine, and many other independent states. What does your research reveal about the current situation of the former Soviet Union?

In January 1973, the North Vietnamese finally signed a cease-fire with the Americans. Two months later, the last American troops came home. In over a decade of fighting, some forty-seven thousand Americans had been killed in action.

In spite of the cease-fire, the Communists did not give up their plan to conquer the South. Soon shooting broke out again between the Communists and South Vietnam's own army, which had been trained and armed by the Americans. For two years the South Vietnamese fought on alone, but finally they were no match for the Communists. In April 1975, the North Vietnamese army captured the South Vietnamese capital of Saigon.

The war was over but times were still hard for the Vietnamese. The war had wrecked the economy of the country. And the Communists took revenge on their old enemies, sending South Vietnamese soldiers and officials to prison camps. Over the next few years hundreds of thousands of Vietnamese would leave their country, fleeing the poverty and oppression. The Communists had made it illegal for them to leave, so they

The Vietnam Memorial in Washington, D.C., commemorates all who died in Vietnam.

had to sneak out of the country. Often crammed together on small, overcrowded fishing boats, they braved the dangers of the open sea. Many of the refugees were drowned when storms sank their boats. Those "boat people" who survived landed in nearby Asian countries like Thailand or Malaysia. From there, some made their way to the United States, and many have become American citizens.

Watergate and the Fall of Richard Nixon

In the early 1970s, the American government was being shaken by a great crisis. For the first time an American president would be forced to resign from office in disgrace.

In 1972, President Richard Nixon ran for reelection as a Republican. Of course the Democratic Party wanted their own candidate to become president. Then in June 1972, five men were arrested in Washington, D.C., for breaking into a Democratic Party office in a building called the Watergate. But these were no ordinary burglars. They were working for a group that was trying to get Nixon reelected. They had broken into the office hoping to find information that would embarrass the Democrats.

At first the American public was not aware of any connection between the Watergate burglars and the people trying to reelect Nixon. Nixon was reelected in November of 1972. But in the following months, the Watergate break-in became a giant political scandal. It turned out that the same group of burglars had been involved in other break-ins. They had stolen personal papers from the president's opponents and put taps on their phones. They had committed serious crimes in an effort to get the president reelected.

We still don't know if Nixon himself ordered these crimes. But in an effort to protect himself and people who worked for him, Nixon did try to stop the investigation of the crimes. By doing so, he was committing another serious crime, called "obstruction of justice." Congress investigated, and it gradually became clear that there were a number of corrupt officials in the Nixon White House.

The investigation went on for two years. Finally, the House of Representatives drew up articles of impeachment against the president. To "impeach" someone is to charge him with serious wrongdoing. According to the Constitution, only the House of Representatives can impeach the president. An impeached president must then be tried in the Senate. Only one American president, Andrew Johnson, has ever gone through such a trial, and (as you might recall from Book Four in this series) he was found not guilty.

The first article of impeachment charged that "Richard M. Nixon has acted in a manner contrary to his trust as President and subversive of constitutional government." Nixon denied committing any crime, but to avoid being impeached, he resigned from office in August 1974. He was succeeded by his vice president, Gerald Ford.

Because of the Watergate scandal, some people became mistrustful of American government and saw the system as completely corrupt. But other people thought just the opposite. They said that Nixon's removal from office proved that the American system worked. After all, it was one of the Founding Fathers' most basic principles that ours is "a government of laws, not of men." And Watergate showed that no one, not even the president, is above the law.

The Women's Liberation Movement

In the 1960s and 1970s, the feminist movement was reborn in America. "Feminism" is the idea that women should have the same rights and opportunities as men. All through the nineteenth and early twentieth centuries, American women had struggled to win such basic rights as the right to vote. (Books Four and Five in this series tell of early feminists like Sojourner Truth, Elizabeth Cady Stanton, and Susan B. Anthony.) When women finally won the right to vote in 1920, many people thought that women had achieved equal standing with men. But this was not yet true.

Women still had fewer opportunities than men. Men were taught that they could be almost anything they wanted to be. A man knew that he could become a soldier, a teacher, a mechanic, a doctor, an artist, or any one of a hundred other things. But women had been trained to believe that their most important goal was to marry and raise children. Most men and women tended to believe the old saying, "A woman's place is in the home."

In 1963, a feminist named Betty Friedan published a book called *The Feminine Mystique*. (A "mystique" is a false way of thinking or feeling.) In her book, Friedan argued that many American women were unhappy because they were not allowed to develop their talents and interests. American girls received educations that opened their minds and made them want to take an active part in the world, but when they grew up, they were told that the only thing they should do was take care of a home. According to Friedan, this "housewife trap" made many women frustrated and angry.

Betty Friedan, here pictured twenty years after the publication of her book The Feminine Mystique, *still works for women's rights.*

Friedan and other feminists also pointed out that when women did work outside the home, they were discriminated against. Usually they could find jobs only in fields where most of the workers were women, like nursing and elementary school teaching. These were hard and important jobs, but they did not pay well, and some men looked down on them as "women's work." And even when a woman did get a job in a "man's" field, she was usually paid less than the men she worked with.

Soon more and more women were drawn to feminism, or the "women's liberation" movement, as it was now called. In 1966, Friedan and other feminists founded a group called NOW. The name had a double meaning; it stood for the National Organization for Women, but it also meant that women were tired of waiting, that they wanted equality with men *now*. NOW soon had thousands of members all over the country.

The Fight for the ERA

NOW called for laws to make sure that men and women would receive the same pay for the same work. It called for the government to set up day-care centers where children could be taken care of while their mothers worked. But NOW's largest goal was to amend the U.S. Constitution.

Back in the 1920s, feminists started fighting for an Equal Rights Amendment (ERA) to the Constitution, but their plan was defeated. In the 1960s, feminists renewed the fight to add to the Constitution an amendment declaring that "equality of rights under the law shall not be denied or abridged by the United States or by any State on account of sex." Feminists felt that, since the Constitution is the ultimate law of the land, it was vital that women's rights be recognized in it.

Finally in 1972, the ERA passed both houses of Congress. Feminists and their supporters rejoiced. But after an amendment is passed by Congress, it has to be ratified (approved) by three quarters of the states. Over half the states ratified the ERA within a year. But in other states there was strong opposition. ERA supporters could not get the three-quarters majority they needed. Today the amendment has not yet been added to the Constitution.

Feminists did not win the battle for the ERA, but they won many others. During the 1970s, the government issued many laws and rules forbidding discrimination against women. Women could no longer be discrimi-

Four generations of women at a demonstration to support the ERA in Illinois.

nated against on the job or anywhere else. Soon women were flocking into jobs that few had ever held before. In 1976 the U.S. military academies were opened to women students for the first time. Women were trained for highly skilled, highly paid jobs in law and medicine. During the 1970s, the number of women doctors more than doubled; the number of women lawyers tripled.

Today women are scientists, construction workers, writers, farmers, police officers, astronauts, governors, and senators. Many women still choose to be homemakers, but now they have other choices as well.

A Birthday Party

On July 4, 1976, the United States celebrated its two-hundredth birthday. Many visitors came to Philadelphia, where the Declaration of Independence had been signed on July 4, 1776. Among the visitors was the queen of England, the great-great-great-great-granddaughter of King George III. At 2 P.M., the Liberty Bell was struck softly with a rubber mallet. (It had to be struck softly so the crack in it wouldn't get any bigger.) At the same moment, all over the nation church bells started ringing. It was a joyous sound.

The nation had come through two hundred years. The way was not easy, and the last few years had been especially difficult. The civil rights movement had forced Americans to face the racism in their midst. The Vietnam War had divided Americans against each other, and ended tragically for America's friends in Vietnam. The Watergate scandal had caused some people to lose faith in the American government.

Fireworks light up the Statue of Liberty during the bicentennial celebration on July 4, 1976.

But in many other ways, Americans continued to work together—as they still do—to ensure, as Martin Luther King, Jr., said, "that one day this nation will rise up and live out the true meaning of its creed . . . that all men are created equal."

On this two-hundredth birthday, Americans wanted to celebrate both their pride in accomplishments of the past and their hopes for achievements yet to come. In New York City, millions of people came together to watch a spectacular sight: over two hundred ships from more than thirty nations swept into New York Harbor and up the Hudson River. Many of these were stately, old-fashioned "tall ships," with the sun dazzling off their sails.

It was a beautiful sight. It was also a reminder—a reminder of the many difficult voyages at the end of which lay a place, and an idea, called America. For the Jamestown settlers, the Ellis Island immigrants, the Vietnamese "boat people," and many others, America was a dream at the end of a hard journey by sea. As the tall ships sailed up the Hudson, they passed the Statue of Liberty, still raising her lamp "beside the golden door."

III.
FINE ARTS

Introduction to the Fine Arts

FOR PARENTS AND TEACHERS

In this section we focus on the Fine Arts in the twentieth century by giving an overview of the many forms of American music today and a historical introduction to the eclectic styles of the visual arts during the last hundred years.

The Music section continues to explain basic elements in music, including minor chords and seventh chords. We discuss sharps and flats and two basic patterns in music, repetition and variation. And we conclude with an overview of contemporary American music, explaining how our music has over the years borrowed many different styles from many different lands. As with many of our other arts, American music—including classical, folk, country, jazz, and show music—reflects our own diverse origins.

Throughout the Music section, we provide songs to help children hear the concepts being taught. As has been our practice in the earlier books in this series, the songs we include for this purpose are widely known. If you or your child do not know the melody for a particular song, you will find it readily available in a library on record or tape. If you read music, you may wish to consult such collections as *Best Loved Songs of the American People* by Denis Agay or *Gonna Sing My Head Off! American Folk Songs for Children* by Kathleen Krull.

In the Visual Arts section we discuss art traditions that led into the modern period, focusing on realism in particular. We then show how artists began breaking away from realism with abstract styles, including those that came to be known as impressionism, expressionism, and cubism. We conclude with a brief introduction to some modern American artists who created works that reflect our culture and landscape.

For further reading:

The Art for Children Series by Ernest Raboff (Harper Collins). Titles include *Van Gogh* and *Picasso*.

Children of Promise: African-American Literature and Art for Young People by Charles Sullivan (Abrams, 1991).

The Getting to Know the World's Greatest Artist Series by Mike Venezia (Children's Press). Artists include Hopper, Monet, Picasso, Klee, and Van Gogh.

First Impressions—Introductions to Art by Gary Schwartz (Abrams). Titles include *Pablo Picasso, Claude Monet,* and *Andrew Wyeth*.

Linnea in Monet's Garden by Christina Bjork (Farrar, Straus & Giroux, 1987).

Music

SHARPS, FLATS, AND MORE ABOUT HARMONY

Sharps and Flats: The Black Keys

So far in this series, we've told you only about the white keys on the piano. What are the black keys for? Within an octave, the black keys give you five more notes to play with, like five more colors for a painting. We call these black keys sharps or flats.

Sharps and flats are shown on a staff by using the sharp and flat signs before the notes. The sharp sign ♯ before a note means that you hit the black key above (to the right of) the note shown, while the flat sign ♭ means that you hit the black key below (to the left of) that note. Look at the keyboard illustration below. The black note just above C and below D can be written either as C♯ or D♭.

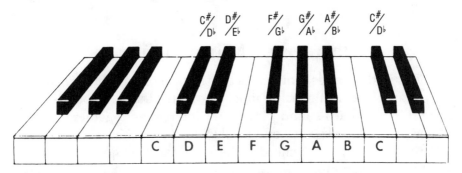

Now put your finger on middle C. Play every key on the keyboard, white and black, up to the next C. Did you notice that every note went up the exact same amount over the note before? The difference between one note and the next closest note on the keyboard is called a "half step."

Two half steps equal a whole step. So the interval between two white keys with a black key between them (such as C and D) is called a whole step. Notice there are times when you hit two white keys in a row *without* any black key between them. Can you find them? That's right: E and F, and B and C. The major scale is made up of whole steps and half steps in this order: 2 whole steps, half step; 3 whole steps; half step.

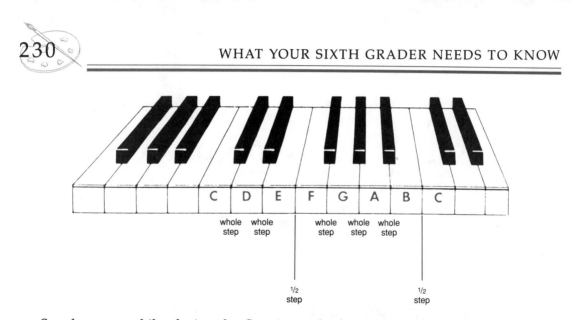

Say the steps while playing the C major scale, from middle C: Whole step, whole step, half step; whole step, whole step, whole step; half step.

As long as you keep this order of whole steps and half steps, you can play a major scale starting with *any* note. Start on the G note, and play just the white keys, counting out the order: (G–A) whole step, (A–B) whole step, (B–C) half step; (C–D) whole step, (D–E) whole step—but wait! the next step (E–F) is only a half step! So instead of F, we play the black note above it, the F♯, to get the whole step. And F♯ is just the right amount, a half step, from our top G! That is why the G major scale and the key of G major have an F♯ in them. Different keys use different numbers of sharps or flats, more or fewer black keys, to make their major scales.

Harmony: Minor Chords

In earlier books in this series, you learned that harmony in music occurs when you play two or more notes at the same time. The notes that are sounded together are called a chord. If the notes sound pleasant or interesting together, that's called harmony. If they sound awful, that's often called "discord." You also learned three important chords: the 1, 4, and 5 chords. These are called major chords, because they have a bright, happy sound. Now we are going to learn about minor chords. Let's make a minor chord, the 6 chord, hitting the 6, 8, and 10 notes. In our key of C major these are the A, C, and E notes, like this:

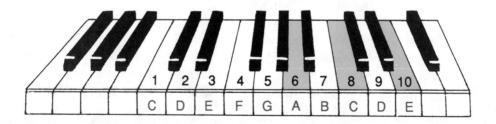

This is called the A minor chord. Does that sound different to you from the other chords we've learned? Many people think this chord sounds sad, while the major chords sound happy. Play a 1 chord (in the key of C, remember, the 1 chord is CEG), and then play the 6 chord, several times. Can you hear how the sound changes? Can you see why people would say it goes from "happy" to "sad"? There are many minor chords, and they are often used in sad songs like the blues. Here are two famous American songs that use minor chords. (The small m next to the capital letter for the chord tells you the chord is minor.)

Sometimes I Feel like a Motherless Child

```
Em                                 C      Em
Sometimes I feel like a motherless child

Am                       Em
Sometimes I feel like a motherless child

                              C
Sometimes I feel like a motherless child

    Em           Am   Em
A long ways from home.

    C7     Em  B7     Em
A long ways from home.
```

Summertime (by George Gershwin)

```
Am                       Dm      Am
Summertime and the livin' is easy.

Dm                                E7
Fish are jumpin', and the cotton is high.

Am                       Dm      Am
Your daddy's rich, and your mama's good-lookin'

    C          Dm7   E7      Am
So hush, little baby, don't you cry.
```

What Is a B7 Chord?

You can make a special version of the B chord by adding an extra note, the seventh note from B, to the chord. The B chord is made up of notes B, D, and F♯. To make the B7 chord you add the seventh note A. There are many 7 chords, and the 7 note is always a whole tone below the octave. Can you figure out how to make the G7 and C7 chords using the same method we used to make the B7?

Can you hear how minor chords have their own distinctive sound? When you listen to a song or other piece of music, try to figure out whether it uses mostly major or minor chords, whether it is in a major or minor key. In classical music, the title of the piece will usually tell you if it's in a major or minor key; for example, Beethoven's Symphony No. 5 in C Minor.

Some songs shift back and forth between major and minor chords. You can hear this shift in the first two lines of this famous song from the Civil War, "When Johnny Comes Marching Home." Sing the song and listen for the change to a happier sound on "hurrah"!

When Johnny Comes Marching Home

Am   C
When Johnny comes marching home again, hurrah! Hurrah!
Am   C
When Johnny comes marching home again, hurrah! Hurrah!
                                    Dm
The men will cheer and the boys will shout

Am   E7
The ladies they will all turn out
                    Am Dm Am   E7   Am   Dm   Am
And we'll all feel glad when Johnny comes marching home.

Major and minor chords are often used to contrast with each other, like light and dark colors in a painting.

Two Simple Ways to Harmonize

Singing harmony is one of the most enjoyable ways to sing a song and make it sound wonderful. Here are two simple ways to harmonize. One way is for one person to sing the melody while others softly hum the notes of the chords that accompany it. You'll find it's lots of fun. Another simple way to harmonize is to sing the same melody shape (which we explain in Book Five) a little higher or lower than the melody. Find a friend and try this with a song you know.

Singing a third higher or lower than the main melody line often makes a pleasant harmony, but the exact interval between the notes will depend on the song. Try different variations! This takes practice, but it can sound great, and just two people can do it.

Rhythm: Syncopation

Regular rhythms repeat over and over in the same way. For example, 1 2 3 4 / 1 2 3 4. Musicians also like to make different rhythms by stressing uneven beats, or by making some beats last longer than others. This gives the rhythm an exciting variety. It can even seem like two rhythms are going at once! This is called "syncopation," and it is often used in African and Latin rhythms. Here is one syncopated rhythm.

1 2 3 1 2 3 1 2

Try it again, and keep repeating it: 1 2 3 1 2 3 1 2 / 1 2 3 1 2 3 1 2. Sounds different, doesn't it? That's because all the accented beats are not spaced evenly apart—not all strong beats follow two unstressed beats. Now say it over and over, keeping the counting going, but tap or clap your hands on the 1 beats. 1 2 3 1 2 3 1 2 / 1 2 3 1 2 3 1 2, etc. See if you can keep this beat going while singing songs in 4/4 time.

Many Calypso songs from the Caribbean islands show the influence of African rhythms and have syncopated rhythms in them. You may know one such song, called "Day-O" or "The Banana Boat Song."

Patterns in Music

Do you know what a pattern is? Here is one you can easily see:

Here's another:

You already know that pictures and designs have patterns you can see. Music is made out of patterns of sound. If you couldn't hear the pattern, you probably wouldn't think it was music. Notice that the patterns above are all made up of groups that repeat themselves. But you can also make interesting patterns by changing the repetitions:

When you change the repeated pattern, it's called a "variation."

Composers use repetition and variation to organize their music. This is very much like nature itself, in which we see patterns repeated and varied. Think of snowflakes, which all have six sides, or maple leaves, which all have the same shape, or even people, who are all similar but who have many variations in height, weight, etc.

Repetition and variation are the basis of jazz music. When a jazz band plays, often one musician will begin by playing the melody of a familiar song, and repeat it two or three times (this is repetition). Then the musicians will do variations on the melody, playing the melody slightly differently each time, adding different things. Different instruments each take their turn to "show off" while changing the melody slightly. Sometimes the changes will be so different from the melody that it's hard to tell how they came from it. But this is the fun of it—to understand how each variation relates to the original melody. Then at the end, one instrument or the whole band will play the melody as it was originally written, so you end, as you began, on another repetition. (Do you know the song "My Favorite Things" from *The Sound of Music*? You might be amazed at how the great jazz saxophonist John Coltrane plays variations on this song in an improvisation that lasts thirteen minutes!)

Some pieces of classical music are called "Theme and Variations," and work the same way. A "theme" is another word for a melody. When you see a piece or a movement called a "Theme and Variations," listen for the repetition and variation. (For example, listen to the first movement of Mozart's piano sonata in A, K.331.)

Building Up to a Climax

Another pattern music uses is to build up to a great climax, and slowly fall off, or become peaceful or resolved. (Pictures, plays, stories, and films often work this way, too.) The music can build in a number of ways: by getting louder, by going faster or slower, by going up higher, by having more instruments play, by changing keys, etc. Usually this is done in steps. The music will build slightly, and fall off just a bit and then build higher still, and fall a bit, over and over until it reaches a great height. To visualize the way music builds to a climax, think of a mountain range getting higher as the music goes along.

When the music builds louder and louder to a climax, it's called a "crescendo." See if you can find this pattern when you listen to a symphony. Sing "The Star-Spangled Banner" and notice how it builds to a great height near the end when you sing "the land of the free," and then finishes peacefully on "the home of the brave."

Choruses

If you have ever heard the song "Jingle Bells," then you have heard a chorus. In "Jingle Bells," the chorus goes like this:

Jingle Bells, Jingle Bells
   Jingle all the way
O what fun it is to ride
In a one-horse open sleigh!

You sing these lines several times, don't you? They get repeated after each new verse. Verses are the sets of lines that come between repetitions of the chorus in a song. Notice that the melody for the verses is the same, while the words or lyrics of each verse change. On the other hand, both the melody and the lines of the chorus are always the same.

In "Jingle Bells," there is a pattern of repetition (in the chorus) and variation (in the verses). You will hear this form of repetition and variation in many songs on the radio. Sometimes the chorus is sung even before the first verse, as in "Jingle Bells," but the chorus always follows the verse, as well. Can you think of some other songs that use a chorus and verses to make patterns of repetition and variation? How about "Swing Low, Sweet Chariot," for example?

What Is American Music?

In 1924, composers were invited to submit original musical compositions for performance at a New York City concert dedicated to answering the question "What is American Music?" There's no simple answer to the question. Because people from many different countries have come to live in the United States, American music embraces a wide variety of styles and traditions from many different cultures. Some of these styles and traditions have mixed to form kinds of music that are distinctively American: jazz, blues, Broadway show tunes, rock-and-roll, all of which have become popular around the world.

One very strong influence in the United States has been African music. Complex rhythms and chants were brought from Africa to America by slaves. Eventually, African music mixed with the musical traditions brought over by European settlers to produce new kinds of music, including spirituals, jazz, the blues, and soul.

The great modern American composer Duke Ellington (1899–1974) is best known for his jazz compositions. Ellington himself didn't like the term "jazz," but preferred to call his music "the music of my people." He became the leader of a jazz band during the "Roaring Twenties," when jazz was growing especially popular among young people. In New York City, at the famous Cotton Club, people would line up

Louis Armstrong on trumpet, Lil Hardin on piano, and Baby Dodds on drums in King Oliver's Creole Jazz Band.

to hear and dance to the music of the Duke Ellington Orchestra. (At this time, the Cotton Club was segregated, so while Ellington and his band were black, the audience was white, with the exception of an occasional famous black entertainer who would be "let in.") Ellington wrote (or cowrote with members of his orchestra) many jazz works that people still enjoy today, including such favorites as "Caravan," "Ko-Ko," "Don't Get Around Much Anymore," and "In a Sentimental Mood." He also wrote some ambitious compositions that merge jazz and classical styles, including orchestral works like *Creole Rhapsody* and *Black, Brown, and Beige.*

Some of the best-loved and most-respected twentieth-century American classical music mixes a variety of styles and influences. For example, if you're familiar with such famous European classical piano concertos as those by Mozart or Beethoven, then you might be surprised by a piano concerto called *Rhapsody in Blue*, by the American composer George Gershwin (1898–1937). Gershwin wrote *Rhapsody in Blue* for the 1924 concert on the theme of "What is American Music?" The *Rhapsody* opens with a slinky, sultry passage for the clarinet that has a distinctively jazzy feel. The concerto was written for "Jazz Band and Piano," though it is often performed and recorded today with a full symphony orchestra.

Some of the greatest examples of how modern American music mixes a variety of styles are the ballet scores by Aaron Copland (1900–1990). In *Rodeo*, for example, Copland made wonderful orchestral music that draws upon traditional cowboy songs and square-dance tunes. In the score for *Appalachian Spring*, Copland wove in the melody of a Shaker hymn called "Simple Gifts" (the Shakers are a deeply religious community in New England, noted for their simple way of life and their fine craftsmanship). Here are the words to "Simple Gifts"; if you know the melody, then listen for it when you hear *Appalachian Spring*, and notice how Copland weaves it into his music, sometimes by simply quoting the tune, sometimes by transforming it into new but recognizable melodies.

'Tis the gift to be simple,
'Tis the gift to be free;
'Tis the gift to come down
Where we ought to be;
And when we find ourselves in the place just right,
'Twill be in the valley of love and delight.
When true simplicity is gained.
To bow and to bend we shan't be ashamed.
To turn, turn will be our delight,
Till by turning, turning we come round right.

Visual Arts

In the Spirit of the Greeks and Romans

In Book Five of this series, we described the history and art of the Renaissance, which took place in Europe from about 1350 to 1600. It was a period when many European artists were inspired by the art of the ancient Greeks and Romans. Even after the Renaissance, artists continued to develop and build upon what they learned from classical Greece and Rome, showing human figures that looked like real people in action as the Greeks and Romans had done.

Here is one example of the classical art that was still being created in Europe in the late eighteenth century, about a hundred years after the Renaissance. It was painted in 1784 by a French artist named Jacques-Louis David (dah-VEED) and is called *Oath of the Horatii*. It depicts the three sons of Horatius, a Roman nobleman, swearing to their father that they will come back from battle either victorious or dead.

Oath of the Horatii *by Jacques-Louis David.*

You can tell from the Roman columns and arches in the background and from the clothing of the people that David painted the people to look like Romans. If you look carefully you will see that David included many details that make the people look very lifelike. You can see the muscles and veins under the men's skins. On the far right, you can see the dimpled joint of the woman's elbow. A strong light creates dark shadows that shade faces and bodies, giving them a rounded look. David's painting looks even more lifelike than much of the Greek and Roman art that inspired it.

Like Real Life

When a work of art shows objects with almost all the exactness and detail of a modern photograph, we say that it is realistic, and part of a style called "realism." Realistic works can be very powerful because people looking at them are reminded of people, things, or events in their own lives.

For example, the people of eighteenth-century France were very enthusiastic about David's *Oath of the Horatii* because they felt it set an example for them. The

French were angry with the aristocrats who were their leaders, and were almost ready to take up arms against them. When French people saw this painting, it reminded them that they should be willing to fight and die for their beliefs. (Keep in mind that five years after David's painting, the French Revolution started.)

David was so popular that Napoleon Bonaparte, who came to power after the French Revolution, made David the head of an art school that was part of Napoleon's government. That position gave David great influence, and many artists came to believe that David's realistic style was the best way to paint. David's realism powerfully influenced artists all over Europe and North America. Gradually people began to believe this style was the standard for fine art.

American Realists: Tanner and Homer

Here is a realistic work that was painted by the African-American artist Henry O. Tanner in 1893. Even if no one ever told you what the painting was about, it would be easy to imagine a story by looking at it. It probably doesn't surprise you that the painting is called *The Banjo Lesson.*

In Tanner's painting a man and a boy both look at a banjo, with their heads close together. Light filtering in from the left makes a bright glow behind their heads, so that we tend to pay attention to this part of the painting. Now look at the position of the man's head and knees. See how they form a triangle with a broad base? Triangles like this tend to give people the feeling of steadiness because the horizontal line of the base looks stable to us. Because the man is painted in a stable, steady shape, he seems to be a secure support for the boy. We feel that the boy is getting strong encouragement from the man. All these things give us the vivid impression that the man and boy are close to one another both emotionally and physically, as they share the experience of playing the banjo.

As a young man, Henry Tanner went to one of the finest art schools in the United States, but when he finished, a very fine artist, he was deeply disappointed to find that he could not make a living by painting. Even though slavery had ended decades earlier, African-

The Banjo Lesson *by Henry O. Tanner.*

Americans were not accepted as equals by whites, and there was still much discrimination against hiring African-Americans. As fine an artist as Tanner was, it was difficult for him to sell his paintings. So in 1891 Tanner left the United States and went to live and study in Paris. *The Banjo Lesson* was painted two years after Tanner arrived there.

It's true that the subjects of *The Banjo Lesson* and *Oath of the Horatii* are not alike. *Oath of the Horatii* shows figures from the classic world of Rome, while *The Banjo Lesson* shows figures from Tanner's own place and time. But both paintings are done in a realistic style. Like many realistic works, both paintings make it easy for us to imagine the story that lies behind them. When Tanner went to school, many years after David died, artists were still taught that realism was the mark of fine art.

About the time Tanner was struggling to gain acceptance as an artist, another American artist, Winslow Homer, was busy painting the seascapes that would make him famous. This one is called *Northeaster*. A northeaster is a storm or gale that blows in from the northeast. In this painting Homer shows the force of such a storm on the coast of Maine. If you were standing on the rocks pictured here, what do you think you would feel on your face? What would you hear?

Homer first learned to draw realistically by illustrating magazines in the 1850s and 1860s. In those days, when photography was still an experimental process, magazines used drawings instead of photographs to show the news. During the Civil War, Winslow Homer earned his living by going to the camps of the Northern armies and drawing scenes for war news. Later he gave up working for magazines so that he could devote himself to perfecting his painting.

Northeaster *by Winslow Homer.*

Then Homer made a move that deeply affected his art. He went to live in an English fishing village on the North Sea coast. For two years he watched the sea and lived with people who had to work around its awesome power. During his time in England, Homer found the sea an endlessly fascinating subject for his paintings. When he moved back to the United States, he lived on the New England coast so he could continue to study and paint the sea. It was so important to Homer to paint the sea realistically that he made a small hut of plate glass, which he could push around on runners on the rocky shore. This shelter gave him enough protection to watch the sea and paint it even during storms!

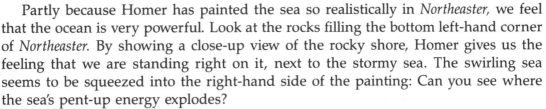
Partly because Homer has painted the sea so realistically in *Northeaster,* we feel that the ocean is very powerful. Look at the rocks filling the bottom left-hand corner of *Northeaster.* By showing a close-up view of the rocky shore, Homer gives us the feeling that we are standing right on it, next to the stormy sea. The swirling sea seems to be squeezed into the right-hand side of the painting: Can you see where the sea's pent-up energy explodes?

When Winslow Homer and Henry Tanner painted, they tried, like most artists, to make their paintings very realistic. But in the years ahead, artists would begin to leave realism and explore new ways of representing the world.

Something New: Impressionism

Here is a water scene as peaceful as *Northeaster* is energetic. This painting, by a French artist named Claude Monet (moh-NAY), is called *Bridge Over a Pool of Water Lilies.* Around 1890, when Monet was fifty, he bought a house in the village of Giverny, France. Three years later he bought land around the house, and began making an enormous garden. Every year he planted more flowers, and he even made a pond so that he could cultivate water lilies. Monet's many paintings of water lilies are some of his most famous works.

Bridge Over a Pool of Water Lilies
by Claude Monet.

Detail of Bridge Over a Pool of Water Lilies.

Hold *Bridge Over a Pool of Water Lilies* a hand's length from your face. Most people see a blurred image—blobs and blotches of paint—when they view Monet's works up close. Now stand at arm's length from the painting. The blobs and blotches turn into water lilies floating on a reflecting pond! If you try the same experiment with *Northeaster,* you will notice a completely different effect. The seascape remains almost as distinct when you look at it close up as when you look at it from farther away.

How did Monet create this unusual effect? The secret lies in the way he brushed paint onto the canvas. Look at this close-up detail of water lilies by Monet. You can see the clumps of oil paint, and even the scratchy marks made by the bristles of Monet's brush. Instead of painting very precisely and smoothly, as was typical for artists of the day, Monet loosely dabbed paint on the canvas.

Monet used a loose brush stroke because he noticed that sunlight changes its position and intensity as the sun travels overhead. Changes in sunlight in turn change the way the landscape looks. Monet wanted to paint the immediate effect of particular qualities of light on the landscape. He would work on a painting for only a half-hour at a time because after that, the light changed. During the time he painted, he didn't try to get every detail down precisely. Instead, he quickly painted his impression of the moment. His loose brush strokes allowed him to work fast and capture the image of a landscape under a fleeting condition of light.

In addition to painting with a loose brush stroke, Monet used vibrant, light colors to suggest the bright colors of the landscape in sunlight. (The photograph in this book shows the pond scene in black and white. You need to imagine the greens, whites, and pinks of Monet's painting, or even better, check your library for a book that offers color reproductions.)

The first time Monet publicly showed a work painted in his original style, the art world was shocked! A realistic style, such as the kind you see in *Oath of the Horatii,* had been the standard for so long that people thought Monet was breaking all the rules of art. Because he painted his *impression* of sunlight on the water, instead of a faithfully rendered, detailed image, the critics scornfully called works by Monet and his friends "impressionism." This was not a compliment: it meant they thought Monet had not finished his work properly.

It took many years for people to appreciate Monet's style. He could barely sell a painting and was often terribly depressed about his debts. But finally, people began to understand the value of his work, and today paintings by Monet and others called Impressionists are some of the best-known pieces of art in the world.

A Night of Fiery Stars

Some artists, like Monet, were interested in showing the marvels of the real world. Others, like Vincent van Gogh (van-GO), wanted to show not just what the eye sees but what the heart and the mind know.

Van Gogh began working as an artist around 1880. Although he was Dutch, he went to live in Paris for a time and became influenced by the impressionistic style of loose brush strokes and bright colors. But Van Gogh wasn't satisfied with working in the impressionist style because it didn't allow him to show enough of what he

Detail of The Starry Night.

The Starry Night
by Vincent van Gogh.

felt. He moved to southern France, and there developed a distinctive style of his own.

One of Van Gogh's paintings, called *The Starry Night*, shows a village under the night sky in southern France. Van Gogh loved vivid colors because they helped him show what he felt when he looked at a landscape. This photograph of *The Starry Night* is in black and white, but the painting is actually filled with brilliant purples, blues, and yellows. The colors are like those of the night sky, but much stronger than you might see in real life.

In addition to using strong colors in his paintings, Van Gogh used the texture of paint itself to help create striking images. In this detail of *The Starry Night*, you can see that Van Gogh's paint is so thick it almost looks like layers of clay. He put paint on the canvas with his brush, a knife, or sometimes right from the paint tube itself, and then made ridges in the paint with his brush. See how the paint seems to ripple out from the moon? The ridges of thick paint make the curved lines stand out more boldly in the painting than color alone could have done.

The total effect of Van Gogh's use of color and texture is electrifying. The whole sky seems to be on the move. Light pulses out from the stars and moon, and the sky almost churns with activity. A dark green cypress tree on the left twists up to the heavens, and the line of the hills seems to follow the light of the stars. In a letter to his brother, Van Gogh once wrote, "The sight of stars makes me dream." In this painting, Van Gogh seems to show us that the stars themselves take part in his dream by reaching toward the sleepy earth with all their vibrant energy.

Although Van Gogh's paintings now sell for millions of dollars, during his own day, few people were willing to buy them. His expressive style seemed strange and shocking to people at that time. Often Van Gogh had to go without food, and he depended on money from his admiring brother in Paris. Although he loved the inspirational landscape of southern France, he had few friends there, and almost no one to talk with about his work. He began to suffer from mental illness, and the townspeople avoided him or made fun of him. Feeling isolated and fearful about his illness, he took his own life less than a year after painting *The Starry Night*.

Unfinished Work?

What is the first thing you notice about this statue? Many people respond that the statue shows a man pondering a serious topic. That makes sense because this statue, called *The Thinker*, was designed to be placed over a set of great doors which would show the things that happened to people in hell. Both *The Thinker* and the doors were designed by Auguste Rodin (row-DAN), an artist who lived and worked in France around the same time as Monet.

Like Monet, Rodin was much criticized for his nontraditional style. In the 1800s there was a strict standard for realistic sculpture, just as there was for painting. People still looked back to the statues of the Greeks and Romans and to artists of the Renaissance for models of excellent sculpture. The marble and bronze statues

they admired were polished to a smooth texture, so some people thought a smooth finish was one of the essential marks of fine sculpture. Notice that the surface of *The Thinker* is wrinkled and rippled. Even though Rodin's statues are realistic and detailed, critics felt that he did not properly finish his work.

Leaving the surface of the statue wrinkled and rippled, though, gives the statue an effect it would not have if it were smooth. Imagine a calm pool of water. Not a breeze stirs. The surface of the pool is as flat as a mirror. Now imagine that wind stirs up the surface of the water. There are ripples and waves everywhere you look. Which image of the pool gives the impression that something is happening? *The Thinker* shows a man in a still, quiet position, but because the "skin" of the figure

The Thinker *by Auguste Rodin.*

shows so much movement, we get the feeling there's a lot happening here. The rippled surface of *The Thinker* adds to the impression that the man must be thinking and feeling a great deal. In this way, Rodin was able to express more than his subject matter alone could show.

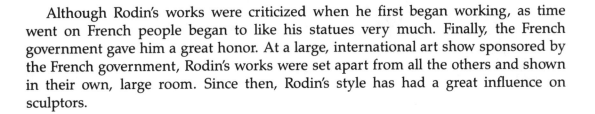
Although Rodin's works were criticized when he first began working, as time went on French people began to like his statues very much. Finally, the French government gave him a great honor. At a large, international art show sponsored by the French government, Rodin's works were set apart from all the others and shown in their own, large room. Since then, Rodin's style has had a great influence on sculptors.

Abstractionism: A Different Way of Seeing

As you have seen in reading about the early criticisms of Monet, Van Gogh, and Rodin, precise realism had become such an accepted standard in Europe and North America that people thought any other style was not fine art. But artists in Europe and America, after coming into contact with art from China, Japan, and Africa, began to realize that there are many other excellent ways for artists to depict feelings and objects. They began to incorporate some aspects of art from other cultures into

their own, particularly the use of nonrealistic forms in which some details are kept simple and others are exaggerated. When an artist represents objects by simplifying and exaggerating shapes or colors, we say that he or she is working in an abstract style.

These three drawings by the Spanish artist Pablo Picasso (Pee-KAH-so) are examples of a bull drawn in realistic and abstract manners. The drawing to the left is realistic. It shows us a lot of details

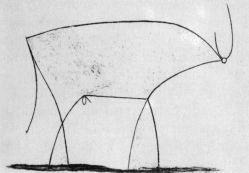

and the full shape of the bull: for example, we see its nostrils and the bristles on its back, and we see that its side and back leg are rounded. This drawing has so much detail that we might be able to identify the actual bull that the artist used as a model, if we saw it.

The other two drawings are abstract. In them you see how the artist works toward making his drawing of the bull as direct and simple as possible. The drawing on the bottom right shows the bare essentials of a bull's shape: its body, tail, legs, and horns. This drawing is so simple that we could not recognize a particular bull by looking at it. Instead, it immediately and forcefully shows us the idea of a bull's shape. (You can read more about Picasso's experiments with abstraction later in this chapter.)

A Navajo Sand Painting

While European artists had developed a tradition of working in a realistic style, other cultures had a long tradition of abstract art forms. Some Native American artists also work in an abstract style. Navajo Indian artists make abstract paintings that don't use oil paints, watercolors, or any kind of wet materials. Their artworks are called sand paintings because the artist's materials are crushed charcoal, cornmeal, crushed rocks, and sand. The artist makes a sand painting by pouring these materials onto the ground according to one of hundreds of traditional designs. It is a delicate task to make this kind of artwork because, as you can imagine, once the materials are poured it is very hard to correct mistakes.

This design is called *Whirling Logs*. The whirling logs are the two bars that cross in the center of the painting to form the shape of the cross. Each end of the cross reaches out to one of the four points of the compass. On the end of each arm of the cross are the figures of a man and a woman. These figures represent Father Sky and Mother Earth. The figure stretched around three arms of the cross is the Rainbow. Because sand paintings express the Navajos' beliefs about gods and the universe, they are considered religious artworks.

Even though the figures in this sand painting are human, they are abstract representations of the human body. Father Sky's head is a circle and Mother Earth's head is a rectangle. Their bodies are long, slender triangles. Their hands are long lines radiating out from a circle. Eyes and mouths are shown as dashes. Every sand painting pattern shows bodies in a slightly different fashion and arranged in different configurations, but all human images are shown with round or rectangular heads, long bodies, and dashes for eyes and mouths. They are "drawn" as distinctly and symmetrically as these are.

For the painting shown in this pho-

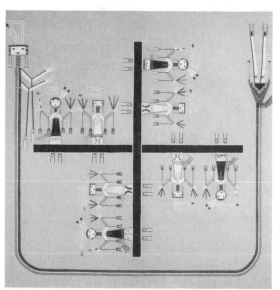

Whirling Logs, *a Navajo sand painting.*

tograph, the materials were glued to a board so that the artwork could be shown in a museum, but real sand paintings are destroyed shortly after they are made. That's because a sand painting has a specific purpose: it is part of a healing ceremony. The Navajo people believe that all parts of the earth work together in harmony and that when a person becomes sick, he or she has fallen out of that harmony. To cure a sick person, a healer must restore that person's harmony. The healer may use a painting because its beauty and harmony are thought to have powerful healing qualities. When the healer finishes the sand painting, the sick person sits in it in order to absorb its beauty. Sometimes part of the painting is also poured on the sick areas of the patient's body. After this part of the ceremony is finished, the sand painting is destroyed and buried so that the illness of the sick person cannot bring evil to others.

A Yoruba Sculpture

Here is an abstract sculpture made by a Yoruba (yuh-ROO-ba) artist from Nigeria, Africa. It is part of a huge hatlike headpiece worn by dancers in a festive ceremony called a *gelede* (guh-LAY-day).

Yoruba artists often make sculptures that are abstract. It is easy to tell that this sculpture shows a human head, but the figure is not entirely realistic. When we look at this sculpture, we can't see the wrinkles that a real human face has. We don't see the contour of cheekbones, eyebrows, or a chin. Instead, the artist carved the human face as if it were made up of basic geometric shapes. The mouth is in the shape of a rectangle. The nose is a vertical ridge with two half-spheres for the nostrils. The face is rounded, almost a perfect oval. The eyes, exaggerated to be larger-than-life, are roughly the shape of half-circles and have thick eyelids. The eyes are so large that we tend to pay the most attention to them, and have to make an effort to focus on the other features of the face.

Just as Picasso's abstract drawing shows the idea of a bull's shape, the Yoruba abstract sculpture shows an idea about human features, not a detailed, realistic image of a particular human face. When you look at this sculpture, you may notice that its round, smooth features create the effect of a pleasant expression, but not an emotional one. The Yoruba believe people should behave calmly and with composure, so they expect sculptures to show this idea, too. Yoruba sculptures vary in appearance according to the individual carver's style and the function of the artwork, but most show rounded, calm faces with the traditional larger-than-life eyes, as this one does.

Yoruba headdress.

A Terrible Cry

Now let's look at another abstract face, but one very different from the calm faces depicted in the Yoruba sculpture.

The year that Van Gogh painted *The Starry Night,* an artist named Edvard Munch (MOONK) traveled from his native Norway to Paris to learn more about painting. There he saw works by many experimental artists, including Van Gogh. Munch applied what he learned in his many works that show images of people with staring, abstract faces set in a dreary landscape.

Have you ever watched a scary movie late at night? Remember how hard it was to get to sleep afterward, how every creak in the dark seemed the sound of some new horror? What if the whole world was your bedroom on a night like that? You might want to scream and run, but you'd be too scared to move or make a noise. When he painted *The Scream,* Edvard Munch expressed that kind of anxiety. He found a way to cry out without making a sound: instead of using his voice to express his feelings, he showed a frozen scream.

When Munch finished one version of *The Scream,* he wrote on the back of it, "I felt a great cry in the whole universe." How did Munch show this? Instead of creating a detailed, realistic face for the screamer, he designed its features to remain simple. Munch used long oval shapes for the eyes and mouth and an indented oval for the face. The line of the face on either side of the mouth repeats the shape of the mouth and then expands outward and upward through the top of the figure's head. On either side of the scream-ing person, Munch made wavy lines that spread up and out so that the shape of the screaming mouth seems to be drawn out and repeated in waving, rip-pling lines. It's as though these lines show the scream echoing through the world around the fig-ure, the whole painting expressing raw emotion.

The Scream *by Edvard Munch.*

Munch made many versions of *The Scream.* He first painted it, then several years later made the lithograph of it you see here. To make a lithograph, an artist draws with a grease-based crayon on a hard surface called a plate. When the drawing is finished, the artist wets the plate. The crayon marks, being water-resistant, do not get wet. Then onto the damp plate the artist rolls ink that clings to the greasy crayon, but not to the wet plate. Finally the artist presses paper against the plate to absorb the ink and make a mirror image of the picture that was drawn on the plate. Often a lithograph, such as this one of *The Scream,* looks like a black-and-white drawing.

Cubes and Triangles

By the early 1900s, people in Europe had seen much art that broke away from the realistic standards of the day. But then Pablo Picasso shocked even the most adventurous artists when he painted this work, *The Ladies of Avignon.* More than any other artist of his time, Picasso experimented with different ways to show the world in an abstract style. At twenty-five, Picasso had been an artist almost all his life, and had already mastered the techniques of realistic art. He was searching for new ways to paint and was inspired by several African artworks, including this mask made by the Fang (FONG) people, and this brass figure made by the Bakota people. When Picasso saw these African works, he realized that African artists had their own standards for art that were very different from European ideas of realistic beauty. African works seemed to Picasso more direct and powerful than European works, and they gave him new ways to think about art.

The Ladies of Avignon *by Pablo Picasso.*

The African artworks Picasso saw were abstract images of the human face. Picasso decided to experiment with ways of showing human features based on African styles of representation. Compare the Fang and Bakota works with the two figures on the right in *The Ladies of Avignon.* Like the faces in the African works, Picasso's faces have triangular noses, long ovals for faces, and dashes for mouths. Because Picasso's figures looked to European artists as though they were made up of cubes and triangles, this style came to be known as cubism.

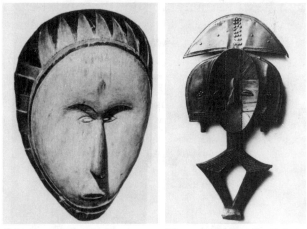

Mask made by the Fang.   *Figure made by the Bakota.*

Although Picasso's cubist style first shocked the art world, it soon attracted a following of artists in Europe and America who saw that it would give them exciting new directions to explore. For the next fifty years, Picasso led the way in cubist and other experimental art forms.

Picasso's Guernica

Have you ever seen a news documentary on war or thought about the suffering that people and animals experience in a war? This cubist painting by Picasso, called *Guernica* (GWERE-neek-a), shows such experiences. On the left side you can see a mother holding her dead child. On the bottom a fallen soldier lies, still clutching his broken sword. Above him rears a horse whose body is pierced with a spear. On the right, a woman on fire is trapped in a burning building. All the bodies look stretched out, or broken and jagged. The figures have open mouths as though they are crying out. The light bulb that shines on the scene gives out a light that looks like crooked, pointed teeth.

Notice that even though there are humans, animals, and buildings in this scene, there seems to be no middle ground or background. Because there is no perspective, figures and forms seem to be crammed together. We get the feeling the figures can't get away from the horrors of war—they are trapped in their suffering.

Guernica is painted in blacks, whites, and grays. Remember how Van Gogh used vivid colors to express his emotions and thoughts about a landscape? Why do you think Picasso did this particular painting *without* bright colors?

Another way Picasso emphasized his subject was to make his work very large. This photograph of *Guernica* is smaller than your two hands, but the real painting is bigger than the wall of most people's living rooms! The painting is so large that a person in the same room is forced to look at it—whether or not she wants to.

Despite its great size, Picasso painted *Guernica* in less than two months. He was in a fury of activity to paint this work because the war that inspired it made him very angry. In 1937 Picasso was living in France, but his home country, Spain, was suffering from a civil war. Picasso was already upset about the war and then he read

Guernica by Pablo Picasso.

a terrible news story. The Spanish government had tested a new way of fighting on a small village called Guernica. It had sent planes over the defenseless village to drop enough bombs to destroy everything in sight. Many of Guernica's people had died, many more had suffered greatly—for an experiment! Picasso was outraged. He decided to paint a scene that would make all who saw it take notice of the brutal event.

Even though it was painted to protest and to commemorate the bombing of Guernica, Picasso's painting shows the kind of suffering that takes place in any war. People had often criticized Picasso because they thought his cubist style served no useful purpose in society: it didn't show the dramas of human life or relate the stories of history; it was not beautiful and so couldn't even be used as simple decoration. But Picasso proved them wrong. He used his cubist style to communicate a tragic message and a warning about war.

In a work like Guernica, *which conveys a strong message, the artist is making a comment on society. Is there something you would like to see changed in your school or society? Can you think of a way you can send a message about this issue in your own work of art?*

Back to Basics: Nonrepresentational Art

This painting is called *Broadway Boogie-Woogie*, and it was painted by the Dutch artist Piet Mondrian (MON-dree-ahn). As you can see, Mondrian's work is not done in a realistic style. But unlike *Starry Night* or *The Scream*, *Broadway Boogie-Woogie* was not painted in order to express Mondrian's reactions to the world around him. Instead, Mondrian is known for a style that we call nonrepresentational: that is, not representing objects at all. (Some people don't agree. They point out that even nonrepresentational art does represent such things as motion and vibration.)

Mondrian wanted mainly to show the visual effects that are made by putting lines and colors together. He said that what was important to him was to show the *relationships* between the most basic elements of art. Some of the paintings that Mondrian is best

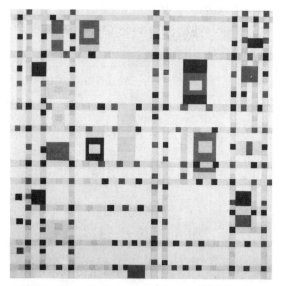

Broadway Boogie-Woogie *by Piet Mondrian.*

known for use only horizontal and vertical lines and the colors red, yellow, blue, black, and white.

Broadway is a street in New York City. *Broadway Boogie-Woogie* was made after Mondrian came to New York to live in the 1940s. He saw New York as a bustling city, with bright lights and activity everywhere. It seemed full of life compared to Europe, whose cities suffered from blackouts and bombing raids during World War II. Music and dancing were favorite forms of entertainment for New Yorkers, and Mondrian loved to dance. He especially liked dancing to the most energetic music in town, boogie-woogie.

Have you ever heard boogie-woogie? It's lively, bouncy, snappy music. Think of these qualities as you look at Mondrian's painting. The painting, like the music, is rhythmic, lively, pulsing.

Pick a song or piece of music you like. Listen to it several times. Then make an artwork that the music inspires.

Lonely Hawks

This painting is called *Nighthawks*. A nighthawk is a nocturnal bird found in North America. People often call it a night owl. Have you ever heard the expression, "He's a night owl"? It means that, like the nighthawk, that person likes being up late at night, when everyone else has gone to bed. In *Nighthawks*, the few people still up are in a small diner. The bright light from the diner makes a strong contrast to the dark streets. At the late hour, the streets are empty of cars and people. Looking at this painting, some people get the feeling that these night owls must be lonely people.

Nighthawks was painted by the American artist Edward Hopper in 1942. As you can see, Hopper preferred realism to the modern trends like abstraction coming from Europe.

Like Winslow Homer, Edward Hopper first learned art techniques by studying to be an illustrator. But he quickly became interested in painting, and went to art school in New York. There he was influenced by a group called the "Ash Can School," which rejected the artworks considered fashionable at the time, like flattering portraits, fruit and flower arrangements, and "pretty" scenes of country and home life. Instead, the Ash Can School painted scenes that ordinary people might encounter on city sidewalks or alleys. Critics made fun of the Ash Can artists, who they said liked to paint things you would see next to ash cans (garbage cans). But Hopper felt that city scenes were fine, real-life subjects for a painting, even if they showed settings that were lonely or unpleasant.

Nighthawks *by Edward Hopper.*

Christina's World

This painting, called *Christina's World*, is by the American artist Andrew Wyeth (WHY-eth). Andrew Wyeth very much admired Edward Hopper's work. Wyeth especially liked the way Hopper painted houses, people, and landscapes that are associated with daily life in the United States. Wyeth also painted daily life. He chose colors and lighting that came to be associated with his work: faded pinks, greens, and blues, and shades of browns, with lighting that comes from an early morning or a late afternoon sun.

Like *Nighthawks*, *Christina's World* is very realistic. For example, we see many real-looking details, like strands of the woman's hair blowing in the wind. In addition, like *Nighthawks*, *Christina's World* seems a lonely scene. There are some important differences between the two paintings, however. Look back at *Nighthawks*. Imagine you are seeing that scene in real life. Where would you be standing? Most people get the clear impression that they are across the street from the diner looking in at the people there. Because they know exactly where they stand, many people get the feeling that they are a part of the world they see in *Nighthawks*. Now look at *Christina's World*. It's hard to tell where a viewer would be standing. The grass seems to rise in front of our eyes, giving us the feeling that we are sitting very close to the ground. But the woman in this painting seems to be below us. It's hard to tell what kind of a view we have, so we don't really know where we stand. Partly for this reason,

Christina's World
by Andrew Wyeth.

people tend to feel a little lost when they look at *Christina's World*. This leads people to identify with the lonely figure, and feel her isolation even more keenly.

Wyeth spent a lot of time studying the people and places he painted. Once he said that by coming to know local people and places intimately, he would find the things about them that speak to everyone, not just those who live where he painted, in Pennsylvania and Maine.

Think of a scene you'd like to draw or paint. Then think of at least four different ways you could picture it, depending on where the viewer of the scene stands. (Remember what you read about the viewers of Nighthawks *and* Christina's World.) *Try to actually make at least two of these variations. You might even ask someone you know to tell you how the two differ. How were they different to make?*

Frank Lloyd Wright

Many people today, when they think of a very modern-looking home, imagine something like this house built at Bear Run, Pennsylvania. But the man who designed it, Frank Lloyd Wright, was ahead of his time. The house, called "Falling Water," was built almost sixty years ago! Wright made huge changes in the way people think about buildings, and his ideas still affect architecture.

Frank Lloyd Wright was born in Wisconsin in 1869 and lived there for much of his childhood and youth. During his teenage years, Wright spent the summers working from 4 A.M. till 8 P.M. on his uncle's farm. As he got used to the hard physical work on the farm, Wright began to enjoy being outdoors in the countryside. He noticed that the curves of the earth and the lines of trees made pleasing designs. He loved the way the natural shapes and colors of the landscape seemed to fit together in a graceful harmony. Many years later, Wright's love of nature shaped his work as an architect by inspiring him to build structures that complemented the landscape. He designed a series of houses called "prairie homes," whose natural-looking materials and flowing shapes seemed to fit in with the features of the surrounding prairie landscape. In addition, Wright designed his prairie homes without an attic, and made the ceiling lower than was common for houses at the time. This was because Wright noticed that, on the flat prairie, a little height makes a big impression. He wanted to make his houses seem as close to the ground as possible so that they would not disturb the lines of the landscape much.

Even though "Falling Water" at Bear Run is not on a treeless prairie, it shows many of the features of Wright's prairie homes. If you look at the outline of the house, you will notice that it is wider than it is tall. Rough-looking stones on the outside of the house look like chips off the stream's boulders. The house also has horizontal slabs that extend out over the stream's bank, parallel to it. It seems as though the house blends in naturally with the stream bank.

As an architect, Wright believed strongly in the idea that "form follows function." For Wright, this meant that an architect should design the form of a building based

"Falling Water" (the Kaufmann House) by Frank Lloyd Wright.

on how it would be used by people. The architect should create a design that makes it easy and pleasant for people to live or work in it. When he was designing his prairie homes, Wright realized that a home's most important function was shelter. He designed roofs that extended far beyond the walls of the house to emphasize the feeling that the home gives protection. Inside the house Wright planned as few walls as possible, so that people could easily walk around. He used natural-looking stones and wood for floors, walls, and ceilings so people would feel the steadiness of solid, natural elements around them. And he built many wide windows, including windows on the corners of rooms, to bring in light and give the home a spacious feel.

During the 1900s, architects looked to Europe for standards in architecture, just as painters had. Although there were architects in the United States who were designing interesting buildings, none had created designs that reflected America's particular landscape and culture. But Wright's prairie homes were an architectural revolution. With these designs, Wright showed architects how to break away from traditions and design buildings that harmonized both with human needs and nature's beauty. As a result, Wright's ideas have affected not just the way American architects look at buildings, but the way modern architects think about design.

IV.

MATHEMATICS

Introduction to Sixth-Grade Mathematics

FOR PARENTS AND TEACHERS

The mathematics sections in *The Core Knowledge Series* are designed as detailed *summaries* of the math that should be mastered in each grade. We hope you will supplement them with continual opportunities for practice. Like the learning of music, the learning of math requires practice: not mindless repetition, but thoughtful and varied practice that approaches problems from a variety of angles, makes use of intuition, and encourages facility at quickly estimating correct results.

The difference between the typical math curriculum in the United States and those employed in countries such as Japan and France, which have more successful math programs, becomes dramatic in the fifth grade. Whereas our students usually spend most of that year on basic arithmetic, Japanese and French students have moved on to the kind of mathematics presented in the fifth-grade book of this series. And by the time they reach the sixth grade, those students are expected to become fluent in and comfortable with a more sophisticated level of mathematics than is presently required of our sixth graders. By mastering the concepts outlined in the mathematics sections of this series, American students—all of them—can attain a similar success. This chapter assumes that students have mastered the techniques for adding, subtracting, and multiplying whole numbers. In Book Six they will continue to learn the arithmetic that will form the basis of algebra, and to pursue studies in geometry. This work includes dividing by decimals, writing fractions as decimals or as percents, learning about proportions and the relationships among proportions, understanding exponents and expanded notation, working with positive and negative integers, and continued practice with word problems. In geometry, students learn to find the area of a circle. They also learn to construct angles and triangles to given specifications and to find the volume of prisms. We continue to detail working with both metric and customary units of measurement, but recommend practicing with metric measures whenever possible, since working with metric measurements can help develop an understanding of place value.

Math is potentially great fun, and math skill yields a sense of accomplishment and self-esteem. Students who master this chapter will have taken great strides toward speaking the language of mathematics—and they will be well prepared for math in the seventh grade and beyond.

Sixth-Grade Mathematics

Place Value, Estimation, Properties, The Symbols ≥, ≤

Trillions

The period after billions is trillions. 10 hundred billions equal 1 trillion. You read the number 314,506,000,000,000 as "three hundred fourteen *trillion*, five hundred six billion."

Instead of writing the zeros in large numbers, we often use a shortened word form. 586,000,000,000 can be written as "586 billion." 3,700,000 can be written as "3.7 million." (700,000 is 7 tenths of a million.) 2,998,810,000,000 can be written as "2 trillion, 998 billion, 810 million."

Hundred Thousandths

hundred thousands	ten thousands	thousands	hundreds	tens	ones	tenths	hundredths	thousandths	ten thousandths	hundred thousandths
				1	2.	3	7	2	0	8

The fifth place to the right of the decimal point is the hundred thousandths' place. You read 12.37208 as "twelve and thirty seven thousand, two hundred eight *hundred thousandths.*" Notice that you read the decimal places in terms of the smallest decimal place value. You can also read 12.37208 as "twelve point three seven two zero eight."

The place values to the right of the ones' place follow the same pattern as the place values to the left of the ones' place. Just as the place to the left of the ten thousands' place is the hundred thousan*ds'* place, so the place to the right of the ten thousandths' place is the hundred thousan*dths'* place. Each place is one tenth the size of the place to its left. For example, there are 10 thousandths in 1 hundredth. You have to add 1 thousandth ten times to 3.67 to make it 3.68.

Decimals are sometimes written in short word form. 0.9612 can be written as "nine thousand, six hundred twelve ten thousandths" or "9612 ten thousandths."

Estimation

When you estimate the answer to a problem, you can round in different ways. How you round will determine how precise or close to the actual answer your estimate is.

To estimate the sum of 12,422 + 36,367, you can round the addends to the nearest ten thousand, thousand, or hundred.

Rounded to ten thousands	Rounded to thousands	Rounded to hundreds	Actual sum
10,000	12,000	12,400	12,422
+ 40,000	+ 36,000	+ 36,400	+ 36,367
50,000	48,000	48,800	48,789

The smaller the place value you round to, the more precise your estimate will be.

Whenever you can, decide whether your estimate is greater or less than the actual answer. When we are working with decimals or mixed numbers, we usually estimate by rounding numbers to the nearest whole number.

$$
\begin{array}{ccc}
 & & \text{Estimate} \\
364.232 & \longrightarrow & 364 \\
\times\ 8.427 & \longrightarrow & \times\ 8 \\
\hline
 & & 2912
\end{array}
\qquad
\begin{array}{ccc}
 & & \text{Estimate} \\
763 & \longrightarrow & 800 \\
\times\ 218 & \longrightarrow & \times\ 200 \\
\hline
 & & 160{,}000
\end{array}
$$

Because both numbers were rounded down, you know that the actual product is greater than 2912.

Because the numbers were rounded in different directions, it is hard to tell whether the actual product is greater or less than 160,000.

$$18\frac{5}{8} - 12\frac{2}{5} \longrightarrow \text{Estimate.}\quad 19 - 12 = 7$$

By rounding $18\frac{5}{8}$ up and $12\frac{2}{5}$ down, we made the difference between them greater. Therefore the actual difference is less than 7.

Properties

In Book Five of this series, you learned some properties of addition and multiplication. Because these properties are true for any numbers, you can write them using what is called a variable, a letter that stands for any number.

> *Commutative Properties: Addition and multiplication are commutative.*
>
> *For any numbers a and b, $a + b = b + a$*
> $$a \times b = b \times a$$

Notice that subtraction and division are *not* commutative. For example, $100 \div 5 \neq 5 \div 100$. (The symbol $\neq$ means "is not equal to.")

> *Associative Properties:*   *Addition and multiplication are associative.*
>
> *For any numbers a, b, and c,* $(a + b) + c = a + (b + c)$
> $(a \times b) \times c = a \times (b \times c)$

Subtraction and division are *not* associative. For example, $(12 - 8) - 4 \neq 12 - (8 - 4)$.

> *Distributive Property:*   *Multiplication is distributive with respect to addition.*
>
> *For any numbers a, b, and c,* $(a + b) \times c = (a \times c) + (b \times c)$

The Symbols ≥, ≤

In Books One and Two of this series, you learned that the symbol > means "is greater than," and the symbol < means "is less than." You can write $7 > 2$ and $2 < 7$.

The symbol ≥ means "is greater than or equal to." You can write $5 \geq 3$ or $3 \geq 3$.

The symbol ≤ means "is less than or equal to." You can write $12 \leq 14$ or $14 \leq 14$.

When you work with the symbols >, <, ≥, or ≤, observe their meaning carefully. The set of odd numbers such that $5 \leq n < 11$ is (5, 7, 9). The smallest whole number such that $n > 5$ is 6. The smallest whole number such that $n \geq 5$ is 5.

When we order numbers from least to greatest, or greatest to least, we sometimes write them with the symbol < or >.

> From least to greatest: $2 < 2.1 < 2.15 < 2.152$
> From greatest to least: $3567 > 3560 > 3507 > 3067$

Expressions, Exponents, Expanded Notation, Order of Operations

Expressions

$12 - 4$ and 8 are both expressions. You can simplify the expression $12 - 4$ by writing it as 8. You simplify an expression written with numbers by writing it in numbers as simply as possible.

Expressions are also written with variables—for example, $8 \times a$. You can find the value of an expression that has a variable for certain values of the variable. We call this evaluating the expression. We can evaluate the expression $8 \times a$ if a has a value of 2 like this: $8 \times a$ is 8×2, which is 16. Here is how you would evaluate the expression $8 \times a$ if $a = 7$:

$$8 \times a = 8 \times 7 = 56.$$

Ways of Writing Multiplication

There are ways of showing multiplication besides using the "$\times$" sign. When variables are being multiplied, the multiplication sign is usually omitted.

$8 \times a$ can be written $8a$.

$z \times w$ can be written zw.

When two numbers are being multiplied, a dot placed between them is sometimes used to show multiplication.

6×8 can be written $6 \cdot 8$.

You can also omit the multiplication sign between two numbers. Then you have to use parentheses to show that you mean 6×8, not 68.

6×8 can be written $6(8)$ or $(6)8$ or $(6)(8)$.

Exponents

An exponent is a small, raised number that shows how many times a number is used as a factor in multiplication. For example, 3^4 is $3 \times 3 \times 3 \times 3$, or 3 used as a factor 4 times. You read 3^4 as "three to the fourth power." The number that is being used as a factor is called the base. In 3^4, 3 is the base and 4 is the exponent.

Here are some examples of how you read and evaluate expressions with exponents.

5^2 is read as "five squared" (or "five to the second power").

$$5^2 = 5 \times 5 = 25$$

4^3 is read as "four cubed" (or "four to the third power").

$$4^3 = (4)(4)(4) = 16(4) = 64$$

2^5 is read as "two to the fifth power."

$$2^5 = 2 \cdot 2 \cdot 2 \cdot 2 \cdot 2 = 32$$

When a number is raised to the second power, we usually read it as "squared." When a number is raised to the third power, we usually read it as "cubed."

Powers of Ten

Powers of ten are very important in working with place value because the decimal system is based on powers of ten.

$10^1 = 10$
$10^2 = 10 \times 10 = 100$
$10^3 = 10 \times 10 \times 10 = 1000$
$10^4 = 10 \times 10 \times 10 \times 10 = 10{,}000$
$10^5 = 10 \times 10 \times 10 \times 10 \times 10 = 100{,}000$
$10^6 = 10 \times 10 \times 10 \times 10 \times 10 \times 10 = 1{,}000{,}000$

(Notice that 10^1 equals 10. A number to the first power is usually simply written as the number itself.)

The number of zeros in each of the numbers 10, 100, 1000, 10,000, . . . tells you what power of ten it is. Because 10,000 has 4 zeros, it is 10^4. Furthermore, the exponent in a power of ten tells you the number of zeros the number has when it is multiplied out. 10^9 has *nine* zeros. 10^9 equals 1,000,000,000, or 1 billion. Examples: 10^3 has three zeros and equals 1000; 100,000 has five zeros and equals 10^5.

Expanded Notation

Remember that you can write a number, such as 365,807, in expanded form or expanded notation. In expanded notation 365,807 is $(3 \times 100{,}000) + (6 \times 10{,}000) + (5 \times 1000) + (8 \times 100) + 7$. You can also write a number in expanded notation using exponents: $365{,}807 = (3 \times 10^5) + (6 \times 10^4) + (5 \times 10^3) + (8 \times 10^2) + 7$. It is a good idea to write numbers in expanded notation with exponents often, so that you get used to this form.

Here are two more examples.

1) $1{,}086{,}520 = (1 \times 1{,}000{,}000) + (8 \times 10{,}000) + (6 \times 1000) + (5 \times 100) + (2 \times 10)$
$= (1 \times 10^6) + (8 \times 10^4) + (6 \times 10^3) + (5 \times 10^2) + (2 \times 10)$

2) $(8 \times 10^4) + (9 \times 10^3) + (4 \times 10^2) + (6 \times 10) + 3$
$= (8 \times 10{,}000) + (9 \times 1000) + (4 \times 100) + (6 \times 10) + 3 = 89{,}463$

Order of Operations

Parentheses ( ) and brackets [ ] tell us which operation is to be done first. You always do the operation in the innermost pair of parentheses or brackets first.

Here is how you would simplify the following expressions.

$$7 \times [(40 - 37) + 6]$$
$$7 \times (3 + 6)$$
$$7 \times 9$$
$$63$$

$$[(27 + 9) \div 2] - 1$$
$$(36 \div 2) - 1$$
$$18 - 1$$
$$17$$

Sometimes expressions are written without parentheses. Then you use a set of rules, called the order of operations, to decide which operations are to be done first.

Order of Operations

Unless parentheses or brackets tell you otherwise:
1. Multiply or divide in order from left to right.
2. Add or subtract in order from left to right.

Here is an example of how you simplify an expression using the order of operations:

$$24 \div 3 + 6 \times 3 - 17 - 2$$
$$8 + 6 \times 3 - 17 - 2$$
$$8 + 18 - 17 - 2$$
$$26 - 17 - 2$$
$$9 - 2$$
$$7$$

Because multiplications and divisions are done before additions or subtractions, expressions are often written in this form:

$$3(6) + 8(2) - 3(3)$$
$$18 + 16 - 9$$
$$34 - 9$$
$$25$$

All the multiplications are performed before any of the additions or subtractions.

Evaluate the expression $3x + 9xy - 10$, if $x = 3$ and $y = 7$.

$$
\begin{aligned}
3x + 9xy - 10 &= 3(3) + 9(3)(7) - 10 \\
&= 9 + 27(7) - 10 \\
&= 9 + 189 - 10 \\
&= 198 - 10 \\
&= 188
\end{aligned}
$$

Calculators and the Order of Operations

Many calculators now available will perform a series of operations using the order of operations. For example, punch the following numbers and operations into a calculator. If it uses the order of operations, the calculator will display the following:

	step 1	step 2	step 3	step 4	step 5	step 6	step 7	step 8
Punch in ⟶	1 0 1 0 −	2 5 ×	3 7 ÷	5 +		2 5 6	=	
Display ⟶	1010	25	37	925	5	825	256	1081

(If your calculator instead performs operations as they are entered, it will give a final answer of 7545.)

This calculator waits to perform the additions and subtractions until it has first done the multiplications and divisions between any + or − sign. The display in step 6 shows that the calculator first divides 925 by 5 and gets 185, then remembers to subtract this quotient from 1010. Because 1010 − 185 = 825, the calculator displays 825.

Many calculators allow you to use parentheses when you want the operations to be performed in a different order. If you would like to calculate 57 + (20.5 × 3.6) − 2.3 and your calculator uses the order of operations, you can simply punch in: 5 7 + 2 0 . 5 × 3 . 6 − 2 . 3 = . The answer will be 128.5.

But if you would like to calculate (57 + 20.5) × (3.6 − 2.3), you can punch in (5 7 + 2 0 . 5) × (3 . 6 − 2 . 3) = , using the (button on the calculator. The answer will be 100.75.

Division

Division Notation

Remember that the fraction bar means the same thing as the division sign. For any numbers a and b, where b ≠ 0, $\frac{a}{b} = a \div b$. The denominator b cannot be 0 because you cannot divide by 0—therefore the denominator of a fraction cannot be zero, either.

Using the rule $\frac{a}{b} = a \div b$, you can calculate the quotient of $\frac{23}{4}$ in three ways: as a whole number with a remainder, as a mixed number, and as a decimal.

As a whole number
with a remainder

$$
\begin{array}{r}
5\ \text{R3} \\
4\ \overline{)2\ 3} \\
-2\ 0 \\
\hline
3
\end{array}
$$

As a mixed number

$$
\begin{array}{r}
5\frac{3}{4} \\
4\ \overline{)2\ 3} \\
-2\ 0 \\
\hline
3
\end{array}
$$

As a decimal

$$
\begin{array}{r}
5.7\ 5 \\
4\ \overline{)2\ 3.0\ 0} \\
-2\ 0 \\
\hline
3\ 0 \\
-2\ 8 \\
\hline
2\ 0 \\
-2\ 0 \\
\hline
0
\end{array}
$$

When there are addition or subtraction operations on either side of the fraction bar, do the addition or subtraction operations first.

$$\frac{6 + 8 + 10}{3} = (6 + 8 + 10) \div 3 = 24 \div 3 = 8$$

$$\frac{30 - 7 + 3}{9(2) - 5} = \frac{23 + 3}{18 - 5} = \frac{26}{13} = 2$$

Dividing by a Decimal

You can multiply the numerator and denominator of a fraction by the same number without changing the value of the fraction.

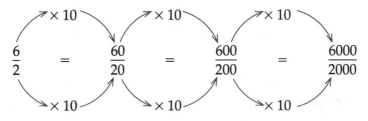

$$\frac{6}{2} = \frac{60}{20} = \frac{600}{200} = \frac{6000}{2000}$$

You can also multiply the divisor and dividend of a division problem by the same number without changing the quotient: you are doing the same thing as multiplying the numerator and denominator of a fraction by the same number.

$$2\overline{)6}^{\,3} \qquad 2 \times 10\,\overline{)6 \times 1\,0}^{\,3} = 2\,0\,\overline{)6\,0}^{\,3} \qquad 2 \times 1\,0\,0\,\overline{)6 \times 1\,0\,0}^{\,3} = 2\,0\,0\,\overline{)6\,0\,0}^{\,3}$$

You need to use this technique when you are dividing by a decimal. Before you divide, multiply the divisor and the dividend by the smallest power of ten that will make the divisor a whole number.

Example: $0.1\,3\,\overline{)8.3\,0\,7}$

The divisor has 2 decimal places. Multiply both the divisor and the dividend by 100. Move the decimal point of each two places to the right.

$$0.1\,3\,\overline{)8.3\,0\,7}$$

Divide. Place the decimal point in the quotient above the decimal point in the dividend.

$$
\begin{array}{r}
63.9 \\
1\,3.\,\overline{)830.7} \\
-\underline{78} \\
50 \\
-\underline{39} \\
11\ 7 \\
-\underline{11\ 7} \\
0
\end{array}
$$

Check by multiplying the original divisor by the quotient.

$$
\begin{array}{r}
6\ 3.9 \\
\times\ 0.1\ 3 \\
\hline
1\ 9\ 1\ 7 \\
6\ 3\ 9\ 0 \\
\hline
8.3\ 0\ 7 \\
\end{array}
$$ ✔ You should get the original dividend.

Sometimes a division problem will not have an exact quotient: you can continue to divide forever without getting a remainder of zero. In that case, we often round a quotient to a certain place. The following example shows how to find the quotient of 2643 ÷ 0.637 to the nearest tenth. If you are rounding to tenths, remember to divide to one place beyond: to hundredths.

$$
\begin{array}{r}
4\ 149.13 \\
0.637\ )\overline{2643.000\ 00} \\
-2548 \\
\hline
950 \\
-637 \\
\hline
31\ 30 \\
-25\ 48 \\
\hline
5\ 820 \\
-5\ 733 \\
\hline
87\ 0 \\
-63\ 7 \\
\hline
23\ 30 \\
-19\ 11 \\
\hline
4\ 19 \\
\end{array}
$$

To the nearest tenth, the quotient of 2643 ÷ 0.637 is 4149.1.

When the quotient is not exact, check by multiplying the rounded quotient by the original divisor.

$$
\begin{array}{r}
4\ 1\ 4\ 9.1 \\
\times\ \ 0.6\ 3\ 7 \\
\hline
2\ 9\ 0\ 4\ 3\ 7 \\
1\ 2\ 4\ 4\ 7\ 3\ 0 \\
2\ 4\ 8\ 9\ 4\ 6\ 0\ 0 \\
\hline
2\ 6\ 4\ 2.9\ 7\ 6\ 7 \\
\end{array}
$$ ✔

The product should equal the original dividend, up to the place to which you rounded. You rounded the quotient to tenths. To the nearest tenth, 2642.9767 is 2643.0, so the division checks.

Note: You can also check the division exactly by using the unrounded quotient. Multiply the unrounded quotient by the divisor and add the remainder to check the division exactly. Use the *original* decimal point in the dividend to find the place value of the remainder.

$$2643 \stackrel{?}{=} (4149.13 \times 0.637) + 0.00419$$
$$2643 = 2643 \quad ✔$$

Dividing by a Decimal in Fraction Form

Decimal divisions are sometimes written as fractions. Use the same method to simplify these fractions that you use with other decimal divisions: multiply the numerator and denominator by the same number so that the denominator is a whole number.

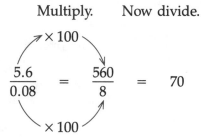

Multiply.   Now divide.

$$\frac{5.6}{0.08} = \frac{560}{8} = 70$$

Multiplying and Dividing by Numbers Close to 1

When you are multiplying or dividing by a number close to 1, estimate in advance whether your answer will be greater than or less than the number you are multiplying or dividing.

1) When you multiply a number by a value greater than 1, the result is a larger number.

$1.2 \times 85 = ?$ **Think:** $1.2 \times 85 > 85$ $1.2 \times 85 = 102$

2) When you multiply a number by a value between 0 and 1, the result is a smaller number. ("Between 0 and 1" does not include 0 or 1.)

$0.8 \times 85 = ?$ **Think:** $0.8 \times 85 < 85$ $0.8 \times 85 = 68$

3) When you divide a number by a value greater than 1, the result is a smaller number.

$85 \div 1.2 = ?$

Think:
$8.5 \div 1.2 < 85$

$85 \div 1.2 = 70.8$, to the nearest tenth

4) When you divide a number by a value between 0 and 1, the result is a larger number.

$85 \div 0.8 = ?$

Think:
$85 \div 0.8 > 85$

$85 \div 0.8 = 106.25$

Multiplying the Dividend and the Divisor by Other Numbers

Sometimes you can divide by a decimal more quickly, even doing the division in your head, if you multiply the dividend and the divisor by a number other than a power of ten. Find a number that will make the divisor a whole number.

$18 \div 4.5 = ?$

so, $18 \div 4.5 = 36 \div 9 = 4$

Think: $4.5 \times 2 = 9$

$15 \div 1.25 = ?$

Think: $0.25 \times 4 = 1$
$1.25 \times 4 = 5$

so, $15 \div 1.25 = 60 \div 5 = 12$

Fractions

Writing Mixed Numbers and Whole Numbers as Fractions

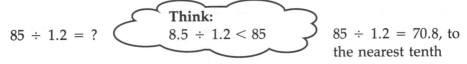

Here are some guidelines for writing mixed numbers and whole numbers as fractions.

1) To write an improper fraction as a mixed number or a whole number, you divide.

$$\frac{18}{5} = 18 \div 5$$

$$5 \overline{)1\,8} \quad \overset{3\frac{3}{5}}{}$$

$$\frac{18}{5} = 3\frac{3}{5}$$

2) To write a mixed number as a fraction, multiply and add. On the number line on page 269, you can see that each whole has 5 fifths. So to change $4\frac{2}{5}$ to a fraction, you must multiply the whole number 4 by $\frac{5}{5}$ to find out how many fifths are in 4 wholes. (Remember $\frac{5}{5}$ = 1. You do not change a number when you multiply it by 1.)

$$4\frac{2}{5} = 4 + \frac{2}{5} = 4 \times \frac{5}{5} + \frac{2}{5} = \frac{20}{5} + \frac{2}{5} = \frac{22}{5}$$

There is a quick way to do this process. Multiply the whole number by the denominator of the fraction, then add the numerator of the fraction. Write this number over the denominator. Here are some examples:

$$4\frac{2}{5} = \frac{(4 \times 5) + 2}{5} = \frac{22}{5} \qquad 2\frac{16}{23} = \frac{(2 \times 23) + 16}{23} = \frac{62}{23}$$

3) To change a whole number to a fraction, multiply the whole number by a name for 1, such as $\frac{1}{1}, \frac{2}{2}, \frac{3}{3}, \frac{4}{4}$.

For example, if you want to write a whole number with a denominator of 7, multiply it by $\frac{7}{7}$.

$$2 = 2 \times \frac{7}{7} = \frac{2 \times 7}{7} = \frac{14}{7}$$

4) If you want to write a whole number as a fraction with a denominator of 1, multiply the whole number by $\frac{1}{1}$.

$$3 = 3 \times \frac{1}{1} = \frac{3 \times 1}{1} = \frac{3}{1}$$

Rule: *Any whole number can be written as a fraction with a denominator of 1.*

Examples: $\quad 7 = \frac{7}{1} \qquad 108 = \frac{108}{1}$

Multiplying Fractions

Here is an example of a situation in which we multiply two fractions. Bob came home and found half of a devil's food cake left. He ate $\frac{2}{3}$ of what was left. How much of the whole cake did Bob eat?

You can see from the picture that Bob ate $\frac{2}{6}$, or $\frac{1}{3}$, of the whole cake. To find $\frac{2}{3}$ of something, you multiply by $\frac{2}{3}$.

$$\frac{2}{3} \times \frac{1}{2} = \frac{2 \times 1}{3 \times 2} = \frac{2}{6} = \frac{1}{3}$$

When you multiply fractions, you multiply the numerators and then multiply the denominators. Always write your answer as a fraction or a mixed number in its lowest terms.

A shortcut for multiplying fractions: If either numerator has a factor in common with either denominator, you can divide them by that common factor before you multiply.

2 is a common factor $\qquad \dfrac{\overset{1}{\cancel{2}}}{3} \times \dfrac{1}{\underset{1}{\cancel{2}}} = \dfrac{1}{3}$

Here is another example, showing both ways of multiplying fractions.

$$\frac{7}{8} \times \frac{2}{7} = \frac{14}{56} = \frac{1}{4} \qquad \dfrac{\overset{1}{\cancel{7}}}{\underset{4}{\cancel{8}}} \times \dfrac{\overset{1}{\cancel{2}}}{\underset{1}{\cancel{7}}} = \frac{1}{4}$$

You make your work much easier by dividing by common factors before you multiply fractions.

Multiplying Whole Numbers and Fractions

In Book Five you learned to multiply a whole number and a fraction like this:

$$4 \times \frac{3}{10} = \frac{4 \times 3}{10} = \frac{12}{10} = \frac{6}{5} = 1\frac{1}{5}$$

You can also think of a whole number as a fraction with a denominator of 1.

$$\frac{4}{1} \times \frac{3}{10} = \frac{12}{10} = \frac{6}{5} = 1\frac{1}{5}$$

You will get the answer either way. As in all fraction multiplication, a good method is to divide by common factors in the numerators and denominators before you multiply.

$$4 \times \frac{3}{10} = \frac{\overset{2}{\cancel{4}} \times 3}{\underset{5}{\cancel{10}}} = \frac{6}{5} = 1\frac{1}{5}$$

Multiplying Mixed Numbers

To multiply mixed numbers, first write them as improper fractions, then multiply. Here are two examples.

$$4\frac{4}{7} \times \frac{3}{4} = \frac{(4 \times 7) + 4}{7} \times \frac{3}{4} = \frac{\overset{8}{\cancel{32}}}{7} \times \frac{3}{\underset{1}{\cancel{4}}} = \frac{24}{7} = 3\frac{3}{7}$$

$$2\frac{1}{4} \times 6\frac{2}{3} = \frac{\overset{3}{\cancel{9}}}{\underset{1}{\cancel{4}}} \times \frac{\overset{5}{\cancel{20}}}{\underset{1}{\cancel{3}}} = \frac{15}{1} = 15$$

You can multiply a whole number and a mixed number in two ways:
1) You can change the mixed number to an improper fraction.

$$5 \times 6\frac{7}{8} = 5 \times \frac{55}{8} = \frac{275}{8} = 34\frac{3}{8}$$

2) You can use the distributive property to multiply the whole number part and the fractional part of a mixed number separately, and then add the products.

$$5 \times 6\frac{7}{8} = (5 \times 6) + (5 \times \frac{7}{8}) = 30 + \frac{35}{8} = 30 + 4\frac{3}{8} = 34\frac{3}{8}$$

It is often simpler to use the second method.

Reciprocals

Two numbers whose product is 1 are reciprocals of each other.

$$\frac{\overset{1}{\cancel{5}}}{\underset{1}{\cancel{6}}} \times \frac{\overset{1}{\cancel{6}}}{\underset{1}{\cancel{5}}} = \frac{1}{1} = 1 \qquad \frac{5}{6} \text{ and } \frac{6}{5} \text{ are reciprocals.}$$

$$7 \times \frac{1}{7} = \frac{7}{7} = 1$$ 7 and $\frac{1}{7}$ are reciprocals.

In general, you can find the reciprocal of a number by exchanging its numerator and denominator: $\frac{5}{6} \diagup\!\!\!\!\diagdown \frac{6}{5}$. If you want to find the reciprocal of a whole number, think of it with a denominator of 1. $\frac{7}{1} \diagup\!\!\!\!\diagdown \frac{1}{7}$

Note: Zero has no reciprocal.

Dividing by Fractions

Here is an example of a situation in which we divide by a fraction. Ann wants to know how many cheese and broccoli pies she can make with 2 heads of broccoli if each pie calls for $\frac{2}{3}$ of a head of broccoli.

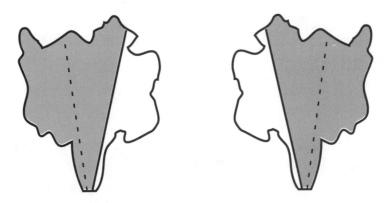

Ann needs to find how many two-thirds there are in 2. She needs to *divide* 2 by $\frac{2}{3}$.

Rule: *To divide by a fraction, multiply by its reciprocal.*

Example: $\qquad 2 \div \frac{2}{3} = 2 \times \frac{3}{2} = \dfrac{\overset{1}{\cancel{2}} \times 3}{\underset{1}{\cancel{2}}} = 3 \quad$ *(The reciprocal of $\frac{2}{3}$ is $\frac{3}{2}$.)*

From the picture you can see that the answer is correct: there are 3 two-thirds in 2. Ann can make 3 broccoli and cheese pies with 2 heads of broccoli. Here are two more examples of dividing with fractions.

$$\frac{3}{5} \div \frac{8}{9} = \frac{3}{5} \times \frac{9}{8} = \frac{27}{40} \qquad \frac{3}{5} \div 9 = \frac{3}{5} \times \frac{1}{\cancel{9}^{^3}} = \frac{1}{15}$$

Dividing with Mixed Numbers

When you are dividing with a mixed number, first write it as an improper fraction. Then multiply by the reciprocal of the divisor. Here are two examples.

$$3\frac{2}{5} \div 2\frac{1}{3} = \frac{17}{5} \div \frac{7}{3} = \frac{17}{5} \times \frac{3}{7} = \frac{51}{35} = 1\frac{16}{35}$$

$$7\frac{1}{3} \div 4 = \frac{22}{3} \div 4 = \frac{\cancel{22}^{^{11}}}{3} \times \frac{1}{\cancel{4}_{_2}} = \frac{11}{6} = 1\frac{5}{6}$$

Estimating Fraction and Mixed-Number Products and Quotients

You can estimate a mixed-number product or quotient by rounding each number to the nearest whole number, and then multiplying or dividing. Here are two examples.

$$15\frac{2}{3} \times 1\frac{3}{4} \qquad\qquad 6 \div 2\frac{1}{6}$$

Estimate: $16 \times 2 = 32$ Estimate: $6 \div 2 = 3$

A Word Problem with Fractions

Maria has $60 to spend this weekend. If she spends $\frac{1}{2}$ of her money on Friday night, and $\frac{2}{3}$ of what is left on Saturday, how much will she have to spend on Sunday?

You must solve a problem like this one in steps.

1) Find $\frac{1}{2}$ of $60. $\frac{1}{2} \times \$60 = \frac{\$60}{2} = \$30$

Maria spends $30 on Friday night. $60 − $30 = $30. She has $30 left.

2) Find $\frac{2}{3}$ of $30. $\qquad \frac{2}{3} \times \$30 = \frac{2 \times \overset{10}{\cancel{\$30}}}{\underset{1}{\cancel{3}}} = \$20$

She spends $20 on Saturday. $30 − $20 = $10. She has $10 left to spend on Sunday.

Notice that although $\frac{1}{2} + \frac{2}{3}$ is more than a whole, Maria still has money left on Sunday. Can you explain why this is so?

Fractions, Mixed Numbers, and Decimals

Decimals as Fractions or Mixed Numbers

You can write any decimal as a fraction or mixed number. First write its decimal places as a fraction with a denominator of 10, 100, 1000, . . . , then reduce this fraction to its lowest terms. The whole-number part of a decimal remains a whole number.

$$0.278 = \frac{278}{1000} = \frac{139}{500} \qquad\qquad 3.6 = 3\frac{6}{10} = 3\frac{3}{5}$$

Decimals greater than 1 are sometimes written as improper fractions. To write a decimal greater than 1 as an improper fraction, write both the whole number and the fractional part of the decimal over a denominator of 10, 100, 1000, . . . Notice that you use the last decimal place to find the correct denominator.

$$3.6 = \frac{36}{10} \qquad\qquad 4.83 = \frac{483}{100}$$

Fractions as Decimals

The most common method for writing a fraction as a decimal is to divide its numerator by its denominator. Remember that $\frac{a}{b} = a \div b$.

1) Sometimes when you divide the numerator of a fraction by its denominator, the division finishes exactly. We say that the division terminates, because to terminate means to end. Here is an example.

$$\frac{1}{8} = 1 \div 8$$

```
        0.1 2 5
  8 ) 1.0 0 0
     − 8
        2 0
     − 1 6
          4 0
        − 4 0
            0
```

$$\frac{1}{8} = 0.125$$

0—The remainder is 0.
The division terminates.

We call 0.125 a terminating decimal, because its decimal places do not go on and on.

2) Sometimes when you divide the numerator of a fraction by its denominator, the division does not terminate. Here is an example.

$$\frac{3}{11} = 3 \div 11$$

```
         0.2 7 2 7
  1 1 ) 3.0 0 0 0
       − 2 2
          8 0
        − 7 7
           3 0
         − 2 2
            8 0
          − 7 7
             3
```

3—The remainder will never become 0. The division does not terminate.

Notice the repeating pattern in the remainders of the division: 8, then 3, then 8, then 3, . . . Also notice the repeating pattern of digits in the quotient: 2, then 7, then 2, then 7, . . . The block of digits "27" will continue to repeat in the quotient for as long as you divide. Therefore, we can write $\frac{3}{11}$ as $0.\overline{27}$, with a bar over the 2 and the 7 to indicate that the digits "27" repeat forever. $0.\overline{27}$ is called a repeating decimal.

$$\frac{3}{11} = 0.\overline{27}$$

It turns out that every division of whole numbers will either eventually terminate or begin to repeat. This means that every fraction can be written as either a terminating or a repeating decimal. Here are some examples.

$$\frac{1}{3} = 0.\overline{3} \qquad\qquad \frac{3}{16} = 0.1875$$

$$\frac{7}{22} = 0.3\overline{18} \qquad\qquad \frac{7}{40} = 0.175$$

Practice writing fractions as either repeating or terminating decimals. Sometimes you may have to divide to many decimal places before you begin to find the pattern in a repeating decimal. For example, write $\frac{2}{7}$ as a repeating decimal.

We sometimes round a repeating or terminating decimal to a certain place value. To the nearest hundredth, $\frac{1}{3}$ is 0.33. To the nearest thousandth, $\frac{3}{16}$ is 0.188.

Sometimes you can write a fraction as a decimal quickly by finding an equivalent fraction that has a power of ten for a denominator. For example, $\frac{2}{5} = \frac{4}{10} = 0.4$.

You can change a fraction to a decimal in this way only when the fraction can be written as a terminating decimal.

The Same Number in Different Forms

Working with decimals, fractions, and mixed numbers shows you that the same number can be written in many different forms. For example, all of the following expressions name the same number.

$$\frac{10}{3} \qquad\qquad 3\frac{1}{3} \qquad\qquad 3.\overline{3} \qquad\qquad 3.333\ldots$$

Always be aware in working with numbers that the same number can appear in many different forms.

Measurement

Customary Units

When doing arithmetic with customary units of measure, you sometimes need to use the equivalences between the different units.

You can calculate 6×2 ft $= 12$ ft easily. To calculate 6×2 ft 7 in, you need to regroup inches as feet. Remember, 12 in $= 1$ ft.

First multiply 7 in by 6.

$$\begin{array}{r} 2\text{ ft} \quad 7\text{ in} \\ \times \qquad 6 \\ \hline 42\text{ in} \end{array}$$

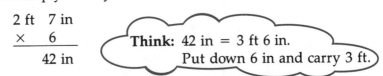

Think: 42 in $= 3$ ft 6 in.
Put down 6 in and carry 3 ft.

$$
\begin{array}{r}
3 \\
2\ \text{ft}\quad 7\ \text{in} \\
\times\qquad 6 \\
\hline
4\!\!\!/2\ \text{in} \\
15\ \text{ft}\quad 6\ \text{in}
\end{array}
$$

To find the difference of 7 gal 1 qt and 4 gal 3 qt, you need to regroup gallons as quarts. Remember, 1 gal = 4 qt.

$$
\begin{array}{r}
6\qquad 5 \\
7\ \text{gal}\quad 1\!\!\!/\ \text{qt} \\
-\ 4\ \text{gal}\quad 3\ \text{qt} \\
\hline
2\ \text{gal}\quad 2\ \text{qt}
\end{array}
$$

Think: 7 gal 1 qt = 6 gal 5 qt.

Metric Units

Learning the prefixes used in the metric system will help you find the equivalences between different metric units, even those that are not often used in this country.

kilo-	*hecto-*	*deka-*	*deci-*	*centi-*	*milli-*
thousand	hundred	ten	tenth	hundredth	thousandth
1000	100	10	0.1	0.01	0.001

The basic unit of length in the metric system is the meter. You can find how many meters are in each of the other units of length by learning the values of the prefixes.

kilometer	hectometer	dekameter	decimeter	centimeter	millimeter
1000 m	100 m	10 m	0.1 m	0.01 m	0.001 m

Prefixes can also help you to understand the metric units of capacity (which are given in terms of liters) or the metric units of mass (which are given in terms of grams). For example, a kiloliter is 1000 L, a milligram is 0.001 g.

Remember that when you calculate with metric measures, you write measurements in a single unit first. Practice writing metric measurements, given in different units, in a single unit.

$$
\begin{aligned}
\text{Example:}\quad 5\ \text{m}\ 7\ \text{dm}\ 3\ \text{cm} &= 5.73\ \text{m} \\
&= 57.3\ \text{dm} \\
&= 573\ \text{cm} \\
&= 5730\ \text{mm}
\end{aligned}
$$

Time

Time in hours is sometimes written in mixed numbers or decimals. To find $3\frac{1}{3}$ hours in hours and minutes, multiply 60 minutes by the fractional part of an hour $(\frac{1}{3})$.

$$\frac{1}{3} \times 60 = 20 \qquad \text{Because } \frac{1}{3}\text{h} = 20\,\text{min}, \qquad 3\frac{1}{3}\text{h} = 3\,\text{h}\,20\,\text{min}.$$

To find 3 hours 48 minutes as a decimal time in hours, write the mixed number $3\frac{48}{60}$ h as a decimal. $3\frac{48}{60} = 3\frac{4}{5}$. Write the fractional part of an hour $\frac{4}{5}$ as a decimal. The whole number part remains unchanged.

$$\frac{4}{5} = 5\overline{)4.0}^{\,0.8} \qquad 3\frac{4}{5} = 3.8 \qquad \text{Therefore, 3 h 48 min} = 3.8\text{ h.}$$

To find 0.3 h in minutes, find 0.3 of 60 minutes.

$$0.3 \times 60 = 18 \qquad \text{Therefore, } 0.3\text{ h} = 18\text{ min}$$

Proportion, Percent

Solving Proportions

A ratio compares one number to another. A proportion is an equation stating that two ratios are equal to each other.

$$\frac{7}{10} = \frac{21}{30} \quad \text{is a proportion.}$$

You read this proportion as "7 is to 10 as 21 is to 30." $\frac{7}{10}$ multiplied by $\frac{3}{3}$ equals $\frac{21}{30}$.

A useful way to solve a proportion that contains a variable is to cross-multiply. Multiply the numerator of each ratio by the denominator of the equal ratio to write a new equation.

Check by cross-multiplying the value you have found for the variable.

$$\frac{n}{20} \diagup\!\!\!\!\diagdown \frac{5}{8}$$

$$n \times 8 = 20 \times 5$$
$$8n = 100$$
$$n = 100 \div 8$$
$$n = 12.5$$

$$\frac{n}{20} = \frac{5}{8}$$

$$\frac{12.5}{20} \diagup\!\!\!\!\diagdown \frac{5}{8}$$

$$100 = 100 \quad \checkmark$$

The two products you get when you cross-multiply are called cross products. Here is a rule about cross products that explains why you can cross-multiply to solve a proportion.

> *Equal ratios have equal cross products.*
>
> If $\frac{a}{b} = \frac{c}{d}$, where b and $d \neq 0$, then $ad = bc$.

It is also true that if two ratios have equal cross products, they are equal. Does $\frac{5}{16} = \frac{1.25}{4}$?

$$(5)(4) \overset{?}{=} (16)(1.25) \qquad \text{So, } \frac{5}{16} = \frac{1.25}{4} \text{ and they are equal ratios.}$$
$$20 = 20 \ \checkmark$$

Setting Up a Proportion

Proportions can help you solve word problems.

Joe is making a piecrust for a slightly larger than normal pie pan. His recipe calls for 7 tb of butter and 5 oz of flour. If Joe decides to make slightly more piecrust by using 6 oz of flour instead of 5 oz, how many tablespoons of butter should he use, to keep the proportion of butter to flour the same?

To solve this problem, you write a proportion, thinking, "7 tb of butter is to 5 oz of flour as n tb butter is to 6 oz of flour."

$$\begin{array}{l} \text{tb butter} \\ \text{oz flour} \end{array} \qquad \frac{7}{5} = \frac{n}{6}$$

Cross-multiply to solve for n.

$$42 = 5n$$
$$5n = 42$$
$$n = \frac{42}{5}$$
$$n = 8.4 \text{ or } 8\frac{2}{5}$$

Joe should use $8\frac{2}{5}$ tb of butter for 6 oz of flour. Because $8\frac{2}{5}$ is very close to $8\frac{1}{2}$, he might use $8\frac{1}{2}$ tb of butter.

Scale Drawings

Here is a table of distances on a map and of the actual distances the map distances represent.

Map distance	1 cm	1.2 cm	2 cm	26 mm	3.2 cm	?
Actual distance	50 km	60 km	100 km	130 km	?	260 km

Scale: 1 cm = 50 km

Figure out the actual distance that is represented by 3.2 cm on the map. You can write a proportion using the scale of 1 cm = 50 km. **Think:** 1 cm is to 50 km as 3.2 cm is to n km.

map distance in cm
actual distance in km
$$\frac{1}{50} = \frac{3.2}{n}$$

Cross-multiply. $1n = 50 \times 3.2 = 160$

3.2 cm on the map represents 160 km of actual distance.

You can also write a proportion to find what the map distance would be, given the actual distance. What map distance would represent 260 km of actual distance?

map distance in cm
actual distance in km
$$\frac{1}{50} = \frac{d}{260}$$
$$260 = 50d$$
$$260 \div 50 = d$$
$$5.2 = d$$

260 km of actual distance would be represented by 5.2 cm on the map.

Proportional Sets of Numbers

At the grocery store, Swiss cheese costs $5.28 a pound. The table of Swiss cheese prices below shows two sets of numbers that are proportional.

Swiss Cheese Prices

Weight of cheese in 1 lb	1	1.25	1.5	2.5
Price of cheese in $	5.28	6.60	7.92	13.20

You multiply each number in the first row by the same number (5.28) to get the number below it in the second row. Therefore we say that the numbers 1, 1.25, 1.5, 2.5 are *proportional* to the numbers 5.28, 6.60, 7.92, and 13.20.

You will find that all the columns have equal ratios. For example, $\frac{1.25}{6.60} = \frac{1.5}{7.92}$. You can check by cross-multiplying:

$$\frac{1.25}{6.60} \overset{?}{=} \frac{1.5}{7.92}$$
$$(1.25)(7.92) \overset{?}{=} (6.60)(1.5)$$
$$9.90 = 9.90 \quad ✔$$

So you can set up a proportion between any two columns—and if there is a number missing in a column, you can set up a proportion to find the missing number. This is what we just did to find the missing numbers in the scale-drawing table, where the map distances are proportional to the actual distances they represent.

You can also work in other ways with proportional sets of numbers. In the table showing Swiss cheese prices, notice that 1 lb + 1.5 lb = 2.5 lb, and $5.28 + $7.92 = $13.20. You could have found the price of 2.5 lb of cheese by adding the price for 1 lb of cheese and the price for 1.5 lb of cheese. How could you have used this method to find the actual distance represented by 3.2 cm in the scale-drawing table?

Also notice in the table for Swiss cheese prices that 2 × 1.25 lb = 2.5 lb, and 2 × $6.60 = $13.20. You could have found the price of 2.5 lb of cheese by multiplying the price of 1.25 lb of cheese by 2. How could you have used this method to find the map distance of 260 km in the scale-drawing table?

Writing Fractions as Percents

Remember that a percent is a ratio of a number to 100. $5\% = \frac{5}{100}$. *Percents are always in hundredths.*

To write a fraction as a percent you can sometimes write an equivalent fraction with a denominator of 100.

$$\frac{2}{5} = \frac{40}{100} = 40\%$$

In general, use the following method to write a fraction as a percent. 1) Write the fraction as a decimal (divide its numerator by its denominator). 2) Write the decimal as a percent. For example, write $\frac{5}{8}$ as a percent.

$$\begin{array}{r} 0.6\,2\,5 \\ 8\,\overline{)5.0\,0\,0} \end{array} \qquad 0.625 = 62.5\%$$

Remember that to write a decimal as a percent, you multiply the decimal by 100, or move its decimal point two places to the right.

When the fraction cannot be written as a terminating decimal, we usually round the percent to a convenient place.

$$11 \overline{)5.0\,0\,0\,0} \quad \frac{0.4\,5\,4\,5\ldots}{} \qquad 11 \overline{)5}$$

is 45% to the nearest percent.
45.5% to the nearest tenth of a percent.
45.45% to the nearest hundredth of a percent.

Sometimes it is more convenient to write a fraction that cannot be written as a terminating decimal, as a mixed number percent. For example, the fraction $\frac{1}{3}$ might be written exactly as $33\frac{1}{3}\%$.

A fraction that cannot be written as a terminating decimal may be written as a mixed number percent by this method: 1) Divide its numerator by its denominator and find the quotient to the hundredth place. 2) Write the remainder as a fraction. 3) Write this quotient as a percent.

$$\frac{2}{3} = 3\overline{)2.0\,0}\quad \begin{array}{r} 0.6\;6\;\frac{2}{3} \\ -\,1.8 \\ \hline 2\;0 \\ -\,1\;8 \\ \hline 2 \end{array}$$

$$\frac{5}{6} = 6\overline{)5.0\,0}\quad \begin{array}{r} 0.8\;3\;\frac{2}{6} \\ -\,4.8 \\ \hline 2\;0 \\ -\,1\;8 \\ \hline 2 \end{array}$$

$$0.66\frac{2}{3} = 66\frac{2}{3}\%$$

$$0.83\frac{2}{6} = 0.83\frac{1}{3} = 83\frac{1}{3}\%$$

Percents Greater than 100%

Just as there can be fractions greater than 1, there can be percents greater than 100%. A whole equals 100%, so 1 = 100%, 2 = 200%, 3 = 300%, . . . In general, to write a whole number or a decimal as a percent, multiply it by 100%, or move its decimal point two places to the right, and add the percent sign. Because 100% = 1, you do not change a number when you multiply it by 100%: 27 = 2700%; 2.867 = 286.7%.

To write a percent as a decimal, divide by 100 or move its decimal point two places to the left: 137.2% = 1.372; 3600% = 36.00 = 36.

To write a mixed number as a percent, work with the whole number part and fractional part separately: $2\frac{3}{5} = 2 + \frac{3}{5} = 200\% + 60\% = 260\%$. You can also write a percent greater than 100% as a mixed number: $375\% = 300\% + 75\% = 3 + \frac{3}{4} = 3\frac{3}{4}$.

Increasing and Decreasing an Amount by a Certain Percent

We often increase an amount by a certain percent, for example, when we are working with a sales tax or a meal tax. To increase an amount by a certain percent, *multiply* the amount by the percent of increase, then *add* this increase to the original amount.

In the city of Grand Elk the meal tax is 6%. What will be the tax on a meal at a restaurant in this city if the pretax bill is $22.65? What will the total bill be?

1) You can calculate 6% of $22.65 in two ways.

$$6\% = 0.06 \text{ or } \frac{6}{100}$$

$$0.06 \times \$22.65 = \$1.359 \quad \text{or} \quad \frac{6}{100} \times \$22.65 = \frac{\$135.9}{100} = \$1.359$$

$1.359 rounds to $1.36.

2) The tax on a meal of $22.65 is $1.36. The total bill is $22.65 + $1.36, or $24.01.

We often decrease an amount by a certain percent, for example, when we want to find a new price after a discount. To decrease an amount by a certain percent, *multiply* the amount by the percent of decrease, and then *subtract* this decrease from the original amount.

During a sale at the department store, all jeans that cost less than $20 are discounted by 35%. All jeans costing $20 or more are discounted by 45%. Natalie likes one pair of jeans marked $18 and another marked $21. What is the discounted price of each pair of jeans?

1) Price of $18 jeans, discounted by 35%.

$$
\begin{aligned}
\text{Discount price} &= \$18 - (\$18)(0.35) \\
&= \$18 - \$6.30 \\
&= \$11.70
\end{aligned}
$$

2) Price of $21 jeans, discounted by 45%.

$$
\begin{aligned}
\text{Discount price} &= \$21 - (\frac{45}{100} \times \$21) \\
&= \$21 - \frac{\$945}{100} \\
&= \$21 - \$9.45 = \$11.55
\end{aligned}
$$

Notice that at the discounted prices the jeans marked $21 are cheaper than the ones marked $18.

Finding What Percent One Number Is of Another

To find what percent one number is of another, you can write the numbers as a fraction, then write the fraction as a percent.

For instance, 21 is what percent of 40?

Think: 21 is what part of 40? $\dfrac{21}{40}$

Write $\frac{21}{40}$ as a percent.

$$\begin{array}{r} 0.525 \\ 40\overline{)21.000} \\ -20\ 0 \\ \hline 1\ 00 \\ -\ 80 \\ \hline 200 \\ -200 \\ \hline 0 \end{array}$$

$0.525 = 52.5\%$

21 is 52.5% of 40.

Here is an example where a fraction cannot be written as a terminating decimal. To the nearest tenth of a percent, what percent of 3 is 5?

Think: 5 is what part of 3? $\dfrac{5}{3}$

$$\begin{array}{r} 1.\ 6\ \ 6\ \ 6\ \ 6 \\ 3\overline{)5.{}^205{}^205{}^205{}^205{}^2} \end{array}$$

$1.6666 = 166.66\%$

166.66% rounds to 166.7%.

To the nearest tenth of a percent, 5 is 166.7% of 3.

Finding an Unknown Number When a Percent of the Number Is Known

A family has to pay 5.6% of its taxable income in state income tax. If it paid $1237.60 in state income tax, what was its taxable income?

You can write an equation to work backward to a number when a percent of the number is known. You know that 5.6% of the taxable income equals $1237.60.

5.6% × taxable income = $1237.60
0.056 × taxable income = $1237.60
0.056n = $1237.60
n = $1237.60 ÷ 0.056
n = $22,100

$$
\begin{array}{r}
\$22\ 100. \\
0.0\ 5\ 6\ )\overline{\$\ 1237.600} \\
-112 \\
\hline
117 \\
-112 \\
\hline
5\ 6 \\
-5\ 6 \\
\hline
0
\end{array}
$$

The family's taxable income was $22,100.

Geometry

Some Signs Used in Geometry

When two segments have the same length, we say that they are congruent. The symbol ≅ means "is congruent to." $\overline{BA}$ and $\overline{CD}$ have the same length. $\overline{BA} \cong \overline{CD}$.

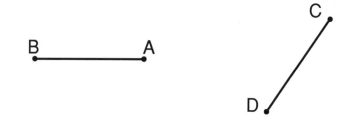

The symbol ‖ means "is parallel to." The symbol ⊥ means "is perpendicular to." (In Book Four, remember, you learned that when two lines intersect to form right angles, we say they are perpendicular.) In the figure at the top of the next page, $\overleftrightarrow{ZC} \parallel \overleftrightarrow{TS}$ (We read this statement: "Line ZC is parallel to line TS"), and $\overleftrightarrow{GH} \perp \overleftrightarrow{TS}$ ("Line GH is perpendicular to line TS").

Parallel lines are defined as two lines in the same plane that do not intersect. (A plane, remember, is a flat surface that goes on forever in all directions.) Can you think of two lines *not in the same plane* that do not intersect and are not parallel? Think about some of the edges of a cube.

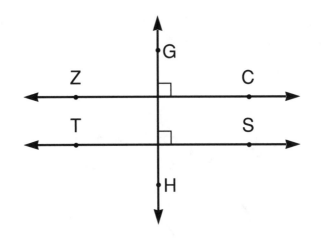

Constructing a Parallelogram

Straightedge.

Many constructions can be made with only
a straightedge and a compass. To construct
parallelogram ABCD, given points ABC, set
the compass to the length of $\overline{AB}$ and draw an arc
with that radius and center C. Then set the compass to
the length of $\overline{CB}$ and draw an arc with that radius and center A. Call the point where the two arcs intersect point D. Use
the straightedge to connect the vertices of the parallelogram.

Compass.

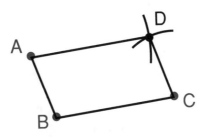

You can use the same method to construct a line through a point A that is parallel
to a given line.

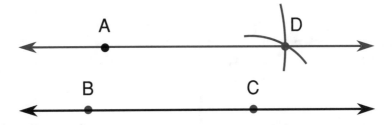

Mark points B and C on the line. Repeat the construction in the preceding example to find point D. Draw $\overleftrightarrow{AD}$. $\overleftrightarrow{AD} \parallel \overleftrightarrow{CB}$. Remember that opposite sides of a parallelogram are parallel.

Constructing a Perpendicular Bisector

The perpendicular bisector of a segment is a line perpendicular to the segment that divides the segment into two congruent segments.

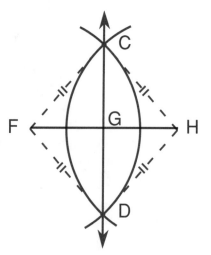

To construct the perpendicular bisector of $\overline{FH}$, draw an arc with center F, as in the diagram. (Make the radius of the arc greater than half the length of $\overline{FH}$.) Draw an arc with the same radius and center H. Label the two points where the arcs intersect C and D. $\overleftrightarrow{CD}$ is the perpendicular bisector of $\overline{FH}$. Point G where $\overleftrightarrow{CD}$ intersects $\overline{FH}$ is the midpoint, or halfway point, of segment $\overline{FH}$, because $\overline{FG} \cong \overline{HG}$. That is why you can also use this method to construct the midpoint of a segment. Notice that $\overline{FC} \cong \overline{HC}$ and $\overline{FD} \cong \overline{HD}$. The perpendicular bisector of $\overline{FH}$ is the set of all points that are the same distance from F and from H. Notice how we mark congruent segments.

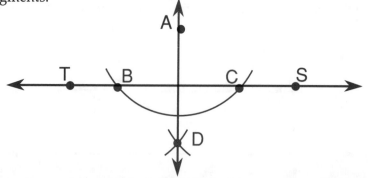

To construct a line perpendicular to $\overleftrightarrow{TS}$ through point A, draw an arc with center A that intersects $\overleftrightarrow{TS}$ at points B and C. Draw arcs with equal radii from points B and C. Call the point where the arcs intersect point D. $\overleftrightarrow{AD} \perp \overleftrightarrow{TS}$.

About Parallel and Perpendicular Lines

1) If two lines are parallel, any line perpendicular to one is also perpendicular to the other.

If $\overleftrightarrow{AB} \parallel \overleftrightarrow{CD}$ and $\overleftrightarrow{AB} \perp \overleftrightarrow{TS}$, then $\overleftrightarrow{CD} \perp \overleftrightarrow{TS}$.

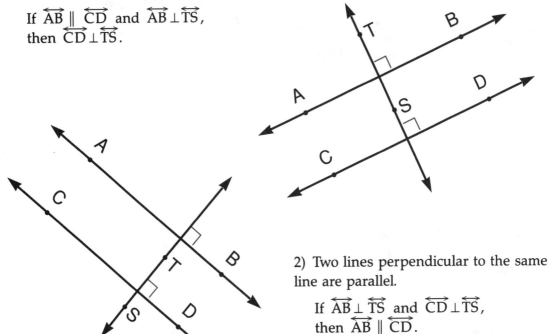

2) Two lines perpendicular to the same line are parallel.

If $\overleftrightarrow{AB} \perp \overleftrightarrow{TS}$ and $\overleftrightarrow{CD} \perp \overleftrightarrow{TS}$, then $\overleftrightarrow{AB} \parallel \overleftrightarrow{CD}$.

Angles

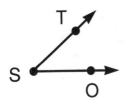

The two rays that form an angle are called the sides of the angle. You can name an angle by three points, using the vertex as the middle point. You can also name an angle by its vertex alone, if no other angle has the same vertex.

∠TSO, or ∠OST, or ∠S

We usually measure an angle in degrees. Two angles that have the same measure are congruent.

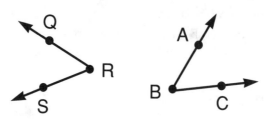

$$m\angle QRS = m\angle ABC$$

(This is read, "The measure of angle QRS equals the measure of angle ABC.")

$$\angle QRS \cong \angle ABC$$

("Angle QRS is congruent to angle ABC.")

A ray that divides an angle into two congruent angles is called a bisector of the angle.

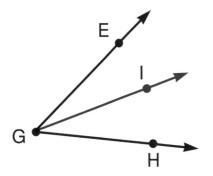

$$\angle EGI \cong \angle HGI$$

Therefore $\overrightarrow{GI}$ is the angle bisector of $\angle EGH$.

Bisecting an Angle

To bisect angle EGH with a straightedge and a compass, draw an arc with center G, and call the points where the arc intersects the sides of the angle X and Y. Then draw an arc with center X, and an arc with an equal radius and center Y. Call the point where the two arcs intersect point Z. $\overrightarrow{GZ}$ is the angle bisector of $\angle EGH$: $\angle EGZ \cong \angle HGZ$.

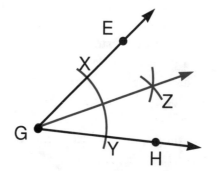

Constructing an Angle Congruent to a Given Angle

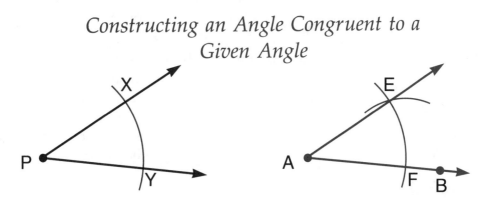

To construct an angle congruent to ∠P, draw $\overrightarrow{AB}$. Draw an arc with center P, and call the points where the arc intersects the sides of the angle X and Y. Then draw an arc with the same radius and center A, and label point F where the arc intersects $\overrightarrow{AB}$. Draw an arc with a radius equal to the length of $\overline{XY}$ and with center F. Call the point where the two arcs intersect point E.   ∠EAF ≅ ∠P.

Congruent Figures and Corresponding Parts

When two figures are congruent, their corresponding parts are congruent. For example, if triangle ABC ≅ triangle XYZ, then the sides and angles of triangle ABC are congruent to the matching or corresponding sides and angles of triangle XYZ.

$$\triangle ABC = \triangle XYZ$$

Therefore:

$\overline{AB} \cong \overline{XY}$	∠A ≅ ∠X
$\overline{BC} \cong \overline{YZ}$	∠B ≅ ∠Y
$\overline{AC} \cong \overline{XZ}$	∠C ≅ ∠Z

Notice how we mark congruent angles.

When you state that two polygons are congruent, be careful to list the matching or corresponding vertices in the same order. For example, you could say of the triangles above that △BCA ≅ △YZX or △CAB ≅ △ZXY. You could not write △BCA ≅ △XYZ, because then you would be falsely saying among other things, that ∠B ≅ ∠X. When the corresponding vertices of congruent polygons are correctly listed, you can read off congruent sides and angles from the order in which the vertices are listed. If quadrilateral GTSO ≅ quadrilateral PIJQ, then you know that ∠G ≅ ∠P, ∠T ≅ ∠I, $\overline{TS} \cong \overline{IJ}$, $\overline{OG} \cong \overline{QP}$, and so on.

Rigid Motions

When two figures are congruent, we use three kinds of rigid motions to make them occupy exactly the same place, or to coincide. The three rigid motions are translation, reflection, and rotation. In a translation, a figure is slid. In a reflection, a figure is flipped over a line. In a rotation, a figure is turned or rotated around a point.

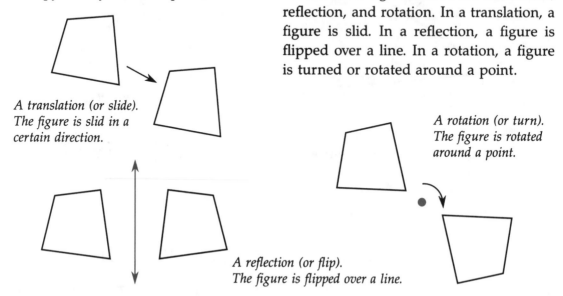

A translation (or slide). The figure is slid in a certain direction.

A rotation (or turn). The figure is rotated around a point.

A reflection (or flip). The figure is flipped over a line.

Here are two examples of the rigid motions you would need to use to make two congruent figures coincide.

You would reflect (or flip) the yellow pentagon over $\overleftrightarrow{XY}$ to make it coincide with the black pentagon.

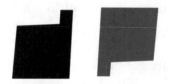

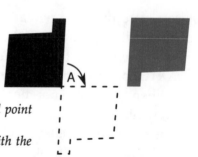

You would rotate the black hexagon around point A in the direction of the arrow, and then translate (or slide) it to make it coincide with the yellow hexagon.

Can you find another combination of rigid motions that would make the two hexagons coincide?

Constructing Triangles

You can use a straightedge and a compass to construct a triangle with certain sides and angles. For example, construct triangle WXY, where $\overline{WX} \cong \overline{AB}$, $\angle WXY \cong \angle S$, and $\overline{XY} \cong \overline{CD}$.

In order to construct this triangle, you must put into practice some of the things you learned on pages 289–91. Here is one way to construct triangle WXY.

1) Open the compass to the length of $\overline{AB}$, and mark off a segment of equal length, $\overline{XW}$.

2) Draw an arc with center S. Call the points where the arc intersects the sides of the angle, points E and F. Draw an arc with the same radius and center X. Call the point where the arc intersects $\overline{XW}$, point H.

3) Draw an arc with a radius equal to the length of $\overline{EF}$ and with center H. Call the point where the two arcs intersect, point G. Draw a ray with endpoint X through point G.

4) Draw an arc with a radius equal to the length of $\overline{CD}$ and center X. Call the point where the arc intersects $\overrightarrow{XG}$, point Y.

5) Use the straightedge to draw $\overline{YW}$.

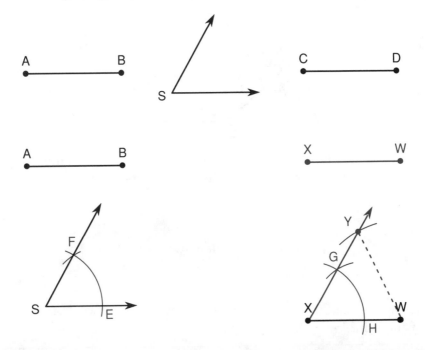

All triangles you construct in this way must be congruent. In the same way, you can construct only one triangle WXY where $\angle$WXY $\cong$ $\angle$D, $\overline{XY}$ $\cong$ $\overline{AB}$, and $\angle$XYW $\cong$ $\angle$C.

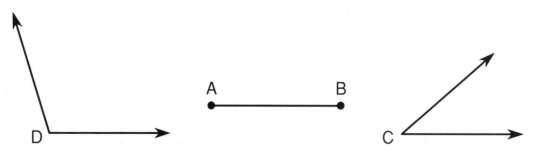

You can also use a ruler and a protractor to construct a triangle, when the measures of some of its sides and angles are given. In Book Five you learned to construct a triangle with sides of a certain length using a ruler and a compass—for example, a triangle with sides of 6 cm, 7 cm, and 8 cm. There is only one triangle ABC you can construct where m$\angle$ABC = 35°, BC = 3 cm, and m$\angle$BCA = 70°. Construct two non-congruent triangles OPS where OP = 4 cm, PS = 3.5 cm, and m$\angle$SOP = 60°.

The Angles of a Triangle

Using a protractor, draw a triangle XYZ, then construct a figure similar to the one below so that $\angle$OST $\cong$ $\angle$X, $\angle$TSL $\cong$ $\angle$Y, and $\angle$LSM $\cong$ $\angle$Z.

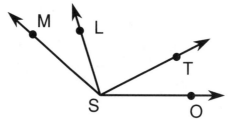

No matter what triangle you draw, $\angle$OSM will be a straight angle. Remember, a straight angle has a measure of 180°. This construction shows you the following property of triangles:

> *The sum of the measures of the angles of a triangle is 180°.*

If you know the measure of any two angles of a triangle, you can always find the measure of the third.

You know that x + 65° + 35° = 180°

$$x = 180° − 65° − 35°$$
$$x = 115° − 35°$$
$$x = 80°$$

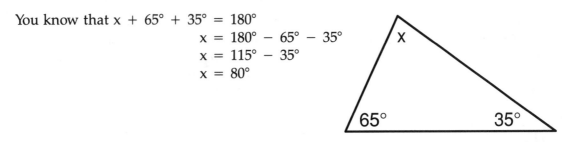

Special Triangles

We classify triangles according to the length of their sides.

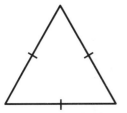

Equilateral triangle
Three sides of equal length

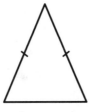

Isosceles triangle
At least two sides of equal length

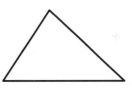

Scalene triangle
No sides of equal length

We also classify triangles according to their angles.

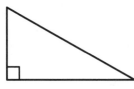

Right triangle
One right angle

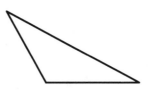

Obtuse triangle
One obtuse angle

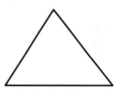

Acute triangle
Three acute angles

Can a triangle have more than one obtuse angle? More than one right angle? Why or why not?

Isosceles Triangles

Isosceles triangles—triangles with at least two congruent sides—have a number of properties.

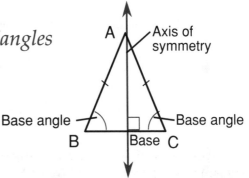

$\triangle ABC$ is an isosceles triangle.
$\overline{AB} \cong \overline{AC}$. Therefore $\angle B \cong \angle C$.

The third side of an isosceles triangle is called the base. The two base angles of an isosceles triangle are congruent.

An isosceles triangle also has an axis of symmetry. An axis of symmetry divides a figure into two parts, in such a way that if you reflected one part of the figure over the axis of symmetry, it would coincide exactly with the other part. The axis of symmetry of an isosceles triangle is also the perpendicular bisector of the base. The height of the triangle from the base to the vertex opposite the base is also a part of the axis of symmetry.

It is also true that a triangle with two congruent angles is an isosceles triangle.

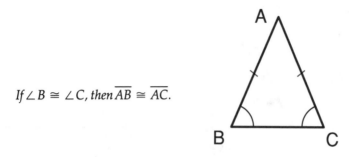

If ∠B ≅ ∠C, then $\overline{AB}$ ≅ $\overline{AC}$.

An equilateral triangle is a special kind of isosceles triangle with all three sides congruent. You can think of it as a triple isosceles triangle: you can find three different pairs of sides that are congruent.

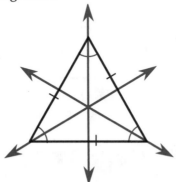

With three pairs of congruent sides, an equilateral triangle has three axes of symmetry and three congruent angles. Because 180 ÷ 3 = 60, each of the angles of an equilateral triangle has a measure of 60°.

Constructing Special Angles

You have learned how to construct a perpendicular bisector and how to bisect an angle. Now you can construct angles that have certain measures without using a protractor. For example, because you can construct a line perpendicular to another line, you can construct a right angle. You can bisect a right angle, to construct an angle of 45° (90 ÷ 2 = 45). You can bisect an angle of 45°, to form an angle of 22.5°. You can construct an equilateral triangle and then bisect one of its angles, to form an angle of 30°. You can construct an angle of 30° next to an angle of 45°, to make an angle of 75°.

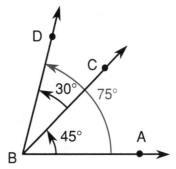

Reflection

As you have already seen, a figure can be reflected (flipped) over a line. A point and a line can also be reflected over a line. We call a line that a figure is flipped over a "line of symmetry." You can reflect a point over a line with or without graph paper.

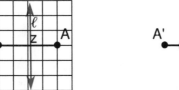

$\overline{A'Z'} \cong \overline{AZ}$

We say that point A is symmetric to point A′ (you read A′ as "A prime") with respect to line *l*, if line *l* is the perpendicular bisector of $\overline{AA'}$.

When a segment is reflected over a line, each point of the segment is reflected over the line. You can reflect a segment over a line by reflecting its endpoints over the line, and then connecting them. A segment and its reflection over a line are congruent.

$\overline{A'B'}$ *is symmetric to* $\overline{AB}$ *with respect to line l.* $\overline{A'B'} \cong \overline{AB}$.

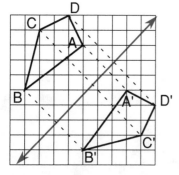

When a polygon is reflected over a line, each point of the polygon is reflected over the line. You can reflect a polygon over a line by first reflecting its vertices over the line and connecting them. The reflected polygon will be congruent to the original polygon.

Notice that if you reflect point A over line *l*, you make an isosceles triangle AXA′ for which line *l* is a line or axis of symmetry. (As its name indicates, the axis of symmetry is a line that divides a figure into identical symmetrical parts.)

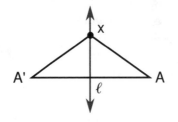

Similarity

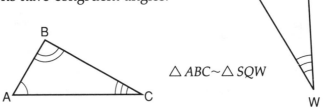

Figures that have the same shape, but not necessarily the same size, are said to be similar. Similar polygons have congruent angles.

$\triangle ABC \sim \triangle SQW$

The sign ~ means "is similar to." Notice that you list vertices of similar polygons so that you can pair the congruent angles: $\angle A \cong \angle S$, $\angle B \cong \angle Q$, $\angle C \cong \angle W$.

You can enlarge or reduce a triangle to make a similar triangle by multiplying the length of each side by the same number. Construct triangle ABC with sides of 3 cm, 5 cm, and 6 cm; then multiply the length of each side by 2, and construct a second triangle, A′B′C′. The two triangles will be similar.

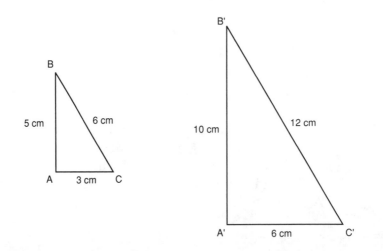

These similar triangles show a property of similar polygons: the lengths of corresponding sides of similar polygons are proportional.

Lengths of sides of triangle ABC (in cm) $\quad\dfrac{3}{6} = \dfrac{5}{10} = \dfrac{6}{12}$
Lengths of sides of triangle A'B'C' (in cm)

You can use similar triangles (or other polygons) to find the length of a missing side by setting up a porportion. If △HIJ and △KRS are similar, then x is to 5 m as 24 m is to 7 m.

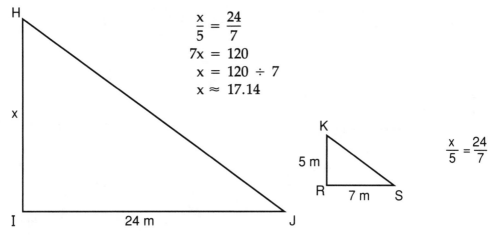

$$\frac{x}{5} = \frac{24}{7}$$
$$7x = 120$$
$$x = 120 \div 7$$
$$x \approx 17.14$$

$$\frac{x}{5} = \frac{24}{7}$$

The missing side is 17.14 m, to the nearest hundredth of a meter. The symbol ≈ means "is approximately equal to."

Properties of Parallelograms: Rhombuses and Rectangles

A parallelogram is a quadrilateral with two pairs of parallel sides. Its opposite sides and opposite angles are congruent. It does not necessarily have any axes of symmetry.

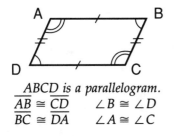

ABCD is a parallelogram.
$\overline{AB} \cong \overline{CD} \qquad \angle B \cong \angle D$
$\overline{BC} \cong \overline{DA} \qquad \angle A \cong \angle C$

A rhombus is a particular kind of parallelogram with all four sides congruent. A rhombus has two axes of symmetry that run along its diagonals.

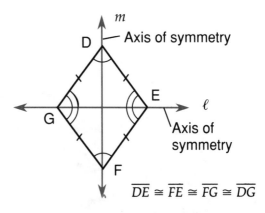

$\overline{DE} \cong \overline{FE} \cong \overline{FG} \cong \overline{DG}$

Notice that if you reflect isosceles triangle DEG over line *l*, you make the rhombus DEFG. Also notice that if you reflect isosceles triangle DGF over line *m* you make the rhombus DGFE. You can think of a rhombus as two isosceles triangles—put together in two different ways.

A rectangle is a parallelogram with four right angles. Its adjacent sides are perpendicular.

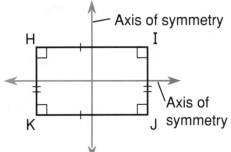

∠*H*, ∠*I*, ∠*J*, ∠*K* are right angles.
KH⊥*HI*, *HI*⊥*IJ*, and so on.

A rectangle has two axes of symmetry that run through the midpoints of the opposite sides.

Because a square is both a rectangle and a rhombus, it has four axes of symmetry—along its diagonals, and through the midpoints of the opposite sides. A square has the properties of a rhombus *and* the properties of a rectangle.

Square ABCD

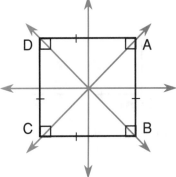

Area and Volume

Area Formulas

Here are some formulas for finding the *areas* and *perimeters* of plane figures. Multiplication signs between variables have been omitted.

Area and Perimeter Formulas

Rectangle	Square	Triangle	Parallelogram
$A = lw$	$A = s^2$	$A = \frac{1}{2}bh$	$A = bh$
$P = 2(l + w)$	$P = 4s$	$P = s1 + s2 + s3$	$P = 2(b + s)$

You can use these formulas to find the area or the perimeter of these figures, or to work backward to find a missing dimension. Example: A rectangle has a length of 12 cm, and a perimeter of 32 cm. What is its area?

To find the area of the rectangle, you need to find its width. Use the formula for the perimeter of a rectangle, and substitute the known values to find the width.

1)
$$P = 2(l + w)$$
$$32 = 2(12 + w)$$
$$32 = 24 + 2w$$
$$32 - 24 = 2w$$
$$8 = 2w$$
$$w = 4$$

2)
$$A = lw$$
$$= (12)(4)$$
$$= 48$$

The area of the rectangle is 48 cm².

A parallelogram has a height of 5 m and an area of 68 m². What is its base?

Formula for the area of a parallelogram:	$A = bh$
Substitute known values for variables:	$68 = b(5)$
Solve for b:	$\dfrac{68}{5} = b$
	$b = 13.6$

The parallelogram has a base of 13.6 m.

The formula for the area of a square is $A = s^2$. The area of a square with sides of 4 cm is 4^2 cm², or 16 cm². That is why we read a number to the second power as "squared." For example, we read 4^2 as "four squared": this is the area of a square with sides 4 units long.

Changing Units of Area

U.S. Customary System	Metric System
$1\ ft^2 = 144\ in^2$	$1\ cm^2 = 100\ mm^2$
$1\ yd^2 = 9\ ft^2$	$1\ dm^2 = 100\ cm^2$
$1\ mi^2 = (1760 \times 1760)\ yd^2$	$1\ m^2 = 100\ dm^2$
$\quad = 3{,}097{,}600\ yd^2$	$1\ km^2 = (1000 \times 1000)\ m^2$
	$\quad = 1{,}000{,}000\ m^2$

Sometimes you need to change from one unit of area to another. Here is a word problem in which you use both km² and m² as units of area.

The United States has an area of about 9.4 million km² and a population of about 235 million people. About how many people on average does the United States have per square kilometer? If the area were divided equally, about how many square meters would there be for each person?

1) To find the average number of people per km², divide 235 million by 9.4 million. 235 million ÷ 9.4 million is the same as 235 ÷ 9.4.

$$
\begin{array}{r}
2\,5. \\
9.4\,\overline{)2\,3\,5.0} \\
-1\,8\,8 \\
\hline
4\,7\,0 \\
-4\,7\,0 \\
\hline
0
\end{array}
$$

There is an average of 25 people for each km² in the United States.

2) There are 1,000,000 m² in a km². If there is an average of 25 people per km², then there are (1,000,000 ÷ 25) m² for each person. 1,000,000 ÷ 25 = 40,000. There are 40,000 m² for each person.

The Circumference of a Circle

Remember that there are π diameters in the circumference of a circle: C = πd. You can also write this equation another way: $\pi = \frac{C}{d}$. So π equals the ratio of the circumference to the diameter of a circle. This ratio π is the same for all circles, but you cannot write it exactly as either a fraction or a decimal. From early times in history, the mathematicians among many peoples of the world have tried to write fractions that were close approximations of π, such as $\frac{256}{81}$ (the Egyptians), $\frac{25}{8}$ (the Babylonians), $\frac{22}{7}$ (the Greeks), $\frac{355}{113}$ (the Chinese). Today mathematicians have written a decimal approximation of π to thousands of decimal places.

$$\pi = 3.14159265358979323846264383 \ldots$$

For most calculations you can use the approximation $\pi \approx 3.14$ or $\pi \approx \frac{22}{7}$. Remember, the symbol ≈ means "is approximately equal to."

> ### Formulas for the Circumference of a Circle
> $$C = \pi d \qquad\qquad C = 2\pi r$$

You can use the formula C = πd or C = 2πr to find the circumference of a circle or of figures made up of parts of circles. Find the perimeters of the two figures that follow.

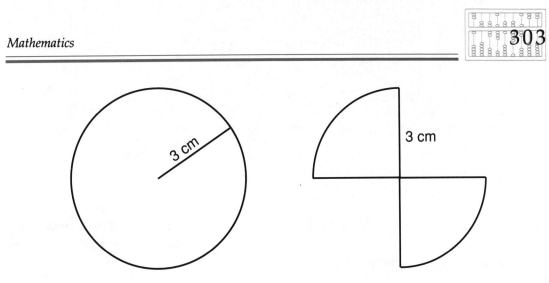

Because you know the radius, use the formula $C = 2\pi r$ to find the circumference of the circle.

$$C \approx 2(3.14)3 \text{ cm} \approx 18.84 \text{ cm.}$$

The second figure is in the shape of two quarter circles, with radius 3 cm. Because there are *two quarter* circles, the perimeter of the figure is one half the circumference of *one complete* circle with a radius of 3 cm, plus four 3 cm lengths.

$$P = \frac{1}{2}(2\pi r) + (4)(r)$$
$$P = \pi(3) \text{ cm} + 4(3) \text{ cm}$$
$$P \approx 3.14(3) \text{ cm} + 4(3) \text{ cm}$$
$$P \approx 21.42 \text{ cm}$$

The Area of a Circle

A square with sides of length r units has an area of r^2 square units.

How many squares with sides the length of the radius are there inside a circle? It turns out that there are more than three such squares, but less than four. There

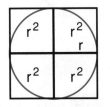

are π squares with area r^2 inside a circle, just as there are π diameters in the circumference of a circle. So we have the following formula for the area of a circle.

> ## Formula for the Area of a Circle
>
> $$A = \pi r^2$$

Using this formula, we can find the area of a circle with a diameter of 7 cm to the nearest tenth of a cm². 1) The radius is $\frac{1}{2}$ of the diameter. $7 \div 2 = 3.5$. The radius of the circle is 3.5 cm. 2) We next substitute the value for the radius into the formula for the area of a circle.

$$A = \pi (3.5)^2$$
$$A = \pi (12.25)$$
$$A \approx 3.14 (12.25)$$
$$A \approx 38.465$$

38.465 cm² rounds to 38.5 cm². To the nearest tenth of a square centimeter, a circle with a diameter of 7 cm has an area of 38.5 cm².

Sometimes, rather than use an approximation for π, we leave π in the answer and write the answer exactly, as in the example that follows:

In this illustration, there are two circles. Suppose we want to find the area of the shaded region. The area of the larger circle: $A = \pi (7)^2 = 49\pi$. The area of the smaller: $A = \pi (5)^2 = 25\pi$. The area of the shaded region is the area of the larger circle minus the area of the smaller circle: $49\pi - 25\pi = 24\pi$. The area of the shaded region is 24π cm².

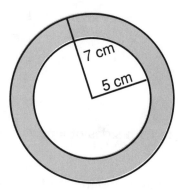

Polyhedrons

A polyhedron is a solid, each face of which is a polygon. Two kinds of polyhedrons are prisms and pyramids.

Prisms have two parallel congruent faces called bases. Prisms are named by the shapes of their bases. You can see that the shape of the base of a prism "runs through" the prism.

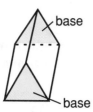
base
base

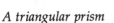
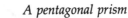
base
base

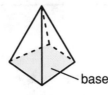
base
base
base

A triangular prism   *A rectangular prism*   *A pentagonal prism*

Pyramids are also named by the shapes of their bases.

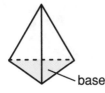
base

base

base

A triangular pyramid   *A square pyramid*   *A pentagonal pyramid*

Cones, spheres, and cylinders are not polyhedrons, because not all of their faces are polygons.

Constructing Cubes and Rectangular Prisms

You can draw many different designs which, when cut out and folded, will make a cube or a rectangular prism. Find two designs different from the one given which, when cut out and folded, will make a cube. Color opposite faces the same color.

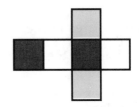

Find two designs different from the one given below, which, when cut out and folded, will make a rectangular prism with dimensions 5 cm, 4 cm, and 3 cm.

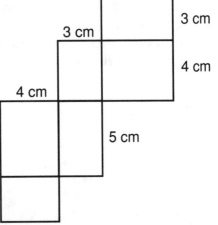

3 cm

3 cm

4 cm

4 cm

5 cm

3 cm

The Volume of Prisms

To find the volume of a rectangular prism, you first multiply the length times the width. The product gives you the area of the base of the rectangular prism. Then you multiply the area of the base by the height to find the volume.

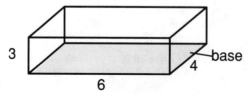

Volume = (6 × 4) × 3.

Volume of a Prism

V = area of base × height, or V = bh

You can find the volume of any prism in the same way, by multiplying the area of its base by its height.

For example, find the volume of this triangular prism:

1) Find the area of the triangular base: b $= \frac{1}{2}$ (3) (4) = 6

2) The height is the other dimension: 7 cm. V = bh = 6 × 7 = 42

7 cm

4cm

3 cm

The volume of the triangular prism is 42 cm³. Notice that you write volume in cubic units.

In Book Five you learned the formulas for the volume of a rectangular prism and a cube: for a rectangle, V = lwh. And for a cube, V = e³ (e is the length of any edge of the cube). You can use these formulas to find the volume of a rectangular prism or cube, or to work backward to find a missing dimension.

If a rectangular prism has a length of 6 cm, a height equal to half its length, and a volume of 63 cm³, what is its width?

Use the formula V = lwh and substitute the values you know. If l = 6 cm, then h = ($\frac{1}{2}$) 6 cm, or 3 cm.

$$63 = (6) \, w \, (3)$$
$$63 = 18w$$
$$\frac{63}{18} = w$$
$$w = 3.5 \qquad \text{The width is 3.5 cm.}$$

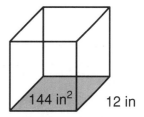
If the base of a cube has an area of 144 in², what is the cube's volume? The area of the base of a cube is an edge times an edge. Because 12 × 12 = 144, each edge must be 12 in long. The cube's volume is 12³ in³, or 1728 in³. Notice that each side of the cube is 1 foot long. We can therefore say that the volume of the cube is 1 ft³ or 1728 in³.

144 in²   12 in

Changing Units of Volume: A Word Problem

U.S. Customary Units	*Metric Units*
$1 \, ft^3 = 1728 \, in^3$	$1 \, cm^3 = 1000 \, mm^3$
$1 \, yd^3 = 27 \, ft^3$	$1 \, dm^3 = 1000 \, cm^3$
	$1 \, m^3 = 1000 \, dm^3$
	$1 \, L = 1 \, dm^3$
	$1 \, L = 1000 \, cm^3$

Sometimes you need to change from one unit of volume to another. For example, a glass that can hold 0.3 L of water can hold how many cm³ of water? 1 L = 1000 cm³, so multiply 0.3 L by 1000 to change liters to cubic centimeters. 0.3 L = 300 cm³. The glass can hold 300 cm³ of water. Notice that a cubic centimeter is the same as a milliliter: 0.3 L = 300 mL = 300 cm³.

Here is an example of a traditional kind of word problem involving volume: Mr. Burke has a large lawn, 45 m by 30 m. He hears that in a neighboring town an afternoon thundershower just brought 25 mm of rain. What volume of water would Mr. Burke need to sprinkle on his lawn so that it also gets the equivalent of 25 mm of rain?

To solve this problem you need to imagine a large, shallow rectangular prism with a base of (45 × 30) m² and a height of 25 mm, and then find its volume. Find the area of the base: 45 × 30 = 1350. Write the height (25 mm) in the same unit as the other dimensions. 25 mm = 0.025 m.

$$V = 1350 \times 0.025$$
$$= 33.75$$

Mr. Burke would need to sprinkle 33.75 m³ of water on his lawn. Because each cubic meter of water has a mass of 1000 kg, or 1 metric ton, he would need to sprinkle more than 33 metric tons of water on his lawn to equal the afternoon thundershower!

Integers

Positive and Negative Numbers

On a Celsius thermometer, 0° (zero degrees) is the temperature at which water freezes. $^{+}20°$ is a common room temperature, and $^{-}10°$ is the outdoor temperature of a very cold winter day.

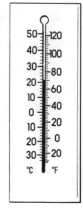

$^{+}20$, or 20, is a positive number. You read it as "positive 20," or just "20."

$^{-}10$ is a negative number. You read it as "negative 10."

You can write positive numbers with or without a $^{+}$ sign: $^{+}3 = 3$ ("positive three = three"); $^{+}4.5 = 4.5$. You must write a negative sign with a negative number.

We can show positive and negative numbers on a number line.

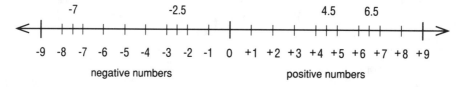

Numbers to the left of 0 on the number line are negative, numbers to the right of 0 are positive. 0 is neither positive nor negative.

Two numbers that are the same distance from zero but in opposite directions are called *opposites*.

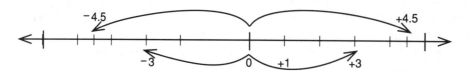

$^{-}3$ and $^{+}3$ are opposites; $^{+}4.5$ and $^{-}4.5$ are opposites. To find the opposite of a number, change its sign: the opposite of $^{-}100$ is $^{+}100$; the opposite of $^{+}100$ is $^{-}100$.
Zero is its own opposite: $^{+}0 = {^{-}0} = 0$.

Examples of Integers

Whole numbers, as opposed to mixed numbers or fractions, are called integers. (The word integer means whole.) The positive integers are the numbers $^+1$, $^+2$, $^+3$, . . . The negative integers are the numbers $^-1$, $^-2$, $^-3$, . . . The set of numbers called integers is made up of the positive integers, the negative integers, and zero.

There are many practical examples of the way we use integers in everyday life. For instance, the twenty dollars we earn at a job is an example of the positive integer $^+20$; the fifteen dollars we pay for groceries is an example of the negative integer $^-15$. To mark the sea floor 250 m below sea level we can use the negative integer $^-250$; to mark a mountain 4807 m above sea level we can use the positive integer $^+4807$.

Opposites

Remember that to find the opposite of an integer (or any number), you change its sign. See what happens when you take the opposite of an integer twice.

take opposite of	$^+5$	$^+3$	$^-7$	$^-10$
take opposite of	$^-5$	$^-3$	$^+7$	$^+10$
	$^+5$	$^+3$	$^-7$	$^-10$

Changing the sign of an integer twice gives you the integer you started with. You can practice changing the signs of integers using the $+/-$ key on your calculator. See what happens when you use the $+/-$ key on a calculator to change the sign of an integer 3 times. What happens when you change the sign 4 times?

Comparing Integers

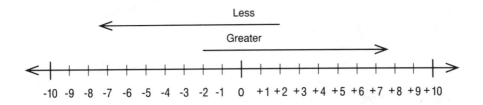

Integers that are farther to the right on the number line are greater than those to their left. $^+5 > {}^+2$ and $^-2 > {}^-5$. Integers that are farther to the left on the number line are less than those to their right. $^-7 < {}^-4$ and $4 < 7$. In general, remember the following rules.

> ## Rules for Integers
>
> 1) *A positive integer is always greater than a negative integer* $(1 > {}^-100)$.
>
> 2) *The farther to the left a negative integer is from zero, the smaller its value* $({}^-1 > {}^-100)$.

Adding Integers

You can show the sum of two integers by using arrows on a number line. Find the sum of ${}^+5 + {}^+3$. Starting at 0, first move 5 units to the right, then 3 units to the right.

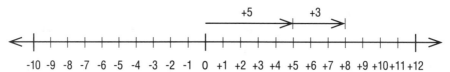

Therefore, ${}^+5 + {}^+3 = {}^+8$. (Remember, positive integers are most often written without positive signs: $5 + 3 = 8$.)

Find the sum of ${}^-5 + {}^-3$. Starting at 0, first move 5 units to the left, then 3 units to the left.

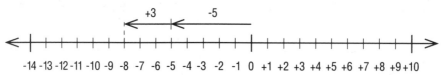

Therefore, ${}^-5 + {}^-3 = {}^-8$. You can add two negative integers the same way you add two positive integers, but because you are moving in the opposite direction, the sum is negative.

> ## Rules for Adding Integers
>
> *The sum of two positive integers is positive.*
> *The sum of two negative integers is negative.*

We have seen how to add integers that have the same sign. Practice using arrows on a number line to see what happens when you add integers with opposite signs.

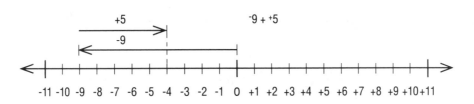

To find the sum of ⁻9 + ⁺5, start at 0. First move left 9 units, then move right 5 units. ⁻9 + ⁺5 = ⁻4.

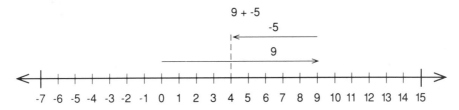

Now find the sum of their opposites. Starting at 0, first move right 9 units, then move left 5 units. 9 + ⁻5 = 4.

Draw your own number lines to show the sum of ⁺5 + ⁻8 and the sum of ⁻5 + ⁺8. See if you can invent your own rules to explain what happens when you add integers with opposite signs. Explain your rules, using examples, to a friend or a parent. Test your rules to make sure you can find several different sums, such as ⁻64 + 41 or ⁺18 + ⁻67.

Notice that ⁻6 + ⁺6 = 0 and 3 + ⁻3 = 0.

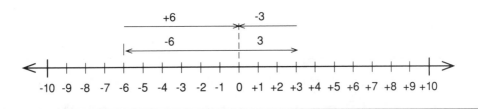

Rule for Adding Opposite Integers

The sum of an integer and its opposite is zero.

Subtracting Integers

Remember that if 9 − 6 = 3, then 6 + 3 = 9. We can also say: the *difference* of 9 and 6 is the number you have to *add* to 6 to get 9. We can define subtraction with integers the same way. The difference of two integers a − b is the number you have to add to b to get a.

Consider ⁻2 − ⁻5. The difference (⁻2 − ⁻5) is the number you have to add to ⁻5 to get ⁻2.

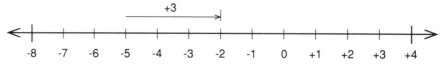

To get from ⁻5 to ⁻2, you add ⁺3. So ⁻2 − ⁻5 = ⁺3. Notice what happens when instead of subtracting ⁻5, you add its opposite: ⁻2 + ⁺5 = ⁻3.

Now try ⁺5 − ⁺7. The difference (⁺5 − ⁺7) equals the number you have to add to ⁺7 to get ⁺5.

⁺5 − ⁺7 = ⁻2. This time, instead of subtracting ⁺7, add its opposite: ⁺5 + ⁻7 = ⁻2. These two examples show a general rule that will always work to subtract an integer.

> ## Rule for Subtracting Integers
>
> *To subtract an integer, add its opposite.*

Here are four more examples:

$$^+3 - {}^+4 = {}^+3 + {}^-4 = {}^-1 \qquad\qquad {}^+5 - {}^-2 = {}^+5 + {}^+2 = {}^+7$$
$$^-3 - {}^+4 = {}^-3 + {}^-4 = {}^-7 \qquad\qquad {}^-5 - {}^-2 = {}^-5 + {}^+2 = {}^-3$$

Adding and Subtracting Integers

Sometimes you need to simplify expressions with integers that have both addition and subtraction operations.

Simplify:

$$^-17 + {}^-12 - {}^+14$$
$$^-29 - {}^+14$$
$$^-29 + {}^-14$$
$$^-43$$

If all the operations in an expression are addition, you can add numbers in whatever order is most convenient. Remember that addition is commutative and associative.

$$^-237 + 86 + 237$$
$$(^-237 + 237) + 86$$
$$86$$

The Coordinate Plane

We can locate a single integer, such as 2 or ¯3, on a number line.

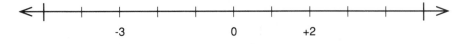

A Coordinate Plane

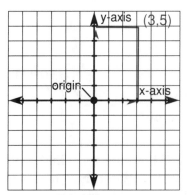

We can locate an ordered pair of integers, such as (3, 5) or (¯2, 4) on a plane, called a *coordinate plane*. A coordinate plane has two lines or axes that are perpendicular to each other: the x-axis, which is horizontal, and the y-axis, which is vertical. The point where the x-axis and the y-axis meet is called the *origin*. When you find the numbers in an ordered pair, you are finding a point on the coordinate plane. The numbers in an ordered pair are called the *coordinates of the point*. They tell where the point is in relation to the origin.

An example: (3, 5). The first coordinate, 3, gives the horizontal distance 3 units to the right from the origin along the x-axis. The second coordinate, 5, gives the vertical distance 5 units up from the origin along the y-axis.

The first coordinate of a point always gives its horizontal distance from the origin along the x-axis; the second coordinate of a point always gives its vertical distance from the origin along the y-axis.

Here is how you would plot some other points on a coordinate plane.

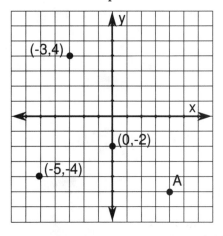

Plot (¯3, 4). Go 3 units from the origin to the left along the x-axis, then 4 units up.

Plot (0, ¯2). The distance from the origin along the x-axis is 0; go 2 units straight down along the y-axis.

Plot (¯5, ¯4). From the origin, go 5 units left, 4 units down.

What are the coordinates of point A? Go 4 units right along the x-axis, 5 units down along the y-axis: (4, ¯5).

The coordinates of the origin are (0, 0).

Working with the Coordinate Plane

Here are some different ways you can work with the coordinate plane.

If ABCD is a rectangle and you are given its coordinates as A ($^-$4, $^-$2), B ($^-$4, ?), C (2, 3), and D (?, ?), you can find the missing coordinates. Solution: Plot the points you are given, A ($^-$4, $^-$2) and C (2, 3). Because you know the figure is a rectangle, you can figure out what the missing coordinates must be:

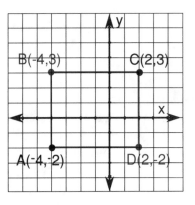

The coordinates of B are ($^-$4, 3); the coordinates of D are (2, $^-$2).

Find the coordinates of the points H, I, J, K. Then take the opposites of each one of the x-coordinates of the points, and make four new points H′, I′, J′, and K′. Draw the new quadrilateral H′I′J′K′. You will find that the quadrilateral H′I′J′K′ is the reflection of HIJK over the y-axis. Draw another new quadrilateral H″I″J″K″, only this time do it by making the y-coordinates of the points H, I, J, and K negative. You will find that this quadrilateral H″I″J″K″ is the reflection of HIJK over the x-axis. Then try adding 3 to the x-coordinate and 5 to the y-coordinate of the points H, I, J, and K. Is this new quadrilateral congruent to the old quadrilateral HIJK? If so, what rigid motion would you use to make them coincide?

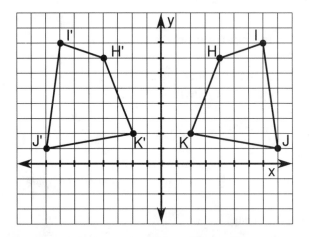

Graphing a Function

The table shows the function "add 3 to each number x."

x	0	1	2	⁻2	⁻1
y = x + 3	3	4	5	1	2

You can make an ordered pair (x, y) for each column in the table. Plot these ordered pairs: (0, 3), (1, 4), (2, 5), (⁻2, 1) (⁻1, 2).

Notice that the points all lie along the yellow line. You can make a graph of a function such as y = x − ⁺4 in the same way: make a table of the values for x and y starting with certain values for x, then plot the ordered pairs on a graph. Using a ruler or straightedge, connect the ordered pairs with a line.

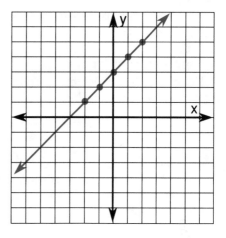

Working with Data: Probability

Mean, Median, Range, and Mode

Here is a set of test scores for a class with 12 students: 87, 84, 92, 84, 72, 77, 59, 51, 84, 72, 99, 69.

Remember that you can find the mean, or average, of the set of scores by adding them up and then dividing the total by the number of scores.

$$\text{Mean} = \frac{87 + 84 + 92 + 84 + 72 + 77 + 59 + 51 + 84 + 72 + 99 + 69}{12}$$

$$= \frac{930}{12} = 77.5$$

The mean of the scores is 77.5.

The median of a set of numbers is the number in the middle of the set when the numbers in the set are ordered by size. When there are an even number of numbers in the set, the median is the average of the middle two numbers.

To find the median score, order the scores from least to greatest: 51, 59, 69, 72, 72, 77, 84, 84, 84, 87, 92, 99. The middle two numbers are 77 and 84.

$$\text{Median} = \frac{77 + 84}{2} = \frac{161}{2} = 80.5.$$

The median score is 80.5.

The range of a set of numbers is the difference between the greatest and the least of the numbers. The highest test score is 99, the lowest 51. $99 - 51 = 48$. The range of the scores is 48.

The mode of a set of numbers is the number that occurs most frequently. The score 84 occurs more frequently than any other—three times. So 84 is the mode of the scores.

A Histogram

A histogram is a kind of bar graph used to show how frequently certain numbers occur in a set of data. Here is a histogram showing in how many games Lyla, a forward for the Awesome Tigers, made a certain number of rebounds.

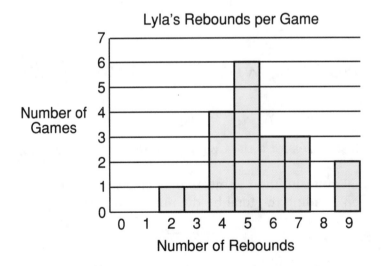

You can easily see that Lyla made 5 rebounds more often than any other number of rebounds. 5 is the mode of the number of rebounds she made in each game.

To find the mean of the number of rebounds she made in each game, you must first find her total number of rebounds.

No. of Rebounds	Games	Total	No. of Rebounds	Games	Total
2	× 1	= 2	6	× 3	= 18
3	× 1	= 3	7	× 3	= 21
4	× 4	= 16	9	× 2	= 18
5	× 6	= 30			

Total rebounds = 2 + 3 + 16 + 30 + 18 + 21 + 18 = 108

To find the mean you also need to find how many games there were, or how many numbers are in the set.

Number of games = 1 + 1 + 4 + 6 + 3 + 3 + 2 = 20

Mean number of rebounds = $\frac{108}{20}$ = 5.4

Lyla made a mean of 5.4 rebounds per game.

You can also use this histogram to find the median and the range of the number of rebounds she made in each game.

Making a Circle Graph

At Fertile Farms this summer, $\frac{1}{2}$ of the land is planted with corn, $\frac{1}{4}$ with soybeans, $\frac{1}{6}$ with alfalfa, and $\frac{1}{12}$ with lettuce and other vegetables. Let's make a circle graph to show the way the crops are planted at Fertile Farms.

Before beginning your circle graph, look at this diagram. Remember that there are 180° in a straight angle? There are two straight angles, or a total of 360°, in a full circle.

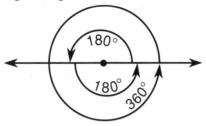

To make a circle graph, you need to find what fraction of 360° (the whole circle) each section should be.

The section for corn is $\frac{1}{2}$ of 360°: $\frac{1}{2}$ × 360° = 180°. The section of the graph representing the corn should have an angle of 180°.

The soybean section is $\frac{1}{4}$ of 360°: $\frac{1}{4}$ × 360° = 90°

Alfalfa: $\frac{1}{6}$ × 360° = 60°

Lettuce and other vegetables: $\frac{1}{12}$ × 360° = 30°

We used a protractor to measure the angle that each section of the circle graph should have; we also gave labels to the sections and a title to the graph.

Crops at Fertile Farms

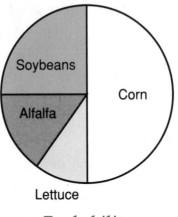

Probability

We write the probability or chance that an event will happen as a ratio. Suppose you want to know what the probability is, with one try, of drawing a red marble out of a bag with four white, three blue, and two red marbles of the same size. The probability of this event is the ratio of the number of outcomes that favor the event to the total number of possible outcomes. There are nine marbles altogether, or nine possible outcomes. There are two red marbles, or two favorable outcomes. So the probability of drawing a red marble is $\frac{2}{9}$. We write: P (red) = $\frac{2}{9}$. (You can read P (red) as "the probability of red.")

What is the probability of drawing either a white or a red marble on one try? There are nine possible outcomes. There are four white and two red marbles, or six favorable outcomes. P (red or white) = $\frac{6}{9}$ = $\frac{1}{3}$.

What is the probability of drawing a yellow marble? There are no yellow marbles, so there are zero favorable outcomes. P (yellow) = $\frac{0}{9}$ = 0. Because there are no yellow marbles, it is impossible that a yellow marble will be drawn. The probability of an impossible event is 0.

What is the probability that either a white, or blue, or red marble will be drawn with one try? There are 4 + 3 + 2, or 9, favorable outcomes, and 9 possible outcomes. P (white, red, or blue) = $\frac{9}{9}$ = 1. Because all the marbles are either white, blue, or red, it is certain that a white, blue, or red marble will be drawn. The probability of an event that is certain is 1.

Possible Outcomes: A Tree Diagram

When you are trying to find a probability, it is sometimes helpful to make a tree diagram to show all the possible outcomes.

Suppose you are playing a game that has a spinner with three equal-sized sections: a black section, a yellow section, and a white section.

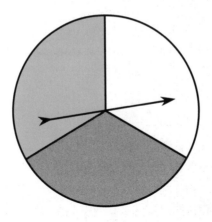

What is the probability of getting white once and yellow once if the spinner is spun twice? Make a tree diagram to show all the possible outcomes.

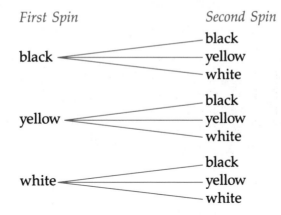

The first column of the tree diagram shows the three possible outcomes if the spinner is spun once: black, yellow, or white. Then the second column shows what can happen on the second spin: each one of the possible outcomes on the first spin can be followed by three possible outcomes on the second spin. You can count that altogether there are nine possible outcomes: nine possible combinations of what can happen on the first spin plus the second spin. There are two outcomes with "one white and one yellow," so the probability of getting one white and one yellow is $\frac{2}{9}$.

What is the probability of getting black at least once, if the spinner is spun twice? There are five outcomes that have at least one "black," so the probability of getting black at least once, if the spinner is spun twice, is $\frac{5}{9}$. Notice that the probability of getting black twice, if the spinner is spun twice, is $\frac{1}{9}$.

V.

NATURAL SCIENCES

Introduction to Life Sciences

FOR PARENTS AND TEACHERS

This section culminates the studies in life sciences begun in the earlier books in this series. Here students continue their study of cellular reproduction; they learn about the origin of genetics in the humble garden of Gregor Mendel and the complex process by which DNA replicates itself; and they are introduced to mutation and adaptation, including symbiotic adaptation. This section also includes a look at types of behavior, distinguishing between inherited behaviors and learned behaviors.

A section on health explains the body's immune system and addresses the related topics of contagious and noncontagious diseases. It also reexamines the skeletal system.

We continue to urge parents and teachers to reinforce and enlarge upon the topics in this section by providing children with opportunities for active, hands-on learning. You may find the following resources helpful:

How Did We Find Out About Our Genes? by Isaac Asimov (Walker, 1983).
Where Did You Get Those Eyes: A Guide to Discovering Your Family History by Kay Cooper (Walker, 1988).
Understanding and Preventing AIDS by Warren Coleman (Children's Press, 1988).
How Animals Behave: A New Look at Wildlife by Donald J. Crump (National Geographic, 1984).
The Skeleton and Movement by Jacqueline Dineen (Silver Burdett, 1988).
Your Immune System by Alan E. Nourse (Franklin Watts, 1989).

Life Sciences

REPRODUCTION, HEREDITY, AND GENETICS

Sexual and Asexual Reproduction

Have you ever heard people say things like, "You have your mother's eyes!" or "You have your father's chin"? You know that even if you do have some features that resemble those of your parents, you don't look exactly like either of them. You also know that sometimes a short-haired gray mother cat will have long-haired

orange kittens. Usually children and animals do resemble their parents, but they are never exact copies of them. Certain other organisms, however, do make exact copies of themselves when they reproduce. Amoeba, for example, divide in half, making two identical new organisms.

There are two different ways of making new individuals: sexual and asexual reproduction. Sexual reproduction occurs through the combination of male and female sex cells. Organisms that reproduce sexually—whether they are cats, ferns, or beluga whales—produce offspring that combine traits from *both* parents. That's why the offspring from sexual reproduction may have slightly different traits from those of either parent.

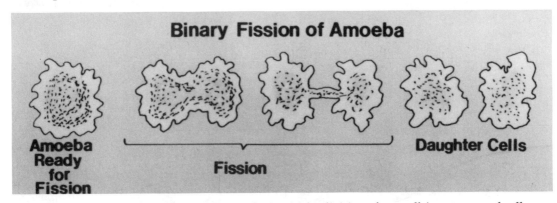

Binary Fission of Amoeba

Amoeba Ready for Fission

Fission

Daughter Cells

"Binary" means composed of two, so binary fission is the division of one cell into two equal cells.

In asexual reproduction there is only one kind of parent cell, which divides into new cells, so all the traits of the offspring are exactly the same as those of the parent. Offspring produced by asexual reproduction are called clones. In Book Five of this series you read about yeasts that reproduce asexually by budding and fungi that reproduce asexually by making spores. There are many methods of asexual reproduction, but the result is always a cell that is identical to its parent.

To live, cells must carry instructions that tell them how to grow, reproduce, and perform many other life processes. These instructions are contained in threadlike cell parts, called chromosomes, located in the nucleus. In ordinary cells of living things chromosomes occur in pairs. Cells with chromosome pairs are called diploid cells. In a special instance during sexual reproduction, cells are made with single chromosomes rather than paired chromosomes. We call cells with single chromosomes haploid cells.

Did you know that you can reproduce a potato by cutting some of the buds, or "eyes," from a raw potato and planting them? The new potato plants will have exactly the same traits as the parent plant. You will have created clones of the original potato through asexual reproduction. Did you also know that your skin cells are constantly dying and being replaced by new cells? You shed and regrow more than a pound of skin a year. To replace these cells, your body employs the very same kind of asexual

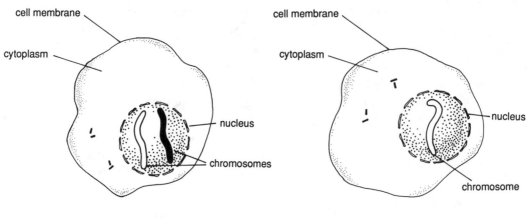

Diploid Cell

cell membrane

cytoplasm

nucleus

chromosomes

Haploid Cell

cell membrane

cytoplasm

nucleus

chromosome

In the diploid cell, chromosomes occur in pairs. In the haploid cell, they are single.

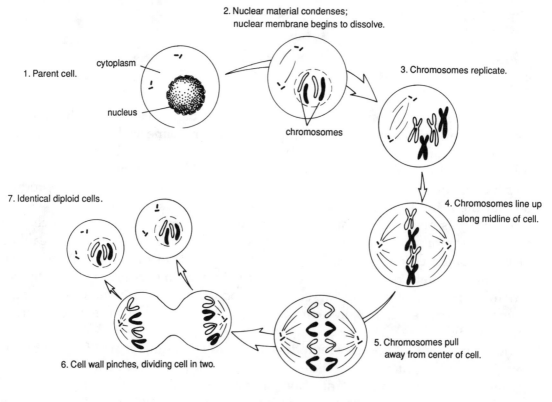

1. Parent cell.

cytoplasm

nucleus

2. Nuclear material condenses; nuclear membrane begins to dissolve.

chromosomes

3. Chromosomes replicate.

4. Chromosomes line up along midline of cell.

5. Chromosomes pull away from center of cell.

6. Cell wall pinches, dividing cell in two.

7. Identical diploid cells.

Mitosis

reproduction by which bacteria, amoebas, and potato buds clone themselves—the process of cell division called mitosis.

During mitosis, the chromosomes in the cell nucleus duplicate themselves. Remember that chromosomes come in pairs, so this means that each chromosome in a pair duplicates itself. The membrane around the nucleus then opens, and the duplicated pairs of chromosomes line up in the middle of the cell. The duplicated chromosomes separate from the original pairs and move to opposite ends of the cell. The cell then splits to form two cells, each of which contains an identical set of chromosome pairs. That is what happens every time an amoeba or one of your own skin cells divides by asexual reproduction.

Sexual reproduction involves a process quite different from asexual reproduction. Organisms that reproduce sexually, such as cats and humans, produce special sex cells for the job. Each sex cell is a haploid cell, containing *half* the number of chromosomes as the rest of the cells in the organism. To form a new organism with the full number of chromosomes, two sex cells must join together.

The process by which a cell makes new haploid sex cells is called meiosis. In meiosis the chromosomes first copy themselves, just as in mitosis.

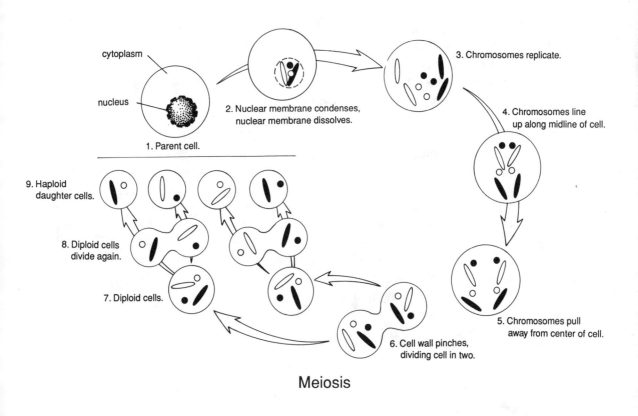

cytoplasm

nucleus

1. Parent cell.

2. Nuclear membrane condenses, nuclear membrane dissolves.

3. Chromosomes replicate.

4. Chromosomes line up along midline of cell.

5. Chromosomes pull away from center of cell.

6. Cell wall pinches, dividing cell in two.

7. Diploid cells.

8. Diploid cells divide again.

9. Haploid daughter cells.

Meiosis

Heredity: A Closer Look at Chromosomes

In both kinds of reproduction, sexual and asexual, the parents' chromosomes are passed to the offspring. To understand how this causes the parents' *traits* to be passed to their offspring, we have to learn more about chromosomes.

Different kinds of organisms have different kinds of chromosomes in their cells. But parents and offspring of the same kind of organism always carry the same number and kind of chromosomes. All radish cells have nine pairs of radish chromo-

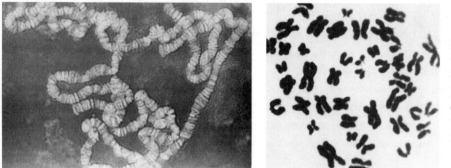

The chromosome of a fruit fly.

The twenty-three pairs of human chromosomes are shown in a photomicrograph, a picture taken with a microscope.

somes, all fruit fly cells have four pairs of fruit fly chromosomes, all cat cells have thirty-eight pairs of cat chromosomes, all human cells have twenty-three pairs of human chromosomes, and all crayfish cells have two hundred pairs of crayfish chromosomes.

Is a crayfish cell with two hundred chromosome pairs more complex than a human cell with twenty-three? No. The number of chromosome pairs in an organism does not determine how complex it is. It's the amount and complexity of the instruction-carrying material in the chromosome that determines the complexity of the organism. That instruction-carrying material, called DNA (short for deoxyribonucleic acid), is a molecule that looks like a twisted ladder. (In the Stories About Scientists section of this book, you can read about Crick and Watson's discovery of DNA's structure.) The DNA molecule can be very long, depending on how complicated its instructions are. A very important feature of DNA is that the instructions it contains can be duplicated and passed to new offspring. That's what happens in the processes of mitosis and meiosis.

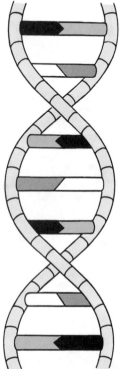

The DNA molecule looks like a twisted ladder.

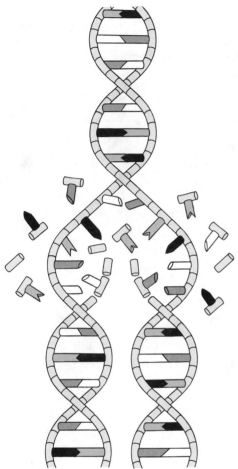

The DNA molecule copies itself exactly.

The ladder-shaped DNA molecule breaks in half right down the middle when it duplicates itself. When it does this, part of each rung of the ladder stays on each side. But each half of each rung has a special shape that will allow *only one kind of new half-rung* to join with it. That means that each half of the long DNA ladder will create one and only one kind of new DNA molecule, and that each half-molecule will be an exact copy of the half of the original DNA molecule.

The strands of DNA contain many different instructions written in special codes. Once scientists figured out that the strands included instructions for "start here" and "stop there," they could tell where one instruction ended and the next began.

The DNA codes, or instructions for making individual traits, are called genes. There are many genes in a single chromosome, and each carries specific pieces of information for the development of the organism. Cats have certain genes for forming tails and others for forming whiskers. Other genes carry information for determining fur and eye color, or ear size and shape. Can you think of some traits you may have inherited from your mother's genes? From your father's?

Because chromosomes come in pairs, the genes that they carry do too. You inherited half your genes from your mother and half from your father. So if one set of genes was for long fingers and one set was for short fingers, would you end up with long or short fingers—or something in between? The study of how traits like these are inherited is called genetics.

Gregor Mendel: The Father of Genetics

As early as 1865, a monk named Gregor Mendel was asking questions about how and why certain traits are inherited by offspring. Growing up on a farm in Austria, Mendel learned as a child to love plants. When he became an adult, he began to investigate how plants inherit their features. He decided to study garden peas because it was easy to protect these plants from accidental fertilization (which would interfere with his experiments) and to distinguish between their traits. Mendel noticed that some pea plants were tall, and some short. There were no plants of medium height. He also noticed that short plants always produced short plants. He observed that peas had seeds that were either green or yellow, and either round or wrinkled. In all, Mendel identified seven different pairs of traits related to plant height, position of blossoms, color and shape of the peas and their pods, and the color of the seed coats. Each of these pairs had two, and only two, forms—for example, tallness and shortness.

Gregor Mendel.

In one of his experiments, Mendel planted seeds from one group of tall pea plants and seeds from another group of short plants. He noticed that all the tall plants produced plants that were tall, and all the short plants produced plants that were short. Mendel called these "pure" plants because they seemed to pass all their traits to their offspring. He decided to cross (or breed) two pure plants to see what would happen.

To crossbreed, Mendel first took pollen from the flower of a pure tall plant and carefully placed it in the flower of a pure short plant. When the seeds from that

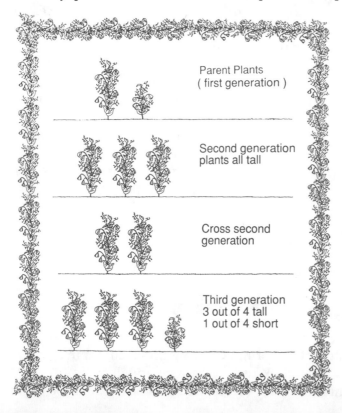

Parent Plants
(first generation)

Second generation
plants all tall

Cross second
generation

Third generation
3 out of 4 tall
1 out of 4 short

This diagram shows you the surprising results Mendel got in the second and third generations of his pea plants. Crossing a tall and a short plant resulted in all tall offspring in the second generation. But crossing two of the tall plants from the second generation resulted in one short plant for every three tall plants.

short plant developed, Mendel put them in the ground and waited for new plants to grow. When the offspring developed, they were all tall! Mendel then took pollen from one of the short plants, and placed it in the flower of a tall plant. When the seeds from that tall plant developed, again all the offspring plants were tall.

Mendel decided to see what would happen if he crossed two tall offspring. After planting the seeds that had developed from the two tall offspring, he noticed that three tall plants grew for every short plant. In other words, three-quarters of these offspring were tall and one-quarter were short. Mendel did similar experiments with the other six pairs of traits he had identified, and noticed the same thing: in every case, one of the pair of traits appeared in three-quarters of the offspring, and the other appeared in one-quarter of the offspring.

Mendel concluded that for every trait, there were two hereditary contributions, one from each parent. He also reasoned that in every pair of traits, one trait would always be stronger than the other. He called the stronger trait the dominant trait, and the weaker trait the recessive trait. Which was the dominant trait in Mendel's crossbreeding between tall and short pea plants? Which was the recessive?

Today we know that these double hereditary contributions are genes located on pairs of chromosomes in the parents' cells. When haploid sex cells, or gametes, combine, offspring inherit a copy of each gene for a given trait from each parent. To predict an offspring's traits, you must know which of the parents' traits are dominant, and which are recessive.

As so often happens to great scientific discoveries, Mendel's work was largely ignored until many years after his death because it was not well understood. Little was known about cell division at the time, and no one could grasp the broad implications of Mendel's findings. Nevertheless, later scientists were able to follow his carefully kept records, and his findings were confirmed in 1900. Mendel is known today as the "Father of Modern Genetics."

Mutations

Sometimes in the DNA copying process, one of the ladder rungs of DNA can be broken or moved. Look at the rabbit in this picture. Something unusual happened here. The parents of this rabbit had brownish fur, but the offspring has white hair and pink eyes. Animals like this are called albinos, from the Latin *albus*, meaning "white." Albinos are a rare occurrence in nature. Some are created when two recessive genes combine during fertilization, but they can also result from an accidental change in the genes. When this happens, it is not because the traits for white hair and pink eyes are present in either of the parents' genes. Instead they are created during meiosis when a gene copies itself

inexactly, and the inexact copy is passed on to the offspring when fertilization occurs. The offspring then has the albino traits that no one in its family has exhibited.

When a gene copies itself inexactly, resulting in a changed gene that produces a new trait, we call this a mutation. The word comes from the Latin *mutare*, meaning "to change." Mutations are not regular or seasonal events. They happen by chance. Sometimes mutations are the result of exposure to chemicals, X-rays, radioactive substances, or even to the sun.

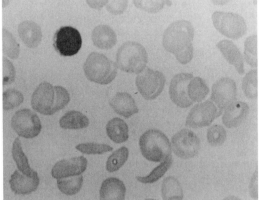

Harmful mutations are not usually passed on through generations, either because the creatures may not be able to create offspring or because they are likely to die before they can do so. An albino rabbit would be easy prey in a forest, for example. But some mutations can be helpful for survival, and they are passed on to offspring long into the future.

For example, consider the story of the peppered moth, which lives in England. Before there were many factories, most of these moths were light gray and mottled with dark specks. This coloring allowed them to blend with the lichen on trees. Only a few of the moths were black, and

The red blood cells in this picture have two shapes, the usual round, flat doughnut-like shape and a sickle shape. The sickle cells result from a harmful mutation called sickle-cell anemia. The sickle cells impair circulation.

they could easily be sighted by birds. Most of the black moths were eaten before they could pass along the gene for blackness to offspring. Then something fascinating happened: in the parts of England where industry was growing, more and more black moths and fewer and fewer gray mottled moths began to be born.

These two pictures allow you to see what hungry birds see. Which moth would you see first on the light, lichen-covered tree? Which on the tree darkened by industrial pollutants?

How did this change arise? The black body color, which was a genetic mutation, helped the moths survive on trees blackened by soot from the new industries. Now it was the light gray moths that were easily seen and eaten by birds. So increasing numbers of black moths passed along the mutation for black coloring to each succeeding generation.

The story of the peppered moth supports Charles Darwin's idea of how new traits develop. This idea, called natural selection, is central to Darwin's theory of evolution, which you read about in Book Four of this series. Many scientists believe Darwin was right that naturally occurring mutations result in traits that allow organisms to better adapt to changes in their environment. These scientists believe that mutations are responsible for the process of evolution. Because it is extremely slow, that process is usually not so easy to detect as the changes in the peppered moth. Scientists think that most forms of evolution normally take thousands of years.

Learning to Live Together

Sometimes species evolve together, forming a special relationship called symbiosis. (The word *symbiosis* is Greek for "living together.") In a symbiotic relationship, two species live together in a way that is usually beneficial to one, sometimes to both. For example, pink lady's-slipper orchids have developed a symbiotic relationship with a species of fungus that grows with the plant's roots. The fungus helps the orchid by increasing the amount of water and nutrients it can take in. The orchid, in turn, serves the fungus by supplying it with carbohydrates.

The red-back cleaner shrimp lives in tropical waters where it removes small parasites from fish. Many cleaner shrimp and fish are brightly colored, probably to advertise their services to the larger fish they clean.

This bumblebee and honeybee are pollinating an aster as they gather nectar. Can you find the "pollen basket" on the bumblebee's leg? The middle segment of the hind leg is flattened and surrounded by long hairs that hold pollen.

There are many other examples of adaptations for mutual benefit in the natural world. Ferocious sharks let tiny fish called wrasse survive by cleaning food from the sharks' sharp teeth. Small birds called plovers scamper into crocodiles' mouths to eat the worm-like leeches that stick to the crocodiles' jaws. Ants herd and protect small bugs called aphids because they love the honeylike liquid they can "milk" from their aphid "cows."

Some of the most colorful and unusual adaptations involve plants that have developed special structures for attracting pollinators (such as bees, birds, or butterflies) to their flowers. The pollinators benefit by having access to food in the form of nectar and pollen, and the plants benefit by having their pollen transferred from anther to stigma, so reproduction can take place. Before an insect can feast on nectar, it must brush up against an anther full of pollen. The pollen sticks to the insect and is either transferred to a sticky pistil, or carried on to the next flower's pistil, where it eventually fertilizes the flower.

Charles Darwin once observed an orchid that had a long, narrow, curved throat with nectar at the bottom. But no creature was known to exist with a beak that could suck the nectar and pollinate the flower. Darwin predicted that someday someone would observe a moth with a long snout that would fit the throat of that particular orchid. And indeed, just such a moth was observed! The two organisms, moth and orchid, must have developed together—to their mutual benefit.

Extinction

Although species can adapt to changes in their environment, adaptation usually takes a long time. Unfortunately, mankind has gained the ability to change the envi-ronment very quickly, and many times organisms cannot adapt quickly enough to survive these changes in the environment. When a whole species dies out, we say the organism has become extinct.

A great many animals and plants are threatened with extinction. Dolphins and whales, gorillas and wild elephants are now classified as endangered animals. In our country, the Florida manatee, the bald eagle, the peregrine falcon, and the California condor face extinction unless we control the fishing, hunting, and land development that threaten these animals and their habitats.

Peregrine falcons like this one are on the endangered species list.

Tropical rainforest.

Sometimes rainforest is cut down so farmers can use the land. In this case, it was cut to mine tin.

Each year, twenty-seven million acres of tropical rainforest—an area the size of Ohio—are cut down for timber or burned to clear the land for agriculture. This translates to the destruction of fifty acres of land per minute, land that is home to a great number of species of plants and animals that live nowhere else in the world. Nearly half of all the world's species of animals and two-thirds of the world's flowering plants are found in the tropical rainforests. It is estimated that by the year 2000, 80 percent of the rainforests will be gone and the species that live there will be facing extinction.

Extinctions can result from entirely natural causes. Dinosaurs, for example, became extinct millions of years ago, before humans appeared on the earth. But most extinctions are now caused by human intervention. Scientists today are worried by the rate at which extinctions are occurring. Our planet is currently losing about three species per day, a rate that is expected to accelerate to three *per hour* in less than ten years. If so, by the year 2000, 20 percent of all the earth's species could be gone forever.

Write a report on one of the endangered species mentioned in the text or on the extinction of a species, such as the passenger pigeon or the gooney bird.

BEHAVIORS OF LIVING THINGS

Instinct

Just as organisms inherit genes for physical characteristics such as fur or petal color, they also inherit genes for certain behaviors. The simplest behaviors are reflexes: you inherited genes for a set of reflexes that cause you to blink your eyes in bright light, snatch your hand away from hot objects, or cough when you inhale smoke.

Animals also inherit genes for behavior patterns more complex than reflexes. These behaviors are known as instincts. Almost all animals inherit the instinct to stay alive. This instinct for self-preservation causes animals to seek food, water, and shelter and to defend themselves against enemies or to run from danger. Rabbits instinctually run when they see danger. Animals also inherit instincts to reproduce and to rear and protect their young. Other examples of instinctive behavior include hibernation and migration. Squirrels and chipmunks hibernate in winter. Birds migrate in winter by instinct.

Here's how scientists tried to test for instinctive behavior in one interesting study. Adult herring gulls

A robin, guided by instinct, feeds its hungry young.

have beaks with red spots. Their chicks peck at the spot as a way of begging for food, and then the parents feed them. When scientists tried to use a simulated beak, to feed herring gull chicks who had never been fed by their parents, they found that the chicks begged for food only if the beak had a red spot on it. Because these chicks had never been fed by their parents, they could not have learned this behavior. Scientists concluded that the chicks' behavior had to be instinctive.

Learning

An instinctive behavior is inherited: you're born with it. In contrast, a learned behavior is developed from experience. Although humans and some animals do inherit an instinct to learn, the content of their learning is determined by their experience.

Instinctive behavior does not change; it stays the same even when circumstances change. Birds migrate in the winter months even when the weather stays warm. But learned behavior is more flexible. Humans don't hibernate in winter, and most humans don't change where they live seasonally. Instead, they have learned to dress warmly and heat their houses. Humans are very adaptable. Generally we don't wait for evolution to change our responses to the environment; instead, learned behavior enables us to respond quickly to changing circumstances.

To learn from an experience, an organism must have a memory to store information to be used later. Memory helps an organism learn through trial and error. In trial-and-error learning, an organism tries to do a task again and again, sometimes making mistakes, but other times succeeding. Eventually the organism figures out what it did to succeed. A mouse will learn how to get through a maze to find food at the end by trying different routes again and again. The mouse eventually remembers which routes don't lead to food and which do.

Animals learn not only by trial and error, but also learn by conditioning, which involves a system of rewards or punishments. If you have a dog, you and your parents probably trained it in this way. A Russian scientist named Pavlov once conducted a famous experiment in conditioning. Pavlov rang a bell every time he offered food to a group of dogs. The dogs would begin to salivate when they were fed. After repeating this action many times, Pavlov continued to ring the bell, but without feeding the dogs. He discovered that the dogs still began to salivate every time he rang the bell.

Conditioned behavior can lead to the development of habits. Habits are learned behaviors that are repeated so often they are performed almost without thinking. They seem almost instinctive. What are some of your good habits? What about bad habits?

Another way animals learn is through imitation. Some young birds learn to fly by imitating their parents. Young eagles learn to hunt by watching their parents and imitating them. You learned to speak by imitating the speech of other people.

Pavlov (center) and his staff.

The maze reflected in the mirror was built for experimental purposes. Although it has fourteen blind alleys, rats can make their way through it quickly.

The young osprey on the left is learning to fly by watching its parent.

Humans can learn through reasoning, building on what they already know. Just like these boys reasoning out a project together, you do this every day, in school and out.

These twins are star college basketball players. Twins, human and animal, provide scientists with a unique opportunity to study nature versus nurture, especially when they have been by some circumstances separated at birth. Why is this so?

Humans and other more advanced animals such as chimps have the ability to learn in the most complex way of all: through reasoning. Reasoning is the process of forming conclusions based on information and experience. It allows us to build on previous knowledge, to put information together to come up with new information—for example, to add 2 and 2 to get 4. One very important result of reasoning is that it enables animals to solve problems and respond to difficulties in their environment even when those difficulties are new to them.

It is sometimes hard to determine whether an animal is able to reason. Scientists are very careful not to assume this ability in a species until they have experimental evidence to prove it exists. There are many studies of dolphins and porpoises that suggest they have highly developed reasoning abilities. It appears that brain size is not as important to reasoning as is the texture of the brain's surface: the smoother the brain surface, the lower the ability of an animal to reason.

How much of an organism's behavior is inherited and how much is learned? No one really knows. This question has been the subject of debate for many years. Because genes are natural in origin and learning is a product of upbringing or nurturing, this debate is known as the "nature versus nurture" controversy.

HUMAN HEALTH

The Immune System and Disease

Fortunately for you, your body fights off harmful germs and chemicals. To get an idea of the way your body does this, think about an ants' nest invaded by predators. When an intruder comes to eat their young or to attack the adult ants, the members of the ant colony resist it. They send a chemical message to each other that acts as an alarm, and they rush toward the intruder to bite it and carry it away. Your body reacts to an invading germ in much the same way. Germs, which scientists call microbes, are actually very small organisms that can be seen only under a microscope. There are many different microbes; they include bacteria, viruses, protozoa, and fungi. The human body has a built-in system of defenses called the immune system, which resists diseases caused by microbes.

The immune system makes use of white blood cells and antibodies to rid the body of intruders. White blood cells attack foreign microbes that appear in your blood. They can even leave the bloodstream to attack microbes found in tissues. The white blood cells surround the intruders and then digest them.

Antibodies work differently. They are not actual cells, but rather special molecules of protein that have the ability to attach themselves to certain parts of invading microbes. Specific antibodies attach themselves to specific foreign proteins, called antigens, that are found in microbes. An antibody and an antigen fit each other like a lock and key. Antibodies lock into the foreign antigens, deactivating their ability to cause harm.

Even after an antigen is deactivated, the antibodies that were made to attack it

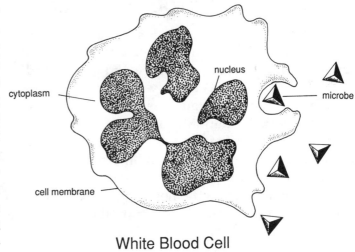

White Blood Cell

A white blood cell attacking a microbe. The nucleus of this cell only looks as if it has many parts. Because you're looking at a cross-section, you don't see the whole nucleus, which is large and many-lobed.

remain in the blood. If a similar invader appears in the future, the antibodies already in the blood can attack the invading microbe and keep it from causing a disease. As a result, some antibodies can protect a person from getting a disease more than once. This protection is called immunity.

antigen

antibody

The antibody fits the antigen just as a key fits a lock.

Have you ever had chicken pox? If you have, you will not get it again, because your body has built up a lifetime immunity to this disease. But other diseases, such as influenza, commonly called the flu, can occur again and again. The viruses that cause the flu are constantly changing the shape of their antigens, so new antibodies have to be created to fight them. You remain sick with the flu until your body creates new antibodies and makes enough white and red blood cells to destroy the viruses.

Microbes: Friends or Foes?

Can we simply stay away from microbes and remain healthy? No. As you read in Book Five of this series, microbes are in the soil, water, and air around you. Microbes are found throughout your house and school, and on your body. Some helpful microbes even live *inside* your body. Your immune system doesn't work to get rid of these microbes, because they are essential for normal body functions, such as digestion.

There are many harmful microbes that the human immune system must recognize and fight. They include certain types of bacteria, fungi, protozoa, flatworms, hookworms, and roundworms. In addition, the immune system must deal with viruses. These harmful microbes enter the human body through a cut in the skin, or through body openings such as the nose or mouth. Other microbes, such as the fungus that causes athlete's foot, simply attach to the skin and cause disease there.

Even before the immune system begins to do its job, the body tries to combat certain microbes and viruses with other defenses. You may have noticed that when you begin to get a cold, you sneeze and cough a lot, and you need to blow your nose frequently. Sneezing and coughing are reflexes that try to expel certain germs from your body. (That's why it's important to cover your mouth when you sneeze or cough to avoid passing these germs to others.)

The reason your nose becomes stuffy or runny is because of increased mucus in your nose, throat, and

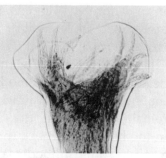

This is a hookworm, a harmful microbe.

sinuses. Mucus is a sticky substance that traps microbes and dust. Tiny hairs in the nose, sinuses, trachea, and bronchi help push the mucus and its harmful matter out of the respiratory system so it can be swallowed and destroyed by stomach acids.

Microbes Are Everywhere

Materials: notebook and pencil
grease pencil
2 flat toothpicks
6 petri dishes with covers
"antiseptic" mouthwash
alcohol

3 cotton swabs
hand lens
agar
regular soap
water

Mark the bottoms of the petri dishes with numbers 1 through 6. Fill each dish with agar. (You can obtain agar with directions for its preparation from a pharmacy or a biological supply house.) Cover petri dish number 1 immediately after the agar cools and hardens. "Wash" the hardened agar in dish 2 with an alcohol-soaked cotton swab, and in dish 3 with a swab soaked with regular soap and water. Leave these uncovered. Take a clean toothpick and gently scrape the inside of your mouth on one side. Rub the toothpick on the agar in dish 4, and repeat this step with a fresh toothpick and dish 5. Now rub the agar in dish 4 with a mouthwash-soaked cotton swab. Do nothing to the agar in dish 6. Leave dishes 4 to 6 uncovered. Place the dishes on a windowsill and leave the window open a crack, or near (not on) a heating vent.

Draw a chart in your notebook with six columns and seven rows. Label your chart like this:

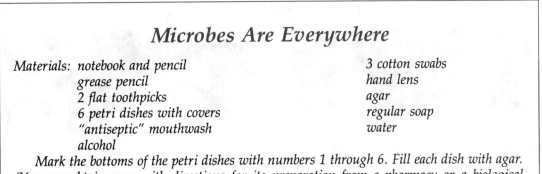

Microbe Experiment

Day / Dish	Day 1	Day 2	Day 3	Day 4	Day 5
Dish 1					
Dish 2					
Dish 3					
Dish 4					
Dish 5					
Dish 6					

Observe each dish with a hand lens and record your observations in the second column, labeled "Day 1." Let the dishes sit overnight for four nights and record your observations at the beginning of each day in the appropriate column. What do you see? Why did it appear? What is the purpose of dishes 1 and 6? Can you explain what happened in dishes 2 through 5?

Sometimes the body becomes oversensitive and reacts to harmless proteins, such as those found in dust and flower pollen, as if they were dangerous. This special sensitivity is called an allergy. It occurs when the body needlessly makes antibodies to combat these harmless proteins. These antibodies cause people to sneeze, get rashes, or even to have difficulty breathing.

Ah-ah-ah-choo!

Infectious Diseases

Sometimes when you get sick, the body's defenses become overwhelmed by the attacking microbes. Suppose the intruder of an ant colony brought more intruders with him, and suppose they could reproduce themselves very quickly. The ants might be able to attack and carry away some of the intruders, but soon they would be outnumbered. The intruders would take over the colony, causing mass destruction. This sounds like a science-fiction movie, but it is exactly what happens inside your body when your immune system is overcome by microbes.

When they are able to enter the body and overpower the immune system, microbes grow and reproduce rapidly, just as you saw if you conducted the experiment

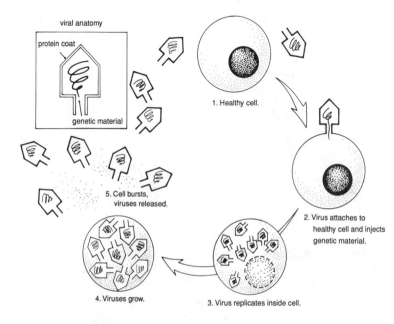

Viral Reproduction

described earlier. This invasion is called an infection. The rapid growth damages the body's cells and leads to what is known as an infectious disease. This is distinguished from diseases that are not caused by infection but by some defect in the body's system. Influenza, for example, is an infectious disease; in contrast, anemia is not an infectious disease, but occurs when the body does not make enough red blood cells.

Different microbes and viruses cause different infectious diseases. Certain types of bacteria are responsible for diseases such as strep throat, tetanus (lockjaw), tuberculosis, and pneumonia. Fungi can cause skin diseases, such as athlete's foot. Malaria is caused by a protozoan.

A virus is little more than DNA in a protective wrapper. Viruses are considered nonliving because they reproduce by invading living cells, where they inject their DNA into the host cell and instruct it to produce more viruses. The viruses multiply and grow until they use up the cell's food. Then the cell bursts, and the viruses are released. They invade other cells and destroy them. In this way, the virus rapidly weakens an organism. Viruses cause infectious diseases in humans that include the common cold, chicken pox, measles, influenza, cancer, and AIDS.

How Disease Is Spread

Infectious diseases that can spread from one person to another, from one animal or plant to another, or from an animal to a person, are called contagious or communicable diseases. When a communicable disease spreads through whole communities it is known as an epidemic. As you may recall from reading about the Middle Ages in Book Four of this series, one famous epidemic in the 1300s killed more than sixty million people. This epidemic, called The Black Death, was the result of a deadly bacterial disease carried by a type of flea that lived on rats.

Another viral disease that is spread from animals to humans is rabies. When an infected animal bites a human, the rabies virus is passed to the human. The word *rabies* comes from a Latin word meaning "rage" or "madness." Rabid animals often appear wildly excited, and increased saliva makes them "foam at the mouth." If untreated, rabies will lead to a very painful death. (Be very careful when approaching all unfamiliar animals, and never attempt to feed or touch them. If you are bitten by any animal, contact a doctor immediately.)

Communicable diseases are spread among humans in a variety of ways. Some microbes can pass from one person to another when they shake

This page of a medieval medical text from Persia shows a man being bitten by a rabid dog and instructs students of medicine how to prevent and treat rabies.

hands, stand close to each other while speaking, or share drinking glasses or eating utensils. Coughing and sneezing can spread diseases—for instance, colds and flu. Some diseases, such as AIDS, are transmitted only through sexual contact or by direct contact with infected blood or other body fluids.

What Is AIDS?

By now you've probably heard of AIDS (Acquired Immune Deficiency Syndrome). AIDS makes it hard or sometimes impossible for a person to resist and fight disease because the AIDS virus (known as HIV) destroys the body's immune system. People with AIDS become very susceptible to infections and certain other diseases, such as pneumonia and some forms of cancer.

People all over the world, from all walks of life, are affected by this disease: AIDS has reached epidemic proportions. Some scientists estimate that as many as 10 million people in the world may already have the virus that causes this painful, deadly disease. Some people carry the AIDS virus but do not have symptoms of the disease themselves. These people can give others the AIDS virus and may someday develop AIDS themselves.

At this time there is no cure for AIDS. The only way to avoid getting AIDS is to avoid contact with infected blood or other body fluids.

You can find out more about AIDS at your local library. One especially humane and informative book is We Have AIDS, by Elaine Landau (Franklin Watts, 1990), in which nine young people with AIDS tell their stories.

The AIDS Memorial Quilt was made to commemorate those who have died of AIDS. Here thousands of people gather on the Capitol lawn to view the quilt and remember their loved ones.

Noncommunicable Diseases

You cannot catch noncommunicable diseases; they are not contagious. Some noncommunicable diseases can, however, be passed from parent to child through their genes: for example, hemophilia, a disease in which the blood does not clot correctly, is a hereditary disease. Other noncommunicable diseases are caused by factors in the environment, such as smog or ultraviolet radiation from the sun. Inhaling smog, like smoking tobacco, can lead to lung disease and may even cause cancer in the lungs and other parts of the body. The sun's ultraviolet rays are thought to contribute to skin cancer in humans.

Poor nutrition causes other noncommunicable diseases. Scurvy, a disease caused by lack of vitamin C, results in bleeding gums and exhaustion. Heart disease and cancer can be brought on by an excess of fat and cholesterol and a lack of vegetables, fruit, and fiber in the diet. Heart disease and cancer are the top two causes of death in America today.

Treatment and Prevention of Disease

Some of the most important developments in medicine have been the discoveries of drugs to treat certain diseases. Antibiotics are drugs that slow the growth of bacteria or kill them without killing the body's cells. The antibiotic called penicillin was discovered in 1928. (You read about penicillin's discoverer, Alexander Fleming, in Book Four of this series.) Used in the treatment of pneumonia, strep throat, and other bacterial diseases, penicillin has saved many lives.

Unfortunately, antibiotics are not helpful in fighting viruses. Because viruses enter cells to attack them, it is difficult to develop drugs that can destroy the viruses without also killing the cells. But scientists have developed a way to strengthen the body's immunity against certain viruses and other germs. This is called vaccination. Vaccines made from small amounts of killed or weakened microbes are used to fight the diseases they cause. Patients swallow or are given an injection of the vaccine.

Do you remember being given shots against disease? When the killed or weakened germs in the vaccine entered your body, your immune system produced antibodies against the disease-causing germ. The antibodies multiplied and remained in your blood to attack any similar germs that might enter your body in the future—before they start multiplying. Just to make sure the antibodies remain in the blood, doctors sometimes give "booster" shots that contain small additional amounts of vaccine. Vaccines have been developed for polio, measles, mumps, and influenza, among others. Which of these diseases have you been vaccinated against?

Drugs: Helpful and Harmful

In addition to drugs that treat or prevent sickness, there are drugs that ease pain. You are probably familiar with aspirin, an over-the-counter pain reliever. "Over-the-counter" means that a medicine can be bought without a doctor's prescription.

When your doctor prescribes a particular drug for you, be sure to follow the instructions on the label very carefully. Prescription drugs are usually stronger than over-the-counter drugs, which is why you need your doctor's approval to take them. Remember, all drugs are potentially dangerous if they are not taken according to directions.

Sometimes people decide to take drugs for reasons other than to cure illness. They may want to change the way they feel, even when they are healthy. This is called drug abuse. Drug abuse can make a person sick, and can even lead to death.

Curiosity often prompts people to try drugs, and some of them, such as alcohol and tobacco, are easy to get. The best way to avoid drug abuse is not to start. Saying no can be difficult, but arming yourself with the knowledge of how drugs can harm you may help.

Doing Your Part to Stay Healthy

A strong, healthy body can do an amazing job of resisting disease. There are many things you can do to keep your body healthy, such as eating proper foods. A balanced diet gives the body the nutrients it needs to function properly.

Getting plenty of sleep is another good habit. A tired, run-down body is like a car that needs a tune-up; it does not function efficiently. Sleep refreshes the body and restores the energy necessary to fight disease.

Exercise is important in reducing stress and keeping the body healthy. Regular, moderate exercise, such as running, dancing, swimming, biking or

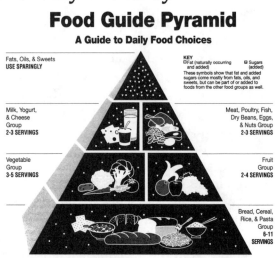

The food pyramid shows you how to eat a balanced diet.

playing a sport, will relieve muscle tension, keep the muscles firm, and make the heart and blood vessels healthy. Exercise, like sleep, makes the body function more efficiently. People who exercise regularly can even strengthen their hearts.

Bones and Muscles

In earlier books in this series you have read about our circulatory and reproductive systems and our senses. Here we examine bones and muscles. Look at the picture of the human skeleton. When you are young, the bones of your skeleton are made up of cartilage and calcium-rich, phosphorus-rich substances. Cartilage is a strong, flexible tissue that pads the ends of bones and protects them from rubbing together at the joints. Cartilage helps two bones that come together move smoothly like the hinges on a door. Feel your kneecap; it is a joint that has lots of cartilage. As you grow, cartilage is replaced by solid minerals (except where two bones come together) and your bones grow longer and more solid.

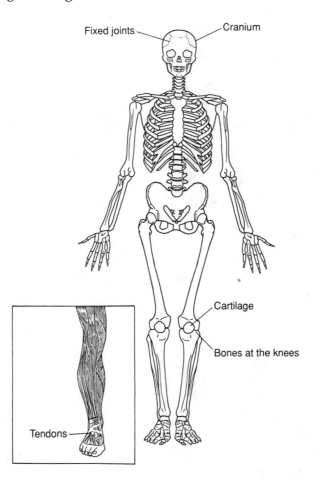

Fixed joints — Cranium

Cartilage

Bones at the knees

Tendons

But bones are not solid all the way through, even in adults. Bones are hollow and are filled with a soft tissue, called marrow, which makes red and white blood cells. Because they are hollow, bones are strong but light in weight. The bone in the upper leg, called the femur, is as strong lengthwise as a bar of steel the same size, but it weighs only about one-fourth as much. Tiny blood vessels run through tunnels in bone tissues, bringing oxygen and nutrients to bone cells and carrying away red and white blood cells and waste.

Tough strips of tissue called ligaments connect bones together. Ligaments help hold bones in place, even at the joints. Tendons, similar to ligaments, allow muscles

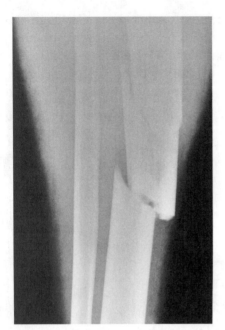

This X-ray shows a broken tibia, the larger inner bone of the lower leg. The other bone, the fibula, is not broken.

to attach to bones. Tendons help muscles move bones when the muscles contract. You can feel your Achilles tendon above your heel and below your calf. Put your hand on your Achilles tendon and then move your foot up and down. Can you feel how it stretches? Slide your hand up your calf and move your foot again. You can feel how the muscles move bones: one group of muscles contracts while another lengthens.

Although they are all very strong, tissues, muscles, cartilage, ligaments, tendons, and bones can withstand only so much strain. You can see how strain can damage tissue if you examine a cooked chicken wing or leg. Remove the skin from the meat (muscle) and bone and see whether you can identify the cartilage, ligaments, and tendons. What happens if you twist the bones from side to side, or bend them too rapidly, the way you might stress your own body during excessive exercise? Strain in the form of overexercise can tear muscles, cartilage, ligaments, and tendons.

It takes even more strain to break bones, but this can happen. Bones give shape to the body and allow it to move. They also protect vital organs such as the heart, lungs, spinal cord, and brain. Your ribs form a cage around your heart and lungs, protecting them from injury. Your backbone protects your spinal cord, and your skull protects your brain, eyes, and inner ears. The part of the skull surrounding the brain is called the cranium. The cranium is made up of many bones. When a baby is born, there are spaces between some of these bones, but as a child gets older, the bones of the cranium grow together and these spaces are closed.

Introduction to Physical Sciences

FOR PARENTS AND TEACHERS

I n this section children are introduced to the properties of light, including color, and to the properties of sound. They will learn about many of the ways we use light and other forms of electromagnetic energy and about some of the technological advances that resulted from a better understanding of light and sound. They are also introduced to fundamental ideas from the field of chemistry.

As always, we have included some hands-on learning activities, but we urge parents and teachers to provide children with further activities to expand upon what they learn here. The following resources complement the topics in this section and many include hands-on activities you may find useful:

The Electromagnetic Spectrum: Key to the Universe by Frank M. Branley (Crowell, 1979).
Experimenting with a Microscope by Maurice Bleifeld (Putnam, 1988).
Lenses! Take a Closer Look by Siegfried Aust (Lerner, 1991).
Light and Color: 35 Science Activities (Educational Insights, 1988). Educational Insights sells other hands-on kits and science equipment for children. For a catalog, write: 19560 South Rancho Way, Dominguez Hills, CA 90220.
Light Fantastic by Philip Watson (Lothrop, Lee & Shepard, 1982).
The Magic of Color by Hilda Simon (Lothrop, Lee & Shepard, 1981).
The Magic of Sound by Larry Kettelkamp (Morrow, 1982).

Physical Sciences

UNDERSTANDING LIGHT

The Nature of Light

L ight is something we take for granted, but life itself could not exist without light. Sunlight is the basic source of energy for living things. Animals, including humans, get their food from plants or from other animals who have gotten their food from plants. And where do the plants get their food? As you learned in Book Five of this series, plants live and grow by using the process of photosynthesis, a word that means "putting things together by light." How is it that plants are able to make food out of light and chemicals? Light has energy. The energy that you get when you eat food came originally from light. But what's the nature of this energy?

For hundreds of years scientists have debated the nature of light. After performing many experiments, Sir Isaac Newton decided that light must be made up of tiny particles. But a Dutch physicist, named Christian Huygens thought that light behaves

Without light from the sun, life as we know it would not exist.

like waves on water and that it must consist of waves. Today we believe that Newton and Huygens were both right: light behaves like particles *and* like waves. When it travels, light acts like the wave you make when you toss a pebble into a pond. When it is being absorbed or given off by matter it acts like particles.

We call particles of light "photons." But they shouldn't be thought of as little specks. Photons are packets of pure energy with no mass. You shouldn't think of light as changing from photon to wave and back again. Light always has the properties of both. If this double nature of light is hard to visualize, don't worry. It's so peculiar that everybody has trouble picturing it.

Visible light is not the only light in the world. There are lots of photons all around us that we can't see. The general term for all these photons—visible and invisible—and the waves associated with them is "electromagnetic radiation." Electromagnetic radiation includes light, X-rays, radio waves, television waves, and even the waves of a microwave oven.

How Fast Does Light Travel?

Light and all other electromagnetic radiation is a very speedy form of energy. In space or in a vacuum, light travels at a rate of about 300,000 kilometers (186,000 miles) per second! Nothing travels faster than light. In the time it takes you to blink your eyes (about a second), light can travel around the earth seven times. In three blinks, light can zip from the earth to the moon and back—a trip that would take you several days in a rocket.

Have you ever noticed the gap in time between a lightning bolt and the clap of thunder that follows? The light and the sound actually occur at the same time, but the light reaches your eye before the sound reaches your ear. That's because light travels about a million times faster than sound, which clocks in at about 0.3 kilometers per second.

Light travels at different speeds depending on the mate-

rial it is traveling through. For example, light travels more slowly through glass and water than through air. Have you ever looked at your leg in a bathtub full of water and noticed that it appeared crooked? The illusion is created because the light is slowed down when it hits the water, and takes a slightly different direction in the water than in the air. Light changes direction again when it leaves the water and returns to the air. You can see the same effect if you look at a pencil partly immersed in a glass of water. This change in direction when light enters glass, water, or other clear materials is called "refraction." (As we will explain later, refraction enables us to have all sorts of cameras, including television cameras. Without refraction, we would have no TV.)

You can try this yourself. Do you see the same illusion?

Rays

Think of a candle burning in the middle of a dark room. What part of the room is the brightest? The darkest? The light gets brighter as you move closer to the candle, dimmer as you move farther away. This happens because light usually moves in rays, which are straight lines that go out in every direction from a source of light. Look at the candle. Do you notice that the lines are very close together near the flame, but get farther apart as they move outward? If you put your finger on the flame in the diagram, you would see that a lot of rays touch your fingertip. As you move your finger away from the center, fewer rays touch your fingertip. As the rays get farther from the center, fewer rays of light hit a unit of area. That's why the light gets dimmer as you move away from the candle.

As we get very far from the candle, any given step we take makes less difference in brightness. Sunlight does not seem much dimmer at sea level than up on a mountain. That's because the sun is so far away from the earth that by the time the rays reach the earth's surface, they are almost parallel to each other. To put this another way:

Rays of light move in every direction from the burning candle, but as the rays get farther from the wick they are farther apart and the light is dimmer.

By the time rays from the sun travel 93 million miles to the earth they are virtually parallel to each other. Can you see how the distance from sea level to mountaintop is very little relative to the great distance the light travels through space?

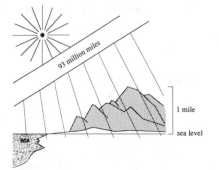

93 million miles

1 mile

sea level

The intensity of sunlight remains fairly constant because the distance from sea level to mountaintop is very small compared to the 93 million miles light travels from the sun to earth.

White Light and the Spectrum

We call the light that we can see coming from the sun "white light." Isaac Newton proved that white light is really a mixture of different colors of light. He did this with a prism, a clear piece of glass or plastic shaped like a wedge. When Newton sent white light from the sun through a prism, he saw that the light became a rainbow of different colors on the wall of his study. To understand why this happened, we need to know why light has different colors.

If you've been lucky enough to see a rainbow more than once, you might have noticed that rainbow colors always come in the same order, from red to orange to yellow to green to blue to violet. All these colors are kinds of light; they are made up of photon/waves. Some photons have more energy than others, which makes them vibrate faster and have a shorter wavelength. (We will explain wavelengths a little later.) Different wavelengths of light make the different colors.

Let's see what happens when we shine white sunlight at an angle through a pane of glass. You already know that light travels more slowly and bends in glass and water. You know that the bending comes from the fact that the glass slows down light. What you can't easily see is that glass slows down and bends some parts of light more than others. It bends violet the most, red the least.

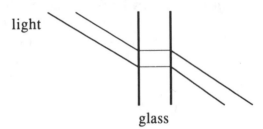

Light bends slightly when it passes through glass.

This is more apparent when light hits a prism at an angle, as in Newton's experiment. The prism shape dramatically bends the colors away from the incoming angle of the white light. Since violet, which has the most energy, is bent the most, it gets sent off toward one end of the prism. Red, which has the least energy, is slowed less and goes toward the other end. All the other colors are spread out between violet and red. Then, as the colored rays leave the prism, the slant of the prism's far side makes the colors angle out from each other even more. As the rays continue to travel in the air, the colors are separated more and more until they hit a wall or other screen. That is how Newton got a beautiful rainbow of colors from white light.

The spread of colors created by the prism is called a spectrum. We have seen that the spectrum for visible light goes from red to violet. Just beyond red there is less energetic radiation, which you can't see, called infrared, which means "below red." You may also have heard of the *more* energetic radiation just above violet, which is

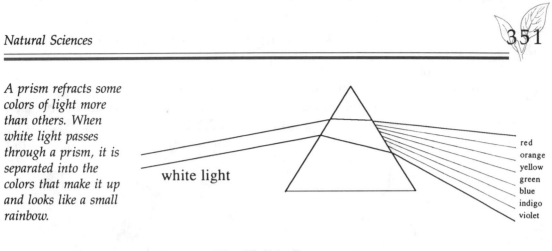

A prism refracts some colors of light more than others. When white light passes through a prism, it is separated into the colors that make it up and looks like a small rainbow.

white light

red
orange
yellow
green
blue
indigo
violet

The Visible Spectrum

red	orange	yellow	green	blue	indigo	violet

This chart shows you the colors of radiation in the spectrum of visible light from the weakest (left) to the strongest (right).

called "ultraviolet." The entire spectrum of what we call electromagnetic radiation goes beyond visible light in both directions, from very low energy radiation to very high energy radiation. All of the waves that make up this spectrum have the special properties of electricity and magnetism, and they can pass through a vacuum. They don't have to bounce off matter to move. That's why sunlight can travel through space to the earth.

The Electromagnetic Spectrum

visible spectrum

radio waves	infrared	red orange yellow green blue indigo violet	ultraviolet	X-rays

Each type of radiation packs its own amount of energy. Scientists have arranged radiation by the amount of energy each type carries. On our chart the weakest (least energetic) radiation is on the left-hand side of the chart, and the strongest is on the right.

Frequency and Wavelength

All electromagnetic radiation consists of photon/waves, which can have more or less energy. What is the difference between a more energetic and a less energetic photon/wave? The difference is in how fast the wave associated with the photon vibrates.

A photon/wave with just a little energy vibrates slowly; one with lots of energy vibrates quickly. If you look at the electromagnetic spectrum again, you might guess that those rays on the left vibrate slowly, and those on the right vibrate quickly.

The word used for how fast the rays vibrate is "frequency." Frequency means how often something happens in a unit of time. When things vibrate slowly, their frequency is low. The frequency of red light is about 375 trillion vibrations per second. The frequency of violet light is about twice as high: about 750 trillion vibrations per second.

Not only light, but all electromagnetic energy travels in vibrating waves. You can get an idea of what these waves are like by observing the waves you make when you drop a pebble into a bowl of water. Notice that the waves radiate out from the center where you dropped the pebble. Notice also that the waves have hills and valleys. The tops of the hills are called crests, and the bottoms of the valleys are called troughs. The distance between one crest and the next is the same as the distance between one trough and the next. This distance is equal to the length of the wave and is called, not surprisingly, the "wavelength."

These ducks are making the same sort of wave you could make by throwing a pebble into the water. The waves radiate outward in larger and larger circles from the ducks in the center.

Each color has its own unique wavelength. Here's why. All the colors of light travel through empty space at the same speed. This means that the length of a wave is determined by just one thing: how fast the photon/wave vibrates. One vibration makes one full wave, and the faster the photon/wave vibrates, the shorter the distance the light travels before a new wave starts.

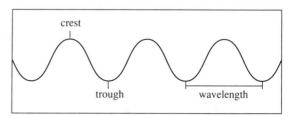

The parts of a light wave.

The Electromagnetic Spectrum

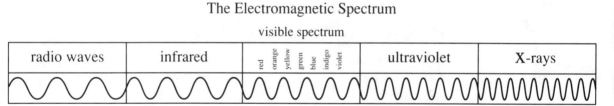

Like the spectrum of visible light, the electromagnetic spectrum can be charted from lower to higher frequency, from longer wavelength to shorter wavelength.

We mentioned that red light vibrates about 375 trillion times a second, and violet about 750 trillion times a second. To find out their wavelengths, you just have to know how fast light travels. The velocity of light is about 300,000 kilometers a second. So to find the length the wave travels during one vibration of violet, you divide 300,000 kilometers by 750 trillion vibrations. (One trillion is 1 with twelve zeros after it, so 750 trillion is 750,000,000,000,000.) The answer to that calculation is that violet has a wavelength of about 0.0004 millimeters, or about 15 millionths of an inch. The red wavelength is about 0.0008 millimeters, or about 30 millionths of an inch.

Uses of Different Rays

The rays of all electromagnetic radiation travel in a straight line. But rays behave in different ways when they hit an object. If they are vibrating very fast (which means they have a lot of energy), they can penetrate certain materials. For example, X-rays are short-wavelength, high-energy rays that can pass through solid objects, including the human body. They allow us to take pictures of the insides of objects by passing through them and leaving an image on a special type of film.

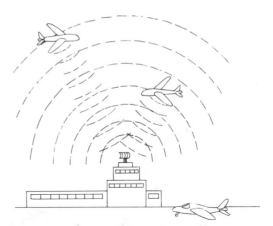

Radar waves, on the other hand, are long, low-energy rays that bounce off objects. We use radar waves to detect objects: airport control towers use radar to track airplanes, and police officers use radar to catch speeders. There are many scientific uses for radar as well. Weather radar is used by meteorologists, pilots, and others to detect storms. Astronomers use radar to measure the distances to other planets. Zoologists can follow the migration of birds, and count the number of birds in flight. Physicists study lightning flashes with radar.

Radar (which is short for Radio Detecting and Ranging) uses radio waves because they travel well through air. By sending a signal and receiving an echo from it, an air traffic controller can tell where an airplane is.

When Light Hits an Object

When light hits an object, the light can pass through it, bounce off it, be absorbed by it, or do any of these in combination. In a swimming pool, you can see the bottom of the pool because the light passes through the water to the bottom and bounces back up to your eyes. You can sometimes see your face reflected from the surface of the pool because some light bounces off the water rather than pass through it.

Window glass is transparent.

Most window shades are translucent.

Thus, water is a substance that lets some light pass through, reflects some light, and absorbs the rest.

Material like water or glass that lets some light pass through unchanged is called "transparent." Material like tissue paper or frosted glass that lets some light through but scatters it is called "translucent." Finally, material like metal or wood that does not let light through at all is called "opaque." Certain opaque objects, like the mirror in a bathroom, bounce almost all the light back into the air instead of absorbing it.

Our eyes can see only two kinds of objects: those that create light, like the sun and stars, and those that reflect light, like the moon and most of the things we come across every day. Since most objects do not make light, we are able to see them only when light bounces off them. We can't see anything in a totally dark room.

Before Newton, people thought that the color of an object changed the color of the light that bounced off it. Newton proved that idea was wrong. He discovered that the color of light that hits an object and then bounces off it never changes. He amazed the members of a London scientific society when he wrote to tell them his experiments proved that objects "have no power to change or alter the colors of any sort of rays."

Why, then, do apples look red? Because, as Newton discovered, many opaque objects absorb some wavelengths of the visible light spectrum, and reflect others. The colors that are reflected are the only ones that you see. An apple absorbs all colors except red, so only the red light

We see red when we look at an apple because it reflects red light but absorbs all other colors.

is reflected and enters the eye. Objects that are a mixture of colors, like purple, reflect several wavelengths back to the eye. Can you guess what wavelengths are reflected by a white piece of paper? What about a black piece of paper? Black absorbs all the colors of the visible light spectrum, so no light is reflected back to the eye. In fact, black is really the absence of light and of color. White, on the other hand, reflects all wavelengths and absorbs none.

Reflectors

How light bounces off a reflecting surface depends on how even the surface is. It's hard to play basketball on a gravel court, because the surface is rough; sometimes the ball goes off in odd directions when it hits the ground. On a paved surface, the ball bounces much more truly. When light bounces off a surface, its photons behave much the same way a ball does when it bounces off a surface. The direction of a photon/wave's bounce is determined by the slant of the surface where the ray hits and the angle at which the ray is traveling. There is a universal rule for all reflecting surfaces: "the angle of incidence equals the angle of reflection." This means that the angle of a ray hitting a surface is the same as its angle leaving the surface.

If the surface is rough, the light scatters: it bounces off at various angles determined by the changing slants of the rough surface. But if the surface is smooth and flat, light bounces off it in a regular way, determined by the consistent angle of the surface. The outgoing rays keep the same relation to each other as the incoming rays had.

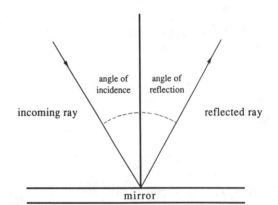

For reflected light, the angle of incidence equals the angle of reflection. This diagram shows you how to measure these angles. At the point where the ray hits the surface, draw a line perpendicular to the surface. Then you measure the angle of incidence from the perpendicular. Once you know its size, you also know and can diagram the angle of reflection.

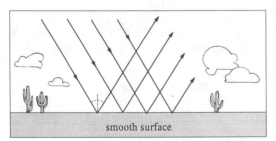

Parallel rays of light which strike a smooth, flat surface are reflected at equal angles.

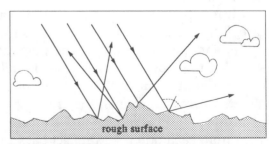

Parallel rays of light which strike an uneven surface are not reflected as parallel rays. Why? Because the reflecting surface is bumpy, and each incoming ray has a different perpendicular.

Flat mirrors are highly polished, very smooth surfaces. When they reflect light, they produce a good likeness of an object. But even though the likeness is good, the image you see in the mirror always seems reversed, left to right. To see how this works, stand in front of a mirror and hold the palm of your *right* hand up to the mirror. Now hold up your left palm and look at it directly, not in the mirror, while you also look at the mirror image of your right palm. It suddenly looks like you have two left hands! Try holding some writing up to the mirror; you'll see that it appears backward too.

Can you write your name like this?

To read this sentence, hold it up to a mirror and read the mirror image.

Curved Reflectors

Mirrors are always smooth, but not always flat. Have you ever seen yourself in a fun-house mirror? These mirrors are curved in ways that can make you look very tall and thin or short and squat. If a mirror curves different ways in different places, different parts of your body will be stretched or shortened.

Why does your body look so strange in a fun-house mirror, and so true to life in a flat mirror? Because curved mirrors reflect light differently than flat mirrors do. Remember that with flat mirrors, light bounces off at the same angle it strikes. This produces a nearly exact image. Curved mirrors, however, change the pathway of bouncing light. Look at the diagrams of curved mirrors to see how this is so.

Mirrors that are curved inward are called concave. They cause parallel light beams to come together and cross each other. The point at which the rays come together—the point at which they focus on one spot—is called the focal point of the mirror. Can you find the focal point in the drawing of the concave mirror? Concave mirrors make objects appear larger than they are.

Mirrors that curve outward are called convex. They cause light rays to bounce away from each other, and reflect back to your eye more of the world beyond. They are often used in rear-view mirrors on trucks and cars. Objects seen in a convex mirror look smaller than they really are.

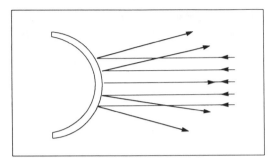

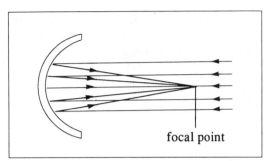

A convex mirror causes light rays to reflect away from each other. These rays do not come together at a focal point.

A concave mirror causes light rays to reflect toward one another, crossing at a focal point.

How a Flashlight Works

If you've ever taken a flashlight apart, you know that the main parts are the batteries, a light source (a small bulb), and a concave mirror. All these parts are essential—the batteries supply the energy for light, the bulb creates the light, and the reflector makes the light illuminate things in the dark. Without the concave mirror, the bulb would not light up anything more than a few inches away. The mirror keeps the light from spreading out.

To see exactly how the mirror does this, you can perform the following experiment on a clear, sunny day. This experiment will be quite safe if you carefully follow these steps. Ask an adult to help you and make sure everyone who takes part in the experiment wears dark, gray sunglasses. Do not look directly at the light of the sun, or at the light reflected from the flashlight mirror. Use small, gentle motions to control the way you shift the mirror so that you do not unexpectedly shine the light into your eyes. If the light bothers your eyes, immediately look away.

Open the top of the flashlight where the bulb is and take out the concave mirror unit with the bulb inside it. Take the mirror unit outside and point it straight toward the bright sun. (Look at the reflected light for only a moment.) You will see something remarkable. If you point the mirror correctly, all the sun rays that hit the mirror will be focused on the tiny filament inside the flashlight—the part that glows when the flashlight is turned on.

You can see what happens from this diagram. Remember, the sun's rays are almost parallel, because the sun is so far away. When these nearly parallel rays hit different parts of the concave mirror, they always bounce off at an angle that is the same as the one they entered. Since the mirror is curved, this angle is different at each point. If the mirror is curved exactly right, all the rays will come together at a single point—the focal point—inside the mirror, just where the filament is.

The light shines on the convex mirror, which reflects it to the focal point at the filament inside the flashlight bulb.

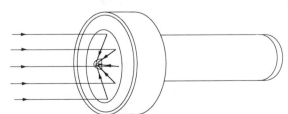

Now think what happens when the filament itself is the source of light. It is exactly the reverse of the experiment with the parallel rays from the sun. As the light from the filament strikes the different parts of the mirror, each ray bounces off at the same angle it entered. Because of the exactly right shape of the concave mirror and the exactly right placement of the bulb, the reflected light rays will all be at the same angle, more or less parallel, as the rays of the sun were. It's only because the rays stay parallel that the flashlight can illuminate objects several yards away.

Refraction and Lenses

A lens is a piece of transparent material, usually glass, with at least one curved surface. While mirrors reflect light, lenses *refract* light. You remember from our discussion of Newton's experiment with the prism that glass bends or refracts light when the light enters or leaves the glass.

Just as there is a rule for reflection, there is also a rule for refraction. When light enters glass from air, it bends toward the perpendicular of the glass surface; when light leaves the glass and enters air, it bends away from the perpendicular of the glass surface. It's easy to remember; light enters toward and leaves away. You can easily see what "toward the perpendicular" means by looking at this diagram of yellow light entering a prism.

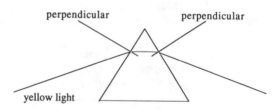

Since the rule is that light bends toward the perpendicular on entering and away from the perpendicular on leaving, what happens when the ray of light is itself perpendicular to the surface? The light isn't bent at all.

When light enters glass from air, it bends toward the perpendicular. When it exits glass into air, it bends away from the perpendicular.

When light hits glass from air at a perpendicular angle, it does not bend at all.

light

glass

Since we already know how a prism bends light, we can now see how a lens bends it. Look at the convex and concave lenses in the diagram. With two prisms, we can make something similar to either one.

The difference between a lens and a pair of prisms is that the surface of the lens is curved rather than straight. That means that the perpendicular to the surface of the lens is changing at every point on the surface. So when the lens is directly facing approaching light rays, as in the picture below, the rays that strike the middle of the lens are at the perpendicular, and are not bent at all; those close to the middle are bent just a little; and the rays hitting the edge of the lens, at a greater angle to the perpendicular, are bent most of all. This means that a convex lens can make parallel light rays converge on a single point—the focal point.

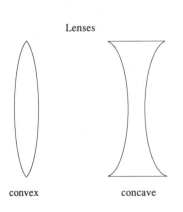

Lenses

convex   concave

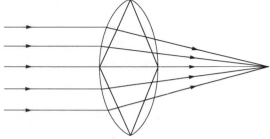

convex lens

The path of light through two prisms stacked to resemble a convex lens.

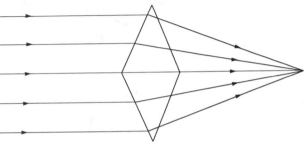

convex

The path of light through a convex lens.

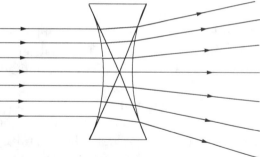

concave

The path of light through a concave lens.

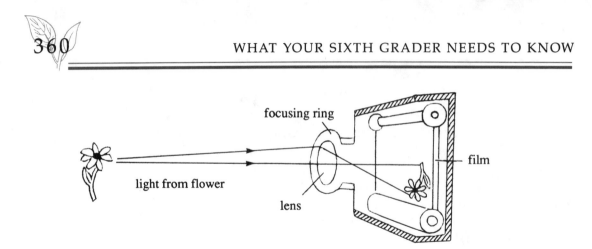

Here you can see the ways a camera is like an eye. How are they different?

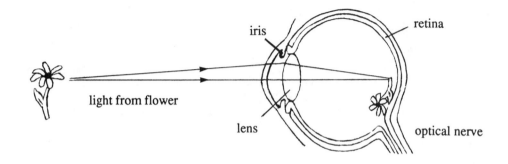

Cameras, Telescopes, and Microscopes

A camera is basically a convex lens in a box, with the film placed behind the lens. The shutter keeps the light out until it is needed to expose the film, and the diaphragm makes the opening bigger or smaller to control the amount of light let through. A camera works remarkably like your eye. The human eye also has a convex lens. It has a shutter—your eyelid—and an iris to control the amount of light that is let through. Your retina is like film, on which images are produced and sent to your brain.

Lenses, in the early days of science, made a new invention possible—the telescope. Scientists looked through telescopes into the night sky and made great discoveries about the universe. The first telescopes were simple affairs. They had a large convex lens at one end of a tube, and a small convex lens, the eyepiece, at the other end. The large lens collected light from a bigger area than the human eye, thus increasing the amount of light brought to the eye and making "invisible" stars visible. In addition, the smaller lens, called the eyepiece, magnified the image from the larger lens, making objects look bigger and closer. This kind of telescope is called a refracting telescope, because it uses lenses, which, as you know, refract light.

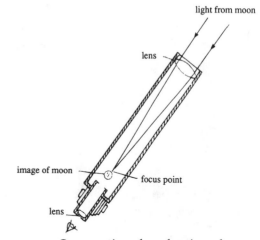

Cross-section of a refracting telescope.

In 1610, Galileo Galilei first looked at the heavens with a refracting telescope of his own making, and was able to see mountains and craters on our moon. His instrument also enabled him to see the moons of the planet Jupiter, and, most remarkable of all, the planet Venus. He saw that Venus had phases just like our moon: sometimes it was very full, an almost perfect disk of light, and at other times it looked only partly full. Galileo could think of only one good explanation for this. Both Venus and the earth must be going around the sun just as the moon goes around the earth.

To see why this is so, you can hold a tennis ball near a lightbulb. When the bulb is between you and the ball, the ball is lit up like the full moon. But when you hold the ball to the side of the bulb, only one side of it seems lit. If you are the earth, and the ball is Venus, you can see why Galileo came to his conclusion. Galileo saw that the earth and the planets must orbit the sun just as the famous astronomer Copernicus had argued about a hundred years earlier. Galileo found strong proof that the sun did *not* revolve around the earth as most people thought at that time. His observations helped change the way people understood our place in the universe.

Later, Sir Isaac Newton invented a marvelous kind of telescope that is still used today—a *reflecting* telescope. Newton realized that the lenses of refracting telescopes made images that were slightly fuzzy because the different colors of the spectrum went through the lenses at different speeds, and each color focused at a slightly different point. Newton reasoned that this problem of fuzziness would be solved if he reflected light rather than refracted it. So, instead of a lens, he used a large concave mirror to collect the light. Then, because the light did not have to go through a refracting medium, the colors stayed together and focused at the same point. An additional advantage of the reflecting telescope was that very little light was lost passing through the glass of lenses. The image was not only sharper but also brighter.

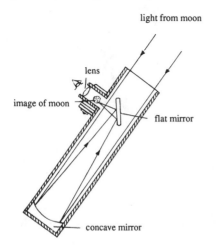

Cross-section of a reflecting telescope.

Microscope with a built-in light source.

Another instrument that makes use of lenses is the microscope. Just as telescopes open up the unseen world in the sky, the microscope introduced humans to the unseen world of very small things on earth. For the first time, people could see that an apparently clear droplet of water from a pond was actually full of swimming creatures. The whole world of single-celled life began to be observed.

A microscope, like a refracting telescope, is a tube with a convex lens at one end and an eyepiece at the other. But the main lens, called the objective lens, isn't large like that of a telescope. It's a small, round lens with a short focal length that gets very close to a small, well-lit object and makes an image that is much bigger than life. The eyepiece magnifies the image still more. A specimen is placed on a slide just beneath the objective lens. For someone to see the specimen, light rays must go through the specimen, pass through the objective lens, and then through the eyepiece. This light can come from a built-in source on the microscope or a mirror that directs surrounding light onto the specimen.

SOUND

The Energy Called Sound

Sound, like light, contains energy in the form of vibrations. But light can travel even through empty space, while sound vibrations can exist only in things that have mass. Sound waves are formed from something made out of matter—almost any kind of matter will do. You can hear sounds in air, under water, and through solid walls. Have you ever heard sound through a wall from a room next door? The sound on one side of the wall may be formed by somebody's vibrating vocal cords, which vibrate the air, which makes the wall vibrate, which vibrates the air on the other side of the wall, which vibrates the air next to the ear, which vibrates our eardrums. The vibrating eardrums in turn vibrate the organs inside our ears, which stimulate nerves that tell our brains we are hearing sounds. Unless a sound causes the air next to our eardrums to vibrate, we can't hear it. People on the moon could not hear sound even if vibrations occurred close by, because there is no air to carry the sound to their ears.

The vibrations of sound are in the form of waves, which travel out in all directions. Sound waves are composed of air vibrating back and forth in the direction of travel. If you hit a drum, it begins vibrating back and forth. This motion compresses and expands the air as the wave travels forward and the air molecules collide with each other. Finally, the colliding air molecules reach your eardrums and cause them to vibrate. From the drum to your eardrum, there is an unbroken connection between molecules.

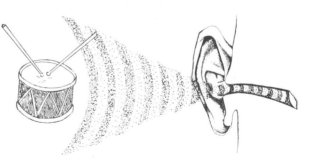

Sound waves travel by causing air molecules to collide with each other. When vibrating air molecules hit your eardrum, the vibrations are relayed by the many parts of the inner ear up the auditory nerve to the brain.

Why Sound Travels Slowly

You know that it usually takes a while before you hear a thunderclap after seeing lightning. It's frightening if the thunder comes right away, because that means the lightning must have struck very close to you. You can tell exactly how far away lightning has occurred by counting how many seconds elapse between seeing the flash and hearing the thunder. The flash of light travels to you almost instantly, but sound travels in air at about 1,000 feet a second. For every second that you count between the flash and the sound, you can estimate 1,000 feet from where the lightning struck. If five seconds elapse, you know that the lightning struck about a mile away from you.

The reason that sound travels at the speed it does is that it is formed by a chain of collisions between molecules of matter, and there is a short interval between the time a molecule is contacted and the time it collides with another molecule.

Have you ever been in a car in a line stopped at a stoplight? If you were far back in the line, did you notice how long it took your car to move after the light turned green? If every driver looked at the stoplight and started instantly when it turned green, then the whole line would move at once. But if each driver waits for the car ahead to move, as they must for safety, it will take quite a while before the fourth or fifth car in the line starts moving. It's that little pause between the moving of one car and the moving of the car behind it that adds up to a long delay for the cars in back. The molecules of air between the sound source and your eardrums are a little like cars in line at a stoplight. By the time motion is transferred through successive collisions of many molecules, a lot of time has elapsed compared to the time it takes for light to travel.

Wavelength and Frequency

Sound waves have wavelengths, just as light waves do. When the vibrations are fast, the wavelengths are short. When the vibrations are slow, the wavelengths are longer. But the wavelengths of sound are *always* much longer than those of light, because sound travels so slowly. The wavelengths of audible sounds range from about one inch to fifty-five feet—quite a bit longer than the 15 millionths of an inch of violet light.

Sounds are best measured by their frequency rather than their wavelength. Here's why. Wavelength depends on the wave's speed of travel. Sound travels at very different speeds in different kinds of matter, so the wavelength of a particular sound changes when the speed changes. The temperature of the air can also change the speed at which sound travels, thus affecting the wavelength, but it does not change the sound's frequency. The frequency of audible sound ranges between 20 and 20,000 "cycles per second," a term used to indicate how often a regular vibration occurs.

The term people use for the frequency of sound is "pitch." Rapid sound vibrations are high pitch, slow ones are low pitch. If a man has a high-pitched voice, he may sound squeaky because his voice has mostly high frequencies. A frequency higher than 800 cycles per second is considered high-pitched, while lower than 200 is low-pitched. A flute is a high-pitched instrument, a tuba a low-pitched one. Symphony orchestras use the mid-level pitch of the "middle-A" note, about 440 cycles per second, to tune all the instruments.

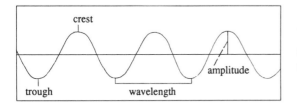

We use the same terms to talk about the parts of sound waves that we use to talk about light waves.

The wave on the bottom has a longer wavelength and therefore a lower pitch than the wave above it. In this diagram the two waves have the same amplitude, but that is not always the case.

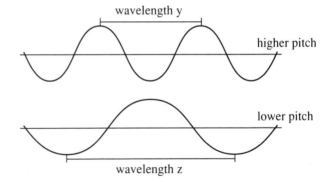

Loudness

The frequency or pitch of a sound doesn't determine the amount of energy being transmitted. With light, the higher the frequency, the greater the energy, but in sound it is often the other way round. It usually takes more energy to make a sound you can hear at 100 cycles a second than to make a sound you can hear at 440 cycles a second. If you have ever watched a band in a parade, you may have noticed that the tuba player has to work harder than the flute player.

In sound, the very same frequencies can have a lot or a little energy. The amount of energy of a frequency determines whether the sound is loud or soft. The loudness of a sound is related to the *amplitude* (AM-plih-tood) of the sound wave. Amplitude means "largeness." The harder you pluck a guitar string (putting more energy into 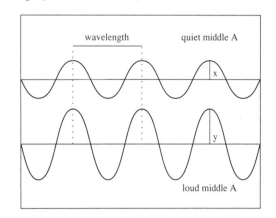 it), the greater the distance the string moves back and forth. The amplitude of the wave increases, and it sounds louder. The frequency for any given guitar string will always be the same no matter how hard or soft you play it, so the pitch is always the same for that string. But the amplitude can vary a lot.

Amplitude or loudness has a very definite physical meaning. It means that the collisions of the molecules that transmit the sound are stronger. When a loud sound hits your eardrums, it makes them move farther and faster back and forth. A loud enough sound can actually damage or even destroy your eardrum and the other parts of your hearing system.

The waves for the loud middle A and the quiet middle A have the same wavelength and travel at the same speed, but the louder wave has a higher amplitude.

Resonance

When you stretch a rubber band, you can pluck it to make a sound. The tighter you stretch the band, the faster the vibrations and the higher the pitch of the sound. But it's not a very loud or interesting sound, and to make it louder and more complex, you could place the rubber band near a box with a hole in it. If the size of the box and the hole are just right, the vibrating band will start air vibrating inside the box. The increased movement of air will make the sound louder, but it will also create some new sounds. This process, by which original sounds make more sounds, is called resonance.

The word resonate means "to sound again." When a vibration like that of the rubber band makes something else vibrate, the new vibrations add new sound waves. These can reinforce the original ones and make the sound much louder. But the new vibrations may contain other frequencies that we call overtones. Overtones are complicated but not very loud sounds that change the quality of the original sound.

If you play a middle A on a piano and on a guitar, even though the notes have the same pitch they will sound different. The reason is that the sounds of both instruments are really a blend of many different vibrations. Not only do the strings of both instruments vibrate, but the bodies of the instruments vibrate as well. Each additional vibration adds its overtones to the sound of A. Because the overtones of a piano and a guitar are different, the sound quality or "tone" of each instrument is different. Characteristic overtones give each instrument its individual sound.

Traveling Faster than Sound

Sound travels through air at about 1,000 feet per second, which is over 700 miles per hour. There are some jet planes that can fly that fast, and even faster. Jet planes that can fly faster than sound are called supersonic. One supersonic jet, called the Concorde, can fly passengers from London to New York in just over three hours, less than half the time a regular jet would take. There is some controversy about using supersonic jets, however, because they make what is called a sonic boom. As the plane exceeds the speed of sound, or "breaks the sound barrier," people on the ground below hear a booming sound almost like a thunderclap. Sometimes sonic booms are so loud that they break windows in houses. As you can imagine, most people do not want supersonic jets breaking the sound barrier just above their houses.

CHEMISTRY

When we study light, movement, and sound, we are learning about the science of physics. When we study matter and how it changes, we are learning about the science of chemistry. The reactions of chemistry enable plants to make food and tissue out of matter and light, and chromosomes to duplicate themselves to form new life. Chemical phenomena transform the food you eat into growth and activity.

If you want to see chemistry at work, try this. Put eight ounces of vinegar into a big glass container. Now slowly sprinkle one teaspoon of baking soda into the vinegar. You'll get lots of fizz. Would you like to know why? This section will explain the chemical reaction that makes this happen.

John Dalton and Atoms

In the early 1800s, an English schoolteacher named John Dalton analyzed the tests and experiments that scientists had written down over many years. Dalton then proposed the idea that all matter is composed of atoms. (Greek thinkers had already suggested this centuries before, but they were unable to prove it, and the theory was dropped.) Meanwhile, scientists began to discover that matter was composed not of few but of many elements; that in fact there were dozens of elements such as hydrogen, silver, and gold.

Elements are fundamental substances that cannot be reduced by chemical reactions to anything else. Dalton figured out that each element is composed of tiny particles called atoms, and that each atom of each element is the same as every other atom for that element—but different from the atoms of any other element. Whenever matter changes, as you saw in the experiment that created fizz with vinegar and baking soda, the atoms themselves do not change; according to Dalton, they just rearrange themselves.

Dalton's basic ideas proved to be correct, although scientists did not become sure that atoms existed until the twentieth century. It's not really surprising that it took so long to prove the existence of atoms. After all, they were far too small to be seen, even with the best microscopes. So all kinds of experiments and analyses had to be brought together over a long period of time before scientists knew the "atomic theory" was correct.

Atoms, Elements, and the Periodic Table

It wasn't until the 1930s that scientists actually figured out how atoms probably work. Several different theories had been proposed, and it was difficult to prove which was the right one.

Scientists discovered that most of the mass of an atom is in its central nucleus, and this nucleus is surrounded by much lighter electrons. They discovered that the nucleus has a positive charge that exactly balances the negative charges on the surrounding electrons.

Once scientists had formed this picture of the atom's structure, they could begin to understand what the chemical elements were and how they worked.

By the late 1800s, scientists had named most of the elements: from hydrogen, the lightest and most plentiful element in the universe, to heavy elements like lead. But they did not understand why the elements acted with each other as they did.

A very important step in understanding the relations of the elements was the discovery by a Russian chemist, Mendeleev, that the properties of the elements repeated themselves at regular intervals, or periodically.

What Mendeleev discovered was that when you arrange the elements in horizontal rows, from lightest to heaviest, after a while you will find another element

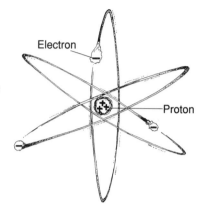

There are several ways of drawing models of atoms. This one of a lithium atom shows you the positive charge in the nucleus and the negative charges of its three electrons.

that has similar properties to the first element in a row. If you put the similar elements in vertical columns you can arrange all the elements in repeating groups. Here is one such column:

> element #3 lithium
> element #11 sodium
> element #19 potassium

These three elements have many similar characteristics. They are all metals, which means that they are shiny and good conductors of heat and electricity; they are dense and solid at room temperature, and can be hammered or drawn into different shapes. They also react with other elements in very similar ways.

Mendeleev made a chart of the periodic repetitions he saw, and a version of his chart, called the "periodic table," has been used ever since to show the relations of the elements. The full periodic table has over a hundred elements, but not all of them repeat their properties every eight elements as lithium, sodium, and potassium do. In fact, the periodic table gets quite complicated in some places. Although no one doubted that Mendeleev had discovered something very remarkable and important, it took many years to figure out why the elements could be arranged in this periodic way.

Explaining the Periods

In the 1920s Niels Bohr, a Danish scientist, proposed that what gave elements their chemical characteristics was mainly one thing: the electrons in each kind of atom. Scientists had already assigned a number to each element, listed from light to heavy on the periodic table, according to the element's number of electrons. So lithium, the third element, had three electrons; sodium, the eleventh element, had eleven electrons, and so on.

Bohr made the inspired guess that the electrons arranged themselves in rings or shells around the nucleus. A shell would be stable and complete when a certain number of electrons filled it. Then a new outer shell would be started.

It turned out that Bohr was basically right. Look at the number of electrons in the shells of lithium, sodium, and potassium. Notice that the total number of electrons is the same as the number of the element. Notice also that each element has a single electron in the outer shell of its atoms. It's the single electron in the outer shell that gives each element many of its chemical and electrical properties.

	Shell #1	Shell #2	Shell #3	Shell #4
element #3 lithium:	2	1		
element #11 sodium:	2	8	1	
element #19 potassium:	2	8	8	1

In general, all chemical reactions are determined by the electrons in the outer shell of atoms. The outer shell of electrons of some elements, such as sodium, can give off an electron easily. And the outer shell of other elements, like oxygen, can take on electrons easily. That's why these two different types of elements tend to

PERIODIC TABLE OF THE ELEMENTS

Key
6 — Atomic number
C — Element's symbol
Carbon — Element's name

Nonmetals

Metals

The symbols shown here for elements 104–109 are being used temporarily until names for these elements can be agreed upon.

1	2	3	4	5	6	7	8	9	10	11	12	13	14	15	16	17	18
1 **H** Hydrogen																	2 **He** Helium
3 **Li** Lithium	4 **Be** Beryllium											5 **B** Boron	6 **C** Carbon	7 **N** Nitrogen	8 **O** Oxygen	9 **F** Flourine	10 **Ne** Neon
11 **Na** Sodium	12 **Mg** Magnesium											13 **Al** Aluminum	14 **Si** Silicon	15 **P** Phosphorus	16 **S** Sulfur	17 **Cl** Chlorine	18 **Ar** Argon
19 **K** Potassium	20 **Ca** Calcium	21 **Sc** Scandium	22 **Ti** Titanium	23 **V** Vanadium	24 **Cr** Chromium	25 **Mn** Manganese	26 **Fe** Iron	27 **Co** Cobalt	28 **Ni** Nickel	29 **Cu** Copper	30 **Zn** Zinc	31 **Ga** Gallium	32 **Ge** Germanium	33 **As** Arsenic	34 **Se** Selenium	35 **Br** Bromine	36 **Kr** Krypton
37 **Rb** Rubidium	38 **Sr** Strontium	39 **Y** Yttrium	40 **Zr** Zirconium	41 **Nb** Niobium	42 **Mo** Molybdenum	43 **Tc** Technetium	44 **Ru** Ruthenium	45 **Rh** Rhodium	46 **Pd** Palladium	47 **Ag** Silver	48 **Cd** Cadmium	49 **In** Indium	50 **Sn** Tin	51 **Sb** Anitomy	52 **Te** Tellurium	53 **I** Iodine	54 **Xe** Xenon
55 **Cs** Cesium	56 **Ba** Barium	57 to 71	72 **Hf** Hafnium	73 **Ta** Tantalum	74 **W** Tungsten	75 **Re** Rhenium	76 **Os** Osmium	77 **Ir** Iridium	78 **Pt** Platinum	79 **Au** Gold	80 **Hg** Mercury	81 **Tl** Thallium	82 **Pb** Lead	83 **Bi** Bismuth	84 **Po** Polonium	85 **At** Astatine	86 **Rn** Radon
87 **Fr** Francium	88 **Ra** Radium	89 to103	104 **Unq** Unniliquadium	105 **Unp** Unnilpentium	106 **Unh** Unnilhexium	107 **Uns** Unnilseptium	108 **Uno** Unniloctium	109 **Une** Unnilennium									

Rare-Earth Elements

Lanthanoid Series

57 **La** Lanthanum	58 **Ce** Cerium	59 **Pr** Praseodymium	60 **Nd** Neodymium	61 **Pm** Promethium	62 **Sm** Samarium	63 **Eu** Europium	64 **Gd** Gadolinium	65 **Tb** Terbium	66 **Dy** Dysprosium	67 **Ho** Holmium	68 **Er** Erbium	69 **Tm** Thulium	70 **Yb** Ytterbium	71 **Lu** Lutetium

Actinoid Series

89 **Ac** Actinium	90 **Th** Thorium	91 **Pa** Protactinium	92 **U** Uranium	93 **Np** Neptunium	94 **Pu** Plutonium	95 **Am** Americium	96 **Cm** Curium	97 **Bk** Berkelium	98 **Cf** Californium	99 **Es** Einsteinium	100 **Fm** Fermium	101 **Md** Mendelevium	102 **No** Nobelium	103 **Lr** Lawrencium

Here's what a periodic table looks like. Can you find some of the elements you've been reading about in this section?

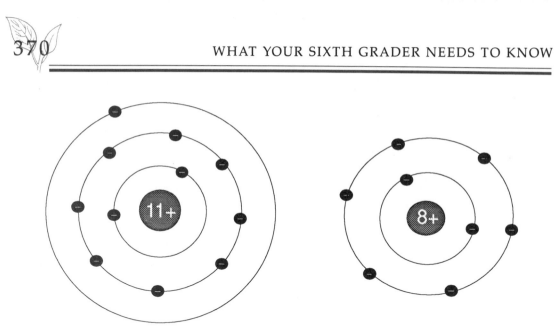

sodium atom

oxygen atom

Sodium is the eleventh element on the periodic table. It has eleven electrons—two in its inner shell, eight in its middle shell, and one in its outer shell. It can give off the single electron in its outer shell easily.

Oxygen is the eighth element in the periodic table. How many shells and how many electrons does oxygen have?

come together, one giving electrons, one taking electrons, to stabilize the outer shell of both kinds of atoms.

Molecules

If the atoms of each element always stayed together, nothing much would happen. There would be no chemical reactions and no life. It's because atoms interact with each other, forming combinations called molecules, that we have chemistry and life.

A molecule is created when two or more atoms join together—either from different elements or from the same element. For example, you know that humans need oxygen to survive. The oxygen in the air you breathe is in the form of molecules; that is, two oxygen atoms joined together. The symbol for oxygen is "O," and the double oxygen molecule can be represented like this:

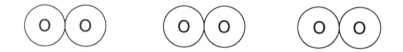

The way chemists indicate a regular molecule of two oxygen atoms is by the symbol O_2. Sometimes lightning can cause this oxygen molecule to break up into its individual atoms:

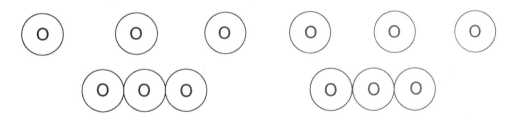

Many of these single oxygen atoms quickly form into oxygen molecules called "ozone," made of three oxygen atoms. You can smell ozone sometimes after a thunderstorm. Because ozone is unstable, many of the ozone molecules will break apart after a while, and regular O_2 molecules will form again.

Compounds

Compounds are molecules made up of atoms of different elements joined together. Here is the chemical formula for water: H_2O. The way you read this formula is "H-two-O." It means that two hydrogen atoms are joined with one oxygen atom to make

Look up oxygen and hydrogen on the periodic table to find out why this model of the oxygen molecule uses a large sphere for the oxygen atom and small spheres for the hydrogen atoms.

one molecule of water. Here's another famous compound: NaCl. It's the chemical formula for table salt. You can read it "N-A-C-L," or "sodium chloride," which is what the letters stand for. This formula means that one atom of sodium (Na) is joined with one atom of chlorine (Cl) to make a molecule of salt.

Here's a rhyme about chemical formulas that shows what a difference a few of these letters and numbers can make.

A model of the NaCl molecule.

> Johnny had the stomach ache.
> He hasn't anymore,
> For what he thought was H_2O
> Was H_2SO_4.

In case you are wondering, H_2SO_4 is the chemical formula for sulfuric acid, a very powerful and poisonous liquid. Poor Johnny!

Acids, Bases, and Chemical Reactions

Now we are ready to get a general idea of what happened when you mixed vinegar with baking soda. In general terms, you were mixing an acid with a base. What is

an acid in chemical terms? It's a compound that has a hydrogen atom (H) that can react with other atoms or molecules when dissolved in water. (Not all compounds that have an H are acids, however. The H has to be willing to give itself up to the water and be free to react.) The chemical formula for an acid always starts with that free H. You already heard the formula for sulfuric acid: H_2SO_4. The formula for hydrochloric acid is HCl, meaning one atom of hydrogen and one of chlorine. The acid in vinegar is a little more complicated, but it also starts with

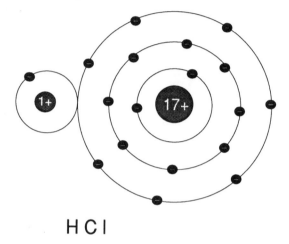

HCl

an H: $HC_2H_3O_2$. The C stands for carbon, you read the formula, "H-C-two-H-three-O-two."

The kind of molecule that wants to join with an acid is called a base, which is a compound that is eager to take up the free hydrogen that an acid has. This can only happen when the acid and base are both dissolved in water or "in solution," and are able to move around and join each other. When they are in solution, the attraction between acids and bases makes them want to join and stay joined.

When acid and base join, a chemical reaction occurs that results in a new compound called a salt. For instance, you can make table salt (NaCl) by joining together the acid HCl (hydrochloric acid) with the base NaOH (sodium hydroxide) when they are dissolved in a water solution. Both HCl and NaOH are poisons, but when they react with each other the result is table salt and water. You can make a formula out of what happens. Notice that it's like an equation. All the elements on the left side still appear on the right, but in different combinations:

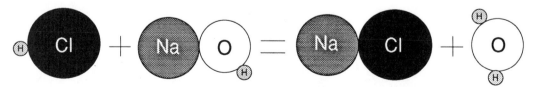

This can be read: "hydrochloric acid plus sodium hydroxide yields sodium chloride plus water."

A similar thing happened when you mixed vinegar and baking soda. You mixed an acid and a base, which made a salt plus a gas (CO_2) that escaped from the solution as fizz. You have heard of this gas before. It's called carbon dioxide, and it's essential to plant growth.

Energy and Chemical Reactions

The joining of an acid and a base is just one kind of chemical reaction. Another kind is oxidation, which occurs when an element or compound joins with oxygen. You may have noticed that iron rusts; that is, it oxidizes when it gets wet. The red-colored rust is iron oxide, a compound made of iron and oxygen.

All chemical reactions take up or give away heat when they occur. When you put baking soda in vinegar, you may have noticed that the liquid felt just a little colder when the fizzing stopped—even colder than it would have been if you had dissolved the soda in plain water. That's because that particular chemical reaction absorbed heat energy from the solution, leaving it colder than it was at first. That doesn't always happen when an acid joins with a base, but there are many chemical reactions, like photosynthesis, that do use energy as they occur. When plants make cells and food, they use energy from sunlight to fuel those chemical reactions.

Then there are chemical reactions that give *off* energy. For example, when your body utilizes the food you eat, it uses chemical reactions that give off the energy you need to run, walk, and talk. It's this chemical energy that keeps you breathing and keeps your heart pumping blood through your body.

Can you think of other chemical reactions that give off energy? What about fire? When you burn wood in a campfire, you are watching chemical energy being

What forms of energy does fire give off?

given off from rapid oxidation. That is what fire is—rapid oxidation. When wood burns, its components are joining with oxygen from the air to make new compounds. The light energy from the sun that had been used by trees to make the wood is being turned back to energy in the form of light and heat.

Matter and Energy Are Not Lost

When you burn wood, generating energy, is there more or less energy in the world than there was before? The answer is that there is exactly the same amount. The energy in the wood was turned into heat and light, but no energy was lost or gained. This is one of the most fundamental laws in physics and chemistry; it is called the law of the conservation of energy. There is a similar law for matter. Matter is not gained or lost in chemical reactions. This is called the law of the conservation of matter.

Here's an experiment you can do to observe the conservation of matter. You can use vinegar and baking soda again. Put about four tablespoons of vinegar in a very small paper cup. Put one half-teaspoon of baking soda in a 12-inch by 12-inch plastic bag, the kind used for storing food. Now, without spilling the vinegar, put the paper cup into the bag. Keeping the cup upright, press the air out of the bag, and then make it air-tight with a twist-tie. Carefully weigh the bag and its contents on a postal scale, noting down the weight. Remove the bag from the scale, and without opening it, pour the vinegar onto the baking soda, allowing the bag to puff up with the CO_2 that is formed. Now weigh the bag again. Though the bag looks more full, you should find no difference in weight because none of the atoms changed or left the bag; they just made themselves into new compounds.

WONDERS OF WATER

Ice Doesn't Sink

Most of the chemical reactions that make life possible depend on substances being dissolved in water. Without water, life as we know it would be impossible.

There's another feature of water that makes it almost unique, and which has a great effect on earthly life. It's the fact that water expands when it changes from a liquid to a solid. When most other liquids freeze, just the opposite happens—they contract and become more dense. The solid form of the substance will sink down to the bottom of the liquid form.

But water is different. When ice forms, it doesn't sink. It floats, because ice is actually lighter than water. Think what that means to people who live in cool climates. If ice sank, a pond or lake would gradually freeze from the bottom up. All the water could eventually freeze, killing the fish and other creatures that live in it. If that happened, life as we know it could not exist. But because ice is lighter than water, it stays on top and actually helps prevent the cold air from freezing the water below.

Why a Watched Pot Never Boils

There's an old saying: "A watched pot never boils." It means that if you are impatient for something to happen, it seems to take even longer. But water really does take a long time to boil. Let's find out why.

It takes only 100 calories of heat to bring a gram of water from 0° to the boiling temperature of 100°. But it takes 540 calories to change that water at 100° to steam at 100°! The amount of heat needed to change a gram of water at 100° from a liquid to a vapor is called its "heat of vaporization." Every liquid has a different heat of vaporization, but water has one of the highest. (You can review phase changes in Book Five of this series.)

In fact, water requires a lot of heat to change any of its phases—from a solid to liquid as well as liquid to gas. To change ice at 0° to water at 0°, it takes 80 calories, which is enough to raise the water temperature from 0° to 80°. The heat needed to change ice to water is water's "heat of fusion." (One of the meanings of fusing is melting.)

By the standards of most liquids, water takes a lot of heat to change its phases, and even a lot to change its temperature within a phase. To raise a gram of water one degree takes one calorie of heat. But to raise a gram of aluminum one degree takes only 0.21 calorie, copper 0.09, and iron 0.11. The amount of heat needed to raise a gram of any substance one degree Celsius is called its "specific heat." Each substance has its own particular specific heat.

We are lucky that water has one of the highest specific heats of any substance. Why? Because this peculiarity of water has a moderating effect on the climate of the world. The changes in air temperature in winter and summer are made less severe, because the water temperature in the oceans changes very, very slowly. And therefore water from the world's oceans cools the air in the summer and warms it in winter.

Did you know that more of the earth's surface is covered with water than with land?
No wonder the oceans have a strong effect on our climate.

Stories of Scientists

Wilbur and Orville Wright

Two brothers, Wilbur and Orville Wright, seem to have been born with a knack for invention. Even as young boys they made wonderful kites and toys that they sold to their friends. They attended school regularly, but much of their knowledge of science and mechanics came from reading and from working with tools. In 1892 the Wright Brothers decided to go into business together, and they opened a shop in their hometown of Dayton, Ohio, where they rented, sold, and built bicycles.

About this time they learned of a man named Otto Lilienthal, who was trying to find a way for human beings to fly. When Lilienthal was killed in a glider accident in 1896, the Wright Brothers decided to continue his experiments. They believed that flying was a problem that could be solved through careful analysis and trial and error. Over the next four years the brothers used all their spare time to study the flight of birds, design flying models, and read everything they could find about aeronautics.

In 1900 Wilbur and Orville Wright began to test double-winged gliders (much like big kites). They kept careful records of their successes and failures and soon discovered why no one had been able to design wings that would enable people to fly: all of the accepted figures concerning air pressure were wrong. The brothers gathered their own correct data by building a six-foot wind tunnel in a corner of their bicycle shop. They built and tested more than two hundred models to determine the best wing design.

The Wright Brothers also built a glider, unlike all previous models. In earlier gliders, the pilot sat in an unsteady upright position, but the Wright glider carried its pilot lying flat on his stomach, to cut down on wind resistance. On the advice of the U.S. Weather Bureau, the Wright Brothers decided to test their glider on the sand dunes near Kitty Hawk, North Carolina. There they glided nearly one thousand times over the next three years, becoming experienced pilots and solving the problems of in-flight balance and steering. They were finally ready to build and test their first real flying machine.

On the bitterly cold morning of December 17, 1903, Orville and Wilbur Wright wheeled their new airplane onto the windy beach at Kitty Hawk. Orville climbed on to pilot the first trial. Powered by a small engine, the airplane coasted along the flat sand, lifted off, and flew one hundred and twenty feet into a strong wind before landing. Success!

The Wright Brothers at Kitty Hawk.

Even though a photographer had captured the momentous moment when the airplane first left the ground, the Wrights' first flight received little attention. Only a few newspapers even mentioned it. But the brothers were not discouraged. They continued to fly in a pasture near their home and to give flying lessons and demonstration flights throughout Europe and the United States. Over time the public became used to the idea of flying, and in 1906 the Wright Brothers received a patent for their airplane. Two years later they began to supply military planes to the U.S. government.

Wilbur Wright died of typhoid fever in 1912. Deeply saddened by the loss of his brother, Orville returned to Dayton, where he remained until his death in 1948. These quiet, hard-working brothers are remembered fondly as the "fathers of flight," and the beach at Kitty Hawk is honored as a national historical monument.

Albert Einstein

When Einstein first developed his theory of relativity in 1905, only a few physicists could understand it. It wasn't until after World War I, in 1919, that the general public was told that Einstein's surprising predictions about space and time and gravity had been proven true by astronomical observations. The world was astonished. From 1919 until his death in 1955, Einstein was the most famous scientist in the world. His flowing white hair, rumpled look, and benign face made him the very image of the genius-scientist.

Born in Germany on March 14, 1879, Albert was not a brilliant student in his early years. But at age twelve, he became enchanted by the logic of geometry, and went on to study physics at a university in Switzerland. After graduating in 1900, Einstein worked as an examiner in the Swiss government's patent office, where he spent long hours helping to decide which patents should be awarded to inventors. But he still found time to earn a doctorate in physics and to write some of the most revolutionary scientific papers the world had ever seen.

In 1905, while still working at the patent office, Albert Einstein published four ground-breaking scientific papers. The first explained the zigzag movements of small particles floating in stationary liquid. This article helped prove the existence of atoms, which not all scientists accepted at the time. The second paper proposed that light is made up of small bundles called quanta (or photons). This paper was to be an early contribution to one of the breakthroughs of modern physics, quantum theory. Einstein's third paper spelled out his "special theory of relativity." His final paper contained the formula $E = mc^2$, the most famous formula in modern science, which means that energy (E) is equivalent to mass (m) times the speed of light squared. This means that mass can be converted to energy—which is exactly what happens when an atom bomb explodes.

Each of these papers was of the highest importance to modern science. Rarely, if ever, had one person (and an unknown patent clerk at that) made so many scientific contributions in a lifetime—much less in the space of a single year. Einstein became a well-respected physicist almost overnight. He left the patent office to be a professor, first in Switzerland, then Prague, and finally in Berlin, where he settled into a position that allowed him to devote almost all of his time to theoretical work. Too absorbed in his studies to take much notice of the progression of World War I, Einstein published an article called "General Theory of Relativity" in 1916. In November of 1919, the Royal Society of London announced that it had proven his theory of relativity by observing, during a total eclipse, that light rays are bent by the gravity of the sun by exactly the amount Einstein had predicted.

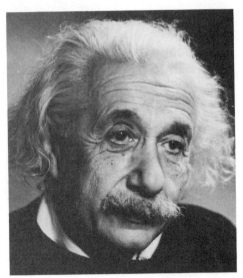

Albert Einstein.

Albert Einstein won the 1921 Nobel Prize for Physics, and he traveled widely during the next two decades, accepting invitations to lecture throughout the world. At home in Germany, however, the increasing prejudice against Jews began to affect even this genius. The Nazis took away Einstein's citizenship, confiscated or destroyed his property, and threw him out of their scientific societies, which no longer allowed Jewish members. When Adolf Hitler became Germany's chancellor in 1933, Einstein left his homeland forever to escape religious persecution. He accepted a full-time position at the new Institute for Advanced Study in Princeton, New Jersey.

Einstein had a strong sense of duty to humanity and was concerned about the potentially terrible consequences of scientific progress. In July of 1939, at the urging of his fellow scientists, he wrote a letter to President Franklin Roosevelt, warning that the Germans were hard at work on an atomic bomb. He urged the United States to begin work on a counter-weapon of its own at once. The great scientist became a kind of unelected statesman, speaking passionately about the need for peace and urging all countries of the world to join under one global government.

His last years were spent in an intense but ultimately unsuccessful search for laws that govern the behavior of everything in the universe. Albert Einstein died peacefully in his sleep on April 18, 1955.

Encouraged by a sense of joyful wonder and a conviction of the mathematical perfection of the world, Einstein discovered truths that extend from the smallest particles of matter to the far reaches of the universe. "The most incomprehensible thing about the world," he once wrote, "is that it is comprehensible."

Percy Lavon Julian

Have you ever known anyone who suffered from arthritis, a painful and crippling disease that attacks the body's joints? Many people who suffer from arthritis use cortisone, one of a group of hormones called steroids, to keep their arthritis under control. Cortisone is cheap and easily available now. But because it once had to be extracted from animals, cortisone cost so much—up to fifty dollars a pill—that only the rich could afford it. Then a brilliant chemist named Percy Lavon Julian figured out how to synthesize cortisone and other important steroids, such as progesterone, from an unlikely source: soybeans.

Percy Julian was born in Montgomery, Alabama, in 1899, when most African-American children had no chance of getting a good education. But Julian's father, a railway mail clerk, and his mother were determined that all six of their children would be educated. The Julian family had a long tradition of schooling; when Julian's grandfather was a slave, his master cut off two of his fingers because he dared to learn to read and write.

It wasn't easy for Percy Julian, but his hard work paid off. He entered DePauw University in Indiana in 1921. He majored in chemistry, and went on to graduate at the top of his class.

Julian knew he wanted to get his Ph.D. (Doctor of Philosophy) and become a research scientist. But he found that in the 1920s very few American universities were willing to admit an African-American into their graduate programs. So Julian took a teaching job at Fisk University, a black college in

Percy Julian.

Nashville, Tennessee. After two years, Harvard University awarded him a fellowship in chemistry, and a year later he completed his master's degree with the highest grades in his program. In 1929 Julian had a chance to start his doctoral work, but he had to go to Vienna, Austria, to do it, because European universities at that time were more open to African-American students than American universities.

In Vienna, Julian began to study soybeans and the proteins they contained to find out what useful products they might produce. He continued to work on soybeans when he came back to America to head the chemistry department at Howard University in Washington, D.C. In 1935, working at his old school, DePauw University, Julian did what a famous chemist at Oxford University had been trying to do for years: he became the first person to synthesize from soybean proteins a drug called physostigmine, used to treat the eye disease glaucoma.

Despite his brilliant success, Julian found that, as an African-American, he was denied the academic positions he deserved. When DePauw wouldn't make him head of its chemistry program, even though his colleagues wanted him appointed, Julian went to work as chief chemist and director of research for the Glidden manufacturing company. It was a major turning point in American science—the first time an African-American had been appointed director of a major laboratory.

The first year Julian worked for Glidden the company started to turn a profit. With the freedom Glidden gave him, Julian continued his research on soybeans. He even found a way to make a firefighting foam out of soybeans; the U.S. Navy called it "bean soup" and used it in World War II to put out fires on shipboard. Julian also manufactured large amounts of synthetic progesterone and testosterone from soy protein. Progesterone is a hormone that can be used to prevent miscarriages among pregnant women; doctors also use it and testosterone, a male hormone, to help fight cancer. Then Julian created from soybeans something called cortexolone, or Substance S. Substance S was almost the same as cortisone produced by animals; it lacked only one oxygen molecule. Julian figured out how to introduce the missing molecule into Substance S, and thus produced the first manmade cortisone.

Julian went on to found his own laboratory. In 1947 the NAACP gave him the Spingarn Award for his achievements. Julian's techniques for synthesizing cortisone and other steroids from soybeans made these important substances widely and cheaply available to doctors and patients who needed them, and earned him a reputation as one of the most brilliant research chemists of our time.

James Watson and Francis Crick

Imagine that you're in a race, running as hard as you can, hoping that you will be the first to reach the finish line. While we all know that this kind of physical competition is exciting, many are surprised to find that intense competition also happens in the field of science. Rivals tried for years to discover the structure of DNA before James Watson, an American, and Francis Crick, an English scientist, finally ran away with the prize.

These two scientists met in 1951 in Cambridge, England, where Crick was a student and Watson was doing research. Sharing a belief that DNA's molecular subunits must be arranged in some simple pattern, the two decided to join forces and investigate the problem. Rosalyn Franklin, Linus Pauling, and several other individuals and teams of scientists were already using X-ray photographs to examine DNA, so Crick and Watson decided to build large-scale models instead.

The two had a hunch that DNA was a spiral, but they made several false starts and mistakes before deducing the full truth. One day when Watson was doodling on a piece of paper, sketching possible combinations of molecular units, he realized that two combinations fit together to form the same shape. This insight soon led Crick and Watson to the final conclusion. DNA is shaped like a ladder twisted into a double spiral or helix. Its "rungs" are pairings of units. Watson and Crick were thrilled by the beauty of the double helix, which enables DNA to duplicate itself simply by "unzipping" down the middle of the "ladder." Once unzipped, each half-rung is able to hook up with a new partner to form a new helix.

Crick and Watson built their model in 1953. They began with pieces of cardboard, but soon switched to thin sheets of color-coded metal cut into the shapes of the complementary pairs. As the pieces were joined with brass rods and screws, the twisting structure of DNA seemed to grow right up out of the table. When it was finished, one complete turn measured nearly two yards.

Watson and Crick wrote a nine-hundred-word paper that introduced the double helix to the world. It began, "We wish to suggest a structure . . . [that

James Watson and Francis Crick with their DNA model.

has] novel features which are of considerable biological interest." This was an understatement, or a kind of joke, because Crick and Watson knew very well that theirs was one of the greatest discoveries in twentieth-century biology. Other scientists accepted the double helix very quickly, because it fit perfectly with their X-ray data and with prior knowledge of the chemistry and functions of DNA.

James Watson and Francis Crick were both awarded the 1962 Nobel Prize in medicine. They joined forces once more in 1957 to investigate the structure of viruses, then parted ways. Crick devoted his time to important research on how genes transfer information from one generation to the next. Watson went on to publish *Double Helix*, a book describing the dramatic quest for DNA, and to teach and head the Cold Spring Biological Laboratories in New York.

Severo Ochoa

Severo Ochoa was born on September 24, 1905, in the town of Luarca, Spain. Ochoa attended the University of Madrid and received a medical degree with honors at the age of twenty-four. The young doctor then traveled and conducted research in a number of laboratories and medical colleges in Germany, England, and Spain, and he began to concentrate on enzymes—proteins that cause or speed up chemical reactions in plants and animals.

Feeling that the opportunities for scientific research and progress were limited in his homeland, Ochoa emigrated to the United States in 1941. (He later became an American citizen.) He taught briefly in St. Louis, Missouri, before joining the staff of New York University's College of Medicine in 1942. For the next thirty years Ochoa worked there as a professor, researcher, and finally chairman of the biochemistry department, studying how chemicals affect important organic processes such as storing and releasing energy and passing genetic information from parent to child.

In the early 1950s Ochoa isolated a key chemical compound that is commonly found in both plant and animal tissue. Dr. Ochoa was the first to realize that this one enzyme had two very important functions. It was a vital agent in photosynthesis—the process by which plants use light to convert water and carbon dioxide into complex sugars and other foods. It served an *opposite* function in animals, acting to change food into carbon dioxide, water, and energy.

Severo Ochoa is best known, however, for making synthetic RNA, an important substance in cells. (You can think of RNA as a messenger with a very important message, because it carries instructions from the DNA of a cell to the cell's cytoplasm. RNA is shaped much like a single or unzipped strand of DNA.) In 1955 Ochoa discovered an enzyme that could be used to cement small molecular units into synthetic RNA. This was the first time in history that

Severo Ochoa.

molecules had been joined in a chain outside of a living organism. This important work earned Severo Ochoa widespread recognition and numerous awards, including the 1959 Nobel Prize in medicine.

Barbara McClintock

Barbara McClintock was born in Hartford, Connecticut, on June 16, 1902. Although her parents encouraged their children to be independent and curious, they strongly opposed Barbara's wish to go to college. But Barbara remained so determined to get an education that she took a job, studied on weekends, and found a tuition-free college: the Cornell School of Agriculture. Barbara enrolled at Cornell in 1919 to study biology. She excelled in a basic genetics class and asked to continue graduate studies in that field, but her request was denied because she was a woman. So after graduation McClintock joined the botany (plant science) department and began an intense study of cells, particularly those of maize, a kind of colorful corn. She became obsessed with finding out why the multicolored patterns on maize didn't follow the strict rules of genetics.

McClintock tilled a small garden where she planted, pollinated, and cultivated her own corn. She harvested the ears and studied the color variations in the kernels under a microscope. She taught herself to identify maize chromosomes and linked each one to the trait it controlled. She received a Ph.D. in 1927 and remained at Cornell for a time as a teacher. Her reputation grew as she used her expertise to map the chromosome pattern in several other species, record the cellular effects of

X-rays, and collaborate with another female scientist to prove that chromosomes can break and form new patterns during meiosis.

McClintock's powers of concentration were remarkable. She once said that she became involved so deeply in her work that she forgot everything else and became part of the cells, letting the chromosomes guide her to truths about themselves. Although McClintock's work earned her an international reputation, the fact that she was a woman kept her from getting a permanent research position or funding. For more than ten years she moved from one short-term position to another, conducting her investigations wherever she could. Finally, in 1941, a friend found a permanent place for her at Cold Spring Harbor, a research facility near New York City.

Barbara McClintock examining an ear of corn.

Fifty years ago, scientists believed that genes were all alike and fixed in their places, much like pearls on a string. But during experiments at Cold Spring, Barbara McClintock discovered genes that can be turned on and off, like a switch, by the presence of other, controller genes. She found that these genes can break off and reinsert themselves in new positions, thereby changing which traits are expressed or repressed. Recognizing that her theory went against the accepted ideas of science, she spent years testing it again and again until she was absolutely certain it was right.

At long last, she presented her evidence at a symposium in 1951. Her detailed and complicated presentation was beyond the comprehension of her colleagues, who asked each other, is she just wrong or has she gone crazy? This was a terrible disappointment. But McClintock did not quit; she said she was "having too much fun." She continued her work throughout the next decades, piling research findings in huge stacks around her office because no one wanted to hear about them.

By the 1960s scientists studying bacteria began to find similar evidence of "jumping genes." Almost overnight, Barbara McClintock began to be showered with honors and prizes. In 1981 she became only the third woman ever to receive a solo Nobel Prize for her research, because, said the Nobel committee, she had worked alone for so many years. When told of this great honor, the seventy-nine-year-old scientist wrote that "it might seem unfair to reward a person for having so much pleasure over the years, asking the maize plant to solve specific problems, and then watching its response."

Illustration and Photo Credits

Demoiselles d'Avignon by Pablo Picasso, Paris (June–July 1907). Oil on canvas, 8′ × 7′8″: 249(a)

Collection, The Museum of Modern Art, New York. Given anonymously. *Broadway Boogie-Woogie* by Piet Mondrian, 1942–43. Oil on canvas, 50″ × 50″: 251

Collection, The Museum of Modern Art, New York. Purchase. *Christina's World* by Andrew Wyeth, 1948. Tempera on gessoed panel, 32¼″ × 47¾″: 254

The Museum of Modern Art Film Stills Archive, New York: 159(b)

Courtesy The Names Project: 342

National Aeronautics and Space Administration: 220

National Archives: 151, 152, 153, 162, 173(b), 175, 180(b), 182(a, b), 183(a, b), 184, 187(a, b), 195, 218(a, b), 232(a)

Nationalgalerie, Berlin: 112

© 1992 National Gallery of Art, Washington, Ailsa Mellon Bruce Fund. *The Bull (Le Taureau)* by Pablo Picasso, 1945. Lithograph on Arches paper (third state): 245(a)

© 1992 National Gallery of Art, Washington, Ailsa Mellon Bruce Fund. *The Bull (Le Taureau)* by Pablo Picasso, 1945. Lithograph on Arches paper (seventh state): 245(b)

© 1992 National Gallery of Art, Washington, Ailsa Mellon Bruce Fund. *The Bull (Le Taureau)* by Pablo Picasso, 1945. Lithograph on Arches paper (eleventh state): 245(c)

Courtesy of National Museum of the American Indian, Smithsonian Institution: 246

National Park Service: 89(a), 90(b), 93(b), 186, 222, 226

New York University Medical Center: 382

Courtesy of The Pace Gallery, New York: 247

© Photo Researchers, Inc. M. W. F. Tweedie, National Audubon Society: 330(b, c)

Courtesy The Prado Museum, Madrid. © 1993 ARS, New York/SPADEM, Paris: 250

Courtesy of Faith Ringgold: 36

Joel Smith: 352(b, c), 364(b)

Smithsonian Institution, Anthropology Department, Catalogue No. 323686: 249(c)

Collection of the Supreme Court of the United States: 201

Texas State Library, Archives Division: 101

Tulane University Library, courtesy of William Ransom Hogan Jazz Archive: 236

United Nations: 128

U.S. Department of Agriculture: 344(a)

U.S. Fisheries and Wildlife Service: 89(b)

U.S. Geological Survey/Hamilton, W. B., 489: 90(a)

University of Virginia Library, Rare Book Division: 43, 45

University of Virginia Medical Center: 346

University of Washington Libraries, Special Collections Division, #14282: 38

Virginia Discovery Museum, photo by Peggy Harrison: 356(b)

Alexandra Webber: 324, 325, 337, 338(a), 340(b)

Meg West: 349(a, b, c), 350, 351(a, b, c), 353, 354(c), 355(a, b, c), 356(a), 357(a, b, c), 358(a, b), 359(a, b, c, d), 360(a, b), 361(a, b), 363, 364(a), 365(b), 370(a, b, c), 371(a, b, c), 372(a, b)

Perry Whidden: 85, 86, 87, 287(a)

Yale University Art Gallery, Mabel Brady Garvan Collection. Barfoot for Darton, *Progress of Cotton #5, Bobbin & Drawing Frames*: 109

Text Credits

Poetry

"Caged Bird" from *Shaker, Why Don't You Sing?* by Maya Angelou. Copyright © 1983 by Maya Angelou. Reprinted by permission of Random House, Inc.

"Harlem" from *Selected Poems of Langston Hughes* by Langston Hughes. Copyright 1948 by Alfred A. Knopf, Inc. Copyright 1951, © 1959 by Langston Hughes. Reprinted by permission of Alfred A. Knopf, Inc.

"Life Is Fine" from *Selected Poems of Langston Hughes* by Langston Hughes. Copyright 1948 by Alfred A. Knopf, Inc. Copyright 1951, © 1959 by Langston Hughes. Reprinted by permission of Alfred A. Knopf, Inc.

"The Negro Speaks of Rivers" from *Selected Poems of Langston Hughes* by Langston Hughes. Copyright 1948 by Alfred A. Knopf, Inc. Copyright 1951, © 1959 by Langston Hughes. Reprinted by permission of Alfred A. Knopf, Inc.

"A Song of Greatness" from *The Children Sing in the Far West* by Mary Austin. Copyright 1928 by Mary Austin; copyright renewed 1956 by Kenneth M. Chapman and Mary C. Wheelwright. Reprinted by permission of Houghton Mifflin Co. All rights reserved.

"Stopping by Woods on a Snowy Evening" by Robert Frost from *The Poetry of Robert Frost* edited by Edward Connely Lathem. Copyright 1923, © 1969 by Holt, Rinehart, Winston. Copyright © 1957 by Robert Frost. Reprinted by permission of Henry Holt & Company, Inc.

"This Is Just to Say" from *The Collected Poems of William Carlos Williams, 1909–1939*, vol. I by William Carlos Williams. Copyright 1938 by New Directions Publishing Corp. Reprinted by permission of the publisher.

"Woman Work" from *And Still I Rise* by Maya Angelou. Copyright © 1978 by Maya Angelou. Reprinted by permission of Random House, Inc.

Songs

"Summertime" (George Gershwin, DuBose Heyward) Copyright 1935 (renewed 1962) by George Gershwin Music, Ira Gershwin Music, and DuBose and Dorothy Heyward Memorial Fund. All rights administered by WB Music Corp. All rights reserved. Used by permission.

Stories

Excerpt from *Animal Farm* by George Orwell, copyright 1946 by Harcourt Brace & Company and renewed 1974 by Sonia Orwell, reprinted by permission of the publisher.

Excerpt of one diary entry from *Anne Frank: The Diary of a Young Girl* by Anne Frank. Copyright 1952 by Otto H. Frank. Used by permission of Doubleday, a division of Bantam Doubleday Dell Publishing Group, Inc.

I Know Why the Caged Bird Sings by Maya Angelou. Copyright © 1970 by Maya Angelou. Reprinted by permission of Random House, Inc.

Index

About the Author

E. D. Hirsch, Jr., a professor at the University of Virginia, is the author or editor of ten books, including *Cultural Literacy*, *The Dictionary of Cultural Literacy*, and *A First Dictionary of Cultural Literacy*. He and his wife Polly live in Charlottesville, where they raised their three children.